Vie

DR   IP

CLAIRE BOOBBYER

CONTENTS

PLANNING YOUR TRIP	04
This is Vietnam	04
Putting it all together	06
Hanoi-Sapa-Halong Bay	08
Hanoi-Hué-Ho Chi Minh City	14
Ho Chi Minh City-Mekong Delta- Angkor Wat	20

HANOI → SAPA → HALONG BAY			25
Hanoi	27	Ha Giang	84
Ninh Binh	53	Pho Bang	86
Mai Chau	60	Dong Van or Meo Vac	88
Son La	62	Ba Be National Park	89
Dien Bien Phu	65	Haiphong	94
Muong Lay	70	Cat Ba Island (for Halong Bay)	
Sapa (opposite page, bottom)	75	(opposite page, top)	99

HANOI → HUÉ → HO CHI MINH CITY	105
Hué	107
Danang	130
Hoi An	137
Kontum	149
Pleiku	153
Buon Ma Thuot	155
Lak Lake	158
Dalat (above)	158
Nha Trang	170
Mui Ne	179
Ho Chi Minh City	185

HO CHI MINH CITY → MEKONG DELTA → ANGKOR WAT			185
Ho Chi Minh City	185	Can Tho (opposite page, middle)	223
Con Dao	210	Sa Dec	225
My Tho	215	Cao Lanh (for Xeo Quit)	227
Ben Tre	218	Chau Doc	231
Tra Vinh	219	Phu Quoc Island (opposite page, bottom)	236
Vinh Long	220	Siem Reap (for Angkor)	241

PRACTICALITIES	261
Ins and outs	262
Best time to visit Vietnam	262
Getting to Vietnam	262
Transport in Vietnam	265
Where to stay in Vietnam	268
Food and drink in Vietnam	269
Essentials A-Z	271
Index	275
Photography credits	287
Credits	288

THIS IS
VIETNAM

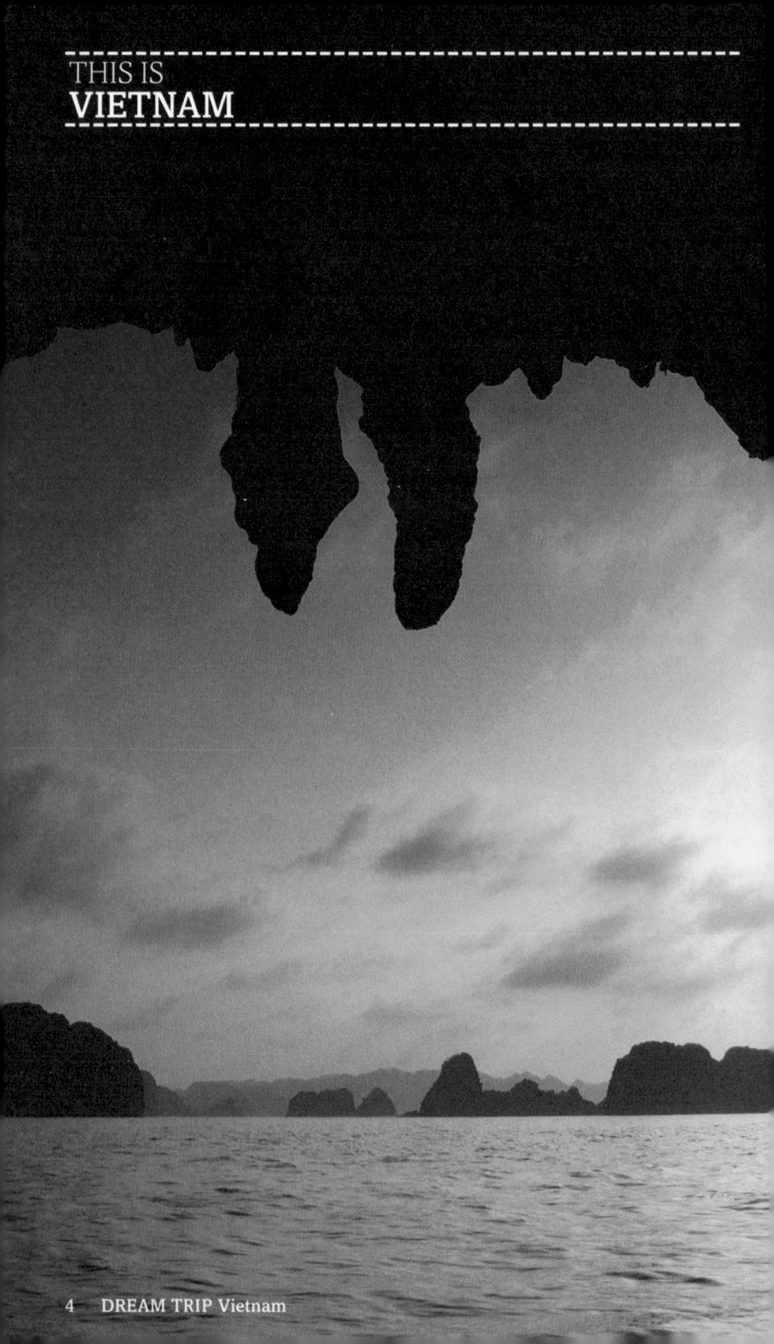

seafood and soups, its historic temples and towns, and the ripple of vibrant green paddy fields that carpet river plains and mountains across this storied land.

From the roof of the country, near the Chinese border, to the wide estuaries of the Mekong Delta in the south, Vietnam's history, food, beaches, pagodas and ethnic minority markets and textiles have always entranced me.

The north pivots around the capital, Hanoi, an elegant city of tree-lined boulevards, French belle-époque buildings, and the antique narrow streets of the old town; while Ho Chi Minh City, an economic powerhouse that trills to the sound of millions of motorbikes, anchors the deep south.

The far north and northwest, dominated by the Hoang Lien and Song Gam mountains, are covered with undulating and high-angled paddy fields tended by the numerous ethnic minorities (Vietnam is home to 53 ethnic groups) who live in these high-altitude lands. The northeast is characterized by the stunning karst island pillars and placid teal waters of Halong Bay.

Between the Communist north and the capitalistic south are more than 3000 km of golden sands, developed primarily in two clusters: Danang and Hoi An, and further south at Nha Trang and Mui Ne. Relatively unvisited are the Central Highlands and the rituals of the ethnic minorities that live in these mountainous folds. While the far south, blanketed with rice paddies, is run through with the watery eight-pronged fingers of the Mekong Delta. While Vietnam's bloody history is evident in giant memorials and museums across the land and embedded in the country's collective memory, go for the Vietnam of the 21st century – its current dynamism and energy is contagious. Where you go depends on your time and budget and how you choose to get around. But in short, the choice of destinations, activities and itineraries is virtually inexhaustible, so careful planning is needed to make best use of your time…

Claire Boobbyer

FIRST STEPS
PUTTING IT ALL TOGETHER

Trains are slow but a wonderful way to experience the countryside.

Vietnam is a very long thin country that offers a variety of destinations encompassing city, seaside and countryside experiences. Arrival in the country will probably be either via the capital, Hanoi, or the economic capital, Ho Chi Minh City (Saigon), so it makes sense to organize an itinerary that starts from one of these cities. Unless on a very short trip, most people try to visit both these urban opposites in order to fully understand the country.

If you have more time, venture further afield into the other provinces too and use these cities as gateways for the beginning and end of a longer tour or even other countries; Vietnam is connected by land, river boats and air to neighbouring Laos and Cambodia.

Vietnam's transport network improves year on year. Domestic flights are key to covering a lot of ground – especially to get to far-flung areas like Phu Quoc and the Con Dao islands. Private buses – called Open Tour Buses – carry thousands of visitors from A to B and are safer than general public buses, although there are long-haul routes that are exceptions to this rule (from Hanoi to Sapa and Hanoi to Cat Ba island, in particular). Trains are slow but a wonderful way to experience the countryside. Self-drive car hire is not permitted in Vietnam but a car with an English-speaking driver and/or guide ensures getting off the beaten track and an insight into local culture.

The three suggested itineraries each cover the northern, central and southern highlights of Vietnam in about a two- to three-week trip. None are written in stone and they are far from exhaustible. Rather they are regional suggestions for travellers wishing to explore a certain part of the country, or for returning visitors to travel somewhere new.

If arriving in Hanoi, an itinerary that starts and finishes there will take in the best of the capital, the Northwest, the Far North and the UNESCO World Heritage Site of Halong Bay.

→ DOING IT ALL

Hanoi → Ninh Binh → Mai Chau → Son La → Dien Bien Phu → Muong Lay → Sapa → Ha Giang → Pho Bang → Dong Van or Meo Vac → Ba Be National Park → Hanoi → Haiphong → Cat Ba Island (for Halong Bay) → Hué → Danang → Hoi An → Kontum → Pleiku → Buon Ma Thuot and Lak Lake → Dalat → Nha Trang → Mui Ne → Ho Chi Minh City → Con Dao → My Tho → Ben Tre → Tra Vinh → Vinh Long → Can Tho → Sa Dec → Cao Lanh (for Xeo Quit) → Chau Doc → Phu Quoc → Siem Reap (for Angkor)

1 Forbidden City detail, Hué 2 Flower garden, Sa Dec

From Hanoi to Ho Chi Minh City, an itinerary can take in Halong Bay, before heading down the spine of Vietnam to incorporate Chinese, Cham and Vietnamese cities in its cluster of central UNESCO World Heritage Sites before heading inland to the remote Central Highlands and/or covering Vietnam's top coastal resorts. This itinerary would end in lively Ho Chi Minh City with an option to fly direct to Cambodia's Siem Reap, the closest town to the world's largest religious complex, the magnificent structures of Angkor Wat. An itinerary that began in Ho Chi Minh City would mean the rural charm of the Mekong Delta could be fully explored. The offshore islands – the paradise of Phu Quoc, and the fascinating wildlife haven and former prison island of Con Dao – could be visited. Further beach time could be planned by travelling a short while north to Nha Trang or Mui Ne.

Alternatively, and if you have more time, combine these three itineraries for a grand tour of Vietnam and Angkor Wat. You could start in Hanoi and finish in Ho Chi Minh City having accommodated a side trip to Cambodia (or the other way around, as both cities are major hubs and open jaw flights are common). By covering everything, you'll get a fantastic insight into the diverse and beautiful scenery that Vietnam has to offer.

For those who have less time or don't want to spend as many hours in a car, this can be speeded up by picking out what interests you from each of the three itineraries and linking the major airports of Hanoi, Hué, Danang, Nha Trang, Dalat, and Ho Chi Minh City by domestic flights and hiring cars and taxis or taking tours from each of these for excursions.

Depending on whether you are a foodie, history buff, beach lover, city fan, or an outdoor adventure enthusiast, will determine how long you stay and explore each destination, but these three itineraries will point you in the right direction for a Dream Trip around Vietnam.

3 Halong Bay 4 Ho Chi Minh City chillies 5 Dalat Cathedral

DREAM TRIP 1
HANOI → SAPA → HALONG BAY

Best time to visit
Winter (November-April)
is usually dry and not
too hot, with average
temperatures of 16°C.
The best months are
December-March.
Avoid Summer (May-
October) is very hot with
average temperatures
of 30°C and has heavy
rainfall and occasional
typhoons. Around Tet
(New Year) transport and
hotels are booked up.

Travelling around the north, outside of Hanoi, takes a little planning as there are few air links and journey times can be long. A three-week holiday is a comfortable amount of time to explore the capital, the UNESCO World Heritage Site of Halong Bay and the mountainous northwest and far north which shelter dozens of ethnic minority villages.

After soaking up the wonders of the tiny capital, Hanoi (page 27), and tasting the abundant food, there are excursions that can be covered by day trips such as former capitals, churches, pagodas and a national park that is home to rare primates.

A Halong Bay (page 92) boat trip is best covered in an organized excursion from Hanoi where your transport to and from Halong City is included. For those who want to get off the beaten track, head to Halong Bay's largest island, Cat Ba (page 99), and explore the beautiful scenery and spot the world's last remaining troupe of white-headed langur.

Travelling west in the other direction is the stunning mountain scenery of Hanoi's Northwest and Far North. These geographical areas can be considered as separate excursions as both can be visited from Hanoi. It is, however, possible to cross high amid the mountains from the Northwest to the Far North in an

1 Sapa landscape 2 Carrying goods through Hanoi 3 Puppets for sale, Hanoi 4 Tran Quoc Pagoda, Hanoi

DREAM TRIP 1
HANOI → SAPA → HALONG BAY

extended mountain tour but remember permits must be
obtained to travel to the far northern province of Ha Giang.

There are two ways to reach the Northwest's 'capital' of Sapa
(page 75): either by road, taking a couple of days and passing
interesting towns and villages overnight; or, for those on a tighter
schedule, by taking the overnight train from Hanoi to Sapa via the
Indochine elegance of the Victoria Sapa carriage or a standard
Vietnam Railways carriage.

If travelling by road, the Mai Chau Valley (page 60) is a highlight
for its stunning rice-paddy covered scenery and the villages of the
White and Black Thai ethnic minority. A night in a valley homestay
or a luxury lodge run by local people is a highlight. History and
warfare buffs will want to detour to Dien Bien Phu (page 65), site of
the disastrous French defeat at the hands of the Vietnamese in 1954
which heralded French withdrawal from Indochina.

The roads plough deeper into the mountains close to the Chinese
border before emerging at the former French hill station of Sapa
(page 75), the trekking capital of Vietnam. It's also the largest Black
Hmong settlement in Vietnam. The indigo-clad Hmong and the

1 French tanks, Dien Bien Phu 2 Bac Ha market 3 Mai Chau Valley 4 Ba Be National Park 5 Ethnic minority family, Sapa

vibrant reds of the clothes of the Dao people characterize the area. Walking the valleys of Sapa and visiting ethnic minority markets – including that of Bac Ha (page 81) – fill the days of most visitors. The more time you have the more off the beaten track you can go in overnight trekking trips.

From Sapa, it's possible to continue by road to the Far North's Ha Giang (page 84) province or, if short of time, return to Hanoi by overnight train.

Most visitors experience the Far North on an organized tour because of the lack of public transport and the need for permits. Trips, mostly lasting seven days, take in the tranquil Thac Ba Lake (page 88) and surrounding tea plantations, before heading way off the beaten track to Xin Man (page 84) and its ethnic minority market. Next, are the Heaven's Gate Pass (page 86), Yen Minh (page 86) and its Sunday market, Sa Phin (page 87) at the centre of the former White Hmong kingdom, Lung Cu (page 88) Vietnam's highest point, the street of ancient houses at Dong Van (page 88) and the oustanding scenery that soars around Meo Vac (page 88), before heading south back to Hanoi via the Ba Be National Park (page 89) and lake with its friendly homestays. The Far North comprises angular limestone sky-scraping mountains on which have been crafted high-altitude paddies. With clear views, there's an otherworldly feeling about this remote region. Adventure junkies might want to tour this route by motorbike – either at the controls or by riding pillion.

The Far North comprises angular limestone sky-scraping mountains on which have been crafted high-altitude paddies...there's an otherworldly feeling about this remote region.

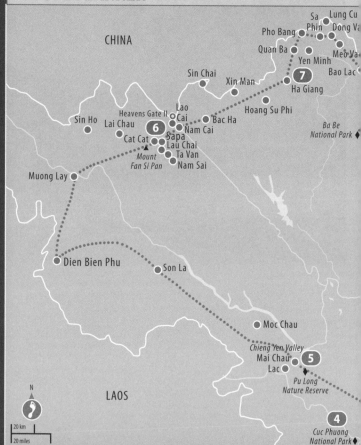

CHINA

LAOS

Sa Phin
Lung Cu
Pho Bang
Dong Va
Quan Ba
Yen Minh
Meo Va
Bao Lac
Sin Chai
Xin Man
Ha Giang
7
Lao Cai
Bac Ha
Hoang Su Phi
Sin Ho
Lai Chau
Heavens Gate II
Nam Cai
6
Cat Cat
Sapa
Ba Be National Park ◆
Lau Chai
Ta Van
Mount Fan Si Pan ▲
Nam Sai
Muong Lay
Dien Bien Phu
Son La
Moc Chau
Chieng Yen Valley
Mai Chau
5
Lac
Pu Long Nature Reserve ◆
4
Cuc Phuong National Park ◆

N
20 km
20 miles

1 Tam Coc 2 Hoan Kiem Lake 3 Lanterns for sale, Hoi An

Cho Ra
Na Phac
Bac Can
Thai Nguyen
Bich Dong
(1) (2)
HANOI
Halong City
(8) Halong Bay
Haiphong
(10)
Perfume
Pagoda
(3)
(9) Cat Ba
Island
Hoa Lu
Ninh Binh
Phat Diem
Gulf of Tonkin
Tam Coc Yen Tu
Mountains

→ WISH LIST

1 Take a stroll around the Hanoi's Old Quarter – the 36 Streets – and experience the clatter of shop and street activity. Settle down for a *bia hoi* and some street food before returning at night to explore these antique streets. 2 Explore Hanoi's tree-framed Hoan Kiem Lake before admiring the belle époque French Quarter buildings of the Opera House, Sofitel Metropole Hotel, and Museum of Vietnamese History. 3 Head out of Hanoi to the popular hilltop pilgrimage spot of the Perfume Pagoda and hire a foot-rowed boat to paddle through the limestone karst and cave landscape of Tam Coc. 4 Take a day or more to head to Cuc Phuong National Park for its butterflies, the endangered primates center, and walks in mountainous tropical forest. 5 Spend a night in the serene Mai Chau Valley which will allow you to soak up the vivid greens of the rice-paddied valleys and meet the local White Thai minority. Those with more time should head further into the valleys to Pu Luong Nature Reserve and Moc Chau. 6 Brave the fresh air and heights of the former French hill station of Sapa to trek past paddy fields to outlying ethnic minority villages. 7 Take a couple of days to explore the heights of Ha Giang province and the roof of Vietnam near the Chinese border. Soaring peaks shelter ethnic minority villages and an old Hmong kingdom palace buried at these giddy heights. 8 Sail out into the teal green waters of Halong Bay on a converted junk. Clamber into the caves of the forested limestone pillars, kayak the bay, and clock the stars as they emerge at night. 9 Head to the often overlooked Cat Ba Island and its sky-high limestone peaks where the island's national park is home to the world's last remaining troupe of white-headed langur. 10 Soak up the untouristy olde-worlde atmosphere of Haiphong. Pedalos and sidecars roam the streets lined with beautiful old French buildings.

2

3

DREAM TRIP 2
HANOI → HUÉ → HO CHI MINH CITY

Best time to visit
The dry season is February-April. Hué can experience heavy rainfall at any time of year but is at its wettest September-January. The hill resorts are cool at night year-round but particularly chilly (4°C) in winter (October-March) but dry with clear blue skies.

Avoid The central region can suffer tropical storms May-November. Around Tet (New Year) transport and hotels are booked up.

This itinerary requires a minimum of three weeks and links the northern and southern itineraries. Those that want to see as much as possible in one trip could combine all three itineraries, or pick out the highlights of each route.

Depending if you are looking for exercise or relaxation first, head either to Vietnam's trekking capital, Sapa (page 75), in the Northwest or to its limestone karst studded Halong Bay for a boat trip in the east. To minimise transport time, head to the mountains, paddy fields and ethnic minority villages of the Sapa valley by train spending the overnight journey in the Indochine luxury of the Victoria carriage or a standard couchette carriage provided by Vietnam Railways. Spending a night or two in the UNESCO World Heritage Site of Halong Bay (page 92) is always a highlight. Different budgets will buy different boat experiences but it's easier to organize this in Hanoi with reputable operators.

To head south to the glorious former capital of Hué (page 107), adventurists can take the train but many people fly. The Nguyen Dynasty ruled Vietnam from 1802-1945 and the remains of their citadel and their geomantically positioned stylised tombs along the fragrantly named Perfume River (page 114), lure historians, romantics and aesthetes.

1 Stone column, Royal Palace, Hué 2 Statues of emperors, Khai Dinh, Hué 3 Perfume River

4

From Hué, many history buffs take day trips to the Demilitarized Zone (DMZ) (page 123). This boundary, established in 1954, ran the width of the country along the 17th Parallel and was the scene of some of the fiercest fighting of the Vietnam War.

South of Hué, Vietnam's most incredible sights and experiences become congested and obvious transport routes are not as logical as they might seem.

Without question, railway fans should take the short train journey from Hué to Danang (page 130). The track clings high above the East Sea as it threads its way through peaks and paddies. The journey is a Vietnam highlight.

Alternatively, head overland to Danang or Hoi An (page 137) by the high-flung Hai Van Pass (page 127). Hoi An is a diminutive old Chinese mercantile town which is a beautiful muddle of ochre

The track clings high above the East Sea as it threads its way through peaks and paddies.

4 Basket boats, Danang Beach

and terracotta shades. Tailors, restaurants and bars as well as the atmosphere of this UNESCO World Heritage Site lure visitors to tour its antique ambience for days. The nearby Cua Dai Beach (page 142) is a further excuse to stay longer. From Hoi An, it is easy to make an excursion to the jungle ruins of My Son (page 143), which was once the spiritual centre of the Cham Empire. At Danang is the world-class museum of Cham Art and the nearby China Beach (page 134), a growing beach resort that was once the deserted R&R sandy stretch for American GIs.

From Hoi An, travel overland to the remote Central Highlands' communities of Kontum (page 149), Pleiku (page 153) and Buon Ma Thuot (page 155) which shelter ethnic minorities and their interesting rituals. Buon Ma Thuot is the coffee capital of Vietnam; nearby Yok Don National Park (page 157) is home to the last wild elephants of Vietnam. For those less keen on overland travel, it's possible to fly from Danang to Pleiku or Buon Ma Thuot and and explore the Central Highlands from there. Arranging private transport will allow you to get off the beaten track and visit the more remote areas. Heading south, you will arrive at the Surrey-meets-France

1 My Son ruin 2 Dalat church 3 Waterfall, Dalat 4 Beach near Nha Trang 5 Scorpion fish, Nha Trang
6 Cao Dai ceremony, Tay Ninh 7 (Next page) Relief from My Son temple

former French hill station of Dalat (page 158), also the honeymoon capital of Vietnam. French villas and waterfalls abound.

From Dalat, it's possible to fly to Ho Chi Minh City, for those short of time, or go overland to Vietnam's beach capital, Nha Trang (page 170). Down the coast is the quieter beach town of Mui Ne (page 180). From Mui Ne, head overland to Ho Chi Minh City. Or, fly from Nha Trang to Ho Chi Minh City.

There are enough sights and foodie experiences in Ho Chi Minh City (page 185) to keep you captured for a few days. The two excursion highlights that can be visited in one day are the wartime Cu Chi Tunnels (page 205) and the outrageously fantastical Cao Dai religion cathedral at Tay Ninh (page 207). From Saigon airport, a roundtrip to Siem Reap (page 241) for Cambodia's Angkor Wat is possible.

There are enough sights and foodie experiences in Ho Chi Minh City to keep you captured for days.

HANOI

Haiphong

Lang Ga

Gulf of Tonkin

3 Vinh Moc
Tunnels   17th Parallel

The Rock Pile   Dong Ha
Khe Sanh

Hué   **1** **2**
Lan Co
LAOS   *Bach Ma* National Park   Danang   **4**
Hai Van Pass   *My Khe Beach*
The Marble Mountains   *Cua Dai Beach*
My Son   Hoi An   **6**
                      5

My Lai
Quang Ngai

Kontum

Bien Ho Lake
Pleiku

*Central
Highlands*   **7**

CAMBODIA   *Yok Don*
National Park   Buon Ma Thuot   *Whale Island*
Lak Lake
*Langbian
Mountain*   Nha Trang
Lat Village   Trai Mat   **9**
Nam Cat Tien   Dalat
National Park   **8**

N

50 km
50 miles
Ho Chi Minh
City   Mui Ne   **10**

→ WISH LIST

1 Imagine the Nguyen emperors and their eunuchs ruling from the impressive imperial city at Hué. 2 Motorbike or boat to the Nguyen Dynasty emperors' tombs geomantically scattered along the banks of the city's Perfume River. 3 Witness the border boundary of Vietnam's 1954-created Demilitarized Zone and enter the extraordinary Vinh Moc Tunnels that sheltered families during the war. 4 Take in Cham art, marble sculpture and the famous curve of China Beach at Danang. 5 Explore the jungle-covered ruins and sculptures of the Cham Empire's spiritual heart at My Son. 6 Bask amid the glorious Chinese mercantile architecture of Hoi An, order clothes at its tailor shops, and indulge in its delicious food before burning the calories in a gentle cycle ride to nearby Cua Dai Beach. 7 Understand the rituals and practices of the Ede, Mnong, Gia-rai and Ba-na minorities in the Central Highlands of Vietnam. The grave-abandonment rituals of the Gia-rai are particularly fascinating. 8 Relax amid the temperate climate of Dalat which boasts French colonial villas and waterfalls. 9 Beach lovers and divers should head to bustling Nha Trang for its clear waters, tropical islands and seafood. 10 Take time to relax and enjoy a more laid-back 'sea, sun and sand' experience at Mui Ne.

DREAM TRIP 3
HO CHI MINH CITY → MEKONG DELTA → ANGKOR WAT

Best time to visit The dry season is November-April with warm days and cool evenings December-March; the hottest months are March-April, before the monsoon, however temperatures are fairly constant throughout the year (average 25-30°C). Avoid The wet season is May-October. Travel in the south and Mekong Delta can be difficult at the height of the monsoon (September-November) with typhoons common in coastal areas. Around Tet (New Year) transport and hotels are booked up.

Transport links in southern Vietnam are not as extensive as those in the rest of the country which means routes must be considered carefully. However, all routes run to and from Ho Chi Minh City, which makes a good base for a few days.

Ho Chi Minh City's (page 185) French architecture sites, war buildings and museums, and Chinese temples and pagodas are the city's backdrop to its lively street life of motorbike and foodie culture, and its soundtrack of economic progress. This is the economic powerhouse of the world's 13th most populous country.

After day trips to see the wartime Cu Chi Tunnels (page 205) and experiencing Mass at the world's most fantastical cathedral – that of the Cao Dai religion in Tay Ninh (page 207) – take a flight to the former French penal colony and former South Vietnam political prison of Con Dao (page 210). Today, Con Dao is a wildlife haven offering Vietnam's best diving opportunities and a range of luxe to budget accommodation.

From Con Dao, fly back to Ho Chi Minh City or, for those short of time, fly direct to one of the delta's major towns, Can Tho (page 223). For those heading to the delta overland, there's a slow introduction by boat and by road to the area's peaceful towns and villages and its lush, fertile lands. The delta's pace of life is slow and a meander

1 Can Tho, Mekong Delta **2** Fishing in Mekong Delta **3** Mekong Delta paddy field

through the towns by way of a private car and boat trips is a perfect way to enjoy this timeless land. Touring the area by public bus is possible but slow and tiresome. The river islands around My Tho (page 215) are carpeted in tropical fruits; laidback Ben Tre (page 218) offers a glimpse into a non-touristy world; Vinh Long is the launchpad for homestays on An Binh Island (page 221) and a small floating market at Cai Be (page 220); Vinh Long (page 220) itself boasts a Khmer flavour; while Sa Dec (page 225) is utterly charming and the former home of French novelist Marguerite Duras, author of *The Lover*. At Xeo Quit (page 228), an exciting boat tour explores a subterranean base of the Viet Cong in swampland. As well as rice paddies, the delta is carpeted in numerous bird sanctuaries to satisfy the keen twitcher.

Can Tho (page 223) is famous for its access to nearby floating markets. Early morning boat trips can be organized independently

A meander through the towns by private car and boat trips is a perfect way to enjoy this timeless land.

4 Cricket, Con Dao island   5 US tank at Cu Chi Tunnels   6 Cathedral, Ho Chi Minh City

DREAM TRIP 3
HO CHI MINH CITY → MEKONG DELTA → ANGKOR WAT

from the river bank at Can Tho or by signing up to various guided boat tours to the markets at Phung Hiep, Phong Dien and Cai Rang. A morning spent watching locals display their wares from poles on their bobbing houseboats is a colourful and memorable experience.

From Can Tho, it's possible to fly direct to Vietnam's newest beach paradise, Phu Quoc (page 236), where the pepper plantation and fish sauce industries rub shoulders with tourism. The island has a diverse range of accommodation from luxury resorts to communal living in beach shacks.

For those wanting more of a delta experience, the border town of Chau Doc (page 231) offers a Khmer flavour, a glimpse into the floating fish farm industry and a holy mountain. From Chau Doc, it's possible to reach Siem Reap (page 244) and Angkor Wat (page 251) via boat. Alternatively, head south to the coastal town of Rach Gia from where there are regular connections to Phu Quoc by boat and by plane.

From Phu Quoc, direct flights link Ho Chi Minh City and Hanoi. Those keen to explore a bit more of Vietnam's coast could fly from Ho Chi Minh City to Nha Trang (page 170), or head overland to Mui Ne (page 180). Dalat and the Central Highlands are also accessible with direct flights linking Ho Chi Minh City with Dalat (page 158), Buon Ma Thuot (page 155) and Pleiku (page 153).

1 Phu Quoc deserted beach 2 Pepper garden on Phu Quoc 3 (Next page) Angkor Wat at sunrise

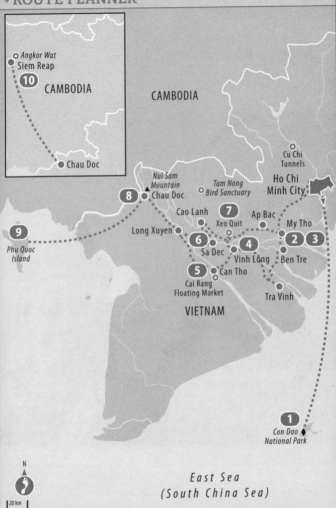

CAMBODIA

Angkor Wat
Siem Reap
(10)
CAMBODIA

Chau Doc

Cu Chi
Tunnels

Ho Chi
Minh City

Nui Sam
Mountain
Chau Doc
(8)

Tam Nong
Bird Sanctuary

Cao Lanh
(7)
Xeo Quit

Ap Bac

My Tho
(2) (3)

Long Xuyen
(6)
Sa Dec

(4)
Vinh Long

Ben Tre

Phu Quoc
Island
(9)

(5)
Can Tho

Cai Rang
Floating Market

Tra Vinh

VIETNAM

(1)
Con Dao
National Park

East Sea
(South China Sea)

N

20 km
20 miles

→ WISH LIST

1 Escape to Con Dao in the East Sea. The prisons' museums, wildlife spotting and unblemished beaches offer a true wilderness adventure. 2 Walk the Mekong riverine islands off My Tho and indulge in the fruits of the land: longans, honey, popcorn and rice whiskey. 3 Marvel at the intricate porcelain-encrusted entrance gate of My Tho's Vinh Trang Pagoda. 4 Spend the night at a homestay on Vinh Long's An Binh Island soaking up the ambience of life on the Mekong Delta. 5 Rise early at Can Tho to visit the colourful and busy floating markets of the Mekong. 6 Explore the quintessential Mekong town of Sa Dec with its market and flower farms. 7 Boat the canals of the Viet Cong base of Xeo Quit passing the cadres' subterranean chambers. 8 Take a boat out to the floating fish farms of Chau Doc and visit the Cham villages, then climb holy Sam Mountain honeycombed with tombs, sanctuaries and temples. 9 Recline on the golden sands of Phu Quoc, Vietnam's castaway island off the south coast. 10 Hop across to Cambodia's Angkor Wat to marvel at the monumental carvings of this vast religious complex.

DREAM TRIP 1:
Hanoi→Sapa→Halong Bay 21 days

Hanoi 2 nights, page 27

Ninh Binh 1 night, page 53
By road from Hanoi (3 hrs)

Mai Chau 1 night, page 60
By road from Hanoi (3-4 hrs)

Son La 1 night, page 62
By road from Mai Chau (3-4 hrs)

Dien Bien Phu 1 night, page 65
By road from Son La (4-5 hrs) or by plane
from Hanoi (1 hr)

Muong Lay 1 night, page 70
From Dien Bien Phu (4 hrs)

Sapa 3 nights, page 75
By road from Dien Bien Phu (10 hrs)
or Muong Lay (7 hrs)
By train from Hanoi via Lao Cai (9½ hrs)
and bus to Sapa (90 mins)

Ha Giang 2 nights, page 84
By road from Sapa (5-8 hrs)

Pho Bang 1 night, page 86
By road from Ha Giang (3 hrs)

Dong Van or Meo Vac 1 night, page 88
By road from Pho Bang (3 hrs) or
Ha Giang (5-6 hrs)

Ba Be National Park 1-2 nights, page 89
By road from Dong Van or Meo Vac (6 hrs)

Hanoi 1 night, page 27
By road from Ba Be National Park (6-8 hrs)

Haiphong 1 night, page 94
By road or by train from Hanoi (2 hrs)

Cat Ba Island (for Halong Bay) 2 nights,
page 99
By boat from Haiphong (35 mins)
or Halong City (4 hrs)

Hanoi 1 night, page 27

DREAM TRIP 1
Hanoi→Sapa→Halong Bay

Vietnam's tiny capital, Hanoi, is beautiful and enchanting, teeming with temples, pagodas and ancient streets, with a fascinating cultural legacy from the colonial to the communist eras. It has a wealth of historic sites, lying as it does at the heart of a region rich in history and landscapes.

Just a couple of hours from Hanoi is Hoa Binh, where villages of the Muong and Dao can be seen, and the beautiful Mau Chau Valley, home to Black and White Thai, whose attractive houses nestle amid the verdant paddies of the hills.

The north of Vietnam is a mountainous region punctuated by limestone peaks and luscious valleys of terraced paddy fields, tea plantations, stilt houses and water hyacinth-quilted rivers. Sapa, in the far northwest, is a former French hill station, home of the Hmong and set in a stunning valley – a popular area for trekking. Scattered around are market towns and villages populated by Vietnam's ethnic minorities. In the far-flung northwest corner, the course of world history was altered at Dien Bien Phu in 1954 when the Vietnamese defeated the French; a vast bronze statue commemorating the victory towers over the town.

One of the least-visited areas of Vietnam, the Far North around Ha Giang, is a beautiful, mainly mountainous region that skirts the Chinese border. Its steep slopes have been carved into rice terracing with paddies shimmering in the strong sun. The sparse populations that live here are predominantly indigenous groups that remain uncorrupted by commercialization.

Closer to Hanoi are a number of worthwhile day and overnight trips: the Perfume Pagoda lies to the southwest; Tam Coc and Cuc Phuong National Park are some three hours south; while the magical Halong Bay with its limestone towers and jagged islands, is three hours to the east.

HANOI AND AROUND

Hanoi is a small city of broad tree-lined boulevards, lakes, parks, weathered colonial buildings, elegant squares and some of the newest office blocks and hotels in Southeast Asia. It lies nearly 100 km from the sea on a bend in the Red River and from this geographical feature the city derives its name – Hanoi – meaning 'within a river bend'.

Hanoi is the capital of the world's 13th most populous country, but, in an age of urban sprawl, the city remains small and compact, historic and charming. Much of its charm lies not so much in the official 'sights' but in the unofficial and informal: the traffic zooming around the broad streets or the cyclos taking a mellow pedal through the Old Quarter, small shops packed with traders' goods or stacks of silk for visitors, skewered poultry on pavement stalls, mobile flower stalls piled on the backs of bikes, the bustle of pedestrians, the ubiquitous tinkle of the ice cream man's bicycle, and the political posters, now raised to an art form, dotted around the city.

At the heart of the city is Hoan Kiem Lake and the famous Sunbeam Bridge. The Old Quarter (36 Streets and Guilds) area, north of the lake, is bustling with commerce, its ancient buildings crumbling from the weight of history and activity. The French Quarter, which still largely consists of French buildings, is south of the lake.

Accessible on a tour from the city, the primates at Cuc Phuong National Park and the waters of Halong Bay make this area one of the most visited in Vietnam.

→ ARRIVING IN HANOI

GETTING THERE
Noi Bai Airport (HAN) is 35 km from Hanoi, a 45- to 60-minute drive, and is the hub for international and domestic flights. The airport minibus service (every 30 minutes or when full, daily 0700-1900, 40,000d), terminates opposite the **Vietnam Airlines office** ① *1 Quang Trung St, T4-3825 0872*. The official **Noi Bai Taxi** ① *T4-3886 5615*, charges a fixed price of 315,000d (four-seat cab) to the city centre. Look for the yellow and white cabs at the front of the airport.

Hanoi is well connected by bus and train with all parts of the country and has plenty of operators to organize tours or arrange onwards transport.

MOVING ON

Air Buses to the airport leave the **Vietnam Airlines** office at regular intervals (0600-1900, one hour, 32,000d). There are flights from Hanoi to Dien Bien Phu (see page 65), Hué (see page 107), Danang (see page 130), Dalat (see page 158), Nha Trang (see page 170) and Ho Chi Minh City (see page 185).

Bus Hanoi has a number of bus stations. The **Southern bus terminal** (out of town but with a linking bus from the north shore of Hoan Kiem Lake) serves destinations south of Hanoi, including Ninh Binh (see page 53) and Cuc Phuong National Park (see page 56). From **Ha Dong bus station**, Tran Phu Road, buses leave for Mai Chau (see page 60) and the Northwest. To get to Haiphong (see page 94) for Halong Bay, buses run from **Luong Yen bus station** and **Giam Lam bus station**, over Chuong Duong Bridge.

Open Tour Buses depart from tour operator offices in the Old Quarter for destinations in the south, including Hué (see page 107), Hoi An (see page 137), Dalat (see page 158), Nha Trang (see page 170), Mui Ne (see page 180) and Ho Chi Minh City (see page 185).

Train The train station (Ga Hanoi) is a short taxi ride from the Old Quarter. There are trains to Ho Chi Minh City (see page 185) and all points on the route south, as well as to Lao Cai (see page 80) for Sapa in the north, and Haiphong (see page 94) for Halong Bay.

GETTING AROUND

At the heart of the city is Hoan Kiem Lake. The majority of visitors make straight for the Old Quarter (36 Streets and Guilds) north of the lake, which is densely packed and bustling with commerce. In the French Quarter, south of the lake, you'll find the Opera House and the grandest hotels, shops and offices. A large block of the city west of Hoan Kiem Lake (Ba Dinh District) represents the heart of the government and the civil and military administration of Vietnam. To the north of the city is the West Lake (Tay Ho District) fringed with the suburban homes of the new middle class and the expat quarter with bars and restaurants.

Hanoi is getting more frenetic by the minute but, thanks to the city's elegant, tree-lined boulevards, walking and cycling outside of rush hours can still be delightful. If you like the idea of being pedalled around town, then a cyclo is the answer but be prepared for some concentrated haggling. There are also motorbike taxis (*xe ôm*), and self-drive motorbikes for hire as well as a fleet of metered taxis. Local buses have also improved, but they are still over-crowded and the network can be difficult to navigate.

BEST TIME TO VISIT

For much of the year Hanoi's weather is decidedly non-tropical. It benefits from glorious Europe-like springs and autumns, when temperatures are warm but not too hot and not too cold. From May until September Hanoi is fearfully hot and steamy. The winter months from November to February can be chilly and Hanoians wrap themselves up well in warm coats, woolly hats, gloves and scarves. Most museums are closed on Mondays.

TOURIST INFORMATION

The privately run **Tourist Information Center** ① *7 Dinh Tien Hoang St, T4-3926 3369, www.ticvietnam.com, daily 0800-2200*, at the northern end of the lake, is proving useful. It provides information and maps and will book hotels and transport tickets at no extra cost; it has currency exchange and ATM. Information is also available from the multitude

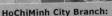

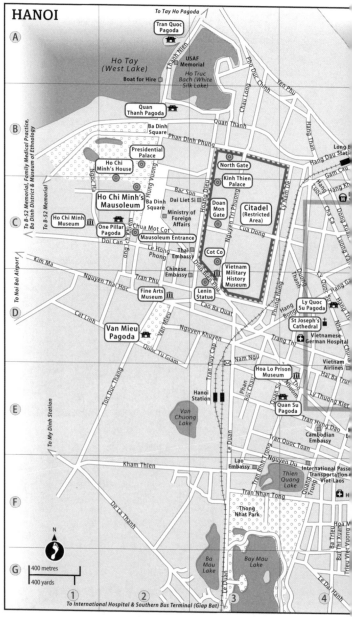

HANOI

To Tay Ho Pagoda

Tran Quoc Pagoda

Ho Tay (West Lake)

USAF Memorial

Boat for Hire

Ho Truc Bach (White Silk Lake)

Quan Thanh Pagoda

Ba Dinh Square

Phan Dinh Phung

Presidential Palace

Ho Chi Minh's House

To B-52 Memorial, Family Medical Practice, Ba Dinh District & Museum of Ethnology

To B-52 Memorial

Ho Chi Minh Museum

Ho Chi Minh's Mausoleum

Ba Dinh Square

Bac Son

Dai Liet Si

Ministry of Foreign Affairs

One Pillar Pagoda

Mausoleum Entrance

Chua Mot Cot

Doi Can

Le Hong Phong

Thai Embassy

Chinese Embassy

Fine Arts Museum

Lenin Statue

Cao Ba Quat

To Noi Bai Airport

Kim Ma

Nguyen Thai Hoc

Tran Phu

Cat Linh

Van Mieu Pagoda

Nguyen Khuyen

Quoc Tu Giam

Ton Duc Thang

To My Dinh Station

Kham Thien

De La Thanh

North Gate

Kinh Thien Palace

Doan Mon Gate

Citadel (Restricted Area)

Cot Co

Vietnam Military History Museum

Long B

Hang Dau Stati

Gam Cau

Quan Thanh

Yen Phu

Hang Than

Thanh Nien

Pho Duc Chinh

Hang Khe

Ly Quoc Su Pagoda

St Joseph's Cathedral

Vietnamese-German Hospital

Vietnam Airlines

Hai Ba Trun

Nam Ngu

Hoa Lo Prison Museum

Quan Su Pagoda

Tran Hung Dao

Ly Thuong Kiet

Cambodian Embassy

Hanoi Station

Van Chuong Lake

Tran Quoc Toan

Lao Embassy

Nguyen Du

International Passe Transportation Viet-Laos

Thien Quang Lake

Tran Nhan Tong

Thong Nhat Park

Ba Mau Lake

Bay Mau Lake

Le Dai Hanh

N

400 metres
400 yards

To International Hospital & Southern Bus Terminal (Giap Bat)

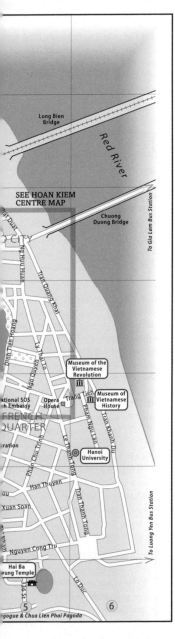

Long Bien
Bridge

Red River

SEE HOAN KIEM
CENTRE MAP

Chuong
Duong Bridge

To Gia Lam Bus Station

Museum of the
Vietnamese
Revolution

Opera
House

Museum of
Vietnamese
History

National SOS
h Embassy

FRENCH
QUARTER

Hanoi
University

Han Thuyen

To Luong Yen Station

Xuan Soan

Nguyen Cong Tru

Hai Ba
rung Temple

5

6

gogue & Chua Lien Phai Pagoda

of tour operators in the city including **Asia Pacific Travel**, 66 Hang Than St, Ba Dinh, T4-3836 4212, www.asiapacifictravel.com, and **Luxury Travel**, www.luxurytravelvietnam.com. Useful websites include www.hanoitourism.gov.vn, www.wordhanoi.com, www.tnhvietnam.xemzi.com/en and www.hanoigrapevine.com.

→ BACKGROUND

The origins of Hanoi as a great city lie with a temple orphan, Ly Cong Uan. Ly rose through the ranks of the palace guards to become their commander and in 1010, four years after the death of the previous King Le Hoan, was enthroned, marking the beginning of the 200-year Ly Dynasty. On becoming king, Ly Cong Uan moved his capital from Hoa Lu to Dai La, which he renamed Thang Long (Soaring Dragon). Thang Long is present-day Hanoi. Hanoi celebrated its 1000th anniversary in 2010.

During the period of French expansion into Indochina, the Red River was proposed as an alternative trade route to that of the Mekong. The French attacked and captured the citadel of Hanoi under the dubious pretext that the Vietnamese were about to attack. Recognizing that if a small expeditionary force could be so successful, then there would be little chance against a full-strength army, Emperor Tu Duc acceded to French demands. At the time that the French took control of Annam, Hanoi could still be characterized more as a collection of villages than a city. From 1882 onwards, Hanoi, along with the port city of Haiphong, became the focus of French activity in the north. Hanoi was made the capital of the new colony of Annam and the French laid out a 2-sq-km residential and business district, constructing mansions, villas and public buildings incorporating both French and Asian architectural styles. At the end of the Second World War, with the French battling to keep Ho Chi Minh and his forces at bay, Hanoi became little more than a service centre. After the French withdrew in 1954, Ho Chi Minh concentrated on building up Vietnam and in particular Hanoi's industrial base.

Although Ho Chi Minh City has attracted the lion's share of Vietnam's foreign inward investment, Hanoi, as the capital, also receives a large amount. But whereas Ho Chi Minh City's investment tends to be in industry, Hanoi has received a great deal of attention from property developers, notably in the hotel and office sectors.

PLACES IN HANOI

Hanoi itself is historical, beauitful and cultured and lies at the heart of a region packed with architecutral and scenic treasures. Like China when it was 'opening up' to Western tourists in the late 1970s, the primary interest lies in the novelty of exploring a city which, until recently, has opted for a firmly socialist road to development and has been insulated from the West. Today, you'll find it enlivened by an entrepeneurial spirit manifest in new shops, bars, companies and building developments.

→HOAN KIEM LAKE AND CENTRAL HANOI

HOAN KIEM LAKE

Hoan Kiem Lake or Ho Guom (the Lake of the Restored Sword) as it is more commonly referred to in Hanoi, is named after an incident that occurred during the 15th century. Emperor Le Thai To (1428-1433), following a momentous victory against an army of invading Ming Chinese, was sailing on the lake when a golden turtle appeared from the depths to take back the charmed sword which had secured the victory and restore it to the lake whence it came. Like the sword in the stone of British Arthurian legend, Le Thai To's sword assures Vietnamese of divine intervention in time of national crisis and the story is graphically portrayed in water puppet theatres across the country. There is a modest and rather dilapidated tower (the **Tortoise Tower**) commemorating the event on an islet in the southern part of the lake. In fact, the lake does contain large turtles; one captured in 1968 was reputed to have weighed 250 kg. The creatures that inhabit the lake are believed to be a variety of Asian softshell tortoise. It is thought that they were the species *Rafetus swinhoei* but a scientist reported that these species were in fact different from Ho Guom tortoises; the Ho Guom tortoise has now been named *Rafetus leloii*. In 2004 the water level fell quite dramatically and turtles were seen more often. The park that surrounds the lake is used by the residents of the city every morning for jogging and t'ai chi (Chinese shadow boxing) and is regarded by locals as one of the city's beauty spots. The light around the lake has a filmic quality, especially in the early morning. When the French arrived in Hanoi at the end of the 19th century, the lake was an unhealthy lagoon surrounded by so many huts that it was impossible to see the shore.

NGOC SON TEMPLE AND THE HUC (SUNBEAM) BRIDGE
① *Daily 0730-1730, 20,000d.*
The northeast corner of Hoan Kiem Lake is the place to have your photo taken, preferably with the **Ngoc Son Temple** in the background. The temple was built in the early 19th century on a small island on the foundations of the old Khanh Thuy Palace. The island is linked to the

shore by the **The Huc (Sunbeam) Bridge**, constructed in 1875. The temple is dedicated to Van Xuong, the God of Literature, although the 13th-century hero Tran Hung Dao, the martial arts genius Quan Vu and the physician La To are also worshipped here. Shrouded by trees and surrounded by water, the pagoda's position is its strongest attribute. To the side of the temple is a room containing a preserved turtle and photographs of the creatures in the lake.

OLD CITY AND 36 STREETS

Stretching north from the lake is the Old City (36 Streets and Guilds or 36 Pho Phuong). Previously, it lay to the east of the citadel, where the emperor had his residence, and was

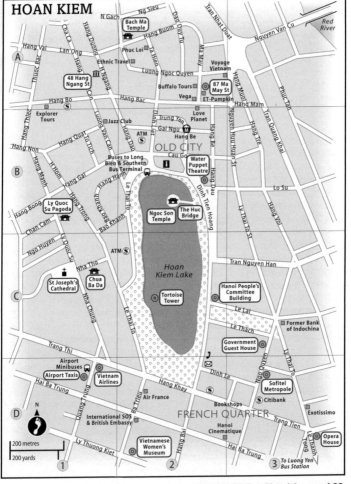

ON THE ROAD

Guild street name meanings and their current trades

Bat Dan St clay bowls
Bat Su ceramic bowls
Hang Bac silver, jewellery
Hang Bo baskets, motorbike stickers, barbecue squid (late night)
Hang Bong cotton
Hang Buom sails, coffee, chocolate, booze
Hang But calligraphy brushes
Hang Can weighing scales
Hang Dao silk (Pho Hang Dao means 'street where red-dyed fabrics are sold'), sewing things, feathers
Hang Dieu smoking pipes, fake brand name handbags
Hang Duong sugar

Hang Gai hemp, silk, souvenirs, galleries, tailor shops
Hang Ma votive paper, headstones
Hang Manh bamboo screens/mats
Hang Non conical hats
Hang Phen St alum sulphate
Hang Quat paper fans, religious artefacts
Hang Thiec tinsmiths, tin ovens
Hang Tre bamboo
Hang Trong drums, boutiques, galleries
Lan Ong traditional medicine
Hang Vai cloth street
Ngo Gach bricks
Thuoc Bac medicine street
To Tich undecorated mats, fruit cups
Yen Thai Alley embroidery

squalid, dark, cramped and disease-ridden. This part of Hanoi has survived surprisingly intact, and today is the most beautiful area of the city. Narrow streets, each named after the produce that it sells or used to sell (**Basket Street**, **Paper Street**, **Silk Street**, etc), create an intricate web of activity and colour (see box, above).

By the 15th century there were 36 short lanes here, each specializing in a particular trade and representing one of the 36 guilds. Among them, for example, were the **Phuong Hang Dao** (Dyers' Guild Street), and the **Phuong Hang Bac** (Silversmiths' Street). In fact, Hang Bac (*hang* means merchandise) is the oldest street in Hanoi, dating from the 13th century. The 36 streets have interested European visitors since they first started coming to Hanoi. For example, in 1685 Samuel Bacon, noted how "all the diverse objects sold in this town have a specially assigned street", remarking how different this was from "companies and corporations in European cities". The streets in question not only sold different products, but were usually also populated by people from different areas of the country – even from single villages. They would live, work and worship together because each of the occupational guilds had its own temple and its own community support networks.

Some of this past is still in evidence: at the south end of Hang Dau Street, for example, is a mass of stalls selling nothing but shoes, while Tin Street is still home to a community of pot and pan menders (and sellers). Generally, however, the crafts and trades of the past have given way to new activities – karaoke bars and tourist shops – but it is remarkable the extent to which the streets still specialize in the production and sale of just one type of merchandise.

The dwellings in this area are known as *nha ong* (**tube houses**). The majority were built at the end of the 19th century and the beginning of the 20th; they are narrow, with shop fronts sometimes only 3 m wide, but can be up to 50 m long (such as the one at 51 Hang Dao). In the countryside the dimensions of houses were calculated on the basis of the owner's own physical dimensions; in urban areas the tube houses evolved so that each house owner could have an, albeit very small, area of shop frontage facing onto the main street; the width was determined by the social class of the owner. The houses tend to be interspersed with courtyards or 'wells' to permit light into the house and allow some space for outside activities like washing and gardening. As geographers Brian Shaw and R Jones note in a paper on heritage conservation in Hanoi, the houses also had a natural air-conditioning system: the difference in ambient temperature between the inner courtyards and the outside street created air flow, and the longer the house the greater the velocity of the flow.

A common wall can sometimes still be seen between tube houses. Built in a step-like pattern, it not only marked land boundaries but also acted as a fire break. The position of the house frontages were not fixed until the early 20th century and consequently some streets have a delightfully irregular appearance. The structures were built of bricks 'cemented' together with sugar-cane juice.

The older houses tend to be lower; commoners were not permitted to build higher than the Emperor's own residence. Other regulations prohibited attic windows looking down on the street; this was to prevent assassination and to stop people from looking down on a passing king. As far as colour and decoration were concerned, purple and gold were strictly for royal use only, as was the decorative use of the dragon. By the early 20th century inhabitants were replacing their traditional tube houses with buildings inspired by French architecture. Many fine buildings from this era remain, however, and are best appreciated by standing back and looking upwards. Shutters, cornices, columns and wrought-iron balconies and balustrades are common decorative features. An ornate façade sometimes conceals the pitched roof behind. There are some good examples on **Nguyen Sieu Street**.

A fear among conservationists is that this unique area will be destroyed as residents who have made small fortunes with the freeing-up of the economy, redevelop their houses insensitively. The desire is understandable: the tube houses are cramped and squalid, and often without any facilities.

48 Hang Ngang Street ① *at the north end of Hang Dao St, before it becomes Hang Duong St, 0800-1130, 1330-1630, 10,000d*, is the spot where Ho Chi Minh drew up the Vietnamese Declaration of Independence in 1945, ironically modelled on the US Declaration of Independence. It now houses a **museum** with black and white photographs of Uncle Ho.

The house at **87 Ma May Street** ① *daily 0800-1200, 1300-1700, 5000d, guide included*, is a wonderfully preserved example of an original shop house now open to the public. The house was built in the late 1800s as a home for a single family. The importance of the miniature interior courtyards providing light, fresh air and gardens can be appreciated. The wooden upstairs and pitched fish-scale-tiled roofs are typical of how most houses would have looked. From 1954 to 1999 five families shared the building as the urban population rose and living conditions declined. The **Bach Ma (White Horse) Temple** ① *76 Hang Buom St*, dating from the ninth century, honours Long Do and is the oldest religious building in the Old Quarter. In 1010, King Ly Thai To honoured Long Do with the title of the capital. It is said that a horse revealed to King Ly Thai To where to build the walls of the citadel.

A walk through **Hang Be Market** (actually on Gai Ngu Street) reveals just how far Hanoi has developed over the past decade. There is a wonderful variety of food on sale – live, dead, cooked and raw. Quacking ducks, newly plucked chickens, saucers of warm blood, pigs' trotters, freshly picked vegetables as well as pickled ones; the quality of produce is remarkable and testimony to the rapid strides Vietnamese agriculture has made. In this market and surrounding streets beautiful cut flowers are on sale.

ON THE ROAD
Asian fusion fashion

The new entrepreneurial streak in Vietnam has proved a catalyst for fabulous design and ingenuity in the fashion world. Although known for the beautiful *ao dai*, the classic-cut trouser tunic of local women, Vietnam was not known for its haute-couture. Nowadays, fashionistas flock for the latest in desirable clothes, bags, shoes and other accessories from the country's designers who have come so far in just a few short years. From the inception of ideas to fabrication to the clothes rails, this has been fashion development on speed. Just 15 years ago, dour communist wear was the nation's lot but since economic liberalization national and international designers have gained fame at home and abroad with some selling to halls of sartorial fame such as **Harrods** and **Harvey Nichols** in London, and **Henri Bendel** in New York. Hollywood actress Cate Blanchett, Shakira Caine, wife of Oscar-winner Sir Michael, and US Senator Hillary Rodham Clinton are all followers of one such designer working under the **Ipa-Nima** label. Christina Yu, a Hong-Kong lawyer, now based in Vietnam, set up glitzy label **Ipa-Nima**. Her bags, clothes and shoes now decorate two shops in Hanoi. Valerie Gregori-McKenzie, a native Frenchwoman who lives in Vietnam, releases beautiful, ethereal clothes, embroidered cushions and bags under the label **Song**. She has two shops gracing Hanoi and Ho Chi Minh City. Sylvie Tran Ha, who is Viet Kieu, set up **SXS** in Ho Chi Minh City, which uses suede, among other materials. Many of these women have combined local materials with ideas, methods and motifs from the ethnic minority clothing of Vietnam. Mai Lam Mai, a Viet Kieu from Australia, has a boutique – Mai's – underneath the Continental Hotel. She sells cutting-edge fashions including a wonderful modern brightly coloured take and twist on the *ao dai*.

Most of the fashion designers using Vietnam as their creative hub are women. The exception to this rule is the elegantly dressed Hoang Khai of the ubiquitous **Khaisilk** empire. **Khaisilk** began as a workshop in Hanoi in 1980. Since then the empire has expanded with shops in Hanoi, Ho Chi Minh City and Hoi An. Now entrepreneurial owner Mr Khai has combined silk with food to create a series of stylish restaurants that are some of the most chic and glamorous in Vietnam. In the hotel domain, he has established the Hoi An Riverside Resort, a peaceful haven just outside Hoi An where attention to detail combined with the setting has produced one of the most exquisite hotels in the country. Mr Khai, who always dresses in black, wins award after award for his silk output and **Khaisilk**, with a winning marketing thrust, has ensured its place as the number one boutique shop in the country.

Venturing further north, is **Cua Quan Chuong**, the last remaining of Hanoi's 16 gates. In the 18th century a system of ramparts and walls was built around Hanoi. Quan Chuong Gate was built in 1749 and rebuilt in 1817.

Further north still, on Dong Xuan Street, is the large and varied **Dong Xuan Market**. This large covered market was destroyed in a disastrous fire in 1994. Stall holders lost an estimated US$4.5 million worth of stock and complained bitterly at the inadequacy of the fire services; one fire engine arrived with no water. The market has been rebuilt. It specializes mainly in clothes and household goods.

To the west, along Phung Hung Street is another live market of fish, dog, birds, vegetables and betel nut. It makes for a wonderful wander.

→ WEST OF HOAN KIEM LAKE

To the west of Hoan Kiem Lake in a little square stands the rather sombre, twin-towered neo-Gothic **Saint Joseph's Cathedral** ① *open 0500-1130*. Built in 1886, the cathedral is important as one of the very first colonial-era buildings in Hanoi finished, as it was, soon after the Treaty of Tientsin which gave France control over the whole of Vietnam. It was at located at the centre of the Catholic Mission. Some fine stained-glass windows remain.

About 100 m in front of the cathedral on Nha Tho Street is a much older religious foundation, the **Stone Lady Pagoda (Chua Ba Da)**, down a narrow alley. It consists of an old pagoda and a Buddhist school. On either side of the pagoda are low buildings where the monks live. Although few of the standing buildings are of any antiquity it is an ancient site and a tranquil and timeless atmosphere prevails. Originally built in 1056 as Sung Khanh Pagoda, by the late 15th century it needed rebuilding. A stone statue of a woman was found in the foundations and was worshipped in the pagoda. By 1767 the walls needed rebuilding. Each time they were built they collapsed. The foundations were dug deeper and the stone statue was found again. Since then the walls have held fast. Although now a pagoda for the worship of Buddha it is clear that the site has had a mixed spiritual history.

North of the cathedral on Ly Quoc Su Street is the **Ly Quoc Su Pagoda**, once home to Minh Khong, a physician and the chief adviser to Ly Than Tong, the Ly dynasty emperor. He became famous in the 12th century after curing the emperor of a disease that other doctors had failed to treat. It was restored in 2010.

→ SOUTH OF HOAN KIEM LAKE

OPERA HOUSE

① *www.hanoioperahouse.org.vn. Not open to the public except during public performances. See the billboards outside or visit the box office for details.*

To the south and east of Hoan Kiem Lake is the proud-looking French-era Opera House. It was built between 1901-1911 by François Lagisquet and is one of the finest French colonial buildings in Hanoi. Some 35,000 bamboo piles were sunk into the mud of the Red River to provide foundations for the lofty edifice. The exterior is a delightful mass of shutters, wrought-iron work, little balconies and a tiled frieze. The top balustrade is nicely capped with griffins. Inside, there are dozens of little boxes and fine decoration evocative of the French era. Having suffered years of neglect the Opera House was eventually lavishly restored, opening in time for the Francophone Summit held in 1997. Original drawings in Hanoi and Paris were consulted and teams of foreign experts were brought in to supervise local craftsmen. Slate was carried from Sin Ho to re-tile the roof, Italians oversaw the relaying of the mosaic floor in the lobby and French artists repainted the fine ornamental details of the auditorium. The restoration cost US$14 million, a colossal sum to spend on the reappointment of a colonial edifice. A Hanoi planning department architect explained that although the Opera House was French in style it was built by Vietnamese hands and represented an indelible part of Vietnamese history.

SOFITEL METROPOLE

① *15 Ngo Quyen St.*

The Metropole, built in French-colonial style in 1901 is an icon of elegance in the French quarter of the city. It quickly became the focal point of colonial life for 50 years. In 1916,

ON THE ROAD
Syndicated loans keep the sharks away

Throughout Vietnam, and indeed across the world wherever there are large numbers of Vietnamese, one will find *hui* in operation. *Hui* (or *ho* as it is called in the north) is a credit circle of 10 to 20 people who meet every month; the scheme lasts as many months as there are participants. In a blind auction the highest bidder takes home that month's capital. Credit is expensive in Vietnam, partly because there are few banks to make personal loans, so in time of crisis the needy have to borrow from money-lenders at crippling rates of interest. Alternatively they can join a *hui* and borrow at more modest rates.

It works like this: the *hui* is established with members agreeing to put in a fixed amount, say 100,000d, each month. Each month the members bid according to their financial needs, entering a zero bid if they need no cash. If, in month one, Mr Nam's daughter gets married he will require money for the wedding festivities and, moreover, he has to have the money so he must bid high, maybe 25,000d. Assuming this is the highest bid he will receive 75,000d from each member (ie 100,000d less 25,000d). In future months Mr Nam cannot bid again but must pay 100,000d to whoever collects that month's pot. Towards the end of the cycle several participants (those whose buffalo have not died and those whose daughters remain unmarried) will have taken nothing out but will have paid in 100,000d (minus x) dong each month; they can enter a zero bid and get the full 100,000d from all participants and with it a tidy profit. There is, needless to say, strategy involved and this is where the Vietnamese love of gambling ("the besetting sin of the Vietnamese" according to Norman Lewis) colours the picture. One day, Mr Muoi wins one million dong on the Vinh Long lottery. He lets it be known that he intends to buy a Honda Dream, but to raise the necessary purchase price he must 'win' that month's *hui* and will be bidding aggressively. In the same month Thuy, Mrs Phuoc's baby daughter, celebrates her first birthday so Mrs Phuoc needs money to throw a lavish *thoi noi* party. She has heard of old Muoi's intentions but doesn't know if he is serious. In case he is, she will have to bid high. On the day, nice Mrs Phuoc enters a knock-out bid of 30,000d but wily old Muoi was bluffing all along and he and the others make a lot of interest that month.

it screened the first movie shown in Indochina. In 1944, Japanese POWs were temporarily housed here. In the 1950s the Vietnamese government appropriated it, named it the **Thong Nhat Hotel**, and used it as a hotel for VIPs; during the Vietnam War years the press and diplomats used it as their headquarters. Many famous celebrities and diplomats have stayed here including Graham Greene (writing *The Quiet American*), Somerset Maugham, Noel Coward, Stephen Hawking, Oliver Stone, Charlie Chaplin, Sir Roger Moore, Jane Fonda, Mick Jagger, Catherine Deneuve, George Bush Senior, Fidel Castro, Robert McNamara, Jacques Chirac and Boutros Boutros Ghali.

MUSEUM OF THE VIETNAMESE REVOLUTION
ⓘ *1 Pham Ngu Lao St, daily 0800-1630, 20,000d.*

The Museum of the Vietnamese Revolution (Bao Tang Lich Su Quoc Gia), housed in an old French villa, traces the struggle of the Vietnamese people to establish their independence. Following the displays, it becomes clear that the American involvement in Vietnam has been just one episode in a centuries-long struggle against foreign aggressors. The 3000 exhibits are dryly presented across 29 rooms and in chronological order. They start with the cover the struggle for independence (1858-1945); the final rooms show the peace and prosperity of reunification: bountiful harvests, the opening of large civil engineering projects, and smiling peasants.

MUSEUM OF VIETNAMESE HISTORY

ⓘ *1 Trang Tien St, T4-325 3518, Tue-Sun 0800-1130, 1330-1630, 15,000d.*

A short distance south of the Museum of the Vietnamese Revolution is the History Museum (**Bao Tang Lich Su**). It is housed in a splendid building, completed in 1931. It was built as the home of the École Française d'Extrême-Orient, a distinguished archaeological, historical and ethnological research institute, by Ernest Hébrard. Hébrard, who was responsible for so many fine colonial-era buildings in Vietnam, here employed a distinctly Indochinese style appropriate to its original and, indeed, its current function. The museum remains a centre of cultural and historical research. The École Française d'Extrême-Orient played an important role in the preservation and restoration of ancient Vietnamese structures and temples, many of which were destroyed or came under threat of demolition by the French to enable the growth of their colonial city. The museum remains a centre of cultural and historical research. The collection spans Vietnamese history from the neolithic to the 20th century of Ho Chi Minh and is arranged in chronological order. Galleries lead from the Neolithic (Bac Son) represented by stone tools and jewellery; the Bronze Age (Dong Son) with some fine bronze drums; Funan and the port of Oc-Eo; Champa is represented by some fine stone carvings of *apsaras*, mythical dancing girls. There are relics such as bronze temple bells and urns of successive royal dynasties from Le to Nguyen. An impressive giant turtle, symbol of longevity, supports a huge stela praising the achievements of Le Loi, founder of the Le Dynasty, who harnessed nationalist sentiment and forced the Chinese out of Vietnam. Unfortunately some of the pieces (including a number of the stelae) are reproductions.

OTHER FRENCH QUARTER BUILDINGS

Other buildings of the 'French Concession' include the impressive **Government Guest House** ⓘ *12 Ngo Quyen St*, diagonally opposite the Metropole. The bright ochre building was the former residence of the French Resident Superior of Tonkin.

The enormous **Post Office** ⓘ *6 Dinh Le St*, facing Hoan Kiem lake, was designed by Henri Cerruti in 1942. Next door is the **Post and Telegraphic Office** ⓘ *75 Dinh Tien Hoang St*, designed by Auguste-Henri Vildieu and completed in 1896. Further up Dinh Tieng Hoang is the **Hanoi People's Committee** building, formerly the town hall and built by Vildieu between 1897 and 1906. The main section at the front dates from the late 1980s and early 1990s demonstrating brutalist communist architecture. Vildieu also designed the **Supreme Court** ⓘ *48 Ly Thuong Kiet*, between 1900 and 1906. It's a fine symmetrical building with a grey-tiled roof, two staircases and balustrades.

Ernest Hébrard, who worked at the Central Services of Urban Planning and Architecture, designed the **Indochina University**, now **Hanoi University** ⓘ *19 Le Thanh Tong St*, which was completed in 1926. It bears a remarkable resemblance to the history museum, which he also designed. Furthermore, Hébrard designed the **Ministry of Foreign Affairs** (then the **Bureau des Finances**) ⓘ *Dien Bien Phu St*, in 1931.

The architecturally remarkable former **Bank of Indochina** ⓘ *49 Ly Thai To St*, was built in 1930 by architect Georges-André Trouvé. Its grey, heavy art deco appearance and isolated position evokes a bit of fear. One wonders what the bank vaults look like inside.

Around 1000 colonial villas are still scattered around Hanoi, especially west of the Old Quarter. Many of them have been superbly restored and are used by embassies.

VIETNAMESE WOMEN'S MUSEUM

ⓘ *36 Ly Thuong Kiet St, T4-3825 9936, www.womenmuseum.org.vn, 30,000d, Tue-Sun 0900-1630.*

A well-curated, fascinating museum containing 25,000 objects and documents that give visitors an excellent insight in to women's roles in Vietnam, past and present. Information on many of the country's 54 ethnic groups is displayed. The museum holds regular exhibitions. Highly recommended.

HOA LO PRISON

ⓘ *1 Hoa Lo, daily 0800-1700, 20.000d, 10,000d for children and students.*

Hoa Lo Prison (Maison Centrale), better known as the **Hanoi Hilton**, is the prison where US POWs were incarcerated, some for six years, during the Vietnamese War. Up until 1969, prisoners were also tortured here. Two US Airforce officers, Charles Tanner and Ross Terry, rather than face torture, concocted a story about two other members of their squadron who had been court-martialled for refusing to fly missions against the north. Thrilled with this piece of propaganda, visiting Japanese communists were told the story and it filtered back to the US. Unfortunately for Tanner and Terry they had called their imaginary pilots Clark Kent and Ben Casey (both TV heroes). When the Vietnamese realized they had been made fools of, the two prisoners were again tortured. The final prisoners were not released until 1973, some having been held in the north since 1964.

At the end of 1992 a US mission was shown around the prison where 2000 inmates were housed in cramped and squalid conditions. Despite pleas from war veterans and party members, the site was sold to a Singapore-Vietnamese joint venture and is now a hotel and shopping complex, **Hanoi Towers**. As part of the deal the developers had to leave a portion of the prison for use as a museum, a lasting memorial to the horrors of war.

'Maison Centrale', reads the legend over the prison's main gate, which leads in to the museum. There are recreations of conditions under colonial rule when the barbarous French incarcerated patriotic Vietnamese from 1896: by 1953 they were holding 2000 prisoners in a space designed for 500. Many well-known Vietnamse were incarcerated here: Phan Boi Chau (founder of the Reformation Party; 1867-1940), Luong Van Can (Reformation Party leader and school founder; 1854-1927), Nguyen Quyen (founder along with Luong Van Can of the School for the Just Cause; 1870-1942) and five men who were later to become general secretaries of the Communist Party: Le Duan (served as general secretary 1976-1986), Nguyen Van Cu (served 1938-1940), Truong Chinh (served 1941-1956 and July-December 1986), Nguyen Van Linh (served 1986-1991) and Do Muoi (served 1991-1997). Less prominence is given to the role of the prison for holding American pilots, but Douglas 'Pete' Peterson, the first post-war American Ambassador to Vietnam (1997-2001), who was one such occupant (imprisoned 1966-1973) has his mug-shot on the wall, as does John McCain (imprisoned 1967-1973), now a US senator.

AMBASSADORS' PAGODA (QUAN SU) AND AROUND

ⓘ *73 Quan Su St.*

In the 15th century there was a guesthouse on the site of the Ambassadors' Pagoda (Quan Su Pagoda) for visiting Buddhist ambassadors. The current structure was built between

ON THE ROAD
Bites but no bark in a Vietnamese restaurant

Quang Vinh's restaurant was the ideal place for the ordeal to come. The palm-thatched house near the West Lake, on the outskirts of the Vietnamese capital Hanoi, was far from the accusing eyes of fellow Englishmen.

It was dark outside. At one table, a Vietnamese couple were contentedly finishing their meal. At another, a man smoked a bamboo pipe. A television at the end of the room showed mildly pornographic Chinese videos.

But then came the moment of truth: could an Englishman eat a dog? Could he do so without his stomach rebelling, without his thoughts turning to labradors snoozing by Kentish fireplaces, Staffordshire bull terriers collecting sticks for children, and Pekinese perched on the laps of grandmothers?

One Englishman could: I ate roast dog, dog liver, barbecued dog with herbs and a deliciously spicy dog sausage, for it is the custom to dine on a selection of dog dishes when visiting a dog restaurant. The meat tastes faintly gamey. It is eaten with noodles, crispy rice-flour pancakes, fresh ginger, spring onions, apricot leaves and, for cowardly Englishmen, plenty of beer.

I had been inspired to undergo this traumatic experience – most un-British unless one is stranded with huskies on a polar ice cap – by a conversation earlier in the week with Do Duc Dinh, a Vietnamese economist, and Nguyen Thanh Tam, my official interpreter and guide.

They were much more anxious to tell me about the seven different ways of cooking a dog, and how unlucky it was to eat dog on the first five days of the month, than they were to explain Vietnam's economic reforms. "My favourite," began Tam, "is minced intestines roasted in the fire with green beans and onions." He remembered proudly how anti-Vietnamese protesters in Thailand in the 1980s had carried placards saying "Dog-eaters go home!"

During the Vietnam War, he said, a famous Vietnamese professor had discovered that wounded soldiers recovered much more quickly when their doctors prescribed half a kilogram of dog meat a day. Dinh insisted I should eat dog in Hanoi rather than Saigon. "I went to the south and ate dog, but they don't know how to cook it like we do in the north," he said. I asked where the dogs came from. "People breed it, then it becomes the family pet." And then they eat it? "Yes," he said with a laugh. I told myself that the urban British, notorious animal lovers that they are, recoil particularly at the idea of eating dogs only because most of them never see the living versions of the pigs, cows, sheep and chickens that they eat in meat-form every day. And the French, after all, eat horses. Resolutely unsentimental, we put aside our dog dinner and went to Vinh's kitchen. Two wire cages were on the floor; there was one large dog in the first and four small dogs in the second. Two feet away, a cauldron of dog stew steamed and bubbled. Vinh told us about his flourishing business. The dogs are transported from villages in a nearby province. A 10 kg dog costs him about 120,000d, or just over US$10. At the end of the month – peak dog-eating time – his restaurant gets through about 30 dogs a day. The restaurant, he said, was popular with Vietnamese, Koreans and Japanese. Squeamish Westerners were sometimes tricked into eating dog by the Vietnamese friends, who would entertain them at the restaurant and tell them afterwards what it was they had so heartily consumed. Source: Extracted from an article by Victor Mallet, *The Financial Times*.

1936 and 1942. Chinese in appearance from the exterior, the temple contains some fine stone sculptures of the past, present and future Buddhas. It is very popular and crowded with scholars, pilgrims, beggars and incense sellers. The pagoda is one of the centres of Buddhist learning in Vietnam (it is the headquarters of the Vietnam Central Buddhist Congregation): at the back is a school room which is in regular use, students often spill-over into the surrounding corridors to listen.

Nearby, on Le Duan Street just south of the railway station, stalls sell a remarkable array of US, Soviet and Vietnamese army-surplus kit.

VIETNAM MILITARY HISTORY MUSEUM AND CITADEL

ⓘ *28 Dien Bien Phu St, T4-3733 6453, www.btlsqsvn.com, Tue-Thu, Sat and Sun 0800-1130, 1300-1630, 30,000d, camera use, 20,000d, ATM and Highlands Coffee Café on site.*

A five-minute walk east from the Fine Arts Museum, is the **Military History Museum** (Bao Tang Lich Su Quan Su). Tanks, planes and artillery fill the courtyard. Symbolically, an untouched Mig-21 stands at the museum entrance while wreckage of B-52s, F1-11s and Q2Cs is piled up at the back. The museum illustrates battles and episodes in Vietnam's fight for independence from the struggles with China (there is a good display of the Battle of Bach Dang River of AD 938) through to the resistance to the French and the Battle of Dien Bien Phu (illustrated by a good model). Inevitably, of course, there are lots of photographs and exhibits of the American War and although much is self-evident, unfortunately a lot of the explanations are in Vietnamese only.

In the precincts of the museum is the **Cot Co**, a flag tower, raised up on three platforms. Built in 1812, it is the only substantial part of the original citadel still standing. There are good views over Hanoi from the top. The walls of the **citadel** were destroyed by the French in 1894 to 1897, presumably as they symbolized the power of the Vietnamese emperors. The French were highly conscious of the projection of might, power and authority through large structures, which helps explain their own remarkable architectural legacy. Other remaining parts of the citadel are in the hands of the Vietnamese army and out of bounds to visitors. Across the road from the museum's front entrance is a **statue of Lenin**.

The **North Gate** of the citadel is on Phan Dinh Phung St and can be visited (10,000d). South on Hoang Dieu is the **Doan Mon Gate** (free, 0800-1130, 1400-1630) where you can nose at the previously off-limits citadel exploration and get a new view of Cot Co and the citadel complex from the roof. The citadel was named a UNESCO World Heritage Site in August 2010.

→ HO CHI MINH'S MAUSOLEUM COMPLEX AND AROUND

HO CHI MINH'S MAUSOLEUM

ⓘ *Summer Tue-Thu, Sat and Sun 0730-1100. Winter Tue-Thu, Sat and Sun 0800-1100, closed 6 weeks from Sep for conservation. Before entering the mausoleum (25,000d), visitors must leave cameras and possessions at the office (Ban To Chuc) on Huong Vuong, just south of and a few mins' walk from the Mausoleum. Visitors must be respectful: dress neatly, walk solemnly, do not talk and do not take anything in that could be construed as a weapon, for example a penknife.* The Vietnamese have made Ho Chi Minh's body a holy place of pilgrimage and visitors march in file to see Ho's embalmed corpse inside the mausoleum (Lang Chu Tich Ho Chi Minh).

The mausoleum, built between 1973 and 1975, is a massive, square, forbidding structure and must be among the best constructed, maintained and air-conditioned buildings in

Vietnam. Opened in 1975, it is a fine example of the mausoleum genre and is modelled closely on Lenin's Mausoleum in Moscow. Ho lies, with a guard at each corner of his bier. The embalming of his body was undertaken by the chief Soviet embalmer Dr Sergei Debrov who also pickled such communist luminaries as Klement Gottwald (President of Czechoslovakia), Georgi Dimitrov (Prime Minister of Bulgaria) and Forbes Burnham (President of Guyana). Debrov was flown to Hanoi from Moscow as Ho lay dying, bringing with him two transport planes packed with air conditioners (to keep the corpse cool) and other equipment. To escape US bombing, the team moved Ho to a cave, taking a full year to complete the embalming process. Russian scientists still check-up on their handiwork, servicing Ho's body regularly. Their embalming methods and the fluids they use are still a closely guarded secret, and in a recent interview, Debrov noted with pleasure the poor state of China's Chairman Mao's body, which was embalmed without Soviet help.

The embalming and eternal display of Ho Chi Minh's body was however contrary to Ho's own wishes: he wanted to be cremated and his ashes placed in three urns to be positioned atop three unmarked hills in the north, centre and south of the country. He once wrote that "cremation is not only good from the point of view of hygiene, but it also saves farmland".

BA DINH SQUARE
In front of Ho Chi Minh's Mausoleum is Ba Dinh Square where Ho read out the Vietnamese Declaration of Independence on 2 September 1945. Following Ho's declaration, 2 September became Vietnam's National Day. Coincidentally 2 September was also the date on which Ho died in 1969, although his death was not officially announced until 3 September.

In front of the mausoleum on Bac Son Street is the **Dai Liet Si**, a memorial to the heroes and martyrs who died fighting for their country's independence. It appears to be modelled as a secular form of stupa and inside is a large bronze urn.

HO CHI MINH'S HOUSE AND THE PRESIDENTIAL PALACE
ⓘ *Ho Chi Minh's house, 1 Bach Thao St, T4-3804 4529; Summer Tue-Thu, Sat and Sun, 0730-1100, 1400-1600, Fri 0730-1100; winter Tue-Thu, Sat and Sun 0800-1100, 1330-1600, Fri 0800-1100; 25,000d; the Presidential Palace is not open to the public.*
From the mausoleum, visitors are directed to Ho Chi Minh's house built in the compound of the former Presidential Palace. The palace, now a Party guesthouse, was the residence of the Governors-General of French Indochina and was built between 1900 and 1908 by Auguste-Henri Vildieu. In 1954, when North Vietnam's struggle for independence was finally achieved, Ho Chi Minh declined to live in the palace, saying that it belonged to the people. Instead, he stayed in what is said to have been an electrician's house in the same compound. Here he lived from 1954 to 1958, before moving to a new stilt house built on the other side of the small lake (Ho Chi Minh's 'Fish Farm', swarming with massive and well-fed carp). The house was designed by Ho and an architect, Nguyen Van Ninh. This modest house made of rare hardwoods is airy and personal and immaculately kept. Ho conducted meetings under the house, which is raised up on wooden pillars, and slept and worked above (his books, slippers and telephones are still here) from May 1958 to August 1969. Built by the army, the house mirrors the one he lived in while fighting the French from his haven near the Chinese border. Behind the house is Ho's bomb shelter, and behind that, the hut where he actually died in 1969.

ON THE ROAD

Quan Am was turned onto the streets by her husband for some unspecified wrong-doing and, dressed as a monk, took refuge in a monastery. There, a woman accused her of fathering, and then abandoning, her child. Accepting the blame (why, no one knows), she was again turned out onto the streets, only to return to the monastery much later when she was on the point of death – to confess her true identity. When the Emperor of China heard the tale, he made Quan Am the Guardian Spirit of Mother and Child, and couples without a son now pray to her.

Quan Am's husband is sometimes depicted as a parakeet, with the Goddess usually holding her adopted son in one arm and standing on a lotus leaf (the symbol of purity).

ONE PILLAR PAGODA (CHUA MOT COT)

Close by is the One Pillar Pagoda, one of the few structures remaining from the original foundation of the city. It was built in 1049 by Emperor Ly Thai Tong, although the shrine has since been rebuilt on several occasions, most recently in 1955 after the French destroyed it before withdrawing from the country. The emperor built the pagoda in a fit of religious passion after he dreamt that he saw the goddess Quan Am (Vietnam's equivalent of the Chinese goddess Kuan-yin) sitting on a lotus and holding a young boy, whom she handed to the emperor. On the advice of counsellors who interpreted the dream, the Emperor built this little lotus-shaped temple in the centre of a water-lily pond and shortly afterwards his queen gave birth to a son. As the name suggests, it is supported on a single (concrete) pillar with a brick and stone staircase running up one side. The pagoda symbolizes the 'pure' lotus sprouting from the sea of sorrow. Original in design, with dragons running along the apex of the elegantly curved tiled roof, the temple is one of the most revered monuments in Vietnam. But the ungainly concrete pillar and the pond of green slime in which it is embedded detract considerably from the enchantment of the little pagoda. Adjacent is the inhabited Dien Huu Pagoda; a sign says they don't like people in shorts, but they are quite friendly and it has a nice courtyard.

HO CHI MINH MUSEUM

ⓘ*19 Ngoc Ha St, T4-3846 3752, Tue-Thu and Sat 0800-1130, 1400-1600, Fri 0800-1130, 25,000d, 460,000d for a guide.*

Overshadowing the One Pillar Pagoda is the Ho Chi Minh Museum – opened in 1990 in celebration of the centenary of Ho's birth. Contained in a large and impressive modern building, likened to a white lotus, it is the best-arranged and most innovative museum in Vietnam. The displays trace his life and work from his early wanderings around the world to his death and final victory over the south.

TEMPLE OF LITERATURE (VAN MIEU PAGODA)

ⓘ*The entrance is on Quoc Tu Giam St, T4-3845 2917, open daily summer 0730-1730, winter 0730-1700, 20,000d, 45-min tour in French or English 100,000d, 8000d for brochure. ATM inside.*

The Temple of Literature is the largest, and probably the most important, temple complex in Hanoi. It was founded in 1070 by Emperor Ly Thanh Tong, dedicated to Confucius who had a substantial following in Vietnam, and modelled, so it is said, on a temple in Shantung,

ON THE ROAD
The examination of 1875

The examinations held at the Temple of Literature and which enabled, in theory, even the most lowly peasant to rise to the exalted position of a Mandarin, were long and difficult and conducted with great formality.

André Masson quotes Monsieur de Kergaradec, the French Consul's, account of the examination of 1875.

"On the morning of the big day, from the third watch on, that is around one o'clock in the morning, the big drum which invites each one to present himself began to be beaten and soon students, intermingled with ordinary spectators, approached the Compound in front of the cordon formed around the outer wall by soldiers holding lances. In the middle of the fifth watch, towards four or five o'clock in the morning, the examiners in full dress came and installed themselves with their escorts at the different gates. Then began the roll call of the candidates, who were thoroughly searched at the entrance, and who carried with them a small tent of canvas, and mats, cakes, rice, prepared tea, black ink, one or two brushes and a lamp. Everyone once inside, the gates were closed, and the examiners met in the central pavilion of the candidates' enclosure in order to post the subject of the composition. During the afternoon, the candidates who had finished withdrew a few at a time through the central gate, the last ones did not leave the Compound until midnight."

Doctor Laureate on his way home. From an illustration by H Oger in 1905.

Going to the examination camp with apparatus (bamboo bed, writing box, bamboo tube for examination papers). From an illustration by H Oger in 1905.

China, the birthplace of the sage. Some researchers, while acknowledging the date of foundation, challenge the view that it was built as a Confucian institution pointing to the ascendancy of Buddhism during the Ly Dynasty. Confucian principles and teaching rapidly replaced Buddhism, however, and Van Mieu subsequently became the intellectual and spiritual centre of the kingdom as a cult of literature and education spread among the court, the mandarins and then among the common people. At one time there were said to be 20,000 schools teaching the Confucian classics in northern Vietnam alone.

The temple and its compound are arranged north-south, and visitors enter at the southern end from Quoc Tu Giam Street. On the pavement two pavilions house stelae bearing the inscription *ha ma* (climb down from your horse), a nice reminder that even the most elevated dignitaries had to proceed on foot. The main **Van Mieu Gate** (Cong Van Mieu Mon) is adorned with 15th-century dragons. Traditionally, the large central gate was opened only on ceremonial occasions. The path leads through the Cong Dai Trung to a second courtyard and the **Van Khue Gac Pavilion** which was built in 1805 and dedicated to the Constellation of Literature. The roof is tiled according to the yin-yang principle.

Beyond lies the **Courtyard of the Stelae** at the centre of which is the rectangular pond or Cieng Thien Quang (Well of Heavenly Clarity). More important are the stelae themselves, 82 in all, on which are recorded the names of 1306 successful examination scholars (*tien si*). Of the 82 that survive (30 are missing) the oldest dates back to 1442 and the most recent to 1779. Each stela is carried on the back of a tortoise, symbol of strength and longevity but they are arranged in no order; three chronological categories, however, can be identified. Fourteen date from the 15th and 16th centuries; they are the smallest and are embellished with floral motifs and yin-yang symbols but not dragons (a royal emblem). Twenty-five stelae are from the 17th century and are ornamented with dragons (by then permitted), pairs of phoenix and other creatures mythical or real. The remaining 43 stelae are of 18th-century origin; they are the largest and are decorated with two stylized dragons, some merging with flame clouds.

Passing the examination was not easy: in 1733, out of some 3000 entrants only eight passed the doctoral examination (*Thai Hoc Sinh*) and became Mandarins – a task that took 35 days. This tradition was begun in 1484 on the instruction of Emperor Le Thanh Tong, and continued through to 1878, during which time 116 examinations were held. The Temple of Literature was not used only for examinations, however: food was also distributed to the poor and infirm, 500 g of rice at a time. In 1880, the French Consul Monsieur de Kergaradec recorded that 22,000 impoverished people came to receive this meagre handout.

Continuing north, the **Dai Thanh Mon** (Great Success Gate) leads on to a courtyard flanked by two buildings which date from 1954, the originals having been destroyed in 1947. These buildings were reserved for 72 disciples of Confucius. Facing is the **Dai Bai Duong** (Great House of Ceremonies), which was built in the 19th century but in the earlier style of the Le Dynasty. The carved wooden friezes with their dragons, phoenix, lotus flowers, fruits, clouds and yin-yang discs are all symbolically charged, depicting the order of the universe and by implication reflecting the god-given hierarchical nature of human society, each in his place. It is not surprising that the communist government has hitherto had reservations about preserving a temple extolling such heretical doctrine. Inside is an altar on which sit statues of Confucius and his closest disciples. Adjoining is the **Dai Thanh Sanctuary** (Great Success Sanctuary), which also contains a statue of Confucius.

To the north once stood the first university in Vietnam, Quoc Tu Giam, which from the 11th to 18th centuries educated first the heir to the throne and later sons of mandarins.

It was replaced with a temple dedicated to Confucius' parents and followers, which was itself destroyed in 1947.

FINE ARTS MUSEUM (BAO TANG MY THUAT)

①*66 Nguyen Thai Hoc St, T4-3733 2131, www.vnfineartsmuseum.org.vn, Tue-Sun 0830-1700, Wed and Sat 0800-2100, 7000d. Free tours in English or French, register in advance, no photography. Restaurant in museum grounds.*

Not far from the northern walls of the Van Mieu Pagoda is the Fine Arts Museum, contained in a large colonial building. The oriental roof was added later when the building was converted to a museum. The ground-floor galleries display pre-20th-century art – from Dongsonian bronze drums to Nguyen Dynasty paintings and sculpture, although many works of this later period are on display in the Museum of Royal Fine Arts in Hué. There are some particularly fine stone Buddhas. The first floor is given over to folk art. There are some lovely works from the Central Highlands and engaging Dong Ho woodblock prints – one block for each colour – and Hang Trong woodblock prints, a single black ink print which is coloured in by hand. There are also some fine lacquer paintings. The top floor contains 20th-century work including some excellent water colours and oil paintings. Contemporary Vietnamese artists are building a significant reputation for their work. There is a large collection of overtly political work, posters and propaganda (of great interest to historians and specialist collectors), and a collection of ethnic minority clothes is exhibited in the annex.

→ **OUTER HANOI**

NORTH OF THE OLD CITY

North of the Old City is **Ho Truc Bach** (**White Silk Lake**). Truc Bach Lake was created in the 17th century by building a causeway across the southeast corner of Ho Tay. This was the site of the 11th-century **Royal Palace** which had, so it is said, 'a hundred roofs'. All that is left is the terrace of Kinh Thien with its dragon staircase, and a number of stupas, bridges, gates and small pagodas.

At the southwest corner of the lake, on the intersection of Hung Vuong, Quan Thanh and Thanh Nien streets is the **Quan Thanh Pagoda** ①*2000d*, originally built in the early 11th century in honour of Huyen Thien Tran Vo (a genie) but since much remodelled. Despite renovation, it is still very beautiful. The large bronze bell was cast in 1677.

To the east of here the Long Bien and Chuong Duong bridges cross the Red River. The former of these two bridges was built as a road and rail bridge by Daydé & Pillé of Paris and named **Paul Doumer Bridge** after the Governor General of the time. Construction was begun in 1899 and it was opened by Emperor Thanh Thai on 28 February 1902. Today it is used by trains, bicycles, motorbikes and pedestrians. Over 1.5 km in length, it was the only river crossing in existence during the Vietnam War and suffered repeated attacks from US planes, only to be quickly repaired. The Chuong Duong Bridge was completed at the beginning of the 1980s.

The much larger **Ho Tay** (**West Lake**) was originally a meander in the Red River. The **Tran Quoc Pagoda**, an attractive brick-red building, can be found on an islet on the east shores of the lake, linked to the causeway by a walkway. It was originally built on the banks of the Red River before being transferred to its present site by way of an intermediate location. The pagoda contains a stela dated 1639 recounting its unsettled history.

A few kilometres north, on the tip of a promontory, stands **Tay Ho Pagoda**, notable chiefly for its setting. It is reached along a narrow lane lined with stalls selling fruit, roses and paper votives and a dozen restaurants serving giant snails with *bun oc* (noodles) and fried shrimp cakes. Dominating it is an enormous bronze bell held by a giant dragon hook supported by concrete dragons and two elephants; notice the realistic glass eyes of the elephants.

However, West Lake is fast losing its unique charm as development spreads northwards. The nouveau riche of Hanoi are rapidly turning the area into a middle-class suburb and new restaurants and bars have clustered around Xuan Dieu Street. New houses go up in an unplanned and uncoordinated sprawl. Nguyen Ngoc Khoi, director of the Urban Planning Institute in Hanoi, estimates that the area of the lake has shrunk by 20%, from 500 ha to 400 ha, as residents and hotel and office developers have reclaimed land. The lake is also suffering encroachment by water hyacinths, which are fed by organic pollutants from factories (especially a tannery) and untreated sewage. The view from Nghi Tam Road, which runs along the Red River dyke, presents a contrasting spectacle of sprawling houses interspersed with the remaining plots of land which are intensively and attractively cultivated market gardens supplying the city with flowers and vegetables.

MUSEUM OF ETHNOLOGY AND B-52 MEMORIALS

ⓘ *8 km west of the city centre in Cau Giay District (Nguyen Van Huyen Rd), T4-3756 2193, www.vme.org.vn, Tue-Sun 0830-1730, 25,000d, photography 50,000d, tour guide, 50,000d. Catch the No 14 minibus from Dinh Tien Hoang St, north of Hoan Kiem Lake, to the Nghia Tan stop; turn right and walk down Hoang Quoc Viet St for 1 block, before turning right at the Petrolimex station down Nguyen Van Huyen; the museum is down this street, on the left. Alternatively take a taxi. Branch of Baguette & Chocolat bakery on site.*

The museum opened in November 1997 in a modern, purpose-built structure. The collection here of some 5000 artefacts, 42,000 photographs and documentaries of practices and rituals is excellent and, more to the point, is attractively and informatively presented with labels in Vietnamese, English and French. It displays the material culture (textiles, musical instruments, jewellery, tools, baskets and the like) of the majority Kinh people as well as Vietnam's 53 other designated minority peoples. While much is historical, the museum is also attempting to build up its contemporary collection. There is a very good shop attached to the museum. The highlight is wandering the gardens at the rear where ethnic minorities' homes have been moved from their ancestral site and painstakingly rebuilt.

On the routes out to the Ethnology Museum are two B-52 memorials. The remains of downed B-52s have been hawked around Hanoi over many years but seem to have found a final resting place at the **Bao Tang Chien Tang B-52 (B-52 Museum)** ⓘ *157 Doi Can St, free.* This curious place is not really a museum but a military hardware graveyard, but this doesn't matter because what everyone wants to do is walk over the wings and tail of a shattered B-52, and the B-52 in question lies scattered around the yard. As visitors to Vietnamese museums have by now come to expect, any enemy objects are literally heaped up as junk while the 'heroic' Vietnamese pieces are painted, tended for and carefully signed with the names of whichever heroic unit fought in them. Here we have anti-aircraft guns, the devastating SAMs that wreaked so much havoc on the USAF and a MIG21. Curiously the signs omit to mention the fact that all this hardware was made in Russia. The size and strength of the B-52 is simply incredible and needs to be seen to be believed.

ON THE ROAD

Vietnamese history honours a number of heroines, of whom the Trung sisters are among the most revered. At the beginning of the Christian era, the Lac Lords of Vietnam began to agitate against Chinese control over their lands. Trung Trac, married to the Lac Lord Thi Sach, was apparently of a 'brave and fearless disposition' and encouraged her husband and the other lords to rise up against the Chinese in AD 40. The two sisters often fought while pregnant, apparently putting on gold-plated armour over their enlarged bellies. Although an independent kingdom was created for a short time, ultimately the uprising proved fruitless; a large Chinese army defeated the rebels in AD 43, and eventually captured Trung Trac and her sister Trung Nhi, executing them and sending their heads to the Han court at Lo-yang. An alternative story of their death has it that the sisters threw themselves into the Hat Giang River to avoid being captured, and turned into stone statues. These were washed ashore and placed in Hanoi's Hai Ba Trung Temple for worship.

On Hoang Hoa Tham Street, between Nos 55 and 57, a sign points 100 m down an alley to the wreckage of a B-52 bomber sticking up out of the pond-like Huu Tiep Lake. There's a plaque on the wall stating that at 2305 on 27 December 1972, Battalion 72 of Regiment 285 shot down the plane. At the time Huu Tiep was a flower village and the lake a lot bigger.

SOUTH OF HANOI

Down Hué Street is the hub of motorcycle sales, parts and repairs. Off this street, for example along Hoa Ma, Tran Nhan Tong and Thinh Yen, are numerous stalls and shops, each specializing in a single type of product – TVs, electric fans, bicycle parts and so on. It is a fascinating area to explore. At the intersection of Thinh Yen and Pho 332, people congregate to sell new and second-hand bicycles, as well as bicycle parts.

Not far away is the venerable **Den Hai Ba Trung (Hai Ba Trung Temple)** ① *open 1st and 15th of each lunar month, 0600-1800, free*, the temple of the two Trung Sisters – overlooking a lake. The temple was built in 1142, but like others, has been restored on a number of occasions. It contains crude statues of the Trung sisters, Trung Trac and Trung Nhi (see box, above), which are carried in procession once a year during February.

Further south still from the Hai Ba Trung, is another pagoda – **Chua Lien Phai**. This quiet pagoda, which can be found just off Bach Mai Street, was built in 1732, although it has since been restored.

Compared with Ho Chi Minh City and the south, Hanoi and its surrounds are rich in places of interest. Not only is the landscape more varied and attractive, but the 1000-year-old history of Hanoi has generated dozens of sights of architectural appeal, many of which can be visited on a day trip.

PERFUME PAGODA

① 50,000d entrance plus 40,000d per person for the boat (maximum 6 people). Taking a tour is the best way to get here.

The Perfume Pagoda (Chua Huong or Chua Huong Tich) is 60 km southwest of Hanoi. A sampan takes visitors along the Yen River, a diverting 4-km ride through a flooded landscape to the Mountain of the Perfume Traces. From here it is a 3-km hike up the mountain to the cool, dark cave wherein lies the Perfume Pagoda. Dedicated to Quan Am (see box, above), it is one of a number of shrines and towers built among limestone caves and is regarded as one of the most beautiful spots in Vietnam. The stone statue of Quan Am in the principal pagoda was carved in 1793 after Tay Son rebels had stolen and melted down its bronze predecessor to make cannon balls. Emperor Le Thanh Tong (1460-1497) described it as "Nam Thien de nhat dong" ("foremost cave under the Vietnamese sky"). It is a popular pilgrimage spot, particularly during the festival months of March and April.

Perfume Pagoda Festival From the sixth day of the first lunar month to the end of the third lunar month (15th-20th day of the second lunar month is the main period). This festival focuses on the worship of the Goddess of Mercy (Quan Am). Thousands flock to this famous pilgrimage site. Worshippers take part in dragon dances and a royal barge sails on the river.

HANDICRAFT VILLAGES

Many tour operators arrange excursions to villages just outside of Hanoi including Van Phuc, where silk is produced, Bat Trang, where ceramics and bricks are made, and Le Mat, a snake village; here visitors can try eating snake meat.

HANOI AND AROUND LISTINGS

WHERE TO STAY

$$$$ InterContinental Hanoi Westlake, 1A Nghi Tam, Tay Ho District, T4-6270 8888, www.ichotelsgroup.com/intercontinental. One of the newer 5-star hotels. Rooms are large with traditional Vietnamese decor. The bar and pool areas face West Lake and are lovely in the early evening when *den choi* (fire-powered paper balloons) drift over the water. Cocktails are good but international prices. In 2012, **InterContinental** opened the **Hanoi Landmark 72** hotel in the tallest building in Vietnam.

$$$$ Sofitel Legend Metropole Hanoi, 15 Ngo Quyen St, T4-3826 6919, www. accorhotels.com. The French colonial-style cream building with green shutters is beautifully and lusciously furnished and exudes style. It boasts a diversity of bars and restaurants. **Le Beaulieu** is one of the finest restaurants in Hanoi. A small pool is boosted by the attractive poolside **Bamboo Bar**. The **Le Spa du Metropole** is seriously chic.

$$$$-$$$ Zephyr, 4-6 Ba Trieu St, T4-3934 1256, www.zephyrhotel.com.vn. A little business-like, but a very popular hotel, largely due to its excellent location within sight of Hoan Kiem Lake and solid service. Serves a good breakfast, including *pho*, and international options.

$$$ Joseph's Hotel, 5 Au Trieu St, T4-3938 1048, www.josephshotel.com. Right near St Joseph's Cathedral, on Au Trieu St –

a cosy street filled with good cafés and shops – **Joseph's Hotel** is small, with just 10 rooms, but all are very well equipped and some have awesome cathedral views from small balconies. Staff are friendly and helpful. Wi-Fi in all rooms. Breakfast included. Highly recommended. Also runs **$$ Joseph's Hang Da**, 6C Duong Thanh St, www.josephshangdahotel.com.

$$ Hanoi Guesthouse, 85 Ma May St, T4-3935 2572, www.hanoiguesthouse.com. Excellent-value rooms. Whitewashed walls, dark wood furnishings and wooden floors. Some with huge windows and plenty of light. Ask to see a few. Recommended.

$$-$ May De Ville Backpackers Hostel, 1 Tai Tuong Lane, 24 Ta Hien St, T4-3935 2468, www.maydevillebackpackershostel. com. Large, bright double and twin rooms which are better than the price tag would suggest. Cheap dorm beds are also available. Has a games room and a home cinema room complete with comfy beanbags.

$ Hanoi Backpackers' Hostel, 48 Ngo Huyen St, T4-3828 5372, www.hanoiback packershostel.com. Dorm rooms and double suites in a house that belonged to the Brazilian ambassador. A friendly and busy place. Breakfast, internet, tea/coffee and luggage store are included. Don't miss the barbecues on the roof terrace. A second **Hanoi Backpackers** is at 9 Ma May St.

RESTAURANTS

Hanoi has Western-style restaurants, coffee bars and watering holes to rival those in Europe, as well as a good number of excellent Vietnamese restaurants.

    Note Dog (*thit chó* or *thit cay*) is a delicacy in the north but is mostly served in shacks on the edge of town – so you are unlikely to order it inadvertently.

$$$ El Gaucho, 99 Xuan Dieu, T4-3718 6991, www.elgaucho.asia. Perhaps the best steak

in town – certainly merits the journey from the city centre. Cool, bare-brick surroundings. Superb cocktails and a good cellar.

$$$ Lá, 25 Ly Quoc Su St, T4-3928 8933. This attractive green and cream building houses a restaurant serving up marvellous Vietnamese and international food. Behind the modest exterior is one of the best-loved restaurants in the city. Traditional Vietnamese menu as well as a range of unpretentious fusion meals and daily specials. The bistro atmosphere is comfortable and the wine list excellent. The small bar is surprisingly well stocked.

$$$-$$ La Badiane, 10 Nam Ngu St, T4-3942 4509, www.labadiane-hanoi.com. La Badiane's French aesthetic stops at the food. Fusion, and of more than Vietnamese and French, is what this restaurant is about and while its intricately decorated plates of seasonal meals won't appeal to everyone there are many who swear this is the best restaurant in town. Service is good, if over attentive at times. Portions have increased but order a starter too if you're hungry. The converted colonial villa is delightful. The set lunch menu is a bargain at US$15.50.

$$ Hanoi Cooking Centre, 44 Chau Long St, T4-3715 0088, http://hanoicookingcentre. com. Run by Aussie cookbook author Tracey Lister, this restaurant, café and cooking centre is housed in a restored colonial villa near Truc Bach Lake. As well as excellent cooking classes, the centre serves dishes rarely seen in Hanoi, such as a seasonal Sunday roast.

$$ KOTO, 59 Van Mieu St, next to Temple of Literature, T4-3747 0337, www.koto.com. au. Mon 0700-1600, Tue-Sun 0700-2130. A training restaurant for under-privileged young people. The food is international, filling and delicious. Upstairs is the **Temple Bar** with Wi-Fi.

$$-$ Chim Sáo, 65 Ngo Hué St, T4-3976 0633, www.chimsao.com. Set in an atmospheric old colonial villa, **Chim Sao** is famous for its speciality Northern Vietnamese food. Don't miss the chicken wings in fish sauce and the sautéed duck. Seating is on the floor upstairs. Ask about a lovely homestay here: www.orientalbridge. com/maison-en.htm. Great rice wine too – try the apple variant.

$$-$ Highway 4, 5 Hang Tre St, T4-3926 4200, www.highway4.com. Open 0900-0200. **Highway 4** has numerous branches throughout Vietnam, but this is the original. It specializes in ethnic minority dishes from North Vietnam (Highway 4 is the most northerly road in Vietnam running along the Chinese border) but now includes a full menu of dishes from other provinces. The chicken with lemongrass and the papaya salad are particularly good. The fruit and rice wines – available in many flavours – are the highlight of this place.

$ Tamarind, 80 Ma May St, T4-3926 0580, www.tamarind-cafe.com. Very smart vegetarian restaurant with a lengthy menu and delicious juices. The Thai glass noodle salad is delicious.

ENTERTAINMENT

Hanoi's main bar street, Ta Hien, heading towards Hang Buom after it has cut across the famous Bia Hoi Corner (at Luong Ngoc Quyen), has been spruced up and is home to more drinking holes than ever. See www.wordhanoi.com, www.tnhvietnam.xemzi.com/en and www.hanoigrapevine.com.

CAMA ATK, Mai Hac De, www.cama-atk. com for what's on. Wed-Sat, 1800-2400. Run by the people behind Hanoi's music promotion collective, **CAMA**, this feels more East London than Hanoi, with superb cocktails, DJ sets and film nights. Happy hour 1800-2000.

Commune, 20A Duong Yen, T4-6684 7903. www.communehanoi.com. A café by day and a bar by night, **Commune** is a social enterprise with an arty vibe. The roof terrace is a great spot for a sundowner looking over West Lake, interesting international menu and good coffee.

Water Puppetry House, 57 Dinh Tien Hoang St, T4-3824 9494, www.thanglong waterpuppet.org. Fabulous shows with exciting live music and beautiful comedy: the technical virtuosity of the puppeteers is astonishing. Admission 100,000d (1st class); 60000d (2nd class); children half price on Sun. This is not to be missed.

NINH BINH AND AROUND

Ninh Binh is capital of the densely populated province of Ninh Binh. It marks the most southerly point of the northern region. The town itself has little to commend to the tourist but it is a useful and accessible hub from which to visit some of the most interesting and attractive sights in the north. Within a short drive lie the ancient capital of Hoa Lu with its temples dedicated to two of Vietnam's great kings; the exquisite watery landscape of Tam Coc, an 'inland Halong Bay', where sampans carry visitors up a meandering river, through inundated grottoes and past verdant fields of rice; the Roman Catholic landscape around Phat Diem Cathedral, spires and towers, bells and smells; and the lovely Cuc Phuong National Park, with its glorious butterflies, flowers and trees. The town of Nam Dinh is a centre for visiting several pagodas in the area before returning to Hanoi to continue the route up to the Northwest Highlands.

ARRIVING IN NINH BINH

Getting there It is a three-hour journey from Hanoi by bus or by train. From Hanoi, the route south runs through expanding industrial towns which, in the last few years have been convulsed with change: road widenings, demolition of old buildings to make way for industrial zones and factories gobbling up 'ricefield' sites. Communities, which for centuries were divided by nothing more than a dirt track, now find themselves rent asunder by four-lane highways, but ancient ties of kith and kin and tradition have yet to adjust. Beyond Phu Ly the limestone karsts start to rise dramatically out of the flat plain.

Moving on It's best to head back to Hanoi by bus or train for onward connections. However, some Open Tour Buses do stop here on the way to Hué.

Getting around Visitors can get to the places around Ninh Binh as a day trip from Hanoi through tour agencies or by taking tours or hiring transport from the hotels in Ninh Binh.

Tourist information Ninh Binh Tourism ① *www.ninhbinhtourism.com.vn*, can arrange tours and transport. The hotels all have good information.

HOA LU

① *6 km north of Ninh Binh and 6 km west of Highway 1, follow signs to Truong Yen, 20,000d.*
Hoa Lu lies about 13 km from Ninh Binh near the village of **Truong Yen**; it is a couple of kilometres signposted off the main road and can be reached by bicycle or *xe ôm*. It was the capital of Vietnam from AD 968 to 1010, during the Dinh and Early Le dynasties. Prior to the establishment of Hoa Lu as the centre of the new kingdom, there was nothing here. But the location was a good one in the valley of the Hong River – on the 'dragon's belly', as the Vietnamese say. The passes leading to the citadel could be defended with a small force, and defenders could keep watch over the plains to the north and guard against the Chinese. The kings of Hoa Lu were, in essence, rustics. This is reflected in the art and architecture of the temples of the ancient city: primitive in form, massive in conception. Animals were the dominant motifs, carved in stone.

A large part of this former capital, which covered over 200 ha, has been destroyed, although archaeological excavations have revealed much of historical and artistic interest. The two principal temples are those of Dinh Bo Linh, who assumed the title King Dinh Tien

Hoang on ascending the throne (reigned AD 968-980), and Le Hoan, who assumed the title King Le Dai Hanh on ascending the throne (reigned AD 980-1009).

The **Temple of Dinh Tien Hoang** was originally constructed in the 11th century but was reconstructed in 1696. It is arranged as a series of courtyards, gates and buildings. The inscription on a pillar in the temple, in ancient Vietnamese, reads 'Dai Co Viet', from which the name 'Vietnam' is derived. The back room of the temple is dedicated to Dinh Tien Hoang, whose statue occupies the central position, surrounded by those of his sons, Dinh Lien (to the left), Dinh Hang Lang and Dinh Toan (to the right). In the AD 960s, Dinh Tien Hoang managed to pacify much of the Red River plain, undermining the position of a competing ruling family, the Ngos, who accepted Dinh Tien Hoang's supremacy. However, this was not done willingly, and banditry and insubordination continued to afflict Hoang's kingdom. He responded by placing a kettle and a tiger in a cage in the courtyard of his palace and decreed: 'those who violate the law will be boiled and gnawed'. An uneasy calm descended on Dinh Tien Hoang's kingdom, and he could concern himself with promoting Buddhism and geomancy, arranging marriages, and implementing reforms. But, by making his infant son Hang Lang heir apparent, rather than Lien (his only adult son), he sealed his fate. History records that the announcement was followed by earthquakes and hailstorms, a sign of dissension in the court, and in AD 979 Lien sent an assassin to kill his younger brother Hang Lang. A few months later in the same year, an official named Do Thich killed both Dinh Tien Hoang and Lien as they lay drunk and asleep in the palace courtyard. When Do Thich was apprehended, it is said that he was executed and his flesh fed to the people of the city.

The **Temple of King Le Dai Hanh** is dedicated to the founder of the Le Dynasty who seized power after the regicide of Dinh Tien Hoang. In fact Le Dai Hanh took not only Hoang's throne but also his wife, Duong Van Nga. Representations of her, Le Dai Hanh and Le Ngoa Trieu (also known as Le Long Dinh), his fifth son, each sit on their own altar in the rear temple. Near this temple the foundations of King Dinh's (10th century) royal palaces were found by Vietnamese archaeologists in 1998.

A short walk beyond Le Dai Hanh's temple is **Nhat Tru Pagoda**, a 'working' temple. In front of it stands a pillar engraved with excerpts from the Buddhist bible (*Kinh Phat*). Opposite Dinh Tien Hoang's temple is a hill, Nui Ma Yen, at the top of which is **Dinh Tien Hoang's tomb**. Locals will tell you it is 260 steps to the top.

TAM COC AND BICH DONG

ⓘ *Daily 0700-1700, 80,000d (1-2 people) for the boat, 30,000d for the grottoes including Bich Dong (a tip and purchase will be requested on the boat). The turning to Tam Coc and Bich Dong is 4 km south of Ninh Binh on Highway 1. A small road leads 2-3 km west to Tam Coc. Tam Coc can easily be reached by bicycle or xe ôm from Ninh Binh or by car from Hanoi (on a day trip). There are a couple of hotels and restaurants.*

Tam Coc means literally 'three caves'. The highlight of this excursion is an enchanting boat ride up the little Ngo Dong River through the eponymous three caves. Those who have seen the film *Indochine*, some of which was shot here, will be familiar with the nature of the beehive-type scenery created by limestone towers, similar to those of Halong Bay. The exact form varies from wet to dry season; when flooded the channel disappears and one or two of the caves may be under water. In the dry season the shallow river meanders between fields of golden rice. You can spot mountain goat precariously clinging to the rocks and locals collecting snails in the water. Women row and punt pitch-and-resin tubs that look like elongated coracles through the tunnels. It is a most leisurely experience and a chance to observe at close quarters the extraordinary method of rowing with the feet. Take plenty of sun cream and a hat. The villagers have a rota for rowing and supplement their fee by trying to sell visitors embroidered table cloths and napkins. On a busy day the scene from above is like a two-way, nose-to-tail procession of waterboats; to enjoy Tam Coc at its best make it your first port of call in the morning.

A short drive to the south is **Bich Dong**. This is much harder work, so not surprisingly it is a lot quieter than Tam Coc. Bich Dong consists of a series of temples and caves built into, and carved out of, a limestone mountain. The temples date from the reign of Le Thai To in the early 15th century. It is typical of many Vietnamese cave temples but with more than the average number of legends attached to it, while the number of interpretations of its rock formations defies belief. The lower temple is built into the cliff face. Next to the temple is a pivoted and carved rock that resonates beautifully when tapped with a stone. Next see Buddha's footprints embedded in the rock (size 12, for the curious) and the tombs of the two founding monks.

Leading upwards is the middle temple, an 18th-century bell, a memorial stone into which are carved the names of benefactors and a cave festooned with rock forms. Here, clear as can be, are the likenesses of Uncle Ho, a turtle and an elephant. More resonant rock pillars follow and a rock which enables pregnant women to choose the sex of their baby: touch the top for a boy and the middle for a girl. But best of all scramble right to the pinnacle of the peak for a glorious view over the whole area. Unfortunately, the view has been marred by a horrible new orange and sickly green concrete building.

PHAT DIEM CATHEDRAL

① *24 km southeast of Ninh Binh in the village of Kim Son, daily 0800-1700, English and French guidebook; 15,000d; there are several services daily. The journey takes in a number of more conventional churches, waterways and paddy fields. Take a motorbike from Ninh Binh or hire a car from Hanoi. Hoa Lu, Tam Coc and Phat Diem can all be comfortably covered in 1 day; there are souvenir shops selling nuoc mam (fish sauce) and Virgin figures side by side.*

Phat Diem Cathedral is the most spectacular of the church buildings in the area, partly for its scale but also for its remarkable Oriental style with European stylistic influences. Completed in 1899, it boasts a bell tower in the form of a pagoda behind which stretches for 74 m the nave of the cathedral held up by 52 ironwood pillars. The cathedral was built under the leadership of parish priest Father Tran Luc between 1875 and 1899. He is buried in a tomb between the bell tower and the cathedral proper. Surrounding the cathedral are several chapels: St Joseph's, St Peter's, the Immaculate Heart's, the Sacred Heart's and St Roch's.

In 1953 French action in the area saw artillery shells damage the eastern wing of the cathedral causing part of the roof to collapse.

The cathedral was bombed in 1972 by Americans who despatched eight missiles. St Peter's Church was flattened, St Joseph's blown to an angle, the cathedral forced to a tilt, the roof tiles hurled to the floor, and 52 of the 54 cathedral doors were damaged. Restoration of different parts of the complex is ongoing.

The approach to the cathedral is impressive: you drive down a narrow valley to be confronted with a statue of Christ the King in the middle of a huge square pond; behind are the cathedral buildings.

The Red River Delta was the first part of the country to be influenced by Western missionaries: Portuguese priests were proselytizing here as early as 1627. Christian influence is still strong despite the mass exodus of Roman Catholics to the south in 1954 and decades of Communist rule. Villages (which are built of red brick, often walled and densely populated) in these coastal provinces may have more than half-a-dozen churches, all with packed congregations, not only on Sundays. The churches, the shrines, the holy grottoes, the photographs of the parish priest on bedroom walls and the holy relics clearly assume huge significance in people's lives.

CUC PHUONG NATIONAL PARK

ⓘ *Nho Quan district, T30-384 8018, www.cucphuongtourism.com, daily 0500-2100, 540,000d, children 20,000d; botanic garden 5000d. 1- to 6-day treks can be arranged with a guide; short treks of a couple of hours are also available (trail to silver cloudy peak and ancient tree; trail to Muong village; wildlife experience tour; night spotting; bicycle tours can also be arranged). Mr Hai who is head of the tour guide section is very helpful and has worked at the park for more than 10 years. A visit to the park can be done as a day trip from Ninh Binh or from Hanoi. Direct access by car only. An organized tour from Hanoi may be a sensible option for lone travellers or pairs, otherwise charter a car or hire a motorbike.*

The park, which is around 120 km south of Hanoi and 45 km west of Ninh Binh, is probably the second most accessible of Vietnam's national parks, and for nature lovers not intending to visit Cat Ba Island, it is worthy of consideration. It is also Vietnam's oldest park, established in 1962. Located in an area of deeply cut limestone and reaching elevations of up to 800 m, the park is covered by 22,000 ha of humid tropical montane forest. It is home to an estimated 2000 species of flora including the giant parashorea, cinamomum and sandoricum trees. Wildlife has been much depleted by hunting; only 117 mammal and 307 bird species and 110 reptile and amphibian species are thought to remain. The government has resettled a number of the park's 30,000 Muong minority people, although Muong villages do remain and can be visited. April and May see fat grubs and pupae metamorphosing into swarms of butterflies that mantle the forest in fantastic shades of greens and yellows.

The **Endangered Primate Rescue Center** ⓘ *www.primatecenter.org, 0900-1100, 1330-1600, limited entrance every 30 mins, 30,000d,* is a big draw in the park. There are more than 30 cages, four houses and two semi-wild enclosures for the 130 animals in breeding programmes; there are some 15 different species and sub-species. The centre is repsonsible for discovering a new species in Vietnam, the grey-shanked douc langur (*Pygathrix cinereus*), in 1997. The centre's work is extremely interesting and it is well worth a visit.

There's also the **Turtle Conservation Center**. Visitors can arrange tours to visit the 16 species kept there. Cuc Phuong also has a botanical garden that is excellent for birdwatching in the early morning as well as listening to the nearby primates' dawn chorus.

Visitors can take a number of trekking tours in the park and also spend the night at homestays with the Muong. Night spotting could enable you to see black giant squirrel, Indian flying squirrel, samba deer and Loris. Birdwatchers could see the rare feathers of the silver pheasant, red-collared woodpecker, brown hornbill and bar-bellied pitta. Two lucky tourists and their guide saw an Asiatic black bear in early 2007.

Facilities at the park headquarters include accommodation, a restaurant, visitor centre and guides' headquarters; a museum is planned. From here you can trek for 25 km camping, accompanied by a guide From headquarters to the park centre is 20 km. The drive will take you past Mac Lake, the path for the walk to the 45-m-high Ancient Tree

(*Tetrameles nudiflora*), and Cave of Prehistoric man. At the park centre you can walk the 7-km paved hike through forest to the 1000-year-old tree (45 m high and 5 m wide) and a 1000-m-long liana (*Entada tonkinensis*) and palace cave. The centre area has accommodation and a restaurant.

NINH BINH AND AROUND LISTINGS

WHERE TO STAY

Ninh Binh is not on the main tourist track but it offers some reliable hotel choices with standard services. There's nothing glamorous – just functional, clean hotels with helpful staff. In addition, staying in Cuc Phuong National Park's various accommodation options is a highlight for some.

Ninh Binh

$$-$ Hoang Hai Hotel, 36 and 62 Truong Han Sieu St, T30-387 5177, www.ninhbinhhotel.com.vn. The 40 rooms are divided into 3 types; the bigger rooms are more expensive.

$$-$ Thuy Anh, 55A Truong Han Sieu St, T30-387 1602, www.thuyanhhotel.com. 37 rooms, with fridge, etc, in this spotless hotel in the town centre; the deluxe rooms come with a view. Breakfast included. Will arrange tours and are a useful source of information. The restaurant is good and there is the **Lighthouse Café** and rooftop garden.

$$ Thanh Thuy's Guesthouse, 128 Le Hong Phong St, T30-3871811, www.hotel thanhthuy.com. A friendly place with cheap rooms and newer, more expensive rooms. Most bathrooms have bathtubs.

Cuc Phuong National Park

There are 3 different areas with accommodation: at the park HQ (1 km from the main gate); at Mac Lake (2 km from the park HQ); or at the park centre (20 km from the main gate).

$$ Headquarters detached bungalow.

$$ Mac Lake Bungalow. 4 bungalows with a/c and private bathroom. These rooms have fan and shared bathrooms with hot water.

$$ Park centre concrete bungalows with en suite and a/c but more expensive than at HQ. The 4 bungalows, are set around a lawn. Electricity only available 1800-2200.

$$-$ Headquarters concrete bungalows with en suite facilities, TV and a/c and fan. These are lined up across the road from the restaurant and are clean and comfortable.

$ Headquarters stilt house.

$ Park centre stilt houses. These are near the start of the 1000-year-old walk. They have shared bathroom facilities and no hot water.

RESTAURANTS

Ninh Binh

$ Hoang Hai Hotel, 36 Truong Han Sieu St, T30-387 5177. Open 0900-2200. This centrally located restaurant has zero atmosphere but service is prompt. Breakfast, lunch and dinner served.

$ Thanh Thuy's Guesthouse, 128 Le Hong Phong St, T30-3871811, www.hotel thanhthuy.com. The portions are generous.

$ Thuy Anh, 55A Truong Han Sieu St, T30-387 1602, www.thuyanhhotel.com.

A choice of Vietnamese fare across a range of prices in the **Roof Top Garden** and **Lighthouse Café**. Buffet dinner available.

Cuc Phuong National Park

$ There are 3 restaurants in the national park at each of the accommodation areas. They serve a limited, and sometimes unavailable, range of food. Vegetarians are catered for. Drinks available.

WHAT TO DO

Ninh Binh

Thanh Thuy's Guesthouse, www.hotel thanhthuy.com. Runs a recommended 3-day trip to the Pu Luong Nature Reserve near Mai Chau. Also trips to local attractions.

Thuy Anh, www.thuyanhhotel.com. Runs tours to Tam Coc, Bich Dong, Hoa Lu, Kenh Ga, Van Long Reserve, Phat Diem and Cuc Phuong. Can also arrange trips to Haiphong, Cat Ba and Halong, as well as trekking.

NORTHWEST

The geology of much of Northwest Vietnam is limestone; the effect on this soft rock of the humid tropical climate and the resulting numerous streams and rivers is remarkable. Large cones and towers (hence tower karst), sometimes with vertical walls and overhangs, rise dramatically from the flat alluvial plains. Dotted with bamboo thickets, this landscape is one of the most evocative in Vietnam; its hazy images seem to linger deep in the collective Vietnamese psyche and perhaps symbolize a sort of primeval Garden of Eden, an irretrievable age when life was simpler and more innocent.

Interwoven into this landscape are the houses of the ethnic minorities, beautiful tiled houses in the main. Passing through you will see people tending paddies in traditional clothing and boys on the backs of buffalo. In the far-flung northwest corner is Dien Bien Phu, the site of the overwhelming defeat of the French in Vietnam in 1954 and now home to the largest monument in Vietnam, erected in 2004 to commemorate the 50th anniversary of the Vietnamese victory.

ARRIVING IN THE NORTHWEST

Getting there and around There are three points of entry for the Northwest circuit: the south around Hoa Binh (reached by road); the north around Lao Cai/Sapa (reached by road or by train); and in the middle Dien Bien Phu, reached by plane or road. Which option you pick will depend upon how much time you have available and how much flexibility you require. It is possible to hire a jeep in Hanoi to do the clockwise circuit via Hoa Binh and Dien Bien Phu and pay off your driver at Sapa leaving you free to return by train.

Another option for those so inclined is to do the whole thing by motorbike. The rugged terrain and relatively quiet roads make this quite a popular choice for many people. It has the advantage of enabling you to to make countless side trips and get to remote and untouched tribal areas. It is not advisable to attempt the whole circuit using public transport as this would involve fairly intolerable levels of discomfort and a frustrating lack of flexibility and would be very time-consuming.

Best time to visit The region is wet from May to September, making travel quite unpleasant at this time. Owing to the altitude of much of the area winter can be quite cool, especially around Sapa, so make sure you go well prepared.

Tourist information The Northwest is not a single administrative area so ask at the province and town tourist authorities for local information. Otherwise tour operators in Hanoi are helpful. There are banks and ATMs in Hoa Binh, Dien Bien Phu, Sapa and Lao Cai.

→ HANOI TO SAPA VIA DIEN BIEN PHU

The road from Hanoi to Dien Bien Phu winds its way for 420 km into the Annamite Mountains that mark the frontier with the Lao People's Democratic Republic. The round trip from Hanoi and back via Dien Bien Phu and Sapa is about 1200 km and offers some of the most spectacular scenery anywhere in Vietnam. The loop can be taken in a clockwise or anti-clockwise direction; the advantage of following the clock is that you'll have the opportunity to recover from the rigours of the journey in Sapa. before continuing the route up to the remote villages of the far north.

ON THE ROAD
People of the North

Ethnic groups belonging to the Sino-Tibetan language family such as the Hmong and Dao, or the Ha Nhi and Phula of the Tibeto-Burman language group are relatively recent arrivals. Migrating south from China only within the past 250-300 years, these people have lived almost exclusively on the upper mountain slopes, practising slash-and-burn agriculture and posing little threat to their more numerous lowland-dwelling neighbours, notably the Thai.

Thus was established the pattern of human and political settlement that would persist in North Vietnam right up until the colonial period – a centralized Viet state based in the Red River Delta area, with powerful Thai vassal lordships dominating the Northwest. Occupying lands located in some cases almost equidistant from Hanoi, Luang Prabang and Kunming, the Thai, Lao, Lu and Tay lords were obliged during the pre-colonial period to pay tribute to the royal courts of Nam Viet, Lang Xang (Laos) and China, though in times of upheaval they could – and frequently did – play one power off against the other for their own political gain. Considerable effort was thus required by successive Viet kings in Thang Long (Hanoi) and later in Hué to ensure that their writ and their writ alone ruled in the far north. To this end there was ultimately no substitute for the occasional display of military force, but the enormous cost of mounting a campaign into the northern mountains obliged most Viet kings simply to endorse the prevailing balance of power there by investing the most powerful local lords as their local government mandarins, resorting to arms only when separatist tendencies became too strong. Such was the political situation inherited by the French colonial government following its conquest of Indochina in the latter half of the 19th century. Its subsequent policy towards the ethnic minority chieftains of North Vietnam was to mirror that of the Vietnamese monarchy whose authority it assumed; throughout the colonial period responsibility for colonial administration at both local and provincial level was placed in the hands of seigneurial families of the dominant local ethnicity, a policy which culminated during the 1940s in the establishment of a series of ethnic minority 'autonomous zones' ruled over by the most powerful seigneurial families.

Highway 6, which has been thoroughly rebuilt along almost the entire route from Hanoi to Son La, leads southwest out of Hanoi to Hoa Binh. Setting off in the early morning the important arterial function of this road is evident. Ducks, chickens, pigs, bamboo and charcoal (the energy and building materials of the capital) all pour in to Hanoi – a remarkable volume of it transported by bicycle. Beyond the city limit the fields are highly productive, with bounteous market gardens and intensive rice production.

→ MAI CHAU

After leaving Hoa Binh, Highway 6 heads in a south-southwest direction as far as the Chu River. Thereafter it climbs through some spectacular mountain scenery before descending into the beautiful Mai Chau Valley. During the first half of this journey, the turtle-shaped roofs of the Muong houses predominate, but after passing Man Duc the road enters the territory of the Thai, Northwest Vietnam's most prolific minority group, heralding a subtle change in the style of stilted-house architecture. While members of the Thai will be encountered frequently on this circuit, it is their Black Thai sub-ethnic group which will be seen most often. What makes the Mai Chau area interesting is that it is one of the few places en route where travellers can encounter their White Thai cousins.

An isolated farming community until 1993, Mai Chau has undergone significant change in just a few short years. Its tranquil valley setting, engaging White Thai inhabitants and superb rice wine make Mai Chau a very worthwhile stop.

BACKGROUND

The growing number of foreign and domestic tourists visiting the area in recent years has had a significant impact on the economy of Mai Chau and the lifestyles of its inhabitants. Some foreign visitors complain that the valley has already gone a long way down the same road as Chiang Mai in northern Thailand, offering a manicured hill-tribe village experience to the less adventurous tourist who wants to sample the quaint lifestyle of the ethnic people without too much discomfort. There may be some truth in this allegation, but there is another side to the coin. Since the region first opened its doors to foreign tourists in 1993, the Mai Chau People's Committee has attempted to control the impact of tourism in the valley. **Lac** is the official tourist village to which tour groups are led (there are some 108 guesthouses), and although it is possible to visit and even stay in the others, by 'sacrificing' one village to tourism it is hoped the impact will be limited. Income generated from tourism by the villagers of Lac has brought about a significant enhancement of lifestyles, not just in Lac but also throughout the entire valley, enabling many villagers to tile their roofs and purchase consumer products such as television sets, refrigerators and motorbikes. Of course, for some foreign visitors the sight of a television aerial or a T-shirt is enough to prove that an ethnic village has already lost its traditional culture, but in Lac they are wily enough to conceal their aerials in the roof space.

LAC (WHITE THAI VILLAGE)

① *Lac is easily accessible from the main road. From the direction of Hoa Binh take the track to the right, immediately before the ostentatious, red-roofed People's Committee Guesthouse. This leads directly into the village of Lac.*

This village is popular with day-trippers and overnight visitors from Hanoi. Turning into the village one's heart may sink: minibuses are drawn up and stilt houses in the centre of the village all sport stickers of Hanoi tour operators. But before you turn and flee take a stroll around the village, find a non-stickered house and by means of gestures, signs, broken English and the odd word of Vietnamese ask whether you can spend the night.

Rent a bicycle from your hosts and wobble across narrow bunds to the neighbouring hamlets, enjoying the ducks, buffaloes, children and lush rice fields as you go. It is a most delightful experience. If you are lucky you will be offered a particularly refreshing tea made from the bark of a tree.

GROTTOES

About 5 km south of Mai Chau on Route 15A is the Naon River on which, in the dry season, a boat can be taken to visit a number of large and impressive grottoes. Others can be reached on foot. Ask your hosts for details.

AROUND MAI CHAU

A number of interesting and picturesque walks and treks can be made in the countryside surrounding Mai Chau. These cover a wide range of itineraries and durations, from short circular walks around Mai Chau, to longer treks to minority villages in the mountains beyond. One such challenging trek covers the 20 km to the village of **Xa Linh**, just off Highway 6. This usually takes between two and three days, with accommodation provided in small villages along the way. Genial host Mr Gia in the Hmong village of **Hung Kia** will warmly welcome you for a couple of dollars per night, copious amounts of rice wine included. Be forewarned that this route can become dangerously slippery in the wet and a guide is required; ask at the People's Committee Guesthouse or in Lac. Expect to pay US\$15-20 for two days and arrange for transport to collect you in Xa Linh.

PU LUONG NATURE RESERVE
① Ba Thuoc Project Office, Trang Village, Lam Xa Commune, Ba Thuoc District, Thanh Hoa, T37-388 0671.

Pu Luong Nature Reserve is a newly protected area of limestone forest southeast of Mai Chau that harbours the endangered **Delacour's langur**, **clouded leopard**, **Owston's civet** and **bear**. Birdwatching is best from October to March. From Ban Sai, 22 km south of Mai Chau, trekkers can visit caves and local Thai and Muong communities. From the south, near the reserve headquarters close to Canh Nang, there is the Le Han ferry crossing. From here visitors can see the traditional water wheels at Ban Cong, trek deep east to Ban Son and then, after overnighting, trek up north back to Highway 6. Also from Le Han, trekkers can overnight in Kim Giao Forest in the west of the reserve before visiting an old French airbase, Pu Luong Mountain (1700 m) and trekking north back to the Mai Chau area. Biking and boat in and around the reserve is also possible. Contact the reserve office or Hanoi tour operators.

MOC CHAU AND CHIENG YEN
North of Mai Chau on the road to Son La is Chieng Yen. Home to 14 villages of Thai, Dao, Muong and Kinh, there are new homestay options with trekking and biking opportunities as well as tea farm visits at Moc Chau. A highlight is the weekly Tuesday market.

→SON LA

The road to Son La is characterized by wonderful scenery and superb Black Thai and Muong villages. The road passes close to several attractive villages each with a suspension footbridge and fascinating hydraulic works. Mini hydroelectric generators on the river supply houses with enough power to run a light or television and water power is also used to husk and mill rice. The succession of little villages located just across the river to the left-hand side of the road between 85 km and 78 km from Son La, affords an excellent opportunity to view Black Thai stilt-house architecture. **Cuc Dua** village at the 84-km mark is photogenic. Typically there is a suspension bridge over the incised river in which you can see fish traps and swimming children as clouds of butterflies flutter by on the breeze.

BACKGROUND
It was not until the 18th century, under the patronage of the Black Thai seigneurial family of Ha, that Son La began to develop as a town. During the late 1870s the region was invaded by renegade Chinese Yellow Flag bands taking refuge after the failed Taiping Uprising. Allying himself to Lin Yung-fu, commander of the pursuing Black Flag forces, Deo Van Tri, Black Thai chieftain, led a substantial army against the Yellow Flags in 1880, decisively defeating and expelling them from the country. Thus Tri established hegemony

over all the Black and White Thai lords in the Son La area, enabling him to rely on their military support in his subsequent struggle against the French – indeed, the chieftains of Son La were to take an active role in the resistance effort between 1880 and 1888.

As the French moved their forces up the Da River Valley during the campaign of 1888, the chieftains of the area were one by one obliged to surrender. A French garrison was quickly established at Son La. As elsewhere in the Northwest, the French chose to reward the chieftains of Son La district for their new-found loyalty by reconfirming their authority as local government mandarins, now on behalf of a colonial rather than a royal master.

While large-scale resistance to French rule in the Northwest effectively ceased after 1890, sporadic uprisings continued to create problems for the colonial administration. The French responded by establishing detention centres throughout the area, known to the Thai as *huon mut* (dark houses). The culmination of this policy came in 1908 with the construction of a large penitentiary designed to incarcerate resistance leaders from the Northwest and other regions of Vietnam. Just one year after the opening of the new Son La Penitentiary, prisoners staged a mass breakout, causing substantial damage to the prison itself before fleeing across the border into Laos.

During the final days of colonial rule Son La became an important French military outpost, and accordingly an air base was built at **Na San**, 20 km from the town. Both Na San air base and the colonial government headquarters in Son La town were abandoned to the Viet Minh in November 1953, on the eve of the Battle of Dien Bien Phu.

PLACES IN SON LA

There is little to see other than the **Son La Provincial Museum** ① *on Youth Hill, just off Highway 6 and near the centre of town, T023 852022, daily 0700-1100, 1330-1730, 10,000d.* The museum building is in fact the town's old French Penitentiary, constructed in 1908, damaged in 1909, bombed in 1952 and now partially rebuilt for tourists. The original 3-m-deep dungeon and tiny cells complete with food-serving hatches and leg-irons, can be seen together with an exhibition illustrating the history of the place and the key individuals who were incarcerated here.

→AROUND SON LA

To reach **Tham Coong** (Coong Caves), walk or drive to the north end of town (Hoa Ban Street); after a few hundred metres (roughly opposite a petrol station) are the tanks of the Son La Water Company; turn left off the road and follow the track gently uphill towards a small group of houses, turning left again just before it forks. Follow the stream or take the path and yomp across the bunds of the rice fields. There are two caves, the wet cave is now fenced off but a scramble up the limestone face brings you to a **dry cave** ① *5000d,* from which the views are lovely. As you have probably come to expect by now in Vietnam, the caves are rather unremarkable, the walk a never-ending joy – with wet feet. The fields, ponds and streams below the caves are a miracle of inventiveness and beauty: stilt houses, gardens, hibiscus hedgerows, poinsettia plants and a range of colours and smells that are particularly appealing in the late-afternoon sunlight. Fish are bred in the ponds covered with watercress (*salad soong*) and what looks like a red algal bloom, but it actually a small floating weed (*beo hoa dau*) fed to ducks and pigs.

Ban Co is a Black Thai village and a visit here can be combined with a trip to Tham Coong. Returning from the caves, rejoin the road then turn left and take a track across the fields and over a small bridge to the village of Co. The village is a largish and fairly ordinary Black Thai settlement but a diverting twilight hour can be spent watching its inhabitants returning from the fields with a fish or duck for the pot and a basket of greens, washing away the day's grime in the stream and settling down to a relaxing evening routine that has changed little in the last few hundred years.

WEST TO DIEN BIEN PHU OR NORTH TO MUONG LAY FROM SON LA

The scenery on leaving Son La is breathtaking. Reds and greens predominate – the red of the soil, the costumes and the newly tiled roofs, and the green of the trees, the swaying fronds of bamboo and the wet-season rice. Early morning light brings out the colours in their finest and freshest hues, and as the sun rises colours transmute from orange to pink to ochre.

Around every bend in the road is a new visual treat. Most stunning are the valley floors, blessed with water throughout the year. Here generations of ceaseless human activity have engineered a land to man's design. Using nothing more than bamboo technology and human muscle, terraces have been sculpted from the hills: little channels feed water from field to field illustrating a high level of social order and common purpose. Water powers devices of great ingenuity: water wheels for raising water from river level to field level, rice mills and huskers and mini electrical turbines. And, in addition, these people, who for centuries have been isolated from outside perceptions of beauty, have produced a fusion of natural and human landscape that cannot fail to please the eye. Shape, form, scale and colour blend and contrast in a pattern of sympathy and understanding wholly lost to the modern world. Then the road climbs away from the river to a village dependent on rain for its water: the grey and red dust and the meagre little houses indicate great poverty and make one realize the importance of a constant water supply.

There is a small and colourful market village 25 km from Son La and 10 km further on is **Thuan Chau**, another little market town where, in the early morning, people of different minorities in traditional dress can be seen bartering and trading. Thuan Chau is a good spot for breakfast and for buying headscarves. The settlements along this route nicely illustrate the law that describes the inverse relationship between the size of a place and the proportion of the population traditionally garbed. The road is remarkably good with crash barriers, mirrors positioned strategically on hair-pin bends and warning signs, which, considering the precipitous nature of the terrain from Thuan Chau to Tuan Giao, and that visibility is often obscured by cloud and fog, is just as well.

Tuan Giao is 75 km and approximately three hours from Son La (accommodation is available). From Tuan Giao travellers have the choice of either going direct to Muong Lay (formerly Lai Chau), or taking the longer route via Dien Bien Phu.

Highway 6 from Tuan Giao heads north across the Hoang Lien Son mountains to Muong Lay. The road climbs up through some spectacular scenery reaching altitudes of around 1800-1900 m. Red and White Hmong villages are passed en route.

The journey from Tuan Giao to Dien Bien Phu on Highway 279 is 80 km (about four hours) and tends to be chosen by those with a strong sense of Vietnamese history.

Situated in a region where even today ethnic Vietnamese still represent less than one-third of the total population, Dien Bien Phu lies in the Muong Thanh Valley, a heart-shaped basin 19 km long and 13 km wide, crossed by the Nam Yum River.

For such a remote and apparently insignificant little town to have earned itself such an important place in the history books is a considerable achievement. And yet the Battle of Dien Bien Phu in 1954 was a turning point in colonial history (see box, page 67). It marked the end of French involvement in Indochina and heralded the collapse of its North African empire. Had the Americans, who shunned French appeals for help, taken more careful note of what happened at Dien Bien Phu they might have avoided their own calamitous involvement just a decade later.

ARRIVING IN DIEN BIEN PHU

Getting there Dien Bien Phu is deep in the highlands of Northwest Vietnam, close to the border with Laos and 420 km from Hanoi (although it feels much further). The airport is 2 km north of town and receives daily flights from Hanoi (one hour). Buses snake their way up from Hanoi (13 hours) via Hoa Binh and Son La; the bus station is close to the centre of town on Highway 12, from where it's an easy walk to the hotels.

Moving on From Dien Bien Phu, there are onward bus connections with Muong Lay (see page 70), Sapa (see page 75) and Lao Cai (see page 80). Expect overland journeys to be slow and sometimes arduous in this mountainous region, but the discomfort is compensated for by the sheer majesty of the landscapes. Alternatively, head directly back to Hanoi by road or by plane.

Getting around The town of Dien Bien Phu with its neat streets is quite easy to negotiate on foot. The battlefield sites, most of which lie to the west of the Nam Yum River,

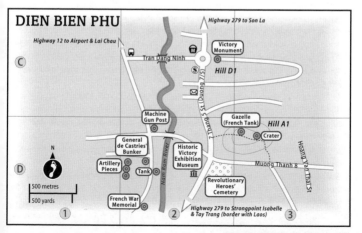

are, however, a bit spread out and best visited by car or by motorbike. Since the majority of visitors arrive in Dien Bien Phu using their own transport, this is not normally a problem.

BACKGROUND

Modern Dien Bien Phu is a growing town. This reflects the decision to make it the provincial capital of the newly created Dien Bien Phu Province and attempts to develop it as a tourist destination.

Settled from an early date, Muong Thanh Valley has been an important trading post on the caravan route between China and Burma for 2000 years. Over the years numerous fortifications were constructed in and around Muong Thanh, the best known being the fabled Citadel of the Thirty Thousand (Thanh Tam Van) built by the Lu during the 15th century. Remnants of this citadel can still be seen today, near Xam Mun.

The early years of the 18th century were a period of acute political instability throughout Vietnam. During this time the Northwest was overrun by armies of the Phe from China's southern Yunnan Province who committed unspeakable acts of barbarism against the inhabitants of the area. In 1751, however, a Vietnamese peasant leader from the Red River Delta named Hoang Cong Chat, whose army had retreated into the region to escape from royal troops, rallied local Lu, Lao and Thai chieftains to his cause and expelled the Phe back across the border to China. Building a new fortress at Ban Phu, Chat set himself up as lord of a large area including most of modern Son La and Lai Chau provinces, winning the hearts of the local people by carrying out important land and taxation reforms.

The town of Dien Bien Phu itself only came into existence in 1841 when, in response to continued Lao, Siamese and Chinese banditry in the area, the Nguyen dynasty ordered the establishment of a royal district governed from a fortified settlement at Muong Thanh.

Occupied by French forces during the course of their major Northwest campaign of 1888-1889, Dien Bien Phu was subsequently maintained as a garrison town. The town fell briefly to Thai insurgents during the latter stages of the 1908 Son La Penitentiary uprising (prompting the suicide of Dien Bien Phu's French commander) and again during the course of the 1914-1916 uprising of Son La chieftains, but perhaps the most serious threat to French rule in the region came in 1918 when the Hmong rebelled against the harsh fiscal policies of the new Governor General Paul Doumer, by refusing to pay taxes in silver coins or to supply opium to the French and taking up arms against the garrison. The insurrection quickly spread east to Son La and south across the Lao border into Samneua, and although the French responded ruthlessly by devastating rebel areas, destroying food crops to provoke famine and setting a high price on the heads of prominent rebels, the revolt persisted until March 1921.

In Vietnam, as elsewhere in Asia, the defeat of the European Allies during the early years of the Second World War utterly shattered the image of Western colonial supremacy, fuelling the forces of incipient nationalism. French attempts to resume their authority in the region in 1945 thus encountered stiff resistance from Viet Minh forces, and in the nine years of fighting which followed, the Northwest became a cradle of national resistance against French colonialism.

Following the French defeat at Hoa Binh in 1952 the Vietnamese Army went on the offensive all over the Northwest, forcing the French to regroup at their two remaining strongholds of Na San (Son La) and Lai Chau. Early the following year, acting in conjunction with Pathet Lao forces, the Viet Minh overran Samneua in upper Laos and proceeded to

ON THE ROAD
Battle of Dien Bien Phu

On 20 November 1953, after a series of French successes, Colonel Christian de Castries and six battalions of French and French-colonial troops were parachuted into Dien Bien Phu. The location, in a narrow valley surrounded by steep, wooded peaks, was chosen specifically because it was thought by the French strategists to be impregnable. From there, they believed, their forces could begin to harry the Viet Minh close to their bases as well as protect Laos from Viet Minh incursions. At the centre of the valley was the all-important airstrip – Colonel de Castries' only link with the outside world.

In his history of Vietnam, Stanley Karnow describes de Castries thus: "Irresistible to women and ridden with gambling debts, he had been a champion horseman, dare-devil pilot and courageous commando, his body scarred by three wounds earned during the Second World War and earlier in Indochina."

In response, the famous Vietnamese General Giap moved his forces, some 55,000 men, into the surrounding area, manhandling heavy guns (with the help, it is said, of 200,000 porters) up the impossibly steep mountainsides until they had a view over the French forces. The French commander still believed, however, that his forces would have the upper hand in any set-piece confrontation and set about strengthening his position. He created a series of heavily fortified strongholds, giving them women's names (said to be those of his numerous mistresses): Anne-Marie, Françoise, Huguette, Béatrice, Gabrielle, Dominique, Claudine, Isabelle and Eliane.

As it turned out, de Castries was not luring the Viet Minh into a trap, but creating one for himself and his men. From the surrounding highlands, Giap had the French at his mercy. The shelling started in the middle of March, and the strongholds fell one by one; Béatrice first and then Gabrielle and Anne-Marie by mid-March until de Castries' forces were concentrated around the airstrip. Poor weather, which prevented the French from using their air power, and human-wave attacks gradually wore the French troops down. By this time, de Castries had withdrawn to his bunker and command had effectively been taken over by his junior officers. A furious bombardment by the heavy guns of the Viet Minh from 1 May led to the final massed assault five days later. On the final night, the Viet Minh taunted the French defenders by playing the *Song of the Partisans*, the theme of the French Resistance, over the garrison's radio frequencies. The colonel's HQ fell on 7 May at 1730 when 9500 French and French-colonial troops surrendered.A small force of paratroopers at the isolated southern position, Isabelle, continued to resist for a further 24 hours. The humiliation at Dien Bien Phu led the French to sue for peace at a conference in Geneva. On 20 July 1954 it was agreed that Vietnam should be divided in two along the 17th parallel: a communist north and a capitalist south. In total, 20,000 Viet Minh and over 3000 French troops were killed at Dien Bien Phu. The Geneva agreement set terms so that the dead from both sides would be honoured in a massive ossuary. But when Ngo Dinh Diem, the President of the Republic of South Vietnam, symbolically urinated over Viet Minh dead in the South rather than bury them with honour, Giap and Ho Chi Minh decided to leave the French dead to lie where they had fallen. Over the nine years of war between the Viet Minh and the French, the dead numbered between a quarter of a million and one million civilians, 200,000-300,000 Viet Minh and 95,000 French-colonial troops. Who was to guess another 20 years of warfare lay ahead.

sweep north, threatening the Lao capital of Luang Prabang. By November 1953 the French colonial government headquarters at Lai Chau (now Muong Lay), just 110 km north of Dien Bien Phu, had also come under siege.

Dien Bien Phu was the site of the last calamitous battle between the French and the forces of Ho Chi Minh's Viet Minh, and was waged from March to May 1954. The French, who under Vichy rule had accepted the authority of the Japanese during the Second World War, attempted to regain control after the Japanese had surrendered. Ho, following his Declaration of Independence on 2 September 1945, thought otherwise, heralding nearly a decade of war before the French finally gave up the fight after their catastrophic defeat here. The lessons of the battle were numerous, but most of all it was a victory of determination over technology. In the aftermath, the French people, much like the Americans two decades later, had no stomach left for a war in a distant, tropical and alien land.

PLACES IN DIEN BIEN PHU

On the sight of the battlefield **General de Castries' bunker** ① *daily 0700-1100, 1330-1700, 5000d*, has been rebuilt and eight of the 10 French tanks (known as bisons) are scattered over the valley, along with numerous US-made artillery pieces.

On **Hill A1** (known as Eliane 2 to the French) ① *daily 0700-1800*, scene of the fiercest fighting, is a bunker, the bison named Gazelle, a war memorial dedicated to the Vietnamese who died on the hill and around at the back is the entrance to a tunnel dug by coal miners from Hon Gai. Their tunnel ran several hundred metres to beneath French positions and was filled with 1000 kg of high explosives. It was detonated at 2300 on 6 May 1954 as a signal for the final assault. The huge crater is still there. The hill is a peaceful spot and a good place from which to watch the sun setting on the historic valley. After dark there are fireflies. Hill A1 was extensively renovated in readiness for Dien Bien Phu's 50th anniversary of the French defeat in 2004.

The **Historic Victory Exhibition Museum** (Nha Trung Bay Thang Lich Su Dien Bien Phu) ① *daily 0700-1100, 1330-1800, 5000d*, is undergoing major renovation until mid-2014 with a reduction in exhibits. It has been renovated and there are photographs and other memorabilia together with a large illuminated model of the valley illustrating the course of the campaign and an accompanying video. It's interesting to

DIEN BIEN PHU BATTLE SITE

The French Garrison, 13 March 1954 shortly before the siege began

GABRIELLE
Ford
Pavie Track
Ban Kéo
ANNE-MARIE
Nam Yum River
BÉATRICE
RLE 41
HUGUETTE
DOMINIQUE
FRANÇOISE
ELIANE
Phony Hill
CLAUDINE
Ban Ong Pet
Baldy Hill
Ban Hong Lech Cang
Ban Na Loi
MARCELLE Evacuated
Ban Papé
Ban Ten
Ban Palech
Ban Bom La
Ban Nhong Nhai
Ban Kho Lai
Auxiliary Airstrip
Ban Hong Cum
N
ISABELLE
WIEME

1 km
1 miles
CLAUDINE French strongholds
------ Barbed-wire systems

note that, while every last piece of Vietnamese junk is carefully catalogued, displayed and described, French relics are heaped into tangled piles.

The **Revolutionary Heroes' Cemetery** ① *opposite the Exhibition Museum adjacent to Hill A1, 0700-1100, 1330-1800*, contains the graves of some 15,000 Vietnamese soldiers killed during the course of the Dien Bien Phu campaign.

Located close to the sight of de Castries' command bunker is the **French War Memorial** (Nghia Trang Phap). It consists of a white obelisk surrounded by a grey concrete wall and black iron gates sitting on a bluff overlooking the Nam Yum River.

Dien Bien Phu's newest sight towers over the town. Erected on Hill D1 at a cost of US$2.27 million, the **Victory Monument** (Tuong Dai Chien Dien Bien Phu) ① *entrance next to the TV station on 6 Pho Muong Thanh (look for the tower and large, gated pond)*, is an enormous, 120-tonne bronze sculpture and is, as such, the largest monument in Vietnam. It was sculpted by former soldier Nguyen Hai and depicts three Vietnamese soldiers standing on top of de Castries' bunker. Engraved on the flag is the motto *Quyet Chien, Quyet Thang* (Determined to Fight, Determined to Win). One of the soldiers is carrying a Thai child. It was commissioned to mark the 50th anniversary of the Vietnamese defeat over the French in 1954.

→DIEN BIEN PHU TO MUONG LAY

It is 104 km on Highway 12 from Dien Bien Phu to Muong Lay (formerly Lai Chau). The road was originally built by an energetic French district governor, Auguste Pavie, and was used by soldiers fleeing the French garrison at Lai Chau to the supposed safety of the garrison at Dien Bien Phu in 1953. Viet Minh ambushes along the Pavie Track meant that the French were forced to hack their way through the jungle and those few who made it to Dien Bien Phu found themselves almost immediately under siege again.

The five-hour journey is scenically interesting and there are a few minority villages – Kho-mú and Thai on the valley floors and Hmong higher up on the way.

The scenery is different from any you will have encountered so far. What is amazing around Son La is the exquisite human landscape. From Dien Bien Phu to Muong Lay what impresses is the scenery in its natural state. It is unfriendly but spectacular. The agents at work here are rivers, rain, heat and gravity, and the raw materials are rock and trees. There are no rice terraces but forested hills in which slash-and-burn farming takes place. This is the land of rockslide and flood. It is geologically young and dangerous; the steep slopes of thinly bedded shales collapse after heavy rain, in contrast to the more solid limestone bands of Son La. The density of population is low and evidence abounds that the living here is harsh. A less romantic side to minority-village life is evident: tiny four-year-old children stagger along with a baby strapped to their back, there is no colourful dress or elaborate costume, just ragged kids in filthy T-shirts.

Pu Ka village, 46 km from Muong Lay, is a White Hmong settlement newly established by the authorities to transplant the Hmong away from their opium fields.

The old town of Muong Lay occupied a majestic setting in a deep and wide valley cloaked in dense tiers of forest. However, the old town was submerged by the Son La Hydroelectric Dam and the new town has been repositioned 100 m up the hill.

BACKGROUND

The history of Lai Chau (the old Muong Lay) is inextricably entwined with that of the Black Thai seigneurial family of Deo who had achieved ascendancy over the former White Thai lords of Muong Lay by the first half of the 15th century. In 1451 the Vietnamese King Le Thai To is recorded as having led a campaign against the Deo family of Muong Lay (then a village 13 km south of the town) for its disloyalty to the crown.

The Deo family in fact comprised a number of separate Black Thai lineages dotted around what is now Northwest Vietnam and the Yunnan Province of China, but it was the marriage during the 1850s of Deo Van Xeng, a wealthy merchant from Yunnan, to the daughter of a Muong Lay Deo chieftain, which established the most notorious line of the Deo family. When his father-in-law died, Xeng seized control of the Muong Lay dominions and, with the support of the royal court in Luang Prabang and the mandarinate of Yunnan, quickly established himself as one of the most powerful lords in the Northwest.

Deo Van Xeng's eldest son, the energetic Deo Van Tri, continued his father's expansionist policies. Allying himself with Chinese Black Flag commander Lin Yung-fu, Tri succeeded in expelling a Chinese Yellow Flag occupation force from Son La, instantly winning the respect and allegiance of the Black and White Thai chieftains of that area. Apart from a small number who stayed and were subsequently integrated into the Thai community, the Black Flags also left the country shortly after this, enabling Tri to assume suzerainty over a large area of Northwest Vietnam.

When French forces launched their campaign to pacify the Northwest, Tri initially took an active part in the resistance, leading a joint Black and White Thai force against the colonial army at the battle of Cau Giay in 1883. Consequently, king-in-exile Ham Nghi appointed Tri military governor of 16 districts. But the garrisoning of French troops at Lai Chau during the campaign of 1888-1889 marked a turning point in the war of resistance and Tri was ultimately obliged to surrender to the French at Lai Chau in 1890.

As elsewhere in the north, the French moved quickly to graft their colonial administrative systems onto those already established by the Nguyen court, and they ensured Deo Van Tri's future co-operation by awarding him the hereditary post of Supreme Thai Chieftain.

After his death in 1915, Tri was succeeded as Governor of Lai Chau by his son Deo Van Long who later took office as mandarin of the colonial government in 1940. However, as the Viet Minh war of resistance got under way in 1945, the colonial government sought to ensure the continued allegiance of ethnic minority leaders by offering them a measure of self-government. Accordingly, in 1947 Muong, Thai, Tay, Hmong and Nung Autonomous Regions were set up throughout the Northwest and, in Lai Chau, Deo Van Long was duly installed as king of the Thai.

King Deo Van Long is remembered with loathing by most older inhabitants of the Lai Chau area. By all accounts he was a tyrant who exercised absolute authority, striking fear into the hearts of the local people by occasionally having transgressors executed on the spot. The ruins of Long's mansion that lay just across the river from Doi Cao (High Hill) used to be open to the public. Deo Van Long's House was originally a plush colonial mansion on Road 127 to Muong Te on the opposite bank of the Da River from High Hill (Doi Cao). Older inhabitants of the six or seven remaining houses recall that for many years Deo Van Long and his family lived in great luxury with a large retinue of servants. Some say that before fleeing the country in 1953, Long had all his servants poisoned so they could not inform the advancing Viet Minh forces of his whereabouts.

During the latter days of French rule, as the security situation began to deteriorate throughout the Northwest, Lai Chau became an important French military base; older citizens of the town remember clearly the large numbers of Moroccans, Algerians and Tunisians who were posted here between 1946 and 1953. The French were finally forced to abandon Lai Chau during the winter of 1953 on the eve of the momentous battle of Dien Bien Phu. Bereft of his colonial masters, a discredited Deo Van Long fled to Laos and then to Thailand, whence he is believed to have emigrated to France. A few remaining relatives still live in the area, but have wisely changed their family name to Dieu.

CONTEMPORARY MUONG LAY

Much of the previous town of Muong Lay dated from 1969-1972, when it was expanded to accommodate the large numbers of Chinese engineers posted here to upgrade the road from Dien Bien Phu to the Chinese border (the Friendship Road). In 1993 the status of capital of Lai Chau Province was transferred from Lai Chau town to Dien Bien Phu, partly in recognition of the latter's growing importance as a hub of economic and tourist activity and partly in deference to the side effects of the massive **Son La hydroelectric power scheme** that has opened in the Da River Valley in which the old Muong Lay rested. (Dien Bien Phu later became capital of its own eponymous province when this was created in 2004). The dam and reservoir are three times bigger than the Hoa Binh complex, the second biggest in Southeast Asia. Some 20,000 have lost their homes due to the US$2.5 billion 2400 MW power station which became fully operational in autumn 2012.

The former **French Colonial Government Headquarters** were used as offices and housed the local hospital. Also, on a terrace above the river, was a former **airfield** (Sang Bay Phap). There's not a great deal to see in the town itself but the surrounding countryside is attractive and it makes a good place to break the journey for those travelling between Dien Bien Phu and Sapa.

➔AROUND MUONG LAY

PHI HAY (WHITE HMONG VILLAGE)

ⓘ *Take Highway 6 in the direction of Tuan Giao until just beyond the 10 km way marker from Muong Lay. Stop next to a group of small shops as the road begins to level out, and walk either steeply down left from the road between two shops, or up the path also to the left of the road, but in the direction of a small school building. Continue for a further 2 km.*

This makes an interesting morning's excursion for those who made the detour via Dien Bien Phu. It offers a snapshot of the stunning scenery along the more direct Muong Lay-Tuan Giao mountain route. Phi Hay village is very old and comprises some 50 houses spread out over a considerable area.

SIN HO

Driving to Sin Ho is hazardous as you need to negotiate the hairpin bends and precipitous drops that characterize the road. If the weather is clear you would be strongly advised to walk some stretches to appreciate the full majesty of the scenery. It will also give you a chance to absorb the delicious cool air, the forest sounds and smells and the wayside flowers. You will also have the opportunity to witness the extraordinary perpendicular fields and to wonder how it is that local farmers can actually harvest slopes on which most people could not even stand.

The first 20 km towards Sin Ho off the main highway is possibly the most spectacular and terrifying drive in Vietnam. After 20 km the road levels off and meanders over the Sin Ho plateau passing hamlets of Red, White and Flower Hmong and Dao minorities. Sin Ho provides little that won't have been seen already, although the Sunday morning market is worthy of note. As with other markets in the region, the Sunday market is an important social occasion.

LAI CHAU (FORMERLY TAM DUONG)

There are some interesting walks to **Na Bo**, a Pu Na (Giay sub-group) minority village, **Giang** (Nhang minority) and **Hon** minority villages. Pu Na and Nhang people are similar in culture and clothes. Na Bo is 7 km from Lai Chau from which Giang is a further 1.5 km and Hon a further 5 km still. Alternatively a motorbike and driver can be hired.

About 35 km southeast of Lai Chau, Highway 4D swings sharply to the northeast and the altitude climbs abruptly into the **Hoang Lien Son range**. Here is harsh mountain scenery on a scale previously unencountered on this circuit of Northwest Vietnam. The geology is hard and crystalline as is the skyline, with sharp jagged peaks punching upwards into the sky. Vertical cliffs drop below and soar above; friendly rolling scenery has been replaced by 3000-m-high mountains. There are buses from Lai Chau to Sapa.

NORTHWEST LISTINGS

WHERE TO STAY

The Northwest offers everything from ecolodges to homestays to functional hotels. The greatest concentration of hotels – and the most attractive are those found in and around Sapa (see page 75).

Mai Chau and Lac

$$$$-$$$ Mai Chau Lodge, a short walking distance southwest of Lac village, T0218-386 8959, www.maichaulodge.com. Owned and operated by **Buffalo Tours** and staffed by locals, there are 16 warmly furnished rooms with modern facilities. The attractive lodge has a restaurant, a bar, pool, sauna and jacuzzi. Bicycling, kayaking, rock climbing and trekking tours are offered. Transfer from Hanoi can be booked.

$ Ethnic Houses, Ban Lac Village. Trips to homestays can be booked direct or booked. Particularly recommended, as the hospitality and easy manner of the people is a highlight of many visitors' stay in Vietnam. Food and local rice wine provided at minimal cost while beer is usually available on an honesty system Avoid the large houses in the centre if possible. **Guesthouse No 6**, T0218-386 7168. (No English), is popular; the owner fought the French at Dien Bien Phu.

Mr Binh's place, Guesthouse No 9, T0218-386 7380. Another good option. In the adjoining, quieter village of Ban Pom Coong, House 3 (aka Hung Tu) is run by an absolutely lovely family and has good views – contact Nga at **Wide Eyed Tours** in Hanoi, T4-2213 2951, to request it, or simply turn up.

Moc Chau and Chieng Yen

Homestays with meals are possible in 2 villages. Contact Son La Province, T022-385 5714, or tour operator **Handspan**, www.handspan.com, in Hanoi, which runs the Moc Chau eco stilt house with the local community, and offer trekking in Ngoc Son Ngo Luong, home to turtles and pangolins.

Dien Bien Phu

$$$-$$ Muong Thanh Hotel, 25 Him Lam-TP, T0230-381 0043. The most upmarket option, this dated, but comfortable, hotel has spacious, retro rooms with TV, a/c, minibar and fan. Wi-Fi, swimming pool complete with bizarre statues (10,000d for non-guests), karaoke, Thai massage and free airport transfer. Tacky souvenir shop. Very overpriced motorbike rentals – hire elsewhere.

$$-$ Nha Khach VP, 7/5 Muong Thanh (behind the lake), T0230-283 0338, thanhhoa.dph@gmail.com. Party-owned hotel right in the middle of town. Absolutely massive suites complete with 1970s style living areas. Doubles are clean and spacious with a/c. Considering the alternatives, a very good option.

$ Hung Ha, No 83, opposite the bus station, T0230-650 4187. Strictly for those on a tight budget, this is the best of a bad lot, but is handy for the station. The balcony rooms aren't so bad, but interior rooms are drab and corridor-facing.

Muong Lay (formerly Lai Chau)

$$ Lan Anh Hotel 1, Thi Xa Rd, Muong Lay, T0230-3509577, hotellananh@yahoo. com. Manager Ms Thuy runs the new **Lan Anh Hotel** offering a/c rooms. The old hotel was submerged with the opening of the hydroelectric power station and this, along with the rest of the town was relocated up the hill. This is the best place to stay in new Muong Lay.

Sin Ho

$ People's Committee Guesthouse, on the right as you enter the town, T23-387 0168. The long, low building is very basic.

Lai Chau (formerly Tam Duong)
$ Phuong Thanh, T23-387 5235, phuong

thanhotel@yahoo.com. 21 fan rooms, hot
water, clean, comfortable, lovely views.

RESTAURANTS

Sapa (see page 75) offers the greatest
variety of choice in the Northwest with
restaurants serving Vietnamese and
international cuisine. Outside of Sapa,
options are more limited.

Dien Bien Phu
The main street, Nguyen Chi Thanh, has
plenty of simple noodle and rice joints, but
they are not places to linger. A few *bia hoi*
also serve *lau* (hotpots); **Phuong Thuy** at
number 60 is busy in the evenings.
$$-$ Muong Thanh Hotel Restaurant,
25 Him Lam-TP, T0230-381 0043. Daily 0600-
2200. Popular with tour groups. A tome of a
menu includes plenty of Vietnamese options,
from familiar pork and chicken dishes to
more offbeat frog and tortoise specialities.
Veggies are catered for with some tofu
dishes. For a quick, inexpensive fix, try the
fried noodles with beef and mushrooms.

$ Lien Tuoi, 64 Street 22, behind the
cemetery, T0230-382 4919. Daily 0700-2200.
Simple local fare, including good fried
spring rolls and grilled chicken. Family-run.

Mai Chau
Most people will eat with their hosts.
Mai Chau town itself has a couple of simple
com pho places near the market. The rice
wine in Mai Chau is excellent, particularly
when mixed with local honey. The **Mai
Chau Lodge** has 2 restaurants.

Muong Lay (formerly Lai Chau)
$ Lan Anh Hotel hi Xa Rd, Muong Lay,
T0230-3509577, hotellananh@yahoo.com.

Sin Ho
Eat early at one of the cafés around the
market. They may only have instant noodles
at night and eggs for breakfast. But, washed
down with the local rice wine, it tastes like a
feast. Wine costs less than US$0.50 a bottle.

WHAT TO DO

Mai Chau
**Mai Chau Ethnic Minority Dance
Troupe**, Thai dancing culminating in the
communal drinking of sweet, sticky rice
wine through straws from a large pot. This

troupe performs most nights in Lac in
one of the large stilt houses; admission is
included as part of the package for people
on tours; otherwise you'll need to make a
small contribution.

SAPA AND AROUND

Despite the countless thousands of tourists who have poured in every year for the past two decades Sapa retains great charm. Its beauty derives from the impressive natural setting high on a valley side with Fan Si Pan, Vietnam's tallest mountain, either clearly visible or brooding in the mist.

Sapa's access point is Lao Cai, which is also the Chinese border crossing. The markets of the region are popular one-day or overnight trips for visitors. One such local market is Bac Ha.

→SAPA

The beauty of the town is a little compromised by the new hotels sprouting up everywhere. Certainly none of the new ones can compare with the lovely old French buildings – pitched roofs, window shutters and chimneys each with their own neat little garden of temperate flora, foxgloves, roses, apricot and plum trees, carefully nurtured by generations of gardeners. Weekends are peak tourist time but during the week the few visitors who remain will have the town to themselves.

ARRIVING IN SAPA
Getting there You get to Sapa either by road as part of the Northwest loop or by overnight train from Hanoi, via Lao Cai (9½ hours). A fleet of minibuses transfers

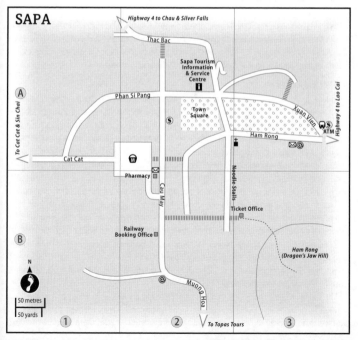

passengers from Lao Cai railway station to Sapa (1½ hours). There are numerous classes of seat or berth on the trains and some hotels have their own private carriages. It is quite easy to make the travel arrangements yourself, but booking with a tour operator removes the hassle. Tour operators in Hanoi sell tours and packages that include treks of various lengths. New comfortable buses now also run the Hanoi–Sapa route (10 hours).

Moving on A railway office in Sapa sells tickets for the journey from Lao Cai back to Hanoi; there are also comfortable buses. Minibuses congregate on the corner next to the church. To continue the route up to the Far North (see page 84), local buses run from from Lao Cai although most people choose to hire a private car with driver or take a tour.

Getting around Sapa is small enough to walk around easily. From Sapa there are a great many walks and treks and the tracks and paths are fun to explore on a Minsk.

Best time to visit At 1650 m Sapa enjoys warm days and cool evenings in the summer but gets very cold in winter. Snow falls on average every couple of years and settles on the surrounding peaks of the Hoang Lien Son Mountains. Rain and cloud can occur at any time of year but the wettest months are May to September with nearly 1000 mm of rain in July and August alone, the busiest months for Vietnamese tourists. December and January can be pretty miserable with mist, low cloud and low temperatures. Spring blossom is lovely but even in March and April a fire or heater may be necessary in the evening.

Tourist information Sapa Tourist Information Center ① *2 Phan Si Pan St, T020-387 1975, www.sapa-tourism.com; Lao Cai branch at 306 Khanh Yet St, T020-625 2506; 0730-1900 (low season closed for lunch).* Free tourist information, tours with local guides including Fan Si Pan, markets and homestays in local villages; tickets booked.

BACKGROUND

Originally a Black Hmong settlement, Sapa was first discovered by Europeans when a Jesuit missionary visited the area in 1918. By 1932 news of the quasi-European climate and beautiful scenery of the Tonkinese Alps had spread throughout French Indochina. Like Dalat in the south it served as a retreat for French administrators when the heat of the plains became unbearable. By the 1940s an estimated 300 French buildings, including a sizeable prison and the summer residence of the Governor of French Indochina, had sprung up. Until 1947 there were more French than Vietnamese in the town, which became renowned for its many parks and flower gardens. However, as the security situation began to worsen during the latter days of French rule, the expatriate community steadily dwindled, and by 1953 virtually all had gone. Immediately following the French defeat at Dien Bien Phu in 1954, victorious Vietnamese forces razed a large number of Sapa's French buildings to the ground.

Sapa was also one of the places to be invaded by the Chinese in the 1979 border skirmish. Chinese soldiers found and destroyed the holiday retreat of the Vietnamese Communist Party Secretary-General, Le Duan, no doubt infuriated by such uncomradely display of bourgeois tendencies.

The huge scale of the Fan Si Pan range gives Sapa an Alpine feel and this impression is reinforced by *haute savoie* vernacular architecture with steep-pitched roofs, window shutters and chimneys. But, with an alluring blend of European and Vietnamese vegetation, the gardeners of Sapa cultivate their foxgloves and apricot trees alongside thickets of bamboo and delicate orchids, just yards above the paddy fields.

PEOPLE

Distinctly oriental but un-Vietnamese in manner and appearance are the Hmong, Dao and other minorities who come to Sapa to trade. Interestingly, the Hmong (normally so reticent) have been the first to seize the commercial opportunities presented by tourism; they are engaging but very persistent vendors of hand-loomed indigo shirts, trousers and skull caps and other handicrafts. Of the craftwork, the little brass and bamboo Jew's-harp is particularly notable. The Dao women, their hands stained purple by the dye, sell clothing on street corners, stitching while they wait for a customer. The girls roam in groups, bracelets, earrings and necklaces jingling as they walk. "*Jolie, jolie*" they say as they push bracelets into your hand and it is hard to disagree. '*Mua mot cai di, mua mot cai di*' (buy one, buy one), the little ones sing, and most people do.

Saturday night is always a big occasion for Black Hmong and Red Dao teenagers in the Sapa area, as youngsters from miles around come to the so-called Love Market to find a partner. The market proved so popular with tourists that the teenagers now arrange their trysts and liaisons in private. The regular market is at its busiest and best on Sunday morning when most tourists scoot off to Bac Ha.

PLACES IN SAPA

Sapa is a pleasant place to relax in and unwind, particularly after the arduous journey from Dien Bien Phu. Being comparatively new it has no important sights but several French buildings in and around are worth visiting.

The small church, built in 1930, dominates the centre of Sapa. Recently rebuilt, the church was wrecked in 1952 by French artillerymen shelling the adjacent building in which Viet Minh troops were billeted. In the churchyard are the tombs of two former priests, including that of Father Jean Thinh, who was brutally murdered. In the autumn of 1948, Father Thinh confronted a monk named Giao Linh who had been discovered having an affair with a nun at the Ta Phin seminary. Giao Linh obviously took great exception to the priest's interference, for shortly after this, when Father Thinh's congregation arrived at Sapa church for mass one foggy November morning, they discovered his decapitated body lying next to the altar.

Ham Rong (Dragon's Jaw Hill) ① *0600-1800, 30,000d, free for children under 5*, on which the district's TV transmitter is stuck, is located immediately above Sapa town centre. Apart from offering excellent views of the town, the path winds its way through a number of interesting limestone outcrops and miniature grottoes as it nears the summit. Traditional dance performances take place on the mountain. The gardens on the lower slopes are a nice place to amble amongst orchids and other flowers.

→TREKS AROUND SAPA

The derelict French seminary is near the village of **Ta Phin**. The names of the bishop who consecrated it and the presiding Governor of Indochina can be seen engraved on stones at the west end. Built in 1942 under the ecclesiastical jurisdiction of the Parish of Sapa, the building was destroyed 10 years later by militant Vietnamese hostile to the intentions of the order.

To get there from Sapa, take the road 8 km east towards Lao Cai then follow a track left up towards Ta Phin; it's 3 km to the monastery and a further 4 km to Ta Phin.

Beyond the seminary, the path descends into a valley of beautifully sculpted rice terraces and past Black Hmong settlements to Ta Phin.

Note You should never just turn up in a village for homestay opportunites; book with a tour operator. Contact **Sapa Tourist Informati**on **Center** ① *Hoang A Tuong's Palace, Bac Ha, T020-378 0662,* to find out about tours and local trekking regulations

MOUNT FAN SI PAN

At a height of 3143 m, Vietnam's highest mountain is a two- or three-day trek from Sapa. It lies on a bearing of 240 degrees from Sapa; as the crow flies it is 9 km but by track it is 14 km and involves dropping to 1200 m and crossing a rickety bamboo bridge before ascending. The climb involves some steep scrambles which are quite nasty in wet conditions. Only

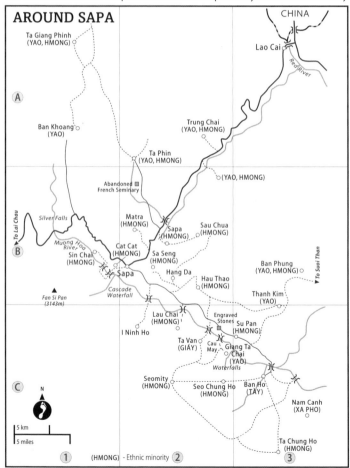

the very fit will make it to the summit. A three-day expedition is recommended. There are few suitable spots for camping other than at the altitudes suggested here: **Day 1**: depart Sapa (1650 m) 0800. Lunch at 1400 m, 1200. Camp at 2285 m; **Day 2**: reach summit late afternoon. Return to camp at 2800 m; **Day 3**: descend to Sapa. A good tour operator, either in Sapa or Hanoi, will provide camping equipment and porters.

LAO CHAI (BLACK HMONG) VILLAGE AND TA VAN (GIÁY) VILLAGE

This is a round trip of 20 km (although cars are usually used for the return journey) taking in minority villages and beautiful scenery. Heading southeast out of Sapa (see map, opposite), past the **Auberge** guesthouse, **Lao Chai** is 6 km away on the far valley side. Follow the track leading from the right-hand side of the road down to the valley floor, cross the river by the footbridge (*cau may*) and then walk up through the rice fields into Lao Chai village. You will find **Ta Van** 2 km further on.

A leisurely stroll through these villages could well be the highlight of a trip to Vietnam. It is a chance to observe rural life led in reasonable prosperity. Wet rice forms the staple income; weaving for the tourist market puts a bit of meat on the table. Here nature is kind, there is rich soil and no shortage of water. Again it's possible to see how the landscape has been engineered to suit human needs. The terracing is on an awesome scale (in places more than 100 steps), the result of centuries of labour to convert steep slopes into level fields which can be flooded to grow rice. Technologically, and in no sense pejoratively, the villages might be described as belonging to a bamboo age. Bamboo trunks carry water huge distances from spring to village; water flows across barriers and tracks in bamboo aqueducts; mechanical rice huskers made of bamboo are driven by water requiring no human effort; houses are held up with bamboo; bottoms are parked on bamboo chairs; and tobacco and other substances are inhaled through bamboo pipes. Any path chosen will lead to some hamlet or other; the Hmong in villages further from Sapa tend to be more reserved and suspicious; their fields and houses are often securely fenced off.

Cross back to the north side of the river by the suspension bridge. A dip in the deep pools of the Muong Hoa River is refreshingly invigorating. Engraved stones are a further 2 km southeast (away from Sapa, that is) by the side of road; they are believed to be inscribed in ancient Hmong. The return walk to Sapa from the inscribed stones is a steady 10-km uphill climb. It's exhausting work but, stimulated by the views and the air and fuelled by hard-boiled eggs and warm Lao Cai beer from roadside shacks, it is a pleasure, not an ordeal. In the late afternoon sun the rice glows with more shades of green than you would have thought possible and the lengthening shadows cast the entire landscape into vivid three-dimensional relief – even through a camera lens.

CAT CAT AND SIN CHAI VILLAGES

ⓘ *40,000d fee for taking the track.*

The track heading west from Sapa through the market area offers either a short 5-km round-trip walk to **Cat Cat** Black Hmong village or a longer 10-km round-trip walk to **Sin Chai** Black Hmong village; both options are accessible without a guide and take in some beautiful scenery. The path to Cat Cat leads off to the left of the Sin Chai track after about 1 km, following the line of pylons down through the rice paddies to Cat Cat village; beyond the village over the river bridge you can visit the **Cascade Waterfall** (from which the village takes its name) and an old French hydroelectric power station that still produces electricity. Sin Chai village is 4 km northwest of here.

The **Silver Falls** are 12 km west of Sapa on the Muong Lay road and are spectacular following rain. They are hardly worth a special visit but if passing it's quite nice to stop for a paddle in the cold pools.

NAM SAI AND NAM CAM

Some 40 km south and southeast of Sapa are the communities of **Nam Sai** and **Nam Cam**, which are being developed for local tourism with the help of NGOs. The area is inhabited by Tay, Xa Pho, Red Dao and Hmong ethnic minorities. Village way of life (including cardamom, mushroom and soybean crop growing) can be explored and homestays are possible. Treks can be arranged to the area or you can travel by car and explore the area from there.

→LAO CAI

Lao Cai is the most important border crossing with China. A two-way flow of people and trade cross through the city each day. But whereas the balance of human traffic is roughly equal, the value of traded goods is highly one-sided: an endless flow of products from China's modern factories wreaks havoc on Vietnam's own hapless state-owned enterprizes struggling to fill quotas of shoddy goods that no one wants to buy. There is a branch of **Sapa Tourism Center** ① *306 Khanh Yen St, T20-362 52506, www.sapa-tourism.com,* very close to the train station.

MOVING ON

The town bus station is on Hong Ha Street and local buses run to Bac Ha (see page 81) and villages in the Far North (see page 84). Ha Giang can be reached comfortably in a day. If you travel from Lao Cai back to Hanoi, the road begins in a beautiful valley where rice, cinnamon (in places the air is scented) and tea are grown. By Viet Tri it has become a drab industrial landscape and remains so all the way back. See also, 'Ha Giang to Hanoi' (page 88) for an alternative route back to Hanoi.

BACKGROUND

An important north–south transit stop for traders with caravans of pack oxen or horses since time immemorial, Lao Cai has changed hands many times over the past thousand years as rival Chinese, Vietnamese and ethnic minority chieftains fought for ascendancy in the region. The town itself dates back at least to 1463, when the Viet kings established it as the capital of their northernmost province of Hung Hoa.

Lao Cai fell to the French in 1889 and thereafter served as an important administrative centre and garrison town. The direct rail link to Hanoi was built during the first decade of the last century, a project notable for the 25,000 Vietnamese conscripted labourers who died during its seven-year construction period.

Following the Vietnamese invasion of Cambodia in late 1978, China, Cambodia's ally, responded in February 1979 by launching a massive invasion of North Vietnam, 'to teach the Vietnamese a lesson'. More than 600,000 Chinese troops were deployed occupying territory from Pa So (formerly Phong Tho) in the Northwest to Cao Bang and Lang Son in the Northeast. From the start of the campaign, however, the poorly trained Chinese forces encountered stiff resistance from local militia and, as the Vietnamese Army got into gear, the Chinese invasion force ground to a halt. After two weeks Chinese troops had penetrated no further than 30 km into Vietnamese territory and, with an estimated 20,000 casualties already incurred by the People's Army, the Chinese government withdrew its troops, declaring the operation "a great success".

Trade with China, much of it illegal, has turned this former small town into a rich community of (dong if not dollar) millionaires and Lao Cai is experiencing something of a construction boom. Huge boulevards flanked by some enormous local government buildings are sprouting up in the main part of town, west of the Red River. In 2006 Lao Cai became a city; by 2020 it looks set to get an airport. Other than for border-crossers Lao Cai holds little appeal.

INTERNATIONAL BORDER CROSSING

The border is open to pedestrians (0700-2200) with the correct exit and entry visas for both countries. Travellers must report to the International Border Gate Administration Center south of the bridge and near the level crossing for passport stamping and customs clearance. Visas into Vietnam must be obtained in Hong Kong or Beijing and must specify the Lao Cai crossing; they normally take a week to process and are not obtainable at the border. Visas for China must be obtained in Hanoi and must also specify the Lao Cai crossing. The Chinese visa costs US$30 but US citizens need to pay US$100; the visa takes four days to be issued. An express 24-hour service costs a further US$20; a two-hour service, a further US$30. **Binh Minh Travel** ① *39 Nguyen Hue, T20-383 6666, www.binhminhtravel.com.vn*, can arrange visas and foreign currency. It costs 10,000d from the train station to the border on a *xe ôm*.

→BAC HA

Around 18 km before Bac Ha the scenery is wonderful; huge expanses of mountains, pine trees and terracing engraved by the winding road as it climbs skywards towards Bac Ha.

Bac Ha itself is really only notable for one thing and that is its Sunday market. That 'one thing', however, is very special. Hundreds of local minority people flock in from the surrounding districts to shop and socialize, while tourists from all corners of the earth pour in to watch them do it. Otherwise there is very little of interest and neither the appeal nor comforts of Sapa.

TOURIST INFORMATION

Bac Ha now has a branch of **Sapa Tourism Center** ① *Hoang A Tuong's Palace, T20-378 0662, www.sapa-tourism.com*. If you have your own transport, arrive early. If you don't, nearly all the hotels and all the tour operators in Sapa organize trips.

PLACES IN AND AROUND BAC HA

The **Sunday market** ① *0600-1400*, draws in the Flower Hmong, Phula, Dao Tuyen, La Chi and Tay – the Tay being Vietnam's largest ethnic minority. It is a riot of colour and fun: the Flower Hmong wear pink and green headscarves; children wear hats with snail motifs and tassles. While the women trade and gossip, the men consume quantities of rice wine and cook dog and other animal innards in small cauldrons. By late morning they can no longer walk so are heaved onto donkeys by their wives and led home.

There are a number of walks to outlying villages. **Pho** village of the Flower Hmong is around 4 km north; **Thai Giang Pho** village of the Tay is 4 km east; and **Na Hoi** and **Na Ang** villages, also of the Tay, are 2 km and 4 km west respectively.

OTHER MARKET VILLAGES

It's also possible to visit the **Can Cau** (Saturday market), **Muong Hum** (Sunday market), **Muong Khuong** (Sunday market), **Coc Ly** (Tuesday market), **Lung Khau Nhin** (Thursday market).

SAPA AND AROUND LISTINGS

WHERE TO STAY

Sapa

A host of guesthouses has sprung up to cater for Sapa's rejuvenation and the appeal of the town has, perhaps, been a little compromised by the new structures. Prices tend to rise Jun-Oct to coincide with northern hemisphere university holidays and at weekends. Hoteliers are accustomed to bargaining; healthy competition ensures fair rates.

$$$$ Topas Ecolodge, 20 km southeast of Sapa, www.topasecolodge.com, (Sapa office: 24 Muong Hoa St, T020-387 1331). 25 bungalows with balconies built from white granite crown a hill overlooking stunning valleys. The walk from reception to the bungalows cuts right through the area's trademark rice terraces. Bungalows are simply furnished and powered by solar energy. The food is good -- evening buffets are a particular treat. Treks and mountain bike rides lead to less touristed Red Dao areas. A new hydroelectric power station in the valley means it is best to request room numbers 101-105 for unspoilt views. For nature, views, peace and an eco-philosophy, the lodge is unique in Vietnam. Highly recommended.

$$$$ Victoria Sapa, T020-387 1522, www.victoriahotels.asia. With 77 rooms, this hotel is the best in town. Comfy, with well-appointed rooms, it is a lovely place in which to relax. In winter there are very welcome open fires in the bar and dining rooms. The food is very good and the set buffets are excellent value. The Health Centre offers everything from the traditional massage to reflexology. The centre, pool, tennis courts and sauna are open to non-guests. Packages available. The hotel has private sleeper carriages on the train from Hanoi to Lai Cai.

$$$ Chau Long Hotel, 24 Dong Loi St, Sapa, T020-3871 245, www.chaulonghotel.com. All rooms here have fantastic views down the valley and private balconies. Cosy decor. Serves an excellent buffet breakfast in the restaurant with a panoramic vista.

$$$ Hmong Mountain Retreat, 6 km along the Ban Ho road, T020-6505 228, www.hmongmountainretreat.com. 5 bungalows and a large, 2-bedroom Hmong House, which is perfect for groups, are set on an isolated rice terrace, complete with a good restaurant. A stay can be combined with trekking to the retreat itself.

$$$ Sapa Rooms, 18 Phan Xi Pang St, T020-650 5228, www.saparooms.com. While the lobby and café is decorated to a very high standard, the rooms offer more of a boutique hostel experience with poor showers.

$$$ Sapa View Hotel, 41 Muong Hoa St, T020-3872 388, http://sapaview-hotel.com. With a Swiss alpine feel, many rooms have jaw-dropping views through large windows and from private balconies. Each room has its own log fire for the colder months. Good restaurant with open kitchen. Very hospitable new manager, David. Highly recommended.

$$ Cat Cat, 46 Phan Xi Pan St, on the Cat Cat side of town through the market. T020-3871946, www.catcathotel.com. The guesthouse has expanded up the hillside, with new terraces and bungalows. Friendly and popular, its 40 rooms represent good value for money, particularly those which offer great views. The hotel has a restaurant and, like most others, arranges tours and provides useful information. Beware other 'Cat Cat' hotel copies.

Lao Cai

$$$ Lao Cai International Hotel, 88 Thuy Hoa St, T20-382 6668, http://www.laocaihotel.com. This grand-looking hotel faces the border gate across the river and has 34 rooms with all facilities. There's a restaurant, health centre and staff can help with obtaining Chinese visas if necessary.

RESTAURANTS

Sapa

There are rice and noodle stalls in the market and along the path by the church.

$$$-$$ The Hill Station, 7 Muong Hoa St, T020-3887 111, www.thehillstation.com. 0800-2300. A blend of Nordic and Hmong design from the Norweigan owners. Cold cuts, cheese boards, gourmet baguettes (probably the priciest in Vietnam) and good wine. Hmong staff trained by the owners.

$$ Red Dao House, 4B Thac Bac St, T020-387 2927. 0900-2400. Homely and warm chalet-style restaurant with very friendly waiting staff. Large range of reasonable Vietnamese food. Gets busy – reserve a table by the front windows.

$$-$ Cha Pa Garden, 23b Cau May St, T020-387 2907, www.chapagarden.com. A peaceful little oasis where you can hide from the street vendors for a romantic meal. Choices include coq au vin and and Swedish meatballs. Extensive wine selection.

$$-$ Quan Ngon Sapa, 2 Phan Xi Pan St, T09-3443 0838, www.quangonsapa.com. It's simply wrong to visit Sapa and not try the local speciality *lau ca hoi* (salmon hot pot). It's served well here, alongside other Vietnamese dishes, in basic, sometimes raucous, surroundings.

$$-$ Sapa Rooms, 18 Phan Xi Pang St, T020-650 5228. An Aussie owner and a Hanoian artist have done a great job decorating this establishment with hilltribe-inspired works. **KOTO**-trained chefs (see page 52) whip up delicious meals. Try the homemade cookie and ice-cream dessert and the Sapa Rooms smoothie.

$ Baguette & Chocolat, Thac Bac St, T020- 387 1766, www.hoasuaschool.com. Daily 0700-2100. A small NGO-run café, with boulangerie attached; lovely home-made cakes for exhausted trekkers, plus baguettes, quiche and burgers. Picnic kits from 90,000d.

ENTERTAINMENT

Sapa

Ethnic minority dancing at Dragon's Jaw Hill (Ham Rong), daily at 0930 and 1500, included in entrance fee; free at **Victoria Sapa** as long as you buy drinks, Sat at 2000; **Sapa View Hotel** has a free nightly performance of ethnic minority music, 1900; a show is also put on regularly at Cat Cat village (included in the entrance fee).

WHAT TO DO

Sapa

Trekking and biking is big business in Sapa – the town is full of trekking paraphernalia and tour companies touting for business. The weather will have a huge impact on how enjoyable your experience is – it is best to head for the hills in spring or autumn. The scenery is most breathtaking in September, when the terraces are chock full of rice and the harvest season begins. It's important to choose the right operator – **Sapa O Chau** is one of the most respected outfits in town. Overnight treks see guests stay in villages in simple homestay accommodation – expect open sleeping quarters, simple meals and plenty of rice wine. In general, the shorter the trek, the less traditional the village you are likely to see. Sapa and Lao Cai province is also home to some excellent cycling. It's possible to arrange overnight cycle treks or cycle the valleys all the way to Dien Bien Phu, stopping at various minority villages en route. For something a little less demanding, **Topas** offer full- and half-day rides either from Sapa town or its ecolodge, 20 km away (see Where to stay).

FAR NORTH

The Far North of Vietnam is a beautiful, mainly mountainous region that skirts the Chinese border. Its steep slopes have been carved into curved rice terracing with paddies shimmering in the strong sun; further north where the steepness increases, majestic limestone mountain peaks will enthrall. The sparse populations that live here are predominantly indigenous groups and, thankfully, they have not yet been corrupted by commercialization to the same extent as their cousins in the Northwest. The way of life in the traditional villages remains just that, traditional; it is not a show put on for the entertainment of tourists. The Far North is still one of the least-visited areas of the country and, as such, it offers the chance to see Vietnamese life as it really is.

ARRIVING IN THE FAR NORTH

Getting there and around Unlike Northwest Vietnam, which has so conveniently aligned its attractions along one road circuit, the Far North is somewhat fragmented although through road links have improved. For much of the area a **permit** is required to visit. Dutch NGO SNV is trying to encourage tourism in this area as the Northern Highlands Trail and is seeking to ease restrictions in the area.

Best time to visit The best time to visit this area is from October until March. Although this is winter and spring, the weather is milder than if you were to visit later in the year.

THE ROAD TO HA GIANG

A worthwhile detour on the way to Ha Giang is via **Xin Man** in the far west of Ha Giang Province. This ethnic minority town mostly draws Hmong, Nung, Tay and Dao minorities, and Sunday market time is busy and hectic. From Xin Man, a road twists and turns towards Hoang Su Phi, passing **Heaven's Gate II** and the **Hoang Su Phi Pass**.

➔HA GIANG

The provincial capital of Ha Giang lies on the banks of the Lo River just south of its confluence with the River Mien, perched picturesquely between the beautiful Cam and Mo Neo mountains. Like Cao Bang and Lang Son, Ha Giang was badly damaged during the border war with China in 1979 and has since undergone extensive reconstruction.

ARRIVING IN HA GIANG

Getting there and around From Hanoi, Highway 2 goes directly to Ha Giang and is serviced by bus from Hanoi's Gia Lam terminal (six to seven hours). Ha Giang can be reached comfortably in a day from Sapa. Within the town, there are a few taxis and also the ubiquitous *xe ôm*.

Moving on Permits for visiting the Dong Van-Meo Vac region (see page 86) must be arranged in the Ha Giang tourist office. 4WD vehicles are recommended in the Far North whatever the season. From Ha Giang, buses run directly back to Hanoi along Highway 2.

Best time to visit There are four distinct seasons in the north (spring, summer, autumn and winter). The best time to visit would be either during autumn or spring.

Tourist information Ha Giang Tourist Company ① *5 Nguyen Trai St, T219-387 5288/ T219-386 7054, www.dulichhagiang.vn, Mon-Fri 0800-1130, 1330-1700*. To visit the surrounding area you will need a special **permit** which the company can obtain for you; 250,000d for up to a group of five and you must hire a local guide.

BACKGROUND

Archaeological evidence unearthed at Doi Thong (Pine Hill) in Ha Giang town indicates there was human settlement in the region at least 30,000 years ago. It was during the Bronze Age, however, that the most important flowering of early culture took place under the Tay Vu. This was one of the most significant tribes of the Hung kingdom of Van Lang, whose centre of power was in the Ha Giang region. Some of the most beautiful Dong Son bronze drums were found in Ha Giang Province, most notably in the Meo Vac region, where the tradition of making bronze drums for ceremonial purposes continues even to this day among the Lolo and Pu Peo communities.

The original settlement in Ha Giang lay on the east bank of the Lo River and it was here that the French established themselves following the conquest of the area in 1886. The town subsequently became an important military base, a development confirmed in 1905 when Ha Giang was formally established as one of four North Vietnamese military territories of French Indochina.

The Ha Giang area saw a number of important ethnic rebellions against the French during the early years of the colonial period, the most important being that of the Dao who rose up in 1901 under the leadership of Trieu Tien Kien and Trieu Tai Loc. The revolt was quickly put down and Trieu Tien Kien was killed during the fighting, but in 1913 Trieu Tai Loc rose up again, this time supported by another family member known as Trieu Tien Tien, marching under the slogans: "No corvées, no taxes for the French; Drive out the French to recover our country; Liberty for the Dao".

Carrying white flags embroidered with the four ideograms *To Quoc Bach Ky* (White Flag of the Fatherland) and wearing white conical hats (hence the French name 'The White Hat Revolt'), the rebels launched attacks against Tuyen Quang, Lao Cai and Yen Bai and managed to keep French troops at bay until 1915 when the revolt was savagely repressed. Hundreds of the insurgents were subsequently deported and 67 were condemned to death by the colonial courts.

PLACES IN HA GIANG

The **Ha Giang Museum** ① *next to Yen Bien Bridge in the centre of town, daily 0800-1130, 1330-1700, free*, contains important archaeological, historical and ethnological artefacts from in and around the region, including a very helpful display of ethnic costumes.

Located close to the east bank of the River Lo in the old quarter of the town, Ha Giang Market is a daily affair although it is busiest on Sunday. Tay, Nung and Red Dao people are always in evidence here, as are members of northern Ha Giang Province's prolific White Hmong.

Doi Thong (Pine Hill) lies just behind the main Ha Giang Market. The pine trees are newly planted but the hill itself is an area of ancient human settlement believed to date back some 30,000 years to the Son Vi period. Many ancient axe-heads and other primitive weapons were discovered on the hill during land clearance; these are now in the local museum and in the History Museum in Hanoi.

This is the northernmost tip of Vietnam, close to the Chinese border and just 30 km south of the Tropic of Cancer. It's an impressive natural setting high on a valley side with Fan Si Pan, Vietnam's tallest mountain, either clearly visible or brooding in the mist.

ARRIVING IN THE DONG VAN-MEO VAC REGION

Getting there All foreign visitors are required to obtain a special permit and take a licensed guide before proceeding beyond Ha Giang into the remote Dong Van-Meo Vac area on the Chinese border including the districts of Quan Ba and Yen Minh. This can be obtained either directly from the local police or alternatively through the **Ha Giang Tourist Company** (see page 85). One possible advantage of booking a tour in Hanoi is that they do it for you, although the permit arrangement must be completed in the Ha Giang tourist office.

Moving on Returning from Meo Vac to Ha Giang head straight to Yen Minh via Highway 176 and Highway 180 bypassing Dong Van and cutting off 22 km. It is a small and windy 50-km road in good condition. From Ha Giang, it's possible to return south to Hanoi via Thac Ba Lake (see 'Ha Giang to Hanoi', page 88).

Alternatively, head south from Meo Vac to Bao Lac and join Highway 3 at Na Phac from where it's possible to visit the Ba Be National Park (see page 89) before returning to Hanoi.

Getting around Local bus services are infrequent and slow. The roads north of Ha Giang have now been sealed are in good condition but the roads are narrow and windy with high mountain slopes. A 4WD vehicle or sturdy motorbike is highly advisable. Ha Giang to Dong Van via Yen Minh is 148 km (five hours); Dong Van to Meo Vac is 22 km (one hour). The most superb scenery is the Dong Van–Meo Vac road.

Note that since both Dong Van and Meo Vac are located very close to the Chinese border, hill-walking by foreigners around both towns is forbidden, making the number of things to do in Dong Van and Meo Vac somewhat limited although Hanoi tour operators can organize four- to seven-day treks in the area.

QUAN BA

Quan Ba is 45 km from Ha Giang. The road climbs up the Quan Ba Pass to '**Heaven's Gate**' – identifiable by the TV transmitter mast to the left of the summit – from where there are wonderful views of the Quan Ba Valley with its extraordinary row of uniformly shaped hills. Quan Ba has a Sunday market, one of the largest in the region, which attracts not only White Hmong, Red Dao, Dao Ao Dai and Tay people but also members of the Bo Y ethnic minority who live in the mountains around the town.

YEN MINH AND PHO BANG

Yen Minh is located 98 km northwest of Ha Giang and is a convenient place to stop for lunch on the way to Dong Van and Meo Vac – a possible overnight stop for those planning to spend longer in the region. It has a Sunday market where, in addition to the groups mentioned above, you'll see Giay, Pu Peo, Co lao, Lolo and the local branch of Red Dao.

ON THE ROAD

Hmong Kings of Sa Phin

While it is clear that Hmong people have lived in the Dong Van-Meo Vac border region for many centuries, the ascendancy of White Hmong in the area is believed to date from the late 18th century, when the powerful Vuong family established its seat of government near Dong Van. In subsequent years the Vuong lords were endorsed as local government mandarins of Dong Van and Meo Vac by the Nguyen kings in Hué and later, following the French conquest of Indochina, by their colonial masters.

Keen to ensure the security of this key border region, the French authorities moved to further bolster the power of the Vuong family. Accordingly, in 1900 Vuong Chi Duc was recognized as king of the Hmong, and Chinese architects were brought in to design a residence befitting his newly elevated status. A site was chosen at Sa Phin, 16 km west of Dong Van; construction commenced in 1902 and was completed during the following year.

During the early years of his reign, Vuong Chi Duc remained loyal to his French patrons, participating in numerous campaigns to quell uprisings against the colonial government. In 1927 he was made a general in the French army; a photograph of him in full military uniform may be seen on the family altar in the innermost room of the house. But, as the struggle for Vietnamese independence got underway during the 1930s, Duc adopted an increasingly neutral stance. Following his death in 1944, Duc was succeeded as king of the Hmong by his son, Vuong Chi Sinh, who the following year met and pledged his support for President Ho Chi Minh.

Built between 1902 and 1903, the house of the former Hmong king faces south in accordance with the geomantic principles which traditionally govern the construction of Northeast Asian royal residences, comprising four, two-storey sections linked by three open courtyards. The building is surrounded by a moat, and various ornately carved tombs of members of the Vuong family lie outside the main gate. Both the outer and cross-sectional walls of the building are made of brick, but within that basic structure everything else is made of wood. The architecture, a development of late 19th-century Southern Chinese town-house style, features *mui luyen* or *yin-yang* roof tiles.

Northwest of Yen Minh right on the Chinese border lies the town of Pho Bang. Time seems to have stood still here with mud construction homes with a second galley floor to house firewood. This is remote but worth the hike for the ambience in the town.

SA PHIN

Crossing the old border into the former demesne of the White Hmong kings the very distinctive architecture of the White Hmong houses of the area becomes apparent; it is quite unlike the small wooden huts characteristic of Hmong settlements elsewhere in North Vietnam. These are big, two-storey buildings, constructed using large bricks fashioned from the characteristic yellow earth of the region and invariably roofed in Chinese style. But it is not only the Hmong who construct their houses in this way – the dwellings of other people of the area such as the Co lao and the Pu Péo are of similar design, no doubt a result of their having lived for generations within the borders of the former Hmong kingdom.

The remote Sa Phin Valley is just 2 km from the Chinese border. Below the road surrounded by conical peaks lies the village of Sa Phin, a small White Hmong settlement of no more than 20 buildings from which loom the twin, white towers of the Hmong royal house, at one time the seat of government in the Dong Van-Meo Vac region, see box, left. The **Sa Phin Tourist Office**, just below the house, provides a guide with a little English, 5000d. A visit to the royal house is fascinating. The Sa Phin market is a treat and is held every 12 days. Duck into the food market and drink beer from bowls with the locals.

LUNG CU
Lung Cu is the most northern point in Vietnam. It is marked by a hillock, flag pole and observation tower. From the top of the hill low mounds and China can be spied. There's an army post there so you'll need to register in the small town before walking up the steep steps.

DONG VAN
This remote market town is itself nothing special (situated 16 km from Sa Phin) but is set in an attractive valley populated mainly by Tay people. However, it does have a street of ancient houses that is very attractive. One has been converted into a café. Dong Van has a Sunday market, but is very quiet at other times of the week. Since the town is only 3 km from the Chinese border, foreigners are not permitted to walk in the surrounding hills or visit villages in the vicinity. (Interestingly no two maps of this part of Vietnam tell the same story.)

MEO VAC
Passing through the **Ma Pi Leng Pass** around 1500 m above the Nho Que River, the scenery is simply awesome. Like Dong Van, Meo Vac is a restricted border area, and foreigners are not permitted to walk in the surrounding hills or visit villages outside the town. Phallic-shaped mountainous peaks and chasms of running rivers make up the scenery. A small market is held every day in the town square, frequented mainly by White Hmong, Tay and Lolo people. Meo Vac is also the site of the famous Khau Vai 'Love Market' held once every year on the 27th day of the third month of the lunar calendar, which sees young people from all of the main ethnic groups of the region descending on the town to look for a partner. The Lolo people, with their highly colourful clothes, make up a large proportion of the town's population. A Lolo village is nearby, up the hill from the town centre.

If you are lucky to pass **Lung Phin**, 15 km after Meo Vac on the way back to Yen Minh on market day you will see the wildest market on the village hillside. It is the most colourful of the markets in the Ha Giang region. This market is held every six days.

HA GIANG TO HANOI
From Ha Giang there is the option to visit Ba Be National Park on the way back to Hanoi (see below). A more direct route is to follow the well-maintained Highway 2, which for much of its route follows the Lo River southwards towards Hanoi, through some wonderful scenery.

Orange groves carpet the hillsides, giving way to tea plantations as the road passes the eastern shores of **Thac Ba Lake**. The delightful little town of **Vinh Tuy**, near the banks of the Lo River, is a possible lunch stop. Boats can be seen on the river most days, dredging the bed for gold. At Thac Ba it's possible to stay in White Trouser Dao communities and take boats out onto the lake.

Heading south, **Tan Quang** is a sizeable market town located some 60 km south of Ha Giang at the junction with Highway 279, the mountain road west to Bao Yen in Lao Cai Province. Tuyun Quang Province has a large ethnic minority population and people from the two main groups of this province, the Tay and the Dao, can be seen.

ⓘ *44 km west of Na Phac on Highway 279, 1 hr from Cho Ra town, T281-389 4014, 20,000d plus 1000d insurance per person. The park centre is located on the eastern shore of Ba Be Lake. It runs many different tours led by English-speaking guides with an expert knowledge of the area and its wildlife. These tours range from 2-hr boat trips to 2-day mountain treks staying overnight in Tay or Dao villages and visiting caves, waterfalls and other local beauty spots.*

Ba Be National Park (Vuon Quoc Gia Ba Be) was established in 1992. It is Vietnam's eighth national park and comprises 23,340 ha of protected area plus an additional 8079 ha of buffer zone. It is centred on the very beautiful Ba Be Lake (*ba be* means 'three basins'), 200 m above sea level. The lake is surrounded by limestone hills carpeted in tropical evergreen forest. The park itself contains a very high diversity of flora and fauna, including an estimated 417 species of plant, 100 species of butterfly, 23 species of amphibian and reptile, 110 species of bird and 50 species of mammal. Among the latter are 10 seriously endangered species, including the Tonkinese snub-nosed langur (*Rhinopitecus avunculus*) and the black gibbon (*Hylobates concolor*). Within the park there are a number of villages inhabited by people of the Tay, Red Dao, Coin Dao and White Hmong minorities.

FAR NORTH LISTINGS

WHERE TO STAY

The Far North includes some of the most remote spots in Vietnam. Here you'll find community lodges, homestays and clean, functional hotels.

The road to Ha Giang
$ Ethnic minority homestay at Thac Ba Lake. Mr Thuong and Miss Nhat offer homestay in the village of Ngoi Tu, Vu Linh, Yen Bai province, T9-7284 5982 (English not spoken). Dinner is US$4.50 and breakfast is US$1.20.

$ Lavie Vu Linh Resort, a sustainable tourism project in Ngoi Tu village, Vu Linh commune, Yen Bai province, www.lavievulinh.com. Sleep in a longhouse on the floor or a private room with en suite. The shared bathroom has the most fabulous bathtub. Hot water is available. Trekking, rafting, fishing, boating, biking and badminton is possible. Dinner is with a local family and costs 110,000d. This is billed as a sustainable tourism project. It has a great lookout across the lake but there is some criticism of the project in the community. It may be better to stay with a local family in the nearby village.

Ha Giang
$$ Pan Hou Village, T219-383 3565, www. panhouvillage.hebergratuit.com, is some distance south of Ha Giang off the main road. You would need to have your own transport to get to this lodge in the mountains. It would be a good place from where to trek which is organized.

$ Huy Hoan Hotel, 10 Nguyen Trai St, T219-386 1288. Follow the main road coming into the town centre and on the left-hand side, just 20 m after the junction of Yen Bien 2 bridge is the hotel. The best hotel in Ha Giang with 41 very comfortable a/c rooms with private bathroom. Very little English is spoken but they are fluent in Chinese. Wi-fi available.

$ Lavie Vu Linh Resort, a sustainable tourism project in Ngoi Tu village, Vu Linh commune, Yen Bai province, www.lavievulinh.com. Sleep in a longhouse on the floor , a rammed earth room with private bathroom, or a private room with en suite. The shared bathroom has the most fabulous bathtub. Hot water is available. Trekking, rafting, fishing, boating, biking and badminton is possible. Dinner is with a local family and costs around 110,000d. This is billed as a sustainable tourism project. It has a great lookout across the lake but there is some criticism of the project in the community. It may be better to stay with a local family in the nearby village.

$ Thon Tha Hamlet (Lam Phuong cooperative), T219-386 0647, T123-852 2447 (mob). Mr Nguyen Van Quyen is in charge of the homestay rota at this picturesque Tay ethnic minority village amid paddy fields, 5 km west of Ha Giang.

Dong Van
$ Cao Nguyen Da (Rocky Plateau Hotel), T219-385 6868. Service is appalling but you've got to dig the orange suede and white retro furniture in the lobby and the clay pot sculpture in the stairwell. 14 overdecorated rooms with small bathrooms. Prices rise at weekends. Breakfast not included.

$ Khai Hoan Hotel, T219-385 6147. A 25-roomed hotel with large rooms; fan only. It's the biggest and cleanest hotel in town. Breakfast not included.

Meo Vac
$ Hoa Cuong Hotel, T219-387 1888. This new 26-roomed hotel is luxurious for these parts. Hot gushing showers and firm beds with crisp linens are most welcome up here.

$ Nho Que Guesthouse, T219-387 2322. A good guesthouse with 12 a/c rooms and hot water showers.

Ba Be National Park
$ Ba Be Hotel, Nguyen Cong Quynh St, Cho Ra, T281-387 6115, about 15 km east of Ba Be National Park. Twin, fan rooms with hot water, shower/toilet. The hotel manager can arrange a whole-day trip including 2 hrs on the river to the lake passing a small ethnic community homestead where you will be fed and filled with rice wine. Opposite the hotel is a 5-day market for Dao and Tay people, some of whom will have walked through the night to get there.
$ Ba Be National Park Guesthouse, T281-389 4026. 62 nice and comfortable a/c rooms with adjoining bathrooms with hot water. Meals available in the park office.
$ Hoanh Tu Homestay, T281-389 4071, T1688-472446 (mob). A lovely homestay with balcony overlooking the lake. Bathrooms are not next to the living quarters.

RESTAURANTS

The road to Ha Giang
$ Nhat Thuy Com Binh Dan (**Common Rice Restaurant**), Xin Man, T219-383 6117. A basic restaurant serving tasty pork dishes, sardines, soups and fried spring rolls.

Ha Giang
$ Com Pho Bo, 200 m from the **Huy Hoan Hotel** on Nguyen Trai St serving simple dishes.
$ Com Vietnam, 1 Quang Trung St, T219-386 8034. Open daily. The menu's not in English but there's chicken, duck, beef, water buffalo, fish and spring rolls.
$ Tourist Company Quan Com Pho, 160 Tran Hung Dao St, corner of Nguyen Trai St. The most traveller-friendly place to eat in Ha Giang. Another restaurant next door. There are numerous other small places to eat down side streets off Tran Hung Dao and on the other side of town near the main market. The Pho Da café is nearby.

Dong Van
$ Pho Co Cafe. A charming café with an interior courtyard and wooden balustrading in an old building. Just drinks on offer.
$ Tien Nhi Restaurant, main road, Dong Van, T219-385 6217. Get yourself a slice of superb roasted pig from here. Failing that a coffee from this friendly restaurant.

WHAT TO DO

Ha Giang
Ha Giang Tourist Company, 160 Tran Hung Dao St, corner of Nguyen Trai St. Permits for Dong Van-Meo Vac region are obtainable here, 250,000d for up to a group of 5; takes 1 hr.

HALONG BAY

Halong means 'descending dragon', and an enormous beast is said to have careered into the sea at this point, cutting the fantastic bay from the rocks as it thrashed its way into the depths. Vietnamese poets (including the 'Poet King' Le Thanh Tong) have traditionally extolled the beauty of this romantic area with its rugged islands that protrude from a sea dotted with sailing junks. Artists have been just as quick to draw inspiration from the crooked islands seeing the forms of monks and gods in the rock faces, and dragon's lairs and fairy lakes in the depths of the caves. Another myth says that the islands are dragons sent by the gods to impede the progress of an invasion flotilla. Historically more believable, if substantially embellished, the area was the location of two famous sea battles, in the 10th and 13th centuries (see box, page 67). The bay is now a UNESCO World Heritage Site.

ARRIVING IN HALONG BAY

Getting there There are two bases from which to explore Halong Bay: Halong City or Cat Ba, while Haiphong makes a good overnight stop on the way to or from the area. Traditionally, visitors went direct to Halong City from Hanoi and took a boat from there. This is still a valid option, especially for those who are short of time. But Cat Ba is becoming increasingly popular as a springboard to Halong Bay, largely because Cat Ba itself is

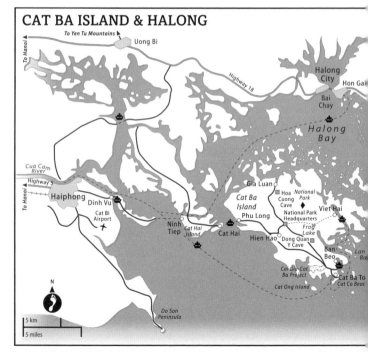

CAT BA ISLAND & HALONG

interesting. Many people, however, take an all-inclusive tour from Hanoi, and if you are short of time, this is your best option.

Getting around Boat tours of the bay can be booked at the Bai Chay Tourist Wharf in Halong City and Cat Ba Town. To see the bay properly allow four to five hours but an overnight trip is enjoyable and preferable. One option is to buy a day ticket for a boat trip and get off at Cat Ba town when it docks thus allowing you a few hours in the bay too. Tour operators in Hanoi, also offer tours of the bay of varying duration.

Best time to visit It can be stormy in June, July and August. July and August are also the wettest months. Winter is cool and dry. The bay is no fun in the rain or fog so get a weather forecast if you can. If there are warnings of cyclones, stay away.

Tourist information In Halong City, **Quang Ninh Tourism** ① *opposite the Halong 1 Hotel and near the Novotel, T033-362 8862, www.halongtourism.com.vn*, is super helpful. 30,000d admission for each cave and attraction. There have been a number of fatal boat accidents in Halong Bay in recent years. Safety standards are not at Western levels. It is best to pay for a more expensive boat run by reputable tour operators rather than the numerous bargain basement offers. Note that it is now not possible to swim from beaches visited on boat tours or to swim directly from boats for safety reasons.

To Cam Pha & Mong Cai

Highway 18

To Bai Tu Long National
Park & Quan Lan Island

key Island

→KARSTS AND CAVES IN HALONG BAY

① Grotto of Wonders, Customs House Cave and Surprise Grotto all charge 30,000d (the Ti Tov cave is 10,000d) and are open 0730-1700. Fees for cave visits and boats to enter caves will not be included in the price of your boat tour. Many are a disappointment with harrying vendors, mounds of litter and disfiguring graffiti. Many are lit but some are not so bring a torch. Rocks can be treacherously slippery, so sensible footwear is advised.

Geologically the tower-karst scenery of Halong Bay is the product of millions of years of chemical action and river erosion working on the limestone to produce a pitted landscape. At the end of the last ice age, when glaciers melted, the sea level rose and inundated the area turning hills into islands. The islands of the bay are divided by a broad channel: to the east are the smaller outcrops of Bai Tu Long, while to the west are the larger islands with caves and secluded beaches.

Among the more spectacular caves are **Hang Hanh**, which extends for 2 km. Tour guides will point out fantastic stalagmites and stalactites that, with imagination, become heroes, demons and animals. **Hang Luon** is another flooded cave that leads to the hollow core in a doughnut-shaped island. It can be swum or navigated by coracle/canoe. **Hang Dau Go** is the cave wherein Tran Hung Dao stored his wooden stakes prior to studding them in the bed of the Bach Dang River in 1288 to destroy the boats of invading Mongol hordes. **Hang Thien Cung** (Heavenly Palace) is a hanging cave, a short 50-m haul above sea level, with dripping stalactites, stumpy stalagmites and solid rock pillars. A truly enormous cave and one of those most visited is **Sung Sot Cave** (Surprise Cave).

→HAIPHONG AND AROUND

Haiphong is still the Vietnam of yesteryear. There are beautiful old French buildings, a peaceful but busy city life where men still pedal ancient cyclos, and sidecars are in generous abundance. There is little to attract the tourist other than an authentic glimpse into life without tourism.

The port of Haiphong was established in 1888 on the Cua Cam River, a major distributory of the Red River. It is the largest port and the second largest city in the north. Over and above its natural attributes Haiphong is blessed with a go-ahead and entrepreneurial People's Committee (no surprises that the district sports Vietnam's first casino) and this attitude is reflected in the bustle in the streets and the industry and vitality of the population. Haiphong's prosperity looks set to redouble with heavy investment in port and communications infrastructure and major investment from overseas in manufacturing plants. Despite this (from the tourists' viewpoint) seemingly inauspicious framework, central Haiphong remains remarkably attractive and its people open and warm.

ARRIVING IN HAIPHONG
Getting there As the north's second city after Hanoi, and the region's premier port, Haiphong is well connected. **Cat Bi**, Haiphong's airport, is 7 km from the city and there are flights from Ho Chi Minh City, Danang and Halong City. The road from Hanoi is now excellent (for Vietnam) and there are frequent bus and minibus connections. Choose a big bus in the interests of comfort and safety. There are trains each day in either direction between the two cities. The 100-km road from Hanoi to Haiphong, the north's principal port, passes through the flood-prone riceland of the Red River Delta. In places the land lies below sea level and a system of dykes and bunds has been built up over the centuries to keep the river in place.

Getting around Central Haiphong is sufficiently compact for most sights to be visited on foot. But a journey from, for example, the railway station to the port, or a trip to the outer temples, merits a taxi, cyclo or *xe ôm*. Because Haiphong does not receive many Western tourists it is not normally possible to rent a motorbike for independent exploring.

Moving on Haiphong is a departure point for Cat Ba Island (one hour by hydrofoil), one of Vietnam's more accessible national parks, and from there with Halong Bay (see page 95). There are regular buses, minibuses and trains back to Hanoi for onward connections. Buses to Halong City (see page 97) leave Lac Long bus station every 15 minutes. There are also buses to Ninh Binh (see page 53) and Hué (see page 107), which leave from the Niem Nghia bus station. From Haiphong's airport it is possible to fly to Ho Chi Minh City, Danang or Halong City.

Tourist information ① *18 Minh Khai St, T31-384 7704, www.haiphongtourism.gov.vn*. Your hotel should be able to provide you with information too

BACKGROUND

Haiphong witnessed the initial arrival of the French in 1872 (they occupied Hanoi a year later) and, appropriately, their final departure from the north at 1500 in the afternoon of 15 May 1955. As the major port of the north, it was subjected to sustained bombing during the war. To prevent petrol and diesel fuel reaching the Viet Cong, nearly 80% of all above-ground tanks were obliterated by US bombing in 1966. The US did not realize that the North Vietnamese, anticipating such action, had dispersed much of their supplies to underground and concealed tanks. This did not prevent the city from receiving a battering, although Haiphong's air defence units are said to have retaliated by shooting down 317 US planes.

PLACES IN HAIPHONG

Much of outer Haiphong is an ugly industrial sprawl that will win no environmental beauty contests. But, considering the bombing the city sustained, there is still a surprising amount of attractive **colonial-style architecture** in the city centre. Central Haiphong is pleasantly green with tree-lined streets.

Right in the heart of town is the **Great Theatre** ① *corner of Tran Hung Dao St and Quang Trung St*, built in 1904 using imported French materials, with a colonnaded front, and facing a wide tree-lined boulevard. In November 1946, 40 Viet Minh fighters died here in a pitched battle with the French, triggered by the French government's decision to open a customs house in Haiphong. A plaque outside commemorates the battle. The streets around the theatre support the greatest concentration of foodstalls and shops.

Other colonial architecture includes the **People's Court** ① *31 Tran Phu St*, a fine French building with shutters; the **post office** ① *5 Nguyen Tri Phuong St*, in an attractive building, and the **bank** (Vietcombank) ① *11 Hoang Dieu St*, a handsome yellow and cream building.

Haiphong Museum (Bao Tang Thanh Pho Hai Phong) ① *66 Dien Bien Phu St, Tue and Thu 0800-1030, Wed and Sun 1930-2130, 2000d*, is an impressive colonial edifice in a wash of desert-sand red, and contains records of the city's turbulent past (some labels are in English).

There are a number of **street markets** and **flower stalls** off Cau Dat Street, which runs south from the theatre, along Tran Nhat Duat and Luong Khanh Thien streets. **Sat Market** is to be found in the west quarter of town, at the end of Phan Boi Chau Street. A market has stood on this site since 1876. The present building is a huge six-storey concrete edifice that has never quite taken off.

Near the centre of town on Me Linh Street is the **Nghe Pagoda** built at the beginning of the 20th century. The pagoda is dedicated to the memory of heroine General Le Chan who fought with the Trung sisters against the Chinese. A festival is held on the eighth day of the second lunar month to commemorate her birthday and offerings of crab and noodles, her favourite foods, are made. There is also an enormous statue of her in front of a cultural building diagonally opposite the Great Theatre.

Du Hang Pagoda ① *1 km south of the city centre on Chua Hang St (take a xe ôm)*, was originally built in 1672 by wealthy mandarin-turned-monk Nguyen Dinh Sach. It has been renovated and remodelled several times since. Arranged around a courtyard, this small temple has some fine traditional woodcarving.

Dinh Hang Kenh (Hang Kenh communal house or *dinh*) ① *2 km south of the centre at 51 Nguyen Cong Tru St*, dates back to 1856. Although built as a communal house, its chief

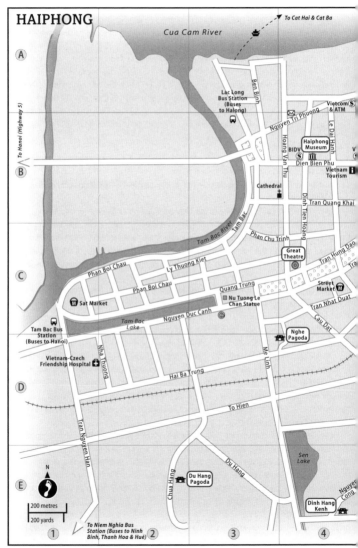

HAIPHONG

function today is as a temple. The main building is supported by 32 columns of ironwood and the wood carvings in the window grilles are noteworthy. From the outside, the roof is the most dramatic feature, tiled in the fishscale style, and ornamented with a number of dragons. The corners of the roof turn up and it appears that the sheer weight is too much, as the roof is now propped up on bricks. There are a number of *dinh* in and around Haiphong, reflecting the traditional importance of Chinese in this area. Today Taiwanese businessmen are counted among the major investors in Haiphong.

Port Entrance
Le Thanh Tong
Hoang Dieu
Tran Phu
Football Pitch
ⓈATM
Khai market
Tran Hung Dao
Vietnam Airlines
Ⓢ Indovina
People's Court
Luong Khanh Thien
Le Loi
Mam Tom Lake
Lach Tray
Stadium
An Bien Lake
⑤ To Cat Bi Airport & Do Son ⑥

→HALONG CITY AND AROUND

The route from Hanoi passes newly industrializing satellite towns whose factories, petrol stations and houses spill onto what were recently paddy fields. After Uong Bi, the scenery improves with the limestone hills which rise out of the alluvial plain giving a foretaste of the better things to come. Following the admission of Halong Bay to UNESCO's hallowed roll of World Heritage Sites, the two small towns of Bai Chay and Hon Gai were, in 1994, collectively elevated in status by the government and dubbed Halong City, a moniker largely ignored by locals. Halong City is an unattractive place with little to recommend it. What appeal it does have is strung along the seafront, which is being spruced up. For reasons unknown, the **Novotel** has opened and the **Sheraton Four Points** is to open.

ARRIVING IN HALONG CITY

Getting there and around Bai Chay bus station is 5 km west of the city, across the water from Hon Gai. There are regular bus connections from Hanoi's My Dinh terminal (four to five hours). Given the paucity of sights in the town, pretty much anywhere of relevance can be reached on foot. For venturing further afield, the town has the usual gangs of *xe ôm* drivers.

Moving on To get to Cat Ba Island (see page 99), take a tourist boat from the Bai

Chay Tourist Wharf. There are regular bus and train connections back to Hanoi for onward connections to other parts of the country.

BACKGROUND

It was at Halong that, arguably, Vietnam's fate under the French was sealed. In late 1882 Captain Henri Rivière led two companies of troops to Hon Gai to seize the coal mines for France. Shortly afterwards he was ambushed and killed and his head paraded on a stake from village to village. His death persuaded the French parliament to fund a full-scale expedition to make all of Vietnam a protectorate of France. As the politician Jules Delafosse remarked at the time: "Let us, gentlemen, call things by their name. It is not a protectorate you want, but a possession."

PLACES IN HALONG CITY

The twin towns, Bai Chay to the west and Hon Gai to the east, separated by a river estuary and now linked by a huge new 903-m-long bridge (10,000d toll), could not be more different. Few visitors made the short ferry crossing to Hon Gai which, with its port and adjacent coal mines, could fairly be described as the industrial end of town.

Bai Chay has made great efforts and not a little progress towards turning itself into a destination rather than merely a dormitory for those visiting Halong Bay. At huge expense a narrow beach has been constructed in front of the hotels; casuarina, palm and flame trees have been planted along the prom, old hotels renovated and new ones built. There is no denying the effect of the plans to create the feel of a seaside town. But the charm is not likely to work its magic with travellers from abroad in the same way that it does with Vietnamese who are drawn in huge numbers, rapidly swamping the little beach every weekend. And, in any case, UNESCO officials have instructed the Vietnamese to stop building new resorts in the area before the unlimited developments threaten the protected bay area. Several large and attractive modern hotels have been built, including the **Halong Plaza**, one of the most luxurious in the country. But quite who is going to occupy all these junior and executive suites is a problem the marketing men appear to have overlooked.

Hon Gai, connected to its neighbour by a US$134 million bridge since December 2006, is, as mining areas go, quite a nice one, but it does not live up to the 'natural wonderland' image **Quang Ninh Tourism** is trying to promote. The port of Hon Gai is busy with plenty of little bamboo and resin coracles (*thung chai*) which are used by the fishermen as tenders to get out to their boats and to bring ashore the catch.

There is a thriving market and near the ferry dock is the 106-m-high **Poem Mountain** (Nui Bao Tho), so named following a visit in 1486 by King Le Thanh Tong who was so taken by the beauty of Halong Bay that he composed a poem celebrating the scenery and carved his verse into the rock. It is quite a scramble up the hill and finding the right path may require some help. At the foot of the mountain nestles the little **Long Tien Pagoda** which dates from the early 20th century. Twenty minutes' walk north up from Hon Gai is a **ruined colonial church** damaged by a bomb in 1972 but the site affords lovely views.

YEN TU MOUNTAINS

The Yen Tu Mountains are 14 km northwest of **Uong Bi** and climb to a maximum elevation of 1068 m. Peppered with pagodas from the 13th to 16th centuries, much has been lost to the ravages of war and climate but stupas and temples of more recent foundation survive. The site has attracted pilgrims since the 13th century when King Tran Nhan Tong abandoned the throne in favour of a spiritual life. He washed the secular dust from his body in the Tam stream and entered the **Cam Thuc (Abstinence) Pagoda**. His 100 concubines traced him here and tried to persuade him of the folly of his ways but despite their undoubted allure he resisted all appeals and clung to his ascetic existence. Distraught by their failure, the poor women drowned themselves. Tran Nhan Tong later built a temple to their memory. Climbing the hills, visiting the temples and admiring the views can take a full day.

→CAT BA ISLAND

Cat Ba occupies a stunning setting in the south of Halong Bay. Much of the island and the seas around are designated a national park and, while perhaps not quite teeming with wildlife (already eaten), it is pleasantly wild and green. Cat Ba's remoteness has been steadily eroded (it only plugged into mains electricity in 1999) and it now represents a handy weekend break for many Hanoians. Despite the growth in numbers of karaoke-loving weekenders, Cat Ba remains an attractive place (minus a few of the uglier buildings) but best of all it is a great springboard into the surrounding waters of Halong Bay and an increasingly popular alternative to Halong City. The chief advantage is that there is a lot to see on the island including the stunning scenery of the interior. Cat Ba, however, will come under intense tourism and ecological pressure with the proposed building of a bridge from Dinh Vu on the mainland to Cat Hai Island (improving the links between the island and the mainland) and the building of the US$600 million 72-ha Cai Gia-Cat Ba urban project for people from Cat Hai Island along with villas, hotels, shopping centres, a marina and entertainment attractions.

ARRIVING IN CAT BA ISLAND

Getting there To get to Cat Ba Island there are several options. From Hanoi, the most commonly used route is the direct bus/boat run by **Hoang Long Co** ① *from Luong Yen Station, Nguyen Khoai St, Hanoi*. The bus runs first to Haiphong (two hours) and then, after a change of buses, 30 minutes to where the boat leaves for Cai Vieng Harbour on Cat Ba Island (35 minutes) and then on to Cat Ba Town by another bus (30 minutes). The entire journey costs 220,000d.

Or get to Haiphong by alternative buses, then take the **Transtour Co** ① *office on the seafront in Haiphong, T31-384 1099, www.transtourco.com.vn*, hydrofoil which runs between Haiphong and Cat Ba in 45 minutes, 130,000-150,000d.

From Halong City, it's possible to jump on a tourist boat for a one-way (four hours) ride for 200,000d from the Bai Chay Tourist Wharf (Halong Road, Halong City, T033-384 6592), daily 0730-1700, to the Gia Luan Wharf. A bus runs from Gia Luan to Cat Bat Town, 15,000d. Ferries also run from Tuan Chau 'Island' to Gia Luan Wharf at 0730 and 0930, 40,000d.

Moving on Hoang Long Co has an office by Cat Ba Harbour, T031-388 6592, from where the boat/bus returns to Hanoi at regular intervals until 1530. There are hydrofoils back to Haiphong or tourist boats to Halong City.

Tourist information ① *18 Minh Khai St, T31-384 7704, www.haiphongtourism.gov.vn*. Your hotel should be able to provide you with information too.

EXPLORING THE ISLAND

Cat Ba is the largest island in a coastal archipelago that includes more than 350 limestone outcrops. It is adjacent to and geologically similar to the islands and peaks of Halong Bay but separated by a broad channel as the map illustrates. The islands around Cat Ba are larger than the outcrops of Halong Bay and generally more dramatic. Cat Ba is the ideal place from which to explore the whole coastal area. It's also the place to try the exhilarating sport of deep water soloing – rock climbing on the karsts with no need for ropes or harnesses, using only the sea as your crash pad. Besides the quality of its scenery it is a more agreeable town in which to stay, although the countless new hotels springing up are slowly eroding the difference. The island is rugged and sparsely inhabited. Outside Cat Ba town there are only a few small villages. Perhaps the greatest pleasure is to hire a motorbike and explore, a simple enough process given the island's limited road network. Half of the island forms part of a national park, see below.

For an island of its size Cat Ba has remarkably few **beaches** – only three within easy access, creatively named **Cat Co 1**, **Cat Co 2** and **Cat Co 3**. The closest of the three is Cat Co 3, home of the Sunrise Resort (the entrance to the beach is via the resort) – the best accommodation on the island. Further up the hill, a long set of steps leads down to Cat Co 1. Cat Co 1 and 3 are linked by a scenic walkway around the headland. Cat Co 2 is reached by a small road that forks left just before Cat Co 1. It features the **Cat Co 2 bungalow complex**: there's food, sun loungers for hire, showers, toilets, lockers, a campground and bungalows (actually minute, ill kitted out shacks). The **Catba Island Resort & Spa** on Cat Co 1 is open to non-guests to use the pool and water slides, US$10; see under Where to stay. There's also a restaurant and drinks here on the beach.

These lie just to the east of town behind a steep hill in the southern fringes of the national park. They are popular with locals and visitors, especially in the late afternoon and at weekends but are also tending to attract tourist paraphernalia and litter, national park status notwithstanding.

On the way to the national park is the **Dong Quan Y Cave** built between 1960 and 1965 and used by the Americans as a hospital. It has 17 rooms and three floors; 20,000d. Near **Gia Luan** village is **Hoa Cuong Cave**, 100 m from the road. From the park headquarters to Gia Luan the scenery is increasingly dramatic with soaring peaks rising out of the flat valley floor. It is so outstandingly beautiful it is almost other-worldly. Gia Luan harbour is used by Halong boats; there's plenty of mangrove, karst scenery, a fishing village (black oysters and snails) and no services. Heading west, passing pine trees, you will arrive at **Hien Hao**, a village of 400 people where water is collected from wells. There's a small temple on the village outskirts; homestay is possible.

Behind the town winds a road, right, up to a peak from where the views of Cat Co 2 and Lan Ha Bay are utterly spectacular. You could walk but the heat may see you on the back of a moto.

Offshore **Monkey Island** can be visited. It is close to Cat Ba and can be combined within a day-long cruise of Halong Bay or shorter four-hour excursion in a small boat. Accommodation is available here.

CAT BA NATIONAL PARK (VUON QUOC GIA CAT BA)

ⓘ *Park office, open 0700-1700; 3 km trek, 15,000d (with guide, 65,000d); 15 km trek 35,000d (with guide 135,000d); park accommodation, 50,000d; 15,000d per meal. Town to park gate, 15 km, is 30 mins on a motorbike.*

The national park, established in 1986, covers roughly half the island and is some 252 km sq. Of this area, a third consists of coast and inland waters. Home to 109 bird and animal species, and of particular importance is the world's last remaining troupe of **white-headed langur** (around 59 animals). Their numbers dropped from around 2500 in the 1960s to 53 in 2000, but following efforts led by the Cat Ba Langur Conservation Project (www.catbalangur.org)., that figure has started to rise slowly, and now reached 65. The primate is critically endangered and on the World Conservation Union 2006 Red List. These elusive creatures (*Trachypithecus poliocephalus poliocephalus*) are rarely spotted and then only from the sea as they inhabit wild and remote cliff habitats. There are also several types of rare **macaque** (rhesus, pig-tailed and red-faced) and **moose deer**. Vegetation ranges from mangrove swamps in sheltered bays and densely wooded hollows, to high, rugged limestone crags sprouting caps of hardy willows. The marine section of the park is no less bounteous: perhaps less fortunate is the high economic value of its fish and crustacea populations, which keeps the local fishing fleet hard at work and prosperous. In common with other coastal areas in the region the potential for snorkelling here is zero.

Visitors are free to roam through the forest but advised not to wander too far from the path. Many hotels arrange treks from the park gate through the forest to **Ao Ech** (Frog Lake) on to the village of **Viet Hai** for a light lunch then down to the coast for a boat ride home. This takes the best part of a day (six to 10 hours) and costs around 250,000d. It is a good way to see the park but those preferring solitude can go their own way or go with a park guide. A short trek leads to the **Ngu Lam Peak** behind the park headquarters. July to October is the wet season when leeches are a problem and mosquitoes are at their worst. Bring leech socks if you have them and plenty of insect repellent. Collar, long sleeves and long trousers advisable.

HALONG BAY LISTINGS

WHERE TO STAY

On land, the choices include Halong City, Haiphong and Cat Ba town on Cat Ba Island in the bay itself. Of the larger cities, Haiphong is more attractive than Halong City. Cat Ba town offers a variety of accommodation. The majority of visitors spend their nights in boats on Halong Bay but Cat Ba Island, itself, warrants further exploration.

Haiphong town

$$$$ Harbour View, 12 Tran Phu St, T31-382 7828, www.harbourviewvietnam.com. Haiphong's most luxurious hotel. Near the river, this under-utilized 122-room hotel has 2 restaurants, a bar, on-site spa.

$$$ Huu Nghi, 60 Dien Bien Phu St, T31-382 3244, www.huunghihotel.vn. Central and, with 11 storeys and 119 rooms, one of Haiphong's largest. It's efficient enough although overpriced. Rooms are fully equipped and quiet. Staff are helpful. Gym, pool and tennis court on site. Popular with Chinese tour groups; breakfast and Wifi included. From the top storey, the view of the port and French colonial buildings is incredible.

Halong City

$$$ Halong Plaza, 8 Halong Rd, Bai Chay, T33-384 5810, www.halongplaza.com. A Thai joint venture with 200 rooms and suites and fantastic views over the sea, especially from upper floors, luxuriously finished, huge bathrooms, every comfort and extravagance, pool, restaurants and engaging staff; a lovely hotel by any standards. The evening dinner buffet is good value and half price for children aged 12 and under.

$$$ Viethouse Lodge, Tuan Chau Island, T33-384 2207, www.viethouselodge.com. With rooms scattered around a hillside this can be a more pleasant alternative to staying in the city. There's a restaurant, bar, games and transport to hire. The island is now connected to the mainland and Halong City by a bridge.

Cat Ba Island

$$$ Sunrise Resort, Cat Co 3, T031-388 7360, www.catbasunriseresort.com. Set right on the beachfront, this is a sizeable resort set around a good pool with plenty of loungers along the sand. The rooms are a little old school, but are well equipped. Many have fantastic ocean views. The best place to stay on the island, hands down. Has 2 dining options, of which the **Fisherman's Grill** is best, serving lunch and dinner al fresco.

$$$-$$ Cat Ba Eco Lodge, 13 km from Cat Ba Town, T031-368 8966, www.suoigoicatbaresort.vn In a beautiful valley, this set of 4 brick stilt houses contain rather basic, but functional rooms with a/c and minibar. Walking trails lead off in to the forest and cooking classes are given. The service, although friendly, can be very haphazard and the food is poor.

$$$-$$ Sea Pearl, opposite the pier, T031-368 8567. A good-value, mid-range option. Many of the rooms have harbour views – those without are less good value. Helpful staff and everything you might expect for the price.

RESTAURANTS

Meals served on the boats vary in standard. The more expensive your boat, the better the cuisine. City hotels offer good cuisine – à la carte and buffets. On Cat Bat Island, there's a good, but limited choice.

Haiphong town

$ Hoa Dai, 39 Le Dai Hanh St, Haiphong, T31-382 2098. Popular with well-off locals. Good Vietnamese food, particularly busy at lunchtime, and welcoming staff.

Halong City

$$$-$$ Co Ngu, Halong Rd, beyond the post office, T33-351 1363, www.halongcongu.com. A large restaurant in a building spread over 3 floors. Everything from fried chicken and salmon dishes to sautéed bladder is served.

$$ Emeraude Café, Co/Royal Park, T33-384 9266. Open 0900-2100. An oasis of comfort food close to the main hotels and restaurants. Free internet and Wi-Fi. Launching point for the *Emeraude* boat tour.

$$ Green Mango, T031-388 7151. This is a very welcome addition to Cat Ba cuisine.

The sesame-encrusted *ahi* tuna on a bed of cellophane noodles is recommended. Other culinary delights include home-smoked duck with vindaloo rice, green mustard and pomegranate jus and warm chocolate pudding, raspberry purée and cream. Indoor and outdoor seating is available.

Cat Ba Island

Cat Ba is full of fish restaurants and there isn't much to distinguish between them all. Most specialize in the popular *lau ca*, or fish hotpot. It's worth trying *pho tom* – the prawn version of the ubiquitous national dish - while on the island.

WHAT TO DO

Halong Bay trips

Many Hanoi tour operators run tours to Halong Bay. Some also offer kayaking trips. Other dedicated Halong Bay operators include:

Asia Outdoors (formerly **Slo Pony Adventures**), Noble House Hotel, Cat Ba Island, T031-368 8450, www.slopony.com. Rock climbing, kayaking, trekking, environmentally conscious boat cruises and other adventures. Slo Pony works directly with the local community on Cat Ba Island, employs domestic and international staff and assists the national park with efforts to protect the endangered langur as well as with the park's conservation efforts.

Auco cruises, 47 Phan Chu Trinh St, Halong City, T04 3933 4545, www.aucocruises.com. Sail further east into Halong Bay's Lan Ha Bay and Bai Tu Long Bay.

Bai Tho, 47 Le Van Huu, Halong City, T04-6278 2659, www.baithojunks.com A well-regarded company offering both mid-range and luxury cruising.

Cruise Halong Co, Suite 328, 33B Pham Ngu Lao St, Halong City, T04-3933 5561, www.cruisehalong.com. Operates the *Halong Ginger* luxury junks and others.

Emeraude Classic Cruises, 46 Le Thai To St, Halong City, T04-3935 1888, www.emeraude-cruises.com. Has one of the best ways to see Halong Bay in style on a reconstructed French paddle steamer, the *Emeraude*.

Life Heritage Resort Halong Bay, T033-625 3000, Halong City, www.life-resorts.com. Private de luxe boats with a living area, sun deck, DVD player and TV and their own captain and staff. Therapy treatments on board.

DREAM TRIP 2:
Hanoi→Hué→Ho Chi Minh City 21 days

Hanoi 2 nights, page 27

Hué 3 nights, page 107
By road from Hanoi (12 hrs)
or sleeper train (14½ hrs)

Danang 1 night, page 130
By road from Hué (3 hrs)
or train from Hué (4 hrs)

Hoi An 2-3 nights, page 137
By road from Danang (1 hr) or Hué (4 hrs)

Kontum 1 night, page 149
By road from Hoi An (8 hrs)

Pleiku 1 night, page 153
By road from Kontum (1-1½ hrs)
or by plane from Danang (50 mins)

Buon Ma Thuot and Lak Lake 2 nights,
pages 155 and 158
By road from Pleiku (4 hrs)

Dalat 2 nights, page 158
By road from Buon Ma Thuot (6 hrs)

Nha Trang 2 nights, page 170
By road from Dalat via Dien Khanh (3-4 hrs)
or from Dalat via Phan Rang (6 hrs)

Mui Ne 2 nights, page 179
By road from Nha Trang (5½ hrs)
By train from Nha Trang to Muong Man
(4 hrs) for Phan Thiet/Mui Ne, then taxi
to Mui Ne (45 mins)

Ho Chi Minh City 2-3 nights, page 185
By road from Phan Thiet (5-6 hrs)
or by train from Phan Thiet (4-5 hrs)

DREAM TRIP 2
Hanoi → Hué → Ho Chi Minh City

Heading south from cultured Hanoi, the historic city of Hué was once Vietnam's capital and home to the last imperial dynasty. Now a World Heritage Site, numerous relics, tombs and palaces sit in peaceful locations along the course of the Perfume River ready to be explored.

The train from Hué to Danang is one of the most country's most spectacular journeys, as the track clings high above the East Sea as it threads its way through peaks and paddies. Danang's Cham Museum is well worth a visit, but most people head straight to Hoi An, an enchanting 17th-century mercantile town in a tranquil riverside setting. During its heyday 200 years ago, when trade with China and Japan flourished, it was a prosperous little port. Much of the merchants' wealth was spent on family chapels and Chinese clan houses that remain little altered today. Nearby, My Son was the spiritual centre of the Cham Empire and is one of the country's most ancient monuments.

The Central Highlands consist of the Truong Son Mountain Range and its immediate environs. The mountains are commonly referred to as the backbone of Vietnam and border Laos and Cambodia to the west. The highlands provide flowers and vegetables to the southern lowlands and have several tea and coffee plantations that supply the whole world. Tourism is an additional source of revenue. Most highlanders belong to one of 26 indigenous groups and, beyond the main towns of Dalat, Buon Ma Thuot, Pleiku (Play Ku) and Kontum, their way of life remains unchanged.

East of the highlands, on the coast, Nha Trang is a seaside resort with diving, boat tours and spas to entice foreign visitors. Further south, Mui Ne has golden sands and the best kitesurfing in Vietnam.

HUÉ AND AROUND

Hué, an imperial city that housed generations of the country's most powerful emperors was built on the banks of the Huong Giang, or 'Perfume River', 100 km south of the 17th Parallel. The river is named after a scented shrub which is supposed to grow at its source.

Hué does, in many respects, epitomize the best of Vietnam and in a country that is rapidly disappearing under concrete, Hué represents a link with the past where the people live in old buildings and don't lock their doors. Whether it is the royal heritage or the city's Buddhist tradition, the people of Hué are the gentlest and the least aggressive in the country. They speak good English and drive their motorbikes more carefully than anyone else.

Just south of the city are the last resting places of many Vietnamese emperors (see page 114). A number of war relics in the Demilitarized Zone (DMZ) can be easily visited from Hué. Also in the region are the nearby Thuan An Beach, the charming Thanh Hoan Covered Bridge, the misty heights of Bach Ma National Park, the Lang Co Peninsula and the stunning Hai Van Pass which should be travelled by train.

ARRIVING IN HUÉ

Getting there Hué's Phu Bai Airport is a 25-minute drive from the city and has connections with Hanoi and Ho Chi Minh City. **Vietnam Airlines** runs a bus service in to town (54,000d) or you can take a taxi. The two bus stations and one railway station are more central and there are connections with Hanoi and Ho Chi Minh City – and all points between. The trains fill up, so advance booking is recommended, especially for sleepers. Hué is also served by Open Tour Buses.

Moving on To get to the airport, a shuttle bus leaves from 20 Ha Noi St one hour 40 minutes before each flight (30 minutes, 40,000d). The Ben Xe Phia Nam bus station serves destinations mostly south of Hué, while buses heading to the north leave from the Ben Xe Phia Bac station at the northwest corner of the Citadel. Open Tour Buses for major destinations can be booked from hotels or tour agencies. The best way to travel to Danang (see page 130) is by train; the four-hour trip is considered one of the most scenic journeys in the world (see box, page 126).

Getting around For the city itself, walking is an option – interspersed, perhaps, with the odd cyclo journey. However, most guesthouses hire out bicycles and this is a very pleasant and slightly more flexible way of exploring Hué and some of the surrounding countryside. A motorbike provides even more flexibility: it makes it possible to fit so much more into a day and this, in Hué, is very important. Boats are available for hire on the river (a pleasant way of getting to the tombs) and there is also the usual array of *xe ôm* motorbike taxis.

Getting to and around the **Imperial Tombs** is easiest by motorbike or car as they are spread over a large area. Most hotels and tour operators organize tours either by minibus, bike or by boat. Set out early if cycling; all the tombs are accessible by bicycle. Finally, boats can be chartered to sail up the Perfume River – the most peaceful way to travel, but only a few of the tombs can be reached in this way.

Best time to visit Hué has a reputation for its bad weather. The rainy season runs from September to January and rainfall is particularly heavy between September and

ON THE ROAD

Nguyen Dynasty Emperors (1802-1945)

Gia Long	1802-1820	Ham Nghi	1884-1885
Minh Mang	1820-1840	Dong Khanh	1885-1889
Thieu Tri	1841-1847	Thanh Thai	1889-1907
Tu Duc	1847-1883	Duy Tan	1907-1916
Duc Duc	1883	Khai Dinh	1916-1925
Hiep Hoa	1883	Bao Dai	1925-1945
Kien Phuc	1883-1884		

November; the best time to visit is therefore between February and August. However, even in the 'dry' season an umbrella is handy. Rainfall of 2770 mm has been recorded in a single month. Humidity levels can be gauged from the trees along Le Loi Street by the Perfume River which sprout mossy ferns from their trunks and branches. Temperatures in Hué can also be pretty cool in winter, compared with Danang, Nha Trang and other places to the south, as cold air tends to get bottled here, trapped by mountains to the south. For several months each year, though, neither fans nor air-conditioning are required.

Tourist information The many tour operators in the city will provide plenty of information and advice.

BACKGROUND

Hué was the capital of Vietnam during the Nguyen Dynasty and is one of the cultural cores of the country. The Nguyen Dynasty ruled Vietnam between 1802 and 1945, and for the first time in Vietnamese history a single court controlled the land from Yunnan (southern China) southwards to the Gulf of Siam. To link the north and south – more than 1500 km – the Nguyen emperors built and maintained the Mandarin Road (Quan Lo), interspersed with relay stations. Even in 1802, when it was not yet complete, it took couriers just 13 days to travel between Hué and Saigon, and five days between Hué and Hanoi. If they arrived more than two days late, the punishment was a flogging. There cannot have been a better road in Southeast Asia or a more effective incentive system. The city of Hué was equally impressive. George Finlayson, a British visitor in 1821-1822 wrote that its "style of neatness, magnitude, and perfection" made other Asian cities look "like the works of children". Although the Confucian bureaucracy and some of the dynasty's technical achievements may have been remarkable, there was continual discontent and uprisings against the Nguyen emperors. The court was packed with scheming mandarins, princesses, eunuchs (see box, page 110) and scholars writing wicked poetry. The female writer Ho Xuan Huong, wrote of the court and its eunuchs: "Why do the twelve midwives who cared for you hate each other? Where have they thrown away your youthful sexual passions? Damned be you if you should care about the twitterings of mice-like lovers, or about a bee-like male gallant caressing his adored one ... At least, a thousand years from now you will be more able to avoid the posthumous slander that you indulged in mulberry-grove intrigues."

In 1883 a French fleet assembled at the mouth of the Perfume River, not far from Hué, and opened fire. After taking heavy casualties, Emperor Hiep Hoa sued for peace, and signed a treaty making Vietnam a protectorate of France. As French influence over Vietnam increased, the power and influence of the Nguyen waned. The undermining effect of the French presence was compounded by significant schisms in Vietnamese society. In particular, the spread of Christianity was undermining traditional hierarchies. Despite the impressive imperial tombs and palace, many scholars maintain that the Nguyen Dynasty was simply too short-lived to have ever had a 'golden age'. Emperor Tu Duc may have reigned for 36 years (1847-1883), but by then the imperial family had grown so large that he had to contend with a series of damaging attempted coups d'état as family members vied for the throne. Although the French, and then the Japanese during the Second World War, found it to their advantage to maintain the framework of Vietnamese imperial rule, the system became hollow and, eventually, irrelevant. The last Nguyen Emperor, Bao Dai, abdicated on 30 August 1945.

Unfortunately for art lovers, the relative peace which descended upon Hué at the end of the Second World War was not to last. During the 1968 Tet offensive, Viet Cong soldiers holed up in the Citadel for 25 days. The bombardment which ensued, as US troops attempted to root them out, caused extensive damage to the Thai Hoa Palace and other monuments. During their occupation of Hué, the North Vietnamese Army forces settled old scores, shooting, beheading and even burning alive 3000 people, including civil servants, police officers and anyone connected with, or suspected of being sympathetic

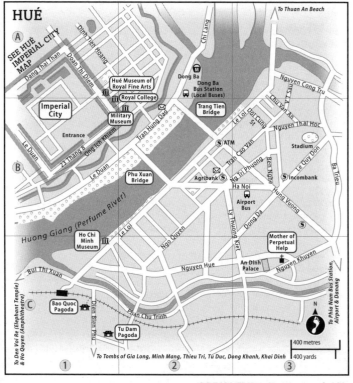

ON THE ROAD

Eunuch power

Eunuchs were key members of the Nguyen Dynasty court in Hué. They were the only men allowed inside the Purple Forbidden City serving the Son of Heaven, the emperor, alongside his wives and concubines. Eunuchs became quite powerful and would play off the concubines against one another. The castrated men, who wore green and red floral gowns with flat, oval hats, arranged the emperor's night time activities and would be bribed by the concubines who wanted to be chosen for that night's sexual adventure. In 1836 Emperor Minh Mang limited their powers so they would not rise to the position of mandarin or become too powerful. He also graded their services. The premier eunuch (clerks) were paid 6 yuans and 0.8 quintals of rice (39.16 kg); the lowliest were the errand boys who earnt one yuan and 0.2 of a quintal of rice (9.8 kg). Some saw this edict as a reaction to the courtier Le Van Duyet, who was himself a eunuch. The employment of eunuchs was abolished in 1914 by Emperor Duy Tan, who reigned between 1907 and 1916.

to the government in Saigon. This action lent support to the notion that, should the north ever achieve victory over the south, it would result in mass killings.

→ PLACES IN HUÉ

IMPERIAL CITY

ⓘ *Entrance to the Imperial City through the Ngo Mon Gate, 23 Thang 8 St, 0700-1700, 80,000d. Guided tours available. English, French, Russian, Mandarin and Japanese spoken. Guiding can last until 1900 after the ticket desk closes.*

The Citadel was built to a design of Vauban (France's 17th-century fortifications designer) and covers 520 sq ha. Its walls are 6.6 m high, 21 m thick and 10,000 m in circumference with 10 entrances topped by watch towers. Inside the Citadel, the Great Enclosure contains the Imperial City and Forbidden City.

The Imperial City is built on the same principles as the Forbidden Palace in Beijing. It is enclosed by 7- to 10-m-thick outer walls, the **Kinh Thanh**, along with moats, canals and towers. Emperor Gia Long commenced construction in 1804 after geomancers had decreed a suitable location and orientation for the palace. The site enclosed the land of eight villages (for which the inhabitants received compensation), and covers 6 sq km; sufficient area to house the emperor and all his family, courtiers, bodyguards and servants. It took 20,000 men to construct the walls alone. Not only has the city been damaged by war and incessant conflict, but also by natural disasters such as floods which, in the mid-19th century, inundated the city to a depth of several metres.

Chinese custom decreed that the 'front' of the palace should face south (like the emperor) and this is the direction from which visitors approach the site. Over the outer moat, a pair of gates pierce the outer walls: the **Hien Nhon** and **Chuong Duc** gates. Just inside are two groups of massive cannon; four through the Hien Nhon Gate and five through the Chuong Duc Gate. These are the **Nine Holy Cannon** (**Cuu Vi Than Cong**), cast in 1803 on the orders of Gia Long from bronzeware seized from the Tay Son revolutionaries. The cannon are named after the four seasons and the five elements, and on each is carved its name, rank, firing instructions and how the bronze of which they are made was acquired. They are 5 m in length, but have never been fired. Like the giant urns outside the Hien Lam Cac (see page 112), they are meant to symbolize the permanence of the empire. Between the two gates is a massive **flag tower**. The flag of the National Liberation Front flew here for 24 days during the Tet Offensive in 1968 – a picture of the event is displayed in Hué's Ho Chi Minh Museum.

Northwards from the cannon, and over one of three bridges which span a second moat, is the **Ngo Mon** (**Royal Gate**) (**1**), built in 1833 during the reign of Emperor Minh Mang. The ticket office is just to the right. The gate, remodelled on a number of occasions since its original construction, is surmounted by a pavilion from where the emperor would view palace ceremonies. Of the five entrances, the central one – the Ngo Mon – was only opened for the emperor to pass through. The other four were for procession participants, elephants and horses. UNESCO has thrown itself into the restoration of Ngo Mon with vigour and the newly finished pavilion, supported by 100 columns, atop the gate now

HUÉ IMPERIAL CITY

100 metres
100 yards

1 Ngo Mon (Royal Gate)
2 Golden Water Bridge
3 Tanks
4 Dai Trieu Nghi (Great Rites Courtyard) & Thai Hoa Palace (Palace of Supreme Harmony)
5 Tu Cam Thanh (Purple Forbidden City)
6 Ta Pavilion
7 Huu Vu Pavilion
8 Central Pavilion, private apartments of the Emperor
9 Quang Minh Palace
10 Royal Reading Pavilion
11 Royal (East) Theatre
12 Hien Lam Cac
13 9 Bronze urns
14 Thé Temple (Temple of Generations)
15 Hung Temple
16 Waiting Pavilion (Huu Ta Dai Lam Vien)

gleams and glints in the sun; those who consider it garish can console themselves with the thought that this is how it might have appeared in Minh Mang's time.

North from the Ngo Mon, is the **Golden Water Bridge** (2) – again reserved solely for the emperor's use – between two **tanks** (3), lined with laterite blocks. This leads to the **Dai Trieu Nghi** (**Great Rites Courtyard**) (4), on the north side of which is the **Thai Hoa Palace** (**Palace of Supreme Harmony**) (4), constructed by Gia Long in 1805 and used for his coronation in 1806. From here, sitting on his golden throne raised up on a dais, the emperor would receive ministers, foreign emissaries, mandarins and military officers during formal ceremonial occasions. In front of the palace are 18 stone stelae, which stipulate the arrangement of the nine mandarinate ranks on the Great Rites Courtyard: the upper level was for ministers, mandarins and officers of the upper grade; the lower for those of lower grades. Civil servants would stand on the left, and the military on the right. Only royal princes were allowed to stand in the palace itself, which is perhaps the best-preserved building in the Imperial City complex. Its red and gold ironwood columns decorated with dragon motifs, symbol of the emperors' power, the tiled floor and fine ceiling have all been restored.

North of the Palace of Supreme Harmony is the **Tu Cam Thanh** (**Purple Forbidden City**) (5). This would have been reserved for the use of the emperor and his family, and was surrounded by 1-m-thick walls: a city within a city. Tragically, the Forbidden City was virtually destroyed during the 1968 Tet offensive. The two **Mandarin Palaces** and the **Royal Reading Pavilion** (see below) are all that survive.

At the far side of the Thai Hoa Palace, are two enormous **bronze urns** (**Vac Dong**) decorated with birds, plants and wild animals, and weighing about 1500 kg each. To either side of the urns are the **Ta** (6) and **Huu Vu** (7) pavilions – one converted into a souvenir art shop, the other a mock throne room in which tourists can pay to dress up and play the part of the emperor for five minutes. The **Royal Reading Pavilion** (10) has been renovated but, needless to say, has no books. On the far side of the palace are the outer northern walls of the citadel and the north gate.

Most of the surviving buildings of interest are to be found on the west side of the palace, running between the outer walls and the walls of the Forbidden City. At the southwest corner is the well-preserved and beautiful **Hien Lam Cac** (12), a pavilion built in 1821, in front of which stand nine massive **bronze urns** (13) cast between 1835 and 1837 on the orders of Emperor Minh Mang. It is estimated that they weigh between 1500 kg and 2600 kg, and each has 17 decorative figures, animals, rivers, flowers and landscapes representing between them the wealth, beauty and unity of the country. The central, largest urn is dedicated to the founder of the empire, Emperor Gia Long. Next to the urns walking northwards is **Thé Temple** (**Temple of Generations**) (14). Built in 1821, it contains altars honouring 10 of the emperors of the Nguyen Dynasty behind which are meant to be kept a selection of their personal belongings. It was only in 1954, however, that the stelae depicting the three Revolutionary emperors Ham Nghi, Thanh Thai, and Duy Tan were brought into the temple. The French, perhaps fearing that they would become a focus of discontent, prevented the Vietnamese from erecting altars in their memory. North of the Thé Temple is **Hung Temple** (15) built in 1804 for the worship of Gia Long's father, Nguyen Phuc Luan, the father of the founder of the Nguyen Dynasty. The temple was renovated in 1951.

UNESCO began the arduous process of renovating the complex in 1983: Vietnam at that time was a pariah state due to its invasion of Cambodia in 1978-1979 and the appeal for funds and assistance fell on deaf ears. It was, therefore, fitting testimony to Vietnam's rehabilitation in the eyes of the world when, in 1993, UNESCO declared Hué a World Heritage Site. Although it is the battle of 1968 which is normally blamed for the destruction, the city has in fact been gradually destroyed over 50 years. The French shelled it, fervent revolutionaries burnt down its buildings, typhoons and rains have battered it, thieves have ransacked its contents and termites have eaten away at its foundations. In some respects it is surprising that as many as a third of the monuments have survived relatively intact.

CITY CENTRE

Just east of the Imperial City is the **Hué Museum of Royal Fine Arts** ① *3 Le Truc St, Tue-Sun 0700-1700, summer (14 Apr-14 Oct) until 1730, 35,000d, no cameras or video cameras, overshoes must be worn and are provided, information in English.* Housed in the Long An Palace, the museum contains a reasonable collection of ceramics, furniture, screens and bronzeware and some stunning, embroidered imperial clothes. In the front courtyard are stone mandarins, cannon, gongs and giant bells. The building itself is worthy of note for its elegant construction with its stunning interior of 128 ironwood columns. It was built by Emperor Thieu Tri in 1845 it was dismantled and erected on the present site in 1909 as the National University Library before being renamed in 1958. The museum was temporarily located at the An Dinh Palace, the former palace of Khai Dinh. It is hoped that the palace, whose frescoes were restored by German experts, will reopen to the public.

Hué Private Museum of Ceramics ① *114 Mai Thuc Loan St*, Hué's first private museum exhibiting ceramic wares from the Ly, Tran, Le and Nguyen dynasties, opened in 2012. The museum, owned by researcher Tran Dinh Son, a leading ceramics expert, is inside the house of a former Nguyen dynasty mandarin, Tran Dinh Ba.

Directly opposite the Royal Fine Arts museum is the **Royal College** ① *2 Le Truc St, daily 0700-1700, free*, established in 1803 and moved to this site in 1908. It is lamentably short of exhibits. Immediately in front is the **Military Museum** ① *23 Thang 8 St (between Dinh Tien Hoang and Doan Thi Diem Sts), T54-352 2397, Tue-Sun 0730-1100, 1330-1700, free.* Missiles, tanks and armoured personnel carriers fill the courtyard.

Further east still, but still on the north bank of the river, next to the Dong Ba bus station, is the covered **Dong Ba Market** ① *Tran Hung Dao St.*

The Perfume River is spanned by two bridges; downstream is the ill-fated **Trang Tien Bridge**, named after the royal mint that once stood at its northern end. It was built in 1896 and destroyed soon after by a typhoon; after having been rebuilt it was then razed once more in 1968 during the Tet Offensive. Upstream is **Phu Xuan Bridge**, built by the US Army in 1970. This carries Highway 1, in other words the main north-south highway, but a new bypass with a huge new river crossing 10 km upriver has seen traffic levels fall.

On the south side of the river is the requisite **Ho Chi Minh Museum** ① *7 Le Loi St, T54-382 2152, Tue-Sun 0730-1100, 1330-1630, 10,000d*, which displays pictures of Ho's life plus a few models and personal possessions. The 'tour' begins at the end of the corridor on the second floor. Some interesting photographs (for example of Ho as a cook's assistant at the Carlton Hotel in London), but does not compare with the Ho Chi Minh Museum in Hanoi.

Further south, the **Bao Quoc Pagoda** ① *just off Dien Bien Phu St to the right, over the railway line*, is said to have been built in the early 18th century by a Buddhist monk named Giac Phong. Note the 'stupa' that is behind and to the left of the central pagoda and the fine doors inscribed with Chinese and Sanskrit characters. Further along Dien Bien Phu Street, at the intersection with Tu Dam Street, is the **Tu Dam Pagoda**. According to the Hué

Buddhist Association this was originally founded in 1690-1695 but has been rebuilt many times. The present-day pagoda was built shortly before the Second World War. In August 1963, the Diem government sent its forces to suppress the monks here who were alleged to be fomenting discontent among the people. The specially selected forces – they were Catholic – clubbed and shot to death about 30 monks and their student followers, and smashed the great Buddha image here.

The skyline of modern Hué is adorned by the striking pagoda-like tower of the **Church of Mother of Perpetual Help**. This three-storey, octagonal steel tower is 53 m high and an attractive blend of Asian and European styles. The church was completed in 1962 and marble from the Marble Mountain in Danang was used for the altar. The church lies at the junction of Nguyen Hue and Nguyen Khuyen streets.

→ ALONG THE PERFUME RIVER AND THE IMPERIAL TOMBS

As the geographical and spiritual centre of the Nguyen Dynasty, Hué and the surrounding area is the site of numerous pagodas and seven imperial tombs, along with the tombs of numerous other royal personages and countless courtiers and successful mandarins.

Each of the tombs follows the same stylistic formula, although at the same time they reflect the tastes and predilections of the emperor in question. The tombs were built during the lifetime of each emperor, who took a great interest in the design and construction – after all they were meant to ensure his comfort in the next life. Each mausoleum, variously arranged, has five design elements: a courtyard with statues of elephants, horses and military and civil mandarins (originally, usually approached through a park of rare trees); a stela pavilion (with an engraved eulogy composed by the emperor's son and heir); a Temple of the Soul's Tablets; a pleasure pavilion; and a grave. Geomancers decreed that they should also have a stream and a mountainous screen in front. The tombs faithfully copy Chinese prototypes, although most art historians claim that they fall short in terms of execution.

THIEN MU PAGODA
ⓘ *It is an easy 4-km bicycle (or cyclo) ride from the city, following the north bank of the river upstream (west).*
Thien Mu Pagoda (the Elderly Goddess Pagoda), also known as the Thien Mau Tu Pagoda, and locally as the **Linh Mu Pagoda** (the name used on most local maps), is the finest in Hué. It is beautifully sited on the north bank of the Perfume River, about 4 km upstream from the city. It was built in 1601 by Nguyen Hoang, the governor of Hué, after an old woman appeared to him and said that the site had supernatural significance and should be marked by the construction of a pagoda. The monastery is the oldest in Hué, and the seven-storey **Phuoc Duyen** (Happiness and Grace Tower), built by Emperor Thieu Tri in 1844, is 21 m high, with each storey containing an altar to a different Buddha. The summit of the tower is crowned with a water pitcher to catch the rain, water representing the source of happiness.

Arranged around the tower are four smaller buildings one of which contains the **Great Bell** cast in 1710 under the orders of the Nguyen Lord, Nguyen Phuc Chu, and weighing 2200 kg. Beneath another of these surrounding pavilions is a monstrous **marble turtle** on which is a 2.6-m-high stela recounting the development of Buddhism in Hué, carved in 1715. Beyond the tower, the entrance to the pagoda is through a triple gateway patrolled by six carved and vividly painted guardians – two on each gate. The roof of

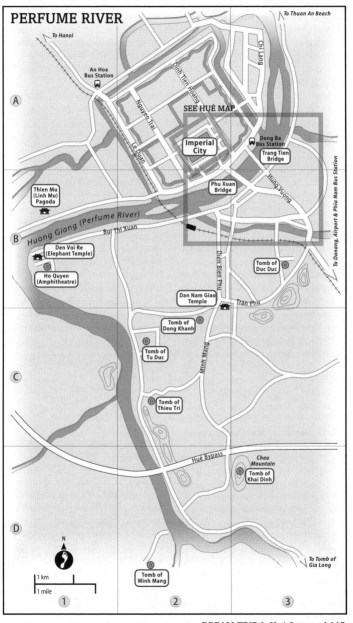

PERFUME RIVER

To Thuan An Beach

To Hanoi

Chi Lang

An Hoa Bus Station

Dinh Tien Hoang

SEE HUÉ MAP

A

Nguyen Trai

Le Duan

Dong Ba Bus Station

Imperial City

Trang Tien Bridge

Thien Mu (Linh Mu) Pagoda

Phu Xuan Bridge

Hung Vuong

To Danang, Airport & Phia Nam Bus Station

Huong Giang (Perfume River)

Bui Thi Xuan

B

Den Voi Re (Elephant Temple)

Ho Quyen (Amphitheatre)

Dien Bien Phu

Tomb of Duc Duc

Dan Nam Giao Temple

Tran Phu

Tomb of Dong Khanh

Minh Mang

Tomb of Tu Duc

C

Tomb of Thieu Tri

Hué Bypass

Chau Mountain

Tomb of Khai Dinh

D

N

1 km

1 mile

To Tomb of Gia Long

Tomb of Minh Mang

1

2

3

the sanctuary itself is decorated with *jataka* stories. At the front of the sanctuary is a brass, laughing Buddha. Behind that are an assortment of gilded Buddhas and a crescent-shaped gong cast in 1677 by Jean de la Croix. The first monk to commit suicide through self immolation, Thich Quang Duc, came from this pagoda (see box, page 199) and the grey Austin in which he made the journey to his death in Saigon is still kept here in a garage in the temple garden.

In May 1993, a Vietnamese – this time not a monk – immolated himself at Thien Mu. Why is not clear: some maintain it was linked to the persecution of Buddhists; others that it was because of the man's frustrated love life.

TOMB OF EMPEROR GIA LONG

ⓘ *Daily 0630-1730, 80,000d for the upkeep of the tomb. Get there by bike or motorbike.*

The Tomb of Emperor Gia Long is the most distant and the most rarely visited but is well worth the effort of getting there. The tomb is overgrown with venerable mango trees, the only sound is bird call and, occasionally, the wind in the trees: otherwise a blessed silence. Devoid of tourists, touts and ticket sellers it is the most atmospheric of all the tombs, and as the political regime in Vietnam is not a fan of Gia Long it is likely to remain this way. However, given the historical changes that were to be wrought by the dynasty Gia Long founded, it is arguably the most significant tomb in Hué. It was built between 1814 and 1820 (see box opposite, for an account of the emperor's burial). Being the first of the dynasty, Gia Long's mausoleum set the formula for the later tombs. There is a surrounding lotus pond and steps lead up to a courtyard with the Minh Thanh ancestral temple, rather splendid in its red and gold. To the right of this is a double, walled and locked burial chamber where Gia Long and his wife are interred (the emperor's tomb is fractionally taller). The tomb is perfectly lined up with the two huge obelisks on the far side of the lake.

Beyond this is a courtyard with five now headless mandarins, horses and elephants on each side; steps lead up to the stela eulogizing the emperor's reign, composed, presumably, by his eldest son, Minh Mang, as was the custom. This grey monolith engraved in ancient Chinese characters remained miraculously undisturbed during two turbulent centuries.

TOMB OF EMPEROR GIA LONG

To River Crossing

Vinh Mau Tomb

Hoang Co Tomb

Thoai Thanh Tomb

Quang Hung Tomb

Thoai Thanh Temple

Gia Thanh Temple

Tomb of Gia Long's second wife

Truong Phong Tomb

Minh Thanh Temple

Gia Long's Tomb

Stela House

N

Obelisks

Not to scale

Gia Long's geomancers did a great job finding this site: with the mountainous screen in front it is a textbook example of a final resting place. Interestingly, despite their getting first choice of all the possible sites, it is also the furthest tomb from the palace; clearly they took their task seriously.

Nguyen Anh, or Gia Long as he was crowned in 1802, came to power with French support. Back in 1787, Gia Long's son, the young Prince Canh, had caused a sensation in French salon life when, along

ON THE ROAD

When the Emperor Gia Long died on 3 February 1820, the thread on the ancestors' altar (representing his soul) was tied. The following day the corpse was bathed and clothed in rich garments, and precious stones and pearls were placed in his mouth. Then a ritual offering of food, drink and incense was made before the body was placed in a coffin made of catalpa wood (*Bignonia catalpa*) – a wood impervious to insect attack.

At this time, the crown prince announced the period of mourning that was to be observed – a minimum of three years. Relatives of the dead emperor, mandarins and their wives each had different forms and periods of mourning to observe, depending upon their position.

Three days after Gia Long's death, a messenger was sent to the Hoang Nhon Pagoda to inform the empress, who was already dead, of the demise of her husband. Meanwhile, the new Emperor Minh Mang had the former ruler's deeds recorded and engraved on golden sheets which were bound together as a book. Then astrologers selected an auspicious date for the funeral, picking 27 May after some argument (11 May also had its supporters). On 17 May, court officials told the heaven, the earth and the dynastic ancestors, of the details for the funeral and at the same time opened the imperial tomb. On 20 May, the corpse was informed of the ceremony. Four days later the coffin left the palace for the three-day journey to its final resting place. Then, at the appointed time, the coffin was lowered into the sepulchre – its orientation correct – shrouded in silk cloth, protected by a second outer coffin, covered in resin, and finally bricked in. Next to Gia Long, a second grave was dug into which were placed an assortment of objects useful in his next life. The following morning, Emperor Minh Mang, in full mourning robes, stood outside the tomb facing east, while a mandarin facing in the opposite direction inscribed ritual titles on the tomb. The silk thread on the ancestors' altar – the symbol of the soul – was untied, animals slaughtered, and the thread then buried in the vicinity of the tomb.

(This account is adapted from James Dumarçay's *The palaces of South-East Asia*, 1991.)

with soldier/missionary Georges Pigneau de Béhaine, he had sought military support against the Tay Son from Louis XVI. In return for Tourane (Danang) and Poulo Condore (Con Dao), the French offered men and weapons – an offer that was subsequently withdrawn. Pigneau then raised military support from French merchants in India and in 1799 Prince Canh's French-trained army defeated the Tay Son at Quy Nhon.

Gia Long's reign was despotic – to his European advisers who pointed out that encouragement of industry would lead to the betterment of the poor, he replied that he preferred them poor. The poor were virtual slaves – the price for one healthy young buffalo was one healthy young girl. Flogging was the norm – it has been described as the 'bamboo's golden age'. One study by a Vietnamese scholar estimated that there were 105 peasant uprisings between 1802 and 1820 alone. For this, and the fact that he gave the French a foothold in Vietnam, the Vietnamese have never forgiven Gia Long. Of him they still say *"cong ran can ga nha"* (he carried home the snake that killed the chicken).

To get to the Tomb of Emperor Gia Long take Dien Bien Phu Street out of town past the railway station. After a couple of kilometres turn right at the T-junction facing pine-shrouded Dan Nam Giao Temple (where Vietnamese emperors once prayed for good weather) and take first left onto Minh Mang. Continue on, passing the sign marking your departure from Hué and taking the right-hand branch of the fork in the road. After a short distance the road joins the river bank and heads for some 2 km towards the river crossing (the new Hué bypass – Highway 1). Follow the riverbank directly underneath this bridge and continue straight on as the road begins to deteriorate. A few metres beyond the Ben Do 1-km milestone is a red sign reading Gia Long Tomb. Down a steep path a sampan is waiting to ferry passengers across this tributary of the Perfume River (bargain); on the far side follow the track upstream for about 1 km. By a café with two billiard tables turn right and then almost immediately turn left. Keep on this path (ask for directions along the way).

TOMB OF EMPEROR MINH MANG

ⓘ *Daily 0630-1730, 80,000d. Get there by bicycle or motorbike. To get there follow the instructions for Gia Long's tomb, but cross the Perfume River using the new road bridge; on the far side of the bridge turn immediately left.*

The Tomb of Emperor Minh Mang is possibly the finest of all the imperial tombs. Built between 1840 and 1843, it is sited among peaceful ponds, about 12 km from the city of Hué. In terms of architectural poise, balance and richness of decoration, it has no peer in the area. The tomb's layout, along a single central and sacred axis (*Shendao*), is unusual in its symmetry; no other tomb, with the possible exception of Khai Dinh (see page 121), achieves the same unity of constituent parts, nor draws the eye onwards so easily and pleasantly from one visual element to the next. The tomb was traditionally approached through the **Dai Hong Mon**, a gate which leads into the ceremonial courtyard containing an array of statuary; today visitors pass through a side gate. Next is the stela pavilion in which there is a carved eulogy to the dead emperor composed by his son, Thieu Tri.

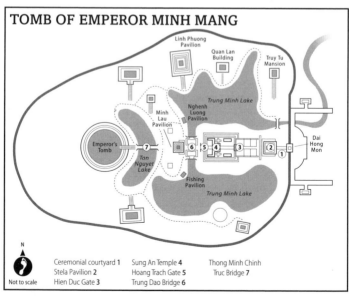

TOMB OF EMPEROR MINH MANG

Linh Phuong Pavilion
Quan Lan Building
Truy Tu Mansion
Trung Minh Lake
Nghenh Luong Pavilion
Minh Lau Pavilion
Emperor's Tomb
Tan Nguyet Lake
Fishing Pavilion
Trung Minh Lake
Dai Hong Mon

N
Not to scale

Ceremonial courtyard **1**   Sung An Temple **4**   Thong Minh Chinh
Stela Pavilion **2**   Hoang Trach Gate **5**   Truc Bridge **7**
Hien Duc Gate **3**   Trung Dao Bridge **6**

ON THE ROAD

Tu Duc's lament

"Never has an era seen such sadness, never a year more anguish. Above me, I fear the edicts of heaven. Below, the tribulations of the people trouble my days and nights. Deep in my heart I tremble and blush, finding neither words or actions to help my subjects.

Alone, I am speechless. My pulse is feeble, my body pale and thin, my beard and hair white. Though not yet 40, I have already reached old age, so that I lack the strength to pay homage to my ancestors every morning and evening. Evil must be suppressed and goodness sought. The wise must offer their counsel, the strong their force, the rich their wealth, and all those with skills should devote them to the needs of the army and the kingdom. Let us together mend our errors and rebuild.

Alas! The centuries are fraught with pain, and man is burdened by fear and woe. Thus we express our feelings that they may be known to the world."

(Taken from *Vietnam*, S Karnow.)

Continuing downwards through a series of courtyards there is, in turn, the **Sung An Temple** dedicated to Minh Mang and his empress, a small garden with flower beds that once formed the Chinese character for 'longevity', and two sets of stone bridges. The first consists of three spans, the central one of which (**Trung Dao Bridge**) was for the sole use of the emperor. The second, single bridge leads to a short flight of stairs with naga balustrades, at the end of which is a locked bronze door (no access). The door leads to the tomb itself which is surrounded by a circular wall.

TOMB OF THIEU TRI

ⓘ *7 km southwest of Hué in the village of Thuy Bang, daily 0630-1730, ticket required only for admission beyond the gatehouse, 80,000d.*

The Tomb of Thieu Tri was built in 1848 by his son Tu Duc, who took into account his father's wishes that it be 'economical and convenient'. Thieu Tri reigned for just seven years and unlike his forebears did not start planning his mausoleum the moment he ascended the throne. Upon his death his body was temporarily interred in Long An Temple (now the Hué Museum of Royal Fine Arts, see page 113). The tomb is in two adjacent parts, with separate tomb and temple areas; the layout of each follows the symmetrical axis arrangement of Minh Mang's tomb which has also inspired the architectural style. The memorial temple area is to the right and reached via a long flight of steps. A gatehouse incorporates Japanese triple-beamed columns (as seen in the Japanese Bridge in Hoi An) and at the back of the courtyard beyond is the temple dedicated to Thieu Tri.

The stela pavilion and tomb are a few hundred yards to the left, unmissable with the two obelisks. Just like his father, Thieu Tri is buried on a circular island reached by three bridges beyond the stela pavilion.

TOMB OF TU DUC

ⓘ *Daily 0630-1730, 80,000d; a return moto trip from the riverbank should be around 50,000d.*

The Tomb of Tu Duc is 7 km from the city and was built between 1864 and 1867 in a pine wood. It is enclosed by a wall, some 1500 m long, within which is a lake. The lake, with lotus and water hyacinth, contains a small island where the emperor built a number of replicas of famous temples – now rather difficult to discern. He often came here to relax, and from the pavilions that reach out over the lake, composed poetry and listened to music. The **Xung Khiem Pavilion**, built in 1865, has recently been restored with UNESCO help and is the most attractive building here. The tomb complex follows the formula described above: ceremonial square, mourning yard with pavilion and then the tomb itself. To the northeast of Tu Duc's tomb are the tombs of his empress, Le Thien Anh and adopted son, Kien Phuc. Many of the pavilions are crumbling and ramshackle – lending the tomb a rather tragic air. This is appropriate: although he had 104 wives, Tu Duc fathered no sons. He was therefore forced to write his own eulogy, a fact which he took as a bad omen. The eulogy itself recounts the sadness in Tu Duc's life. A flavour of its sentiment can be gleaned from a confession he wrote in 1867 following French seizure of territory. It was shortly after Tu Duc's reign that France gained full control of Vietnam.

TOMB OF DUC DUC
ⓘ *11 Tan Lang St, 2 km south of the city centre, daily 0630-1730, 55,000d.*
Despite ruling for just three days and then dying in prison, Emperor Duc Duc (1852-1883) has a tomb, built in 1899 by his son, Thanh Thai, on the spot where, it is said, the body had been dumped by gaolers. (Duc Duc was dethroned by the court for his pro-French sympathies). Emperors **Thanh Thai** and his son **Duy Tan** are buried in the same complex. Unlike Duc Duc, though, both were strongly anti-French and were, for a period, exiled in

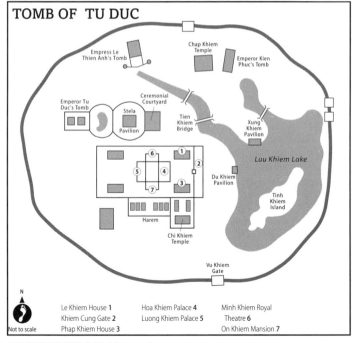

TOMB OF TU DUC

Empress Le Thien Anh's Tomb

Chap Khiem Temple

Emperor Kien Phuc's Tomb

Emperor Tu Duc's Tomb

Ceremonial Courtyard

Stela Pavilion

Tien Khiem Bridge

Xung Khiem Pavilion

Luu Khiem Lake

⑥ ①
②
⑤ ④ Du Khiem Pavilion
⑦ ③

Harem

Chi Khiem Temple

Tinh Khiem Island

Vu Khiem Gate

N
Not to scale

Le Khiem House **1**
Khiem Cung Gate **2**
Phap Khiem House **3**

Hoa Khiem Palace **4**
Luong Khiem Palace **5**

Minh Khiem Royal Theatre **6**
On Khiem Mansion **7**

Réunion Island, Africa. Although Thanh Thai later returned to Vietnam and died in Vung Tau in 1953, his son Duy Tan was killed in an air crash in central Africa in 1945. It was not until 1987 that Duy Tan's body was repatriated and interred alongside his father Thanh Thai. The tomb is in three parts: the Long An Temple; Duc Duc's tomb to the south; and Thanh Thai and Duy Tan's tombs adjacent to each other.

TOMB OF DONG KHANH

ⓘ *The Tomb of Dong Khanh is 500 m from Tu Duc's tomb (walk up the path on the other side of the road from the main entrance to Tu Duc's tomb – the path is partly hidden in amongst the stalls), daily 0630-1730, 55,000d.*

Dong Khanh was the nephew and foster son of Emperor Tu Duc. His tomb was built in 1889, it is the smallest of the imperial mausoleums, but nonetheless one of the most individual; it was not completed until 1923 under the authority of his son Khai Dinh. Unusually, it has two separate sections. One is a walled area containing the usual series of pavilions and courtyards and with a historically interesting collection of personal objects that belonged to the emperor. The second, 100 m away, consists of an open series of platforms. The lower platform has the honour guard of mandarins, horses and elephants along with a stela pavilion; the third platform is a tiled area which would have had an awning; and the highest platform is the tomb itself. The tomb is enclosed within three open walls, the entrance protected by a dragon screen (to prevent spirits entering).

TOMB OF KHAI DINH

ⓘ *Daily 0630-1730, 80,000d. Get there by motorbike or bicycle. As for Gia Long's tomb, continue under the new river crossing, but turn immediately left, through a collection of small shops and head straight on, over a small crossroads and parallel to the main road. From the riverbank a return moto trip should be around 50,000d.*

The Tomb of Khai Dinh is 10 km from Hué. Built between 1920 and 1931, it is the last of the mausoleums of the Nguyen Dynasty and, by the time Khai Dinh was contemplating the afterlife, brick had given way in popularity to the concrete that is now beginning to deteriorate. Nevertheless, it occupies a fine position on the Chau Mountain facing southwest towards a large white statue of Quan Am, also built by Khai Dinh. The valley, used for the cultivation of cassava and sugar cane, and the pine-covered mountains, make this one of the most beautifully sited and peaceful of the tombs. Indeed, before construction could begin, Khai Dinh had to remove the tombs of Chinese nobles who had already selected the site for its beauty and auspicious orientation. A total of 127 steep steps lead up to the Honour Courtyard with statuary of mandarins, elephants and horses. An octagonal Stela Pavilion in the centre of the mourning yard contains a stone stela engraved with a eulogy to the emperor. At the top of some more stairs are the tomb and shrine of Khai Dinh, containing a bronze statue of the emperor sitting on his throne and holding a jade sceptre. The body is interred 9 m below ground level (see box, page 122, for a description of Khai Dinh's interment). The interior is richly decorated with ornate and colourful murals (the artist incurred the wrath of the emperor and only just escaped execution), floor tiles and decorations built up with fragments of porcelain. It is the most elaborate of all the tombs and took 11 years to build. Such was the cost of construction that Khai Dinh had to levy additional taxes to fund the project. The tomb shows distinct European stylistic influences; Khai Dinh himself toured France in 1922, three years before he died.

ON THE ROAD
The funeral of Khai Dinh

On 6 November 1925, Dai-Hanh-Hoang-Khai-Dinh, King of Annam, 'mounted the dragon's back,' or, in other words, died. Seven diamonds were put in the mouth of the corpse, which was washed, embalmed, dressed in state robes, placed in a huge red and gold lacquer coffin and covered over with young tea leaves. Ten days later official mourning was inaugurated with the sacrifice of a bullock, a goat and a pig. A portrait of the late monarch, painted on silk, was placed on the throne. Paper invocations were burnt, massed lamentations rent the air four times daily for 60 days.

All Annam was in Hué, dressed in its best and brightest. Packed sampans swarmed about the bridge. Gay shrines lined the way, hung with flowers and paper streamers. Bunting, citron and scarlet, fluttered in the breeze. Route-keepers in green and red held the crowds in check, chasing small boys out of the way, whacking them over their mushroom hats. At the head of the column were two elephants, hung with tassels and embroidered cloths and topped with crimson *howdahs* and yellow umbrellas. Never have I seen animals so unutterably bored. They lolled against each other, eyes closed – and slumbered. But for an occasional twitch of an ear or tail they might have been dead. Their boredom was understandable when you came to think of it. An elephant is a long-lived beast. These two were full-grown; elderly, even. It is possible that they featured at the obsequies of Thieu-Tri, and there have been innumerable royal funerals since. At one period kings weren't stopping on the throne of Annam long enough to get the cushions warm. What was a very novel and splendid exhibition to me was stale stuff to these beasts. "All very fine for you, mister", they might have said. "First time and all that. Can drop out and buy yourself a drink any time you like. All very well for you, Henry, in a featherweight gent's suiting; but what about us, tight-laced front and back with about a ton of passengers, brollies, flags and furniture up top?" An old bearded mandarin in a coat of royal blue struck with a wooden hammer on a silver gong. The procession began to shuffle forward – somebody in front had found means to rouse the elephants, apparently.

Some 160 trained porters, clad in black and white, crouched under the red lacquer poles of the giant bier – slips of bamboo had been placed between their teeth to stop them from chattering. Slowly, steadily, keeping the prescribed horizontal, the huge thing rose. Six tons it weighed and special bridges had to be built to accommodate it. Slowly, steadily it moved towards us, preceded by solemn-stepping heralds in white; flagbearers in sea-green carrying dragon banners of crimson and emerald, blue and gold. The second day was spent in getting the coffin from Nam-Gio to the mausoleum and was a mere repetition of the first. The actual interment took place on the morning of the third day. In a few minutes the mourners were out in the daylight again and the vault doors were being sealed. The spirit of Khai-Dinh was on its way to the Ten Judgement Halls of the Infernal Regions, to pass before the Mirror of the Past wherein he would see all his deeds reflected, together with their consequences; to drink the Water of Forgetfulness, and pass on through transmigration to transmigration till he attained the Pure Land and a state of blessed nothingness. And Bao-Dai – weeping bitterly, poor little chap – reigned in his stead.

(Adapted from *The Voyage from London to Indochina*, Crosbie Garstin.)

AMPHITHEATRE AND ELEPHANT TEMPLE

ⓘ *Free. Get there by bicycle or motorbike. Head about 3 km west of Hué railway station on Bui Thi Xuan St; turn left up a paved track opposite 203 Bui Thi Xuan St; the track for the Elephant Temple runs in front of the amphitheatre (off to the right).*

Ho Quyen (Amphitheatre) lies about 4 km upstream of Hué on the south bank of the Perfume River. The amphitheatre was built in 1830 by Emperor Minh Mang as a venue for the popular duels between elephants and tigers. Elephants were symbolic of emperors and strength whereas tigers were seen as anti-imperial beasts and had their claws removed before the fight. This royal sport was in earlier centuries staged on an island in the Perfume River or on the river banks, but by 1830 it was considered desirable for the royal party to be able to observe the duels without placing themselves at risk from escaping tigers. The amphitheatre is said to have been last used in 1904 when, as was usual, the elephant emerged victorious: "The elephant rushed ahead and pressed the tiger to the wall with all the force he could gain. Then he raised his head, threw the enemy to the ground and smashed him to death," wrote Crosbie Garstin in *The Voyage from London to Indochina*. The walls of the amphitheatre are 5 m high and the arena is 44 m in diameter. At the south side, beneath the royal box, is one large gateway (for the elephant) and, to the north, five smaller entrances for the tigers. The walls are in good condition and the centre is filled either with grass or immaculately tended rows of vegetables, depending on the season.

Den Voi Re, the Temple of the Elephant Trumpet, dedicated to the call of the fighting elephant, is a few hundred metres away. It is a modest little place and fairly run down with a large pond in front and contains two small elephant statues. Presumably this is where elephants were blessed before battle or perhaps where the unsuccessful ones were mourned.

→ NORTH OF HUÉ

THE DEMILITARIZED ZONE (DMZ)

ⓘ *Most visitors see the sights of the DMZ, including Khe Sanh and the Ho Chi Minh Trail, on a tour. A 1-day tour of all the DMZ sights can be booked from any of Hué's tour operators from around 200,000d, depart 0600, return 1800-2000.*

The incongruously named Demilitarized Zone (DMZ), scene of some of the fiercest fighting of the Vietnam War, lies along the Ben Hai River and the better-known **17th Parallel**. The **Hien Luong Bridge** on the 17th Parallel is included in most tours. The DMZ was the creation of the 1954 Geneva Peace Accord, which divided the country into two spheres of influence prior to elections that were never held. Like its counterpart in Germany, the boundary evolved into a national border, separating communist from capitalist but, unlike its European equivalent, it was the triumph of communism that saw its demise.

At **Dong Ha**, to the north of Hué, Highway 9 branches off the main coastal Highway 1 and heads 80 km west to the border with Laos. Along this route is **Khe Sanh** (now called Huong Hoa), the site of one of the most famous battles of the war. The battleground is 3 km from the village. There's also a small **museum** ⓘ *30,000d*, at the former Tacon military base, surrounded by military hardware.

A section of the **Ho Chi Minh Trail** runs close to Khe Sanh. This is another popular but inevitably disappointing sight, given that its whole purpose was to be as inconspicuous as

ON THE ROAD

Battle at Khe Sanh (1968)

Khe Sanh (already the site of a bloody confrontation in April and May 1967) is the place where the North Vietnamese Army (NVA) tried to achieve another Dien Bien Phu (see page 65); in other words, an American humiliation.

One of the NVA divisions, the 304th, even had Dien Bien Phu emblazoned on its battle streamers. General Westmoreland would have nothing of it, and prepared for massive confrontation. He hoped to bury Ho Chi Minh's troops under tonnes of high explosive and achieve a Dien Bien Phu in reverse. But the American high command had some warning of the attack: a North Vietnamese regimental commander was killed while he was surveying the base on 2 January and that was interpreted as meaning the NVA were planning a major assault. Special forces long-range patrols were dropped into the area around the base and photo reconnaissance increased. It became clear that 20,000-40,000 NVA troops were converging on Khe Sanh.

With the US Marines effectively surrounded in a place which the assistant commander of the 3rd Marine Division referred to as "not really anywhere", there was a heavy exchange of fire in January 1968. The Marine artillery fired 159,000 shells, B-52s carpet-bombed the surrounding area, obliterating each 'box' with 162 tonnes of bombs. But, despite the haggard faces of the Marines, the attack on Khe Sanh was merely a cover for the Tet offensive – the commanders of the NVA realized there was no chance of repeating their success at Dien Bien Phu against the US military. The Tet offensive proved to be a remarkable psychological victory for the NVA – even if their 77-day seige of Khe Sanh cost many thousands (one estimate is 10,000-15,000) of NVA lives, while only 248 Americans were killed (43 of those in a C-123 transporter crash). Again, a problem for the US military was one of presentation. Even Walter Cronkite, the doyen of TV reporters, informed his audience that the parallels between Khe Sanh and Dien Bien Phu were "there for all to see".

---

possible and anything you see was designed to be invisible, from the air at least. However, it's worthy of a pilgrimage considering the sacrifice of millions of Vietnamese porters and the role it played in the American defeat (see box, opposite).

Tours to the DMZ usually also include the **Tunnels of Vinh Moc** ① *13 km off Highway 1 and 6 km north of Ben Hai River, 25,000d*, which served a similar function to the better-known Cu Chi Tunnels in the south. They evolved as families in the heavily bombed village dug themselves shelters beneath their houses and then joined up with their neighbours. Later the tunnels developed a more offensive role when Viet Cong soldiers fought from them. Some regard these tunnels as more 'authentic' than the 'touristy' tunnels of Cu Chi.

The **Rock Pile** is a 230-m-high limestone outcrop just south of the DMZ. It served as a US observation post, with troops, ammunition, Budweiser and prostitutes all being helicoptered in. Although it was chosen as an apparently unassailable position, the sheer walls of the Rock Pile were eventually scaled by the Viet Cong.

BACH MA NATIONAL PARK AND HILL STATION

① *T054-389 7360 www.vietnamnationalparks.org, national park entry 20,000d. Using your own transport go south down Highway 1 from Hué and turn off at the small town of Cau Hai. From here it is about 3 km to the park entrance and the national park office. Visitors must report*

ON THE ROAD
Ho Chi Minh Trail

The Ho Chi Minh trail was used by the North Vietnamese Army to ferry equipment from the North to the South via Laos. The road, or more accurately roads (there were between eight and 10 to reduce 'choke points') were camouflaged in places, allowing the NVA to get supplies to their comrades in the South through the heaviest bombing by US planes. Even the use of defoliants such as Agent Orange only marginally stemmed the flow.

The road was built and kept operational by 300,000 full-time workers and by another 200,000 part-time North Vietnamese peasant workers. Neil Sheehan, in his book *A Bright Shining Lie*, estimates that at no time were more than one-third of trucks destroyed and by marching through the most dangerous sections, the forces themselves suffered a loss rate of only 10-20%.

Initially, supplies were transported along the trail by bicycle; later, as supplies of trucks from China and the Soviet Union became more plentiful, they were carried by motorized transport. By the end of the conflict the Ho Chi Minh trail comprised 15,360 km of all-weather and secondary roads. One Hero of the People's Army is said, during the course of the war, to have carried and pushed 55 tonnes of supplies a distance of 41,025 km – roughly the circumference of the world.

The Ho Chi Minh Trail represents perhaps the best example of how, through revolutionary fervour, ingenuity and weight of people (not of arms), the Viet Cong were able to vanquish the might of the USA.

But American pilots did exact a terrible toll through the years. Again, Sheehan writes: "Driving a truck year in year out with 20-25 to perhaps 30% odds of mortality was not a military occupation conducive to retirement on pension."

The cemetery for those who died on the trail at Truong Son, Quang Tri Province, covers 16 ha and contains 10,306 named headstones; many more died unnamed and unrecovered.

---

here. Cars and minibuses are available from here. Accommodation is available. It is busiest on summer weekends; Mar/Apr are particularly worthwhile for the rhododendron blossom.

The French established a great many hill stations in Vietnam. Dalat was the only one to really develop as a town. Others, like Sapa, were rejuvenated a few years ago and yet others, like Bach Ma, had been forgotten about until very recently. Only now are the ruins of villas being uncovered, flights of steps unearthed and old gardens and ponds cleared. Bach Ma was established as a hill station in 1932 when the construction of a road made it accessible. By the outbreak of the Second World War there were 139 villas and a hotel. Recognizing its natural beauty and biological diversity the French gave it protected status. In 1991 the Vietnamese government classified it as a national park with 22,031 ha at its core and a further buffer zone of 21,300 ha. The area is rugged granite overlain in places by sandstone rising to an altitude of 1448 m at the summit of Bach Ma. There are a number of trails past waterfalls, through rhododendron woods and up the summit trail overlooking the remains of colonial villas.

Climatically it is at least 7°C colder than the coastal plain and annual rainfall of 8000 mm falls mainly between September and January, which is when the leeches are most active. The mammal species of the park have yet to be comprehensively surveyed and so far only 48 species of mammal have been confirmed. Included in this figure, however, are some

ON THE ROAD
By train from Hué to Danang

The train journey from Hué to Danang is regarded as not just one of the most scenic in Vietnam, but in the world.

Paul Theroux in his book *The Great Railway Bazaar* recounts his impressions as the train reached the narrow coastal strip, south of Hué and approaching Danang.

"The drizzle, so interminable in the former Royal Capital, gave way to bright sunshine and warmth; 'I had no idea,' I said. Of all the places the railway had taken me since London, this was the loveliest. We were at the fringes of a bay that was green and sparkling in bright sunlight. Beyond the leaping jade plates of the sea was an overhang of cliffs and the sight of a valley so large it contained sun, smoke, rain, and cloud – all at once – independent quantities of colour. I had been unprepared for this beauty; it surprised and humbled me ... Who has mentioned the simple fact that the heights of Vietnam are places of unimaginable grandeur? Though we can hardly blame a frightened draftee for not noticing this magnificence, we should have known all along that the French would not have colonized it, nor would the Americans have fought so long, if such ripeness did not invite the eye to take it." (Penguin, London, 1977)

As the mist descends, or the sea slips out of sight the interior view comes sharply into focus. Used ragged flannels dangle from the overhead racks, litter is chucked on the floor and the smell of of squid and pepper pervades the carriage. Train staff walk through the train, not stopping to shut the doors of the a/c carriage, drawing tuts all round. They are followed by locals pushing trolleys of coffee in coke bottles that are topped up with the syrupy dollop of condensed milk poured from cans. People with shoes off and legs outstretched onto the armrest of the chair in front listen to the odd bit of piped Vietnamese classical music amid the chatter. A woman dressed in purple eats a purple ice cream.

species of special interest such as the **red-shanked douc langur** and the buff-cheeked or **white-cheeked gibbon**.

Birdlife here is particularly interesting. Four restricted range species are the **Annam partridge, crested argus, short-tailed scimitar babbler** and the **grey-faced tit babbler**. The most characteristic feature of Bach Ma's birdlife is the large number of pheasants. Of the 12 species of pheasant recorded in Vietnam, seven have been seen in the park. A subspecies of the silver pheasant lives here and **Edwards' pheasant**, believed extinct until it was rediscovered in 1996, was seen just outside the park buffer zone. There are many other species of interest including the **red-collared woodpecker, Blyth's kingfisher** and the **coral-billed ground cuckoo**.

LANG CO

The road from Hué to Lang Co passes through many pretty, red-tiled villages, compact and surrounded by clumps of bamboo and fruit trees which provide shade, shelter and sustenance. And, for colour, there's the bougainvillea – which through grafting produces pink and white leaves on the same branch. Just north of Hai Van Pass lies the once idyllic fishing village of Lang Co (about 65 km south of Hué) on a spit of land, which has a number of cheap and good seafood restaurants along the road. Shortly after crossing the Lang Co lagoon, dotted with coracles and fish traps, the road begins the long haul up to **Hai Van Pass** but the majority of traffic now diverts through the tunnel.

Apparently, in the first year of his reign, Emperor Khai Dinh visited Lang Co and was so impressed that he ordered the construction of a summer palace. This, it seems, was never carried out, not even by his son Bao Dai who was so fond of building palaces. There are several guesthouses and tourist resorts on Lang Co, some of the resorts with the poorest standards of rooms in the entire country. However, it has also seen luxury hotel development in recent years and Vietnam's first integrated resort opened here in 2012.

HAI VAN PASS

Hai Van Pass (Deo Hai Van, 'Pass of the Ocean Clouds' or, to the French, Col des Nuages) lies 497 m above the dancing white waves that can be seen at its foot. In historic times the pass marked the border between the kingdoms of Vietnam and Champa. The mountains also act as an important climatic barrier trapping the cooler, damper air-masses to the north and bottling it up over Hué, which accounts for Hué's shocking weather. They also mark an abrupt linguistic divide, with the Hué dialect (the language of the royal court) to the north, the source of bemusement to many southerners.

The pass is peppered with abandoned pillboxes and crowned with an old fort, originally built by the dynasty from Hué and used as a relay station for the pony express on the old Mandarin Road. Subsequently used by the French, today it is a pretty shabby affair collecting wind-blown litter and sometimes used by the Army for a quiet brew-up and a smoke. Looking back to the north, stretching into the haze is the littoral and lagoon of Lang Co. To the south is Danang Bay and Monkey Mountain, and at your feet lies a patch of green paddies which belong to the leper colony, accessible only by boat.

Highway 1 passes through the village of **Nam O**, once famous for firework manufacture. Pages of old school books were once dyed pink, laid out in the sun to dry, rolled up and filled with gunpowder. But, alas, no more. Like other pyrotechnical villages, Nam O has suffered from the government's ban on firecrackers. Just south of Nam O is **Xuan Thieu Beach**, dubbed 'Red Beach II' by US Marines who landed here in March 1965, marking the beginning of direct intervention by the USA in the Second Indochina War. The tarmac and concrete foundations of the military base still remain.

HUÉ AND AROUND LISTINGS

WHERE TO STAY

Most hotels lie to the south of the Perfume River, although there are a couple to the north in the old Vietnamese part of town. Hué suffers from a dearth of quality accommodation but this has improved in recent years.

$$$$ Laguna Lang Co, Phu Loc, T054-369 5881, including the **Banyan Tree Lang Co**, www.banyantree.com, and the **Angsana Lang Co**, www.angsana.com. Massive development recently opened along the coast just north of Lang Co. The **Banyan Tree** offers 49 villas with pools along with the signature **Banyan Tree Spa**.

$$$$ Vedana Lagoon Resort & Spa, Zone 1, Phu Loc, T054-381 9397, www.vedanalagoon.com. This resort, 30 mins south of the city at Phu Loc, is set on a lagoon with villas – some with pools – over-water stilt bungalows, houseboats and a spa.

$$$$-$$$ La Residence Hotel & Spa, 5 Le Loi St, T054-383 7475, www.la-residence-hue.com. For lovers of art deco, this is an essential place to stay. Home of the French governor of Annam in the 1920s, it has been beautifully restored with 122 rooms, a restaurant, lobby bar, spa and swimming pool. The rooms in the original governor's residence are the most stylish, with 4-poster beds; other rooms are extremely comfortable too, with all mod cons. Filling breakfasts and free internet. Highly recommended.

$$$$-$$$ The Pilgrimage Village, 130 Minh Mang Rd, T054-388 5461, www.pilgrimagevillage.com. Tastefully designed rooms in a lush garden setting that looks beautiful in the rain (common in Hué) ranging from honeymoon and pool suites to superior rooms. The rooms in small houses with 4-posters and private pools are very romantic and recommended. There are 2 restaurants including **Junrei** (see Restaurants), a number of places to drink, a beautiful and atmospheric spa (the Vietnamese aromatherapy massage is outstanding) open to outside guests also, and a massive lap pool. Morning yoga, cooking and t'ai chi classes are available.

$$$ Gerbera Hotel, 38 Le Loi St, T054-393 6688, www.gerberahotelhue.com.vn. This former **Mercure** brings a new class of hotel to Hué with 110 rooms a pool and restaurant. The hotel location is downtown and rooms are super comfortable.

$$$ Saigon Morin, 30 Le Loi St, T054-382 3526, www.morinhotel.com.vn. One of the best hotels in Hué, this is still recognizable as the fine hotel built by the Morin brothers in the 1880s. Arranged around a courtyard with a small pool, the rooms are large and comfortable. The courtyard is a delightful place to sit in the evening and enjoy a quiet drink. The **Morin** is famed for its Royal Dinner pageant.

$$$ Villa Hué, 4 Tran Quang Khai St, T054-383 1628, www.villahue.com. 12-room hotel in an attractive building used by the Hué Tourism College to train future hotel managers. All rooms are spacious and comfortable. Vietnamese and Western food is served at the restaurant. there's a lobby bar and an outdoor seating area in the courtyard. Cooking classes are offered. Recommended.

$ Canh Tien Guesthouse, 9/66 Le Loi St, T054-382 2772, http://canhtienhotel.chez-alice.fr. 12 rooms with fan or a/c. Cheaper rooms have fans; the most expensive have a balcony. Welcoming family. Station pick-up. Can help with tours and bike hire.

$ Hué Backpackers' Hostel, 10 Pham Ngu Lao St, T054-382 6567, www.vietnambackpackershostels.com. A fabulous travellers' focus with a bar downstairs and ultra-clean rooms and dorms upstairs with a lovely balcony over the street for chilling. Tours offered too. Prices include breakfast.

RESTAURANTS

Hué cuisine is excellent; delicately flavoured and painstakingly prepared. Hué dishes are robust, notably the famed *bun bo Hué* (round white noodles in soup, with slices of beef, laced with chilli oil of exquisite piquancy). Restaurants for locals tend to close early; get there before 2000. Traveller cafés and restaurants keep serving till about 2200.

$$$-$ Junrei, Pilgrimage Village, 130 Minh Mang Rd, T054-388 5461. Open 0600-2200. Lovely stylized restaurant building serving delicious Vietnamese *bun bo Hué* and passion fruit mousse among other delights. Western menu too. Attentive service.

$$ La Carambole,19 Pham Ngu Lao St, T054-381 0491. Daily 0700-2300. One of the most popular restaurants in town with tourists. It is incredibly busy especially in the evening when the imperial-style dinner of 7-8 courses is recommended.

$$-$ Mediterraneo D2 Hué, 7 Ben Nghe St, T054-381 9849. Some of the softest pizza in Vietnam. Highly recommended. Ice cream served in the double courtyard set-up.

$$-$ Tropical Garden Restaurant, 27 Chu Van An St, T054-384 7143. Dine al fresco in a small leafy garden just a short walk from the Perfume River. Beef soup with starfruit and mackerel baked in pineapple. Touristy, with traditional music performances.

$ Lac Thanh, 6A Dinh Tien Hoang St, T054-352 4674 and **$ Lac Thien**, 6 Dinh Tien Hoang St, T054-352 7348. Arguably Hué's most famous restaurants, run by schismatic branches of the same deaf-mute family in adjacent buildings. You go to one or the other: under no circumstances should clients patronize both establishments! **Lac Thien** serves excellent dishes from a diverse and inexpensive menu, and the family is riotous and entertaining, but service has been known to be slack.

$ Lien Hoa, 3 Le Quy Don St. Vegetarian restaurant that is bustling every night with locals. No English menu, but the waiting staff are getting used to foreign customers and will help guide you. Extremely good value.

$ Mandarin, 24 Tran Cao Van St, T054-382 1281, www.mrcumandarin.com. Recently moved to larger premises but still with the owner's lovely photographs adorning the walls. Serves a variety of cheap food. Travel services and bike rental available. Mr Cu is one of the most helpful café owners in the whole of Vietnam. Highly recommended.

ENTERTAINMENT

Bus and boat tours to the Imperial Tombs are organized by tour operators and hotels.

Rent a **dragon boat** and sail up the Perfume River with private singers and musicians; tour offices and major hotels will arrange groups.

For something more authentic, do as the locals do and rent a *dap vit*, or duck pedalo for an hour.

See a **Royal Court performance** in the Imperial City's theatre or listen to performers during the **Saigon Morin's** evening buffet.

DANANG AND AROUND

Danang is Vietnam's third largest port and a commercial and trading centre of growing importance. The city has a frenetic buzz but no real charm and no sense of permanence. Only a few French buildings survive, near the river. Few cities in the world, however, have such spectacular beaches on their doorstep let alone three UNESCO World Heritage Sites (Hué, Hoi An and My Son) within a short drive.

Originally Danang was known as Cua Han (Mouth of the Han River). When the French took control they renamed it Tourane, a rough transliteration of Cua Han. Then it acquired the title Thai Phien, and finally Danang. The city is sited on a peninsula at the point where the Han River flows into the East Sea. An important port from French times, Danang gained world renown when two US Marine battalions landed here in March 1965 to secure the airfield. They were the first of a great many more who would land on the beaches and airfields of South Vietnam.

ARRIVING IN DANANG

Getting there The airport is on the edge of the city; a taxi into town is 100,000d and takes five to 10 minutes. Danang is extremely well connected with flights from most major cities. The train station is 2 km west of town and is on the north–south railway line linking Hanoi and Ho Chi Minh City. There are also regular bus and minibus connections with all major cities in the south as far as Ho Chi Minh City, and in the north as far as Hanoi. The new bus station is at Hoa Minh, 7 km north of the city. Open Tour Buses stop in the town centre.

Moving on Many people choose to base themselves in Hoi An, which is one hour by bus or 40 minutes by taxi. From Danang railway station there are Express trains to Hanoi, Ho Chi Minh City and Hué as well as trains to smaller places such as Quang Ngai (see page 146), from where it's possible to visit My Lai (see page 146), and all stops south along the coast. From Danang, Highway 14 winds its way on a very scenic route into the Central Highlands towards Kontum (see page 149) and on towards Dalat (see page 158). Buses do run along this route, however many people choose to fly from Danang to Pleiku (see page 153) or Buon Ma Thuot (see page 155) and explore the highlands from there by private car.

Getting around Danang is a sizeable town, rather too large to explore on foot, but there is an abundance of taxis and *xe ôm*. Bicycles and motorbikes are available for hire from most hotels and guesthouses.

Tourist information Sinh Tourist ⓘ *154 Bach Dang St, T511-384 3259, www.the sinhtourist.vn*, is helpful and can book bus tickets. Tour operators are also a good place to get information and book onward transport. The website http://indanang.com is worth consulting for news and events.

BACKGROUND

Danang lies in a region of great historical significance. Fairly close to the city – but often not particularly easy to reach – lies My Son – the ruins of the powerful kingdom of Champa, one of the most glorious in ancient Southeast Asia. The Cham were probably of Indonesian descent, and Chinese texts give the date AD 192 as the year when a group of tribes formed a union known as Lin-Yi, later to become Champa. The polytheistic religion of Champa was a fusion of Buddhism, Sivaism and local elements – and later Islam – producing an abundance of religious (and secular) sculptures and monuments. Siva is represented as a *linga* (phallic symbol). The kingdom reached its apogee in the 10th and 11th centuries but, unlike the Khmers, Champa never had the opportunity to create a capital city matching the magnificence of Angkor. For long periods the Cham were compelled to pay tribute to the Chinese, and after that they were dominated in turn by the Javanese, Annamese (the Vietnamese) and then the Khmers. The Cham state was finally eradicated in 1471, although there are still an estimated 90,000 Cham living in central Vietnam (mostly Brahmanists and Muslims). Given this turbulent history, it is perhaps surprising that the Cham found

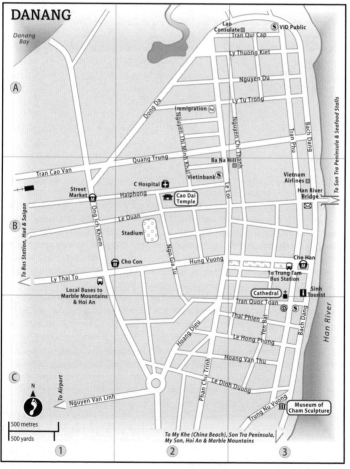

ON THE ROAD
Kingdom of Champa

The powerful kingdom of Champa was one of the most glorious in ancient Southeast Asia. Chinese texts suggest that in AD 192 a group of tribes, probably of Indonesian descent, formed a union known as Lin-Yi, later to become Champa. The first Champa capital, Tra Kieu (fourth to 10th centuries), was about 30 km from Danang, but the kingdom's territories extended far afield and other major sites included Dong Duong (eighth to 10th centuries), Po Nagar, Thap Mam and Cha Ban. Tra Kieu, My Son (page 143) and Dong Duong were the three most important centres of the kingdom.

The polytheistic religion of Champa was a fusion of Buddhism, Sivaism, local elements and, later, Islam, and was expressed in an abundance of religious (and secular) sculptures and monuments. The kingdom reached its apogee in the 10th and 11th centuries but, unlike the Khmers, Champa never had the opportunity to create a capital city matching the magnificence of Angkor. For long periods the Cham were compelled to pay tribute to the Chinese and, after that, they were dominated in turn by the Javanese, Annamese (the Vietnamese) and then the Khmers. The Cham kingdom was finally eradicated in 1471, although there are still an estimated 90,000 Cham living in central Vietnam (mostly Brahmanists and Muslims). Given this turbulent history, it is perhaps surprising that the Cham found any opportunity for artistic endeavours. It should perhaps be added that since the demise of the kingdom, the number of Cham sculptures has increased enormously as forgers have carved more of these beautiful images.

any opportunity for artistic endeavours. It should perhaps be added that since the demise of the kingdom, the number of Cham sculptures has grown enormously as forgers have carved more of these beautiful images.

Danang today has a population of 800,000, making it the fourth largest city in Vietnam. Its position, roughly equidistant between Hanoi and Ho Chi Minh City, gives Danang strategic significance. Danang Bay is a marvellous natural harbour and the port is the third busiest in the country after Ho Chi Minh City and Haiphong. Danang represents modern Vietnam and is a pointer to the way many of Vietnam's towns will look in not so many years to come. Its transformation in the past 20 years has been quite remarkable. It has undergone a whirlwind-like period of growth and continues to expand at a phenomenal rate. The city is ringed by huge dual carriageways and new roads have been driven out into the empty spaces beyond. Within months of the new roads' arrival they are fleshed out with factories, shops and houses. The new River Han Bridge has opened up the Son Tra Peninsula for commercial development (there are several resorts including the **Son Tra Resort** and the future **InterContinental**), which has added a major new dimension to Danang's expansion. **China Beach** (see page 134) stretching from Danang to Hoi An is rapidly disappearing under concrete as hotel expansion advances at a very rapid rate. The Han River is large enough to take passenger cruise liners which are arriving in greater numbers. Danang and its region need sensitive development from a far-sighted and disciplined authority if both its commercial and tourist potential is to be realized. Currently commercial interests are dominant and risk swamping irreplaceable tourist attractions.

DANANG MUSEUM OF CHAM SCULPTURE

ⓘ *At the intersection of Trung Nu Vuong and Bach Dang Sts, T0511-357 2414, www. chammuseumdanang.vn, daily 0700-1730, 30,000d. The museum booklet (US$9) has been written as an art history, not as a guide to the collection, and is of little help. However, there are now books to Champa art which extensively catalogue the exhibits, US$8. Labels are in English. Guided tours are held 0800-1000 and 1400-1630, 5 people minimum.*

The museum was established by academics of the École Française d'Extrême Orient and contains the largest display of Cham art anywhere in the world. The museum buildings alone are worth the visit: constructed in 1916 in a beautiful setting, the complex is open-plan in design, providing an environment in which the pieces can be exhibited to their best advantage. There are a number of rooms each dedicated to work from a different part of Champa: **Tra Kieu**, **My Son** and **Dong Duong** and a new extension. Because different parts of Champa flowered artistically at different times from the fourth to the 14th centuries, the rooms show the evolution of Cham art and prevailing outside influences from Cambodia to Java. One problem with the display is the lack of any background information. The pieces are wonderful, but the visitor may leave the museum rather befuddled by the display.

Principal periods are: My Son E1 (early eighth century); Hoa Lai (early ninth century); Dong Duong (late ninth century); Late Tra Kieu (late 10th century); Thap Mam (12th to 13th century); Po Klong Garai (13th to 16th century).

Tra Kieu was the earliest Cham capital sacked by the Chinese in the fifth century. Some 40 km southwest of Danang, little remains today but the pieces on display at the museum testify to a lively and creative civilization. An altar is inscribed with scenes from the wedding story of Sita and Rama from the Ramayana, a Hindu epic.

Many pieces from My Son illustrate the Hindu trinity: Brahma the Creator, Vishnu the Preserver and Siva the Destroyer. Ganesh, the elephant-headed son of Siva, was a much-loved god and is well represented here.

At the end of the ninth century Dong Duong replaced My Son as the centre of Cham art. At this time Buddhism became the dominant religion of court although it never fully replaced Hinduism. The Dong Duong room is illustrated with scenes from the life of Buddha. From this period faces become less stylistic and more human and the bodies of the figures more graceful and flowing. The subsequent period of Cham art is known as the late Tra Kieu style. In this section there are *apsaras*, celestial dancing maidens whose fluid and animated forms are exquisitely captured in stone. Thereafter Cham sculpture went into artistic decline. The Thap Mam style (late 11th to early 14th century) sees a range of mythical beasts whose range and style is unknown elsewhere in Southeast Asia. Also in this room is a pedestal surrounded by 28 breast motifs. It is believed they represent Uroha, the mythical mother of the Indrapura (My Son, Tra Kieu, Dong Duong) nation, but its significance and that of others like it is unknown.

The museum has a new collection with objects from Quang Tri, Tra Kieu, Quang Nam, Thap Mam-Binh Dinh, An My, Chien Dan, Qua Giang-Khue Trung and Phu Hung in its extension. One of its most outstanding pieces is a bronze with golden eyes, perfect breasts and stretched earlobes. It is the Avalokites Vara, an image of the Bodhisattva of compassion and dates from the ninth century.

OTHER PLACES IN DANANG

Danang's **Cao Dai Temple** ① *63 Haiphong St*, is the second largest temple in Vietnam. The priest here is particularly friendly and informative – especially regarding Cao Dai-ism and its links with other religions. Services are meant to be held at 0600, 1200, 1800 and 2400 (but it does not always appear to be open during these times). **Danang Cathedral** ① *156 Tran Phu St, 0500-1700, Mass is held 6 times on Sun*, built in 1923, is single-spired with a sugary-pink wash. The stained-glass windows were made in Grenoble, in 1927, by Louis Balmet who was also responsible for the windows of Dalat Cathedral (see page 161).

→ AROUND DANANG

DANANG TO HOI AN

① *Head south through Danang towards Highway 1 then take road 604 to Hoa Nhon, Hoa Phong and Hoa Phu. It's easily accessible by motorbike from Danang, or else you can take a tour.*
Bana is a recently rehabilitated hill station. It is 38 km west of Danang on Chua Mountain (Nui Chua). The mountain rises to a height of 1467 m, while Bana itself is tucked in to the hillside at an altitude of 1200 m. The view in all directions is spectacular, the air is fresh and cool and encompassed into each day are four seasons: morning is spring, noon the summer, afternoon is autumn and night the winter. Bana was founded in 1902 by the French, who brought their febrile and palsied here to convalesce in a more benevolent clime. Flora and fauna are diverse and interesting, and villas have been fashioned from the foundations of former French fabrications, some of which accept guests. A new cable car leads up to the mountain and the hotels. Packages can be arranged.

CHINA BEACH (MY KHE BEACH)

An R&R retreat during the war, My Khe became popular with American soldiers, who named it China Beach. It became a fabled resort celebrated in rock songs. Since 1975, however, it has been called T20 Beach, after the military code used by the North Vietnamese Army. Today the whole area, including the hotels, still belongs to the Vietnamese Army. It was a quiet area until relatively recently but now resonates to the sound of construction clatter. This once-abandoned, wild stretch of beach is now nearly all sectioned off for massive hotel development. Only several kilometres of a 30-km stretch between Danang and Hoi An remains untainted. For those who knew it just a few years ago before the mammoth construction boom, the transformation is quite incredible. It has miles and miles of fine white sand, clean water and a glorious setting: the hills of Monkey Mountain to the north and the Marble Mountains clearly visible to the south. At times, there is a dangerous cross-current and undertow.

MARBLE MOUNTAINS (NUI NON NUOC)

① *12 km from Danang and 20 km from Hoi An. Many visitors stop off at Marble Mountain en route to Hoi An, daily 0600-1700, 15,000d.*
The Marble Mountains overlook the city of Danang and its airfield, about 12 km to the west. The name was given to these five peaks by the Nguyen Emperor Minh Mang on his visit in 1825 – although they are in fact limestone crags with marble outcrops. They are also known as the mountains of the five elements (fire, water, soil, wood and metal). An important religious spot for the Cham, the peaks became havens for communist guerrillas during the war owing to their commanding view over Danang airbase. From here, a force with

sufficient firepower could control much of what went on below, and the guerrillas harried the Americans incessantly. The views from the mountain sides, overlooking Danang Bay, are impressive although they will be less impressive once every chain resort on the planet has made its stake on the beach. On the Marble Mountains are a number of important sights, often associated with caves and grottoes formed by chemical action on the limestone rock.

At the foot of the mountains is a village with a large number of shops selling marble carvings. Touts try to inveigle tourists into 'their' shop; do not follow them, it is not their shop but they get paid commission. Go into whichever shop you fancy.

Of the mountains, the most visited is **Thuy Son**. There are several grottoes and cave pagodas in the mountain which are marked by steps cut into the rock. The **Tam Thai Pagoda**, reached by a staircase cut into the mountain, is on the site of a much older Cham place of worship. Constructed in 1825 by Minh Mang, and subsequently rebuilt, the central statue is of the Buddha Sakyamuni (the historic Buddha) flanked by the Bodhisattva Quan Am (a future Buddha and the Goddess of Mercy), and a statue of Van Thu (symbolizing wisdom). At the rear of the grotto is another cave, the **Huyen Khong Cave**. Originally a place of animist worship, it later became a site for Buddhist pilgrimage. The entrance is protected by four door guardians. The high ceiling of the cave is pierced by five holes through which the sun filters and, in the hour before midday, illuminates the central statue of the Buddha Sakyamuni. In the cave are various natural rock formations which, if you have picked up one of the young cave guides along the way, will be pointed out as being stork-like birds, elephants, an arm, a fish and a face.

A few hundred metres to the south on the right is a track leading to **Chua Quan The Am**, which has its own grotto complete with stalactites, stalagmites and pillars. Local children will point out formations resembling the Buddha and an elephant.

NON NUOC BEACH

A 1-km walk from Marble Mountain, this huge, white sandy beach was developed as a beach resort for Russians after 1975. This perhaps explained the ugliness of the concrete **Non Nuoc Beach Resort**, which has been demolished and replaced by the **Sandy Beach Resort**. There's also the popular backpacker joint, **Hoa's Place**. Heading further south is the new **Montgomerie Links** golf course (www.montgomerielinks.com).

DANANG AND AROUND LISTINGS

WHERE TO STAY

Hyatt Regency Danang, Mercure Danang, Novotel Danang Premier Han River, Intercontinental Danang Sun Peninsula Resort, Lifestyle Resort Danang (to become Pullman Danang), FusionMaia (Asia's first all-inclusive spa resort), Meliã Danang, and Fusion Alya (a specialist culinary resort with free cooking classes) have all opened in Danang town and along the pristine beaches of the Danang coastline in the last 2 years.

$$$$ Furama Resort, Bac My An Beach, 8 km from Danang, T0511-384 7888, www.furamavietnam.com. 198 rooms and suites beautifully designed and furnished. It has 2 pools, 1 of which is an infinity pool overlooking the private beach, the other is surrounded by gardens. All its facilities are first class. Watersports, diving, mountain biking, tennis and a health centre offering a number of massages and treatments. Operates a free and very useful shuttle to and from the town, Marble Mountains and Hoi An. Fantastic breakfast and delicious beachside evening BBQs.

$$$ Bamboo Green Central, 158 Phan Chu Trinh St, T0511-382 2996, www.bamboogreenhotel.com.vn; and Bamboo Green Harbourside (a somewhat tenuous claim), 177 Tran Phu St, T0511-382 2722, www.bamboogreenhotel.com. Both are well-run, well-equipped, comfortable, business-type hotels with efficient staff and in central locations offering excellent value for money.

$ Hoa's Place, 215/14 Huyen Tran Cong Chua St, China Beach, T0511-396 9216. Right by the beach and a hit with backpackers, this place is run by the very friendly and talkative manager, Hoa. A laidback, but busy hangout. The small rooms, in 3 buildings, have fans (a/c costs extra), and private bathrooms. Surfboard rentals and communal dinners.

RESTAURANTS

Seafood is excellent here – head to the simple beachside restaurants. On the long strip, near the roundabout, Loc Chao is a great choice with delicious crab and cheesey scallops. Check out www.danangcuisine.com for the lowdown on street food.

$$$-$$ The Waterfront, 150-152 Bach Dang St, T09-3507 5580, www.waterfrontdanang.com. 0900-2400. Very cool 2-storey restobar serving innovative cuisine and top-drawer cocktails. Great, minimalist design. The lobster tortellini is delectable. Recommended.

$ Ba Vi, 166 Le Dinh Duong St. 1100-2000 (variable). Serves absolutely fantastic renditions of 2 regional specialities, my quang ca loc (noodles with fish) and my quang tom thit (noodles with prawn and pork). Simple place with bare metal tables. Perfect for a quick lunch.

$ Bread of Life, 4 Dong Da St, T0511-356 5185, www.breadoflifedanang.com. Closed Sun. Provides training and jobs for deaf people. The pizzas are very tasty. Baked goods and other comfort food too. Motorbike rental.

WHAT TO DO

Buffalo Tours, 20 Trung Nu Vuong St, T083-827 9170, www.buffalotours.com. Long-standing, well-respected agency with excellent staff and guides.

Da Boys Surf, Furama Resort, see Where to stay, www.daboyssurf.com. Surfing lessons from this newcomer on the Danang stretch. Also sells watersports equipment.

HOI AN AND AROUND

The ancient town of Hoi An (formerly Faifo) lies on the banks of the Thu Bon River. During its heyday 200 years ago, when trade with China and Japan flourished, Hoi An became a prosperous little port. Much of the merchants' wealth was spent on family chapels and Chinese clan houses which remain little altered today. Today Hoi An is seeing a late but much-deserved revival: the river may be too shallow for shipping but it is perfect for tourist boats; the silk merchants may not export any produce but that's because all they can make leaves town on the back of satisfied customers.

Hoi An's tranquil riverside setting, its diminutive scale (you can touch the roof of many houses), friendly and welcoming people and its wide array of shops and galleries have made it one of the most popular destinations for foreign travellers. There is plenty to see of historical interest, there is a nearby beach and, as if that were not enough, it has superb and inexpensive restaurants.

ARRIVING IN HOI AN

Getting there There are direct minibus connections with Ho Chi Minh City, Hanoi, Hué and Nha Trang. The quickest way of getting from Hanoi or Ho Chi Minh City is by flying to Danang and then getting a taxi from the airport direct to Hoi An, around 400,000d, 40 minutes.

Moving on There are direct minibus connections with Ho Chi Minh City, Hanoi, Hué and Nha Trang (see page 170), as well as Open Tour Buses to major tourist destinations north and south. However, you must return to Danang (one hour by bus or 40 minutes by taxi) for onward connections by train or plane.

Getting around Hoi An is compact and quite busy and is best explored on foot. Guesthouses hire out bicycles. Motos are banned from the old town centre on Monday, Wednesday, Friday and Saturday and every evening; when they are not, the mix of traffic and tourist pedestrians is an uncomfortable experience.

Best time to visit The Full Moon Festival is held on the 14th day of the lunar month. The town converts itself into a Chinese lantern fest and locals dress in traditional costume. The old town is pedestrianized for the night, lighting is reduced and poetry is recited and music played in the streets. Candles are lit and floated in plastic lotus flowers along the river; it is an exceptionally pretty sight.

Tourist information Entrance to most historic buildings is by sightseeing ticket, 90,000d for three days, on sale at **Hoi An tourist offices** ① *see map for locations, T510-386 1327, www.hoianworldheritage.org.vn, open 0700-1730*, which has English-speaking staff, car and minibus hire and guides to Hoi An. Sights in Hoi An are open for the same hours or a bit longer. The sightseeing ticket is segregated into five categories of different sights, allowing visitors admission to buildings in two of the categories. It is valid for 24 hours. If you want to see additional sites and have used up your tokens you must buy additional tickets. The tourist kiosks provide a good map. At least a full day is needed to see the town properly.

ON THE ROAD

Silk worms

Sericulture was introduced to Vietnam from China more than 1000 years ago, where the process had remained secret for years. Today Vietnam cultivates 20,000 ha of mulberry bushes which yield 1500-1800 tons of silk, around 1.8% of world output.

More recently, silk-making was developed in North Vietnam during Chinese rule and in 1975, on reunification, it was brought to Dalat. Silkworm larvae are fed mulberry leaves for about a month. They are then ready to construct their cocoons when they start rejecting food. For three days they secrete a sticky substance that binds a 750-m-long fibre into a cocoon. On completion the cocoon is plunged into boiling water to soften the thread and kill the caterpillars. Single threads are too weak and so the thread of 10 cocoons is spun into one yarn used to weave the silk. The caterpillars are then fried and eaten as a delicacy.

BACKGROUND

Hoi An is divided into five quarters, or 'bangs', each of which would traditionally have had its own pagoda and supported one Chinese clan group. The Chinese, along with some Japanese, settled here in the 16th century and controlled trade between the islands of Southeast Asia, East Asia (China and Japan) and India. Portuguese and Dutch vessels also docked at the port. During the Tay Son rebellion (1771-1788) the town was almost totally destroyed, although this is not apparent to the visitor. By the end of the 19th century the Thu Bon River had started to silt up and Hoi An was gradually eclipsed by Danang as the most important port of the area. Hoi An has emerged as one of the most popular tourist destinations in Vietnam and there has been no diminution in its status, in fact quite the reverse: walking along Tran Phu Street you'll see more Western than Vietnamese faces.

Hoi An's historic character is being submerged by the rising tide of tourism. Although remaining physically intact, virtually every one of its fine historic buildings either markets some aspect of its own heritage or touts in some other way for the tourist dollar; increasingly it is coming to resemble the 'Vietnam' pavilion in a Disney theme park. Nevertheless, visitors to Hoi An are charmed by the gentleness of the people and the sedate pace of life. The tempo has picked up in recent years, however, and although the police are vigilant in guarding Hoi An's morals (try getting even a foot massage in the historic core), every boat and café owner by the river will attempt to press passers-by into using their services.

Most of Hoi An's more attractive buildings and assembly halls (*hoi quan*) are found either on, or just off, Tran Phu Street. Tran Phu stretches west to east from the Japanese Covered Bridge to the market, running parallel to the river. People are friendly and will generally not mind inquisitive, but polite, foreigners.

The **Japanese Covered Bridge (Cau Nhat Ban)** ① *Tran Phu St, 1 token; keep your ticket to get back*, also known as the Pagoda Bridge, the Faraway People's Bridge and, popularly, as the Japanese Covered Bridge, is Hoi An's most famous landmark. The bridge was built in the 16th century. On its north side there is a pagoda, Japanese in style, for the protection of sailors. At the west end of the bridge are statues of two dogs, and at the east end, of two monkeys – it is said that the bridge was begun in the year of the monkey and finished in the year of the dog. Some scholars have pointed out that this would mean a two-year period of construction, an inordinately long time for such a small bridge; they maintain that the two animals represent points of the compass, WSW (monkey) and NW (dog). Father Benigne Vachet, a missionary who lived in Hoi An between 1673 and 1683, notes in his memoirs that the bridge was the haunt of beggars and fortune tellers hoping to benefit from the stream of people crossing over it. Its popular name reflects a long-standing belief that it was built by the Japanese, although no documentary evidence exists to support this. One of its other names, the Faraway People's Bridge, is said to have been coined because vessels from far away would moor close to the bridge.

Just east of the Covered Bridge is the **Museum of Sa Huynh Culture** ① *149 Tran Phu St, 1 'museum' token, daily 0700-2100*. Housed in an attractive colonial-era building the museum contains a modest collection of mostly pottery unearthed at Sa Huynh, 120 km south of Hoi An. The artefacts, dating from around 200 BC, are significant because they have called into question the previous understanding that the only cultures native to Central Vietnam have been the Cham and the Viet.

Just south of the Covered Bridge is **Bach Dang Street** which runs along the bank of the Thu Bon River. Here there are boats, activity and often a cooling breeze. The road loops round to the Hoi An Market (see below). The small but interesting **French Quarter** around Phan Boi Chau Street is worth taking time over. At No 25 you can visit an 1887 building that has belonged to the same family for four generations, US$2. The French-speaking owner is happy to talk. The colonnaded fronts are particularly attractive. As everywhere in historical quarters in Vietnam visitors should raise their gaze above street level to appreciate the architectural detail of upper floors, which is more likely to have survived, and less likely to be covered up.

Heading east along Tran Phu Street, the **Museum of Trade Ceramics** ① *80 Tran Phu St, 1 'museum' token, daily 0700-2100*, was opened with financial and technical support from Japan. It contains a range of ancient wares, some of them from shipwrecks in surrounding waters. There are also architectural drawings of houses in Hoi An. Upstairs, from the front balcony, there is a fascinating roofscape.

At the east end of Tran Phu Street, at No 24, close to the intersection with Nguyen Hué Street, is the **Ong Hoi An Pagoda** ① *one token*. This temple is in fact two interlinked pagodas built back-to-back: **Chua Quan Cong**, and behind that **Chua Quan Am**. Their date of construction is not known, although both certainly existed in 1653. In 1824 Emperor Minh Mang made a donation of 300 luong (1 luong being equivalent to 1½ oz of silver) for the support of the pagodas. They are dedicated to Quan Cong and Quan Am, respectively.

Adjacent to Ong Hoi An Pagoda is **Hoi An Museum of History and Culture** ⓘ *13 Nguyen Hué St, 1 'museum' token, 0700-2100,* housed in a former pagoda. The museum sets the history of the town in its trading context with sections on all the main cultural influences.

Virtually opposite the Ong Hoi An Pagoda, is the **Hoi An Market (Cho Hoi An)**. The market extends down to the river and then along the river road (Bach Dang Street). At the Tran Phu Street end is a market selling mostly dry goods. Numerous cloth merchants and seamstresses will produce made-to-measure shirts in a few hours. The riverside of the market is the fish market which comes alive at 0500-0600 as boats arrive with the night's catch.

ASSEMBLY HALLS (HOI QUAN)

Chinese traders in Hoi An (like elsewhere in Southeast Asia) established self-governing dialect associations or clan houses which owned their own schools, cemeteries, hospitals and temples. The clan houses (*hoi quan*) may be dedicated to a god or an illustrious individual and may contain a temple but are not themselves temples. There are five *hoi*

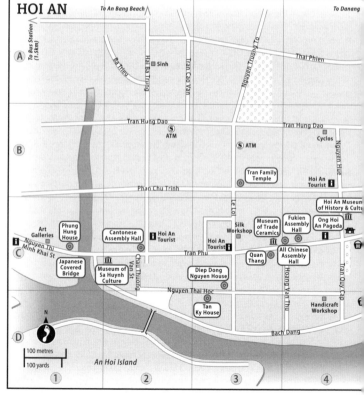

quan in Hoi An, four for use by people of specific ethnicities: Fukien, Cantonese, Hainan, Chaozhou and the fifth for use by any visiting Chinese sailors or merchants.

Strolling east from the Covered Bridge down Tran Phu Street all the assembly halls can be seen. Merchants from Guangdong would meet at the **Cantonese Assembly Hall (Quang Dong Hoi Quan)** ① *176 Tran Phu St, 1 'assembly hall' token*. This assembly hall is dedicated to Quan Cong, a Han Chinese general and dates from 1786. The hall, with its fine embroidered hangings, is in a cool, tree-filled compound and is a good place to rest.

Next is the **All Chinese Assembly Hall (Ngu Bang Hoi Quan)**, sometimes referred to as **Chua Ba (Goddess Temple)** ① *64 Tran Phu St, free*. Unusually for an assembly hall, it was a mutual aid society open to any Chinese trader or seaman, regardless of dialect or region of origin. Chinese vessels tended to visit Hoi An during the spring, returning to China in the summer. The assembly hall would help ship-wrecked and ill sailors and perform the burial rites of merchants with no relatives in Hoi An. Built in 1773 as a meeting place for all five groups (the four listed above plus Hakka) and also for those with no clan house of their own, today it accommodates a Chinese School, Truong Le Nghia, where children of the diaspora learn the language of their forebears.

The **Fukien Assembly Hall (Phuc Kien Hoi Quan)** ① *46 Tran Phu St, 1 'assembly hall' token*, was founded around 1690 and served Hoi An's largest Chinese ethnic group, those from Fukien. It is an intimate building within a large compound and is dedicated to Thien Hau, goddess of the sea and protector of sailors. She is the central figure on the main altar, clothed in robes, who, together with her assistants, can hear the cries of distress of drowning sailors. Immediately on the right on entering the temple is a mural depicting Thien Hau rescuing a sinking vessel. Behind the main altar is a second sanctuary, which houses the image of Van Thien whose blessings pregnant women invoke on the lives of their unborn children.

With a rather more colourful history comes the **Hainan Assembly Hall (Hai Nam Hoi Quan)** ① *10 Tran Phu St, 100 m east of the Fukien Assembly Hall, free*. It was founded in 1883 in memory of the sailors and passengers who were killed when three ships were plundered by an admiral in Emperor Tu Duc's navy. In his defence the admiral claimed the victims were pirates and some sources maintain he had the ships painted black to strengthen his case.

Exquisite wood carving is the highlight of the **Chaozhou (Trieu Chau Assembly Hall)**

① *362 Nguyen Duy Hieu St, 1 'assembly hall' token*. The altar and its panels depict images from the sea and women from the Beijing court, presumably intended to console homesick traders.

MERCHANTS' HOUSES

Just west of the Japanese Bridge is **Phung Hung House** ① *4 Nguyen Thi Minh Khai St, 1 'old house' token*. Built over 200 years ago it has been in the same family for eight generations. The house, which can be visited, is constructed of 80 columns of ironwood on marble pedestals. During the floods of 1964, Phung Hung House became home to 160 locals who camped upstairs for three days as the water rose to a height of 2.5 m.

Tan Ky House ① *101 Nguyen Thai Hoc St, 1 'old house' token*, dates from the late 18th century. Built by later generations of the Tan Ky family (they originally arrived in Hoi An from China 200 years earlier), it reflects not only the prosperity the family had acquired but also the architecture of their Japanese and Vietnamese neighbours, whose styles had presumably worked their influence on the aesthetic taste and appreciation of the younger family members.

Diep Dong Nguyen House ① *80 Nguyen Thai Hoc St*, with two Chinese lanterns hanging outside, was once a Chinese dispensary. The owner is friendly, hospitable and not commercially minded. He takes visitors into his house and shows everything with pride and smiles.

Quan Thang ① *77 Tran Phu St, 1 'old house' token*, is another old merchant's house, reputed to be 300 years old.

Tran Family Temple ① *on the junction of Le Loi and Phan Chu Trinh Sts, 1 'old house' token*, has survived for 15 generations; the current generation has no son which means the lineage has been broken. The building exemplifies well Hoi An's construction methods and the harmonious fusion of Chinese and Japanese styles. It is roofed with heavy *yin* and *yang* tiling which requires strong roof beams; these are held up by a triple-beamed support in the Japanese style (seen in the roof of the covered bridge). Some beams have Chinese-inspired ornately carved dragons. The outer doors are Japanese, the inner are Chinese. On a central altar rest small wooden boxes which contain the photograph or likeness of the deceased together with biographical details; beyond, at the back of the house, is a small, raised Chinese herb, spice and flower garden with a row of bonsai trees. As with all Hoi An's family houses guests are received warmly and courteously and served lotus tea and dried coconut.

→ AROUND HOI AN

CUA DAI BEACH AND AROUND

A white-sand beach with a few areas of shelter, **Cua Dai Beach** ① *4 km east of Hoi An; you must leave your bicycle (5000d) or motorbike (10,000d) just before Cua Dai Beach in a car park; the first shop kiosk on the beach at the end of the road offer lockers for 20,000d*, is a pleasant 20-minute bicycle ride or one-hour walk from Hoi An. Head east down Tran Hung Dao Street or, for a quieter route, set off down Nguyen Duy Hieu Street, which peters out into a walking and cycling path. This is a lovely route past paddy fields and ponds; nothing is signed but those with a good sense of direction will make their way back to the main road a kilometre or so before Cua Dai and those with a poor sense of direction can come to no harm. Behind the beach are a handful of hotels where food and refreshments can be bought.

Four kilometres north of Hoi An, off the new dual carriageway, is **An Bang Beach** where a collection of popular beach bars has gathered.

ON THE ROAD

My Lai – rewriting history

It was thought that pretty much everything that happened that awful day in My Lai was known. Thirty years ago Hugh C Thompson Jr and Lawrence Colburn received medals for heroism under enemy fire, but in 1998 the US Army corrected an oversight: there was no enemy in My Lai; or rather, the enemy was the US.

Thompson, a 24-year-old helicopter pilot, Colburn, his gunner, and a third man, Glenn U Andreotta (who was later killed in action) stopped the My Lai massacre before more people were killed. Thompson spotted women and children hiding in a bunker and put his helicopter down between them and advancing American soldiers. He called up another chopper and between them they evacuated the 10 civilians. At the same time Thompson reported the massacre to his CO who called off all action in the sector, thus ending the killing.

On 7 March 1998, at the Vietnam Veterans Memorial in Washington, the two survivors, Thompson and Colburn, were awarded the highest medal for bravery not involving conflict with an enemy.

The **Cham Islands** are 15 km from Cua Dai Beach and clearly visible offshore. There are seven islands in the group – Lao (pear), Dai (long), La (leaf), Kho (dry), Tai (ear), Mo (tomb) and Nom (east wind). Bird's nests are collected here. You can visit the fishing villages and snorkel and camp overnight (contact http://www.vietnamscubadiving.com/).

MY SON

① *Daily 0630-1630, 60,000d. Cham performance Tue-Sun 0930 and 1030. It is not clear how thoroughly the area has been de-mined so it is advisable not to stray too far from the road and path. Take a hat, sun cream and water as it is hot and dry.*

To get to My Son from Danang, drive south on Highway 1 and turn right towards Tra Kieu after 34 km (some 2 km after crossing the Thu Bon River). Drive through Tra Kieu to the village of Kiem Lam. Turn left; the path to My Son is about 6 km further along this road. At this point is the ticket office, a short bamboo bridge crossing and a 2-km jeep ride (included in the ticket price) with a 500-m walk at the end to My Son where there are toilets, refreshments and the Cham performance. My Son can be reached just as easily from Hoi An (45 km); take Phan Dinh Phung out of town. Turn left onto the main road (heading away from Danang) at Vinh Dien, the first sizeable settlement some 8 km from Hoi An, and follow this busy road for 18 km to the market town of Nam Phuoc where a large signpost points the way right to My Son. The road is well signposted from here. Alternatively, it's a 1½-hour trip each way by *Honda ôm*, as a half-day coach tour, or a full-day boat excursion.

Declared a World Heritage Site by UNESCO in 1999, My Son is one of Vietnam's most ancient monuments. Weather, jungle and years of strife have wrought their worst on My Son. But arguably the jungle under which My Son remained hidden to the outside world provided it with its best protection, for more has been destroyed in the past 40 years than the previous 400. Today, far from anywhere, My Son is a tranquil archaeological treasure with some beautiful buildings and details to look at. Not many visitors have time to make an excursion to see it which makes it all the more appealing to those that do. The thin red bricks of which the towers and temples were built have been carved and the craftsmanship of many centuries remains obvious today. The trees and creepers have been pushed back but My Son remains cloaked in green; shoots sprout up and one senses that were its custodians to turn their backs for even a short time My Son would be reclaimed by the forces of nature.

Tra Kieu, My Son and Dong Duong are the three most important centres of the former Cham Kingdom. My Son is located about 60 km south of Danang (28 km west of Tra Kieu) and consists of more than 70 monuments spread over a large area. The characteristic Cham architectural structure is the tower, built to reflect the divinity of the king: tall and rectangular, with four porticoes, each of which is 'blind' except for that on the west face. Because Cham kings were far less wealthy and powerful than the *deva-rajas* (god kings) of Angkor, the monuments are correspondingly smaller and more personal. Originally built of wood (not surprisingly, none remains), they were later made of brick, of which the earliest (seventh century) are located at My Son. These are so-called Mi-Son E1 – the unromantic identifying sequence of letters and numbers being given, uncharacteristically, by the French archaeologists who rediscovered and initially investigated the monuments in 1898. Although little of these early examples remains, the temples seem to show similarities with post-Gupta Indian forms, while also embodying Chen-La stylistic influences. Bricks are exactly laid and held together with a form of vegetable cement probably the resin of the day tree. It is thought that on completion, each tower was surrounded by wood and fired over several days in what amounted to a vast outdoor kiln.

It is important to see My Son in the broader context of the Indianization of Southeast Asia. Not just architecture but spiritual and political influences are echoed around the region. Falling as it did so strongly under Chinese influence it is all the more remarkable to find such compelling evidence of Indian culture and iconography in Vietnam. Indeed this was one of the criteria cited by UNESCO as justification for its listing. Nevertheless one of the great joys of Cham sculpture and building is its unique feel, its graceful lines and unmistakable form. Angkor in Cambodia is the most famous example but Bagan in Burma, Borobudur in Java and Ayutthaya in Thailand, with all of which My Son is broadly contemporaneous, are temple complexes founded by Hindu or Sivaist god kings. In all these places Buddhism appeared in the seventh century and by the 11th century was in the ascendent with the result that, My Son excepted, these are all widely regarded as Buddhist holy sites. The process whereby new ideas and beliefs are absorbed into a pre-existing culture is known as syncretism. The Hindu cult of *deva-raja* was developed by the kings of Angkor and later employed by Cham kings to bolster their authority. The king was the earthly representative of the god Siva. Sivaist influence at My Son is unmissable. Siva is one of the Hindu holy trinity, destroyer of the universe. Siva's dance of destruction is the very rhythm of existence and hence also of rebirth. Siva is often represented, as at My Son and other Cham relics throughout Vietnam, by the lingam, the phallus. My Son was obviously a settled city whose population is unknown but it seems to have had a holy or spiritual function rather than being the seat of power and it was, very probably, a burial place of its god kings.

Much that is known of My Son was discovered by French archaeologists of the École Française d'Extrême-Orient. Their rediscovery and excavation of My Son revealed a site that had been settled from the early eighth to the 15th centuries, the longest uninterrupted period of development of any monument in Southeast Asia. My Son architecture is notable for its use of red brick which has worn amazingly well. Sandstone plinths are sometimes

ON THE ROAD

Son My (My Lai) massacre

The massacre at Son My (see page 146) was a turning point in the American public's view of the war, and the role that the USA was playing. Were American forces defending Vietnam and the world from the evils of communism? Or were they merely shoring up a despotic government which had lost all legitimacy among the population it ostensibly served?

The massacre occurred on the morning of 16 March 1968. Units from the 23rd Infantry Division were dropped into the village of Son My. The area was regarded as an area of intense communist presence – so much so that soldiers referred to the villages as Pinkville. Only two weeks beforehand, six soldiers had been killed after stumbling into a mine field. The leader of the platoon that was charged with the job of investigating the hamlet of My Lai was 2nd Lieutenant William Calley. Under his orders, 347 people, all unarmed and many women and children, were massacred. Some of Calley's men refused to participate, but most did.

Neil Sheehan, in his book *A Bright Shining Lie*, wrote: "One soldier missed a baby lying on the ground twice with a .45 pistol as his comrades laughed at his marksmanship. He stood over the child and fired a third time. The soldiers beat women with rifle butts and raped some and sodomized others before shooting them. They shot the water buffalos, the pigs, and the chickens. They threw the dead animals into the wells to poison the water. They tossed satchel charges into the bomb shelters under the houses. A lot of the inhabitants had fled into the shelters. Those who leaped out to escape the explosives were gunned down. All of the houses were put to the torch".

In total, more than 500 people were killed at Son My; most in the hamlet of My Lai, but another 90 at another hamlet (by another platoon) in the same village.

The story of the massacre was filed by Seymour Hersh, but not until November 1969 – 20 months later. The subsequent court-martial only convicted Calley, who was by all accounts a sadist. He was sentenced to life imprisonment, but had served only three years before President Nixon intervened on his behalf (he was personally convicted of the murder of 22 of the victims). As Sheehan argues, the massacre was, in some regards, not surprising. The nature of the war had led to the killing and maiming of countless unarmed and innocent peasants; it was often done from a distance. In the minds of most generals, every Vietnamese was a potential communist; from this position it was only a small step to believing that all Vietnamese were legitimate targets.

used, as are sandstone lintels, the Cham seemingly – like the Khmer of Angkor – never having learnt the art of arch building, one of the few architectural techniques in which Europe was centuries ahead of Asia. Linga and yoni, the female receptacle into which the carved phallus was normally inserted, are also usually made of sandstone. Overwhelmingly, however, brick is the medium of construction and the raw material from which Hindu, Sivaist and Buddhist images and ornaments are so intricately carved.

Unfortunately, My Son was a Viet Cong field headquarters and therefore located within one of the US 'free fire' zones and was extensively damaged – in particular, the finest sanctuary in the complex was demolished by US sappers. Of the temple groupings, Groups A, E and H were badly damaged in the war. Groups B and C have largely retained their temples but many statues, altars and linga have been removed to the Cham Museum in Danang. Currently Group C is being restored by UNESCO; the F building is covered in cobwebs and propped up by scaffolding.

→ SOUTH TO DALAT VIA THE COAST

The north–south train continues from Danang to Dalat hugging the coast. There are a number of worthwhile stop-offs en route, which can also be visited as excursions from Hoi An. See also the 'North of Nha Trang' section, page 175.

QUANG NGAI

Quang Ngai is a modest provincial capital on Highway 1, situated on the south bank of the Tra Khuc River and 130 km from Danang. Few people stay here as facilities are still pretty basic. Its greatest claim to fame is its proximity to **Son My** – the site of the **My Lai massacre** (see box, page 145). There is an extensive **market** running north from the bus station, along Ngo Quyen Street (just east of Quang Trung Street or Highway 1). Also in the city is a citadel built during the reign of Gia Long (1802-1820).

SON MY (MY LAI)

① 13 km from Quang Ngai, 10,000d to contribute to the upkeep of the memorial. Motorbikes and taxis can take the track to Son My from the main road.

Just over 1 km north of town on Highway 1, soon after crossing the bridge over the Tra Khuc River, is a plaque indicating the way to Son My. Turn right, and continue for 12 km to the subdistrict of Son My where one of the worst, and certainly the most publicized, atrocities committed by US troops during the Vietnam War occurred (see box, page 145). The massacre of innocent Vietnamese villagers is better known as the My Lai Massacre – after one of the four hamlets of Son My. In the centre of the village of Son My is a memorial with a military cemetery 400 m beyond. There is an exhibition of contemporaneous US military photos of the massacre and a reconstruction of an underground bomb shelter; the creek where many villagers were dumped after being shot has been preserved.

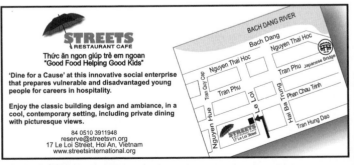

HOI AN AND AROUND LISTINGS

WHERE TO STAY

Hoi An offers some of the loveliest accommodation in the country – spa hotels, beautiful town resorts, beach resorts, boutique hotels and backpacker hotels are all available. Here, you're spoilt for choice.

$$$$ Life Heritage Resort Hoi An, 1 Pham Hong Thai St, T0510-391 4555, www. life-resorts.com. Small, colonial-style resort and spa in an excellent riverside location next to the town. Rooms are spacious and extremely comfortable. There's a restaurant, elegant café and cosy bar on site. Great staff. Highly recommended.

$$$$ Nam Hai, Hamlet 1, Dien Duong Village, 11 km north of Hoi An, 30 km south of Danang on Ha My Beach, T0510-394 0000, www.ghmhotels.com. A stunning creation of 100 beachside villas overlooking the East Sea. Raised platforms inside the villas create a special sleeping and living space envleoped in white silk drapes; egg-shell lacquered baths in black marble surround are incorporated into the platform. Facilities include excellent restaurants, 3 lovely pools, library, sports facilities and a spa.

$$$$ Victoria Hoi An Beach Resort & Spa, Cua Dai Beach, T0510-392 7040, www. victoriahotels.asia. A charming, resort right on the beach with 109 beautifully furnished rooms facing the sea or the river. There's a large pool, good restaurant, bars, live music and dancing, kids' club, sports facilities and charming service. Free shuttle into town.

$$$$-$$$ Ancient House Resort, 377 Cua Dai St, T0510-392 3377, http://ancienthouseresort.com. A beautiful, small hotel set around a garden. There is a pool, shop, billiards, free shuttle to town and beach, free bicycle service and a restaurant. Behind the hotel is a traditional Ancient House producing rice noodles.

$$$ Ha An Hotel, 6-8 Phan Boi Chau St, T0510-386 3126, http://haanhotel.com. This is a lovely hotel with a flourishing courtyard garden. Rooms have ethnic minority decor but are on the small side. The overall ambience is delightful and relaxing.

$$ An Huy Hotel, 30 Phan Boi Chau St, T0510-386 2116, www.anhuyhotel.com. Opposite **Brother's Café**, with courtyards that create a breeze and shutters that keep the noise out. Spacious rooms are beautifully decorated in Japanese style and the staff are very friendly.

$$ Betel Garden Homestay, 161 Tran Nhan Tong St, T051-392 4165, www.betelgardenhomestay.com. Set in pretty gardens, this welcoming family set-up has good-sized rooms, alfresco dining all day, and free bikes for the short trip to the heart of town or the beach.

$ Phuong Dong Hotel, 46 Ba Trieu St, T051-0391 6339. A 10-min walk from town, this ultra-budget option has small but clean rooms. Some are larger, so ask to see a few. Wi-Fi.

RESTAURANTS

A Hoi An speciality is *cao lau*, a noodle soup with slices of pork and croutons, traditionally made with water from one particular well; lots of stalls sell it along the river at night. The quality of food in Hoi An, especially the fish, is outstanding and the value for money is not matched by any other town in Vietnam. Bach Dang St is particularly pleasant in the evening, when tables and chairs are set up along the river.

$$$-$$ Secret Garden, 132/2 Tran Phu St, off Le Loi St, T0510-391 1112, www. secretgardenhoian.com. An oasis amid downtown Hoi An. Superior and attentive service in a delightful courtyard garden with delicious dishes. Try the sublime thin slices of beef with garlic and pepper, lemon juice, soya sauce, and black sesame oil or the star fruit soup. Live music is played nightly and there's a cooking school. Touristy, but recommended.

$$ Streets Restaurant Café, 17 Le Loi St, T0510-391 1948, www.streetsinternational. org. A professional training restaurant for disadvantaged youngsters (including a Hoi An specialties tasting menu) that serves up very tasty Vietnamese and Western cuisine in a lovely old property. Recommended.

$$ Son Restaurant, 177 Cua Dai Rd, T09-8950 1400, www.sonhoian.com. 0900-2200. Set in a beautiful position right on the river outside town en route to Cua Dai Beach. Excellent food all round, particularly the white rose. Tasty fresh fruit smoothies. Top lunch spot. Highly recommended.

$$-$ Mango Rooms, 111 Nguyen Thai Hoc St, T0510-391 0839, www. mangorooms.com. Enjoy slices of baguette layered with shrimp mousse served with a mango coconut curry or the delicious ginger and garlic-marinated shrimps wrapped in tender slices of beef and pan-fried with wild spicy butter and soy-garlic sauce; the seared tuna steak with mango salsa is outstanding. Complimentary tapas-style offerings such as tapioca crisps are a welcome touch. Highly recommended.

$ Cargo Club, 107-109 Nguyen Thai Hoc St, T0510-391 1227, www.restaurant-hoian. com. Extremely popular venue for filling Vietnamese and Western fodder including club sandwiches, Vietnamese salads and fajitas. The service is quicker downstairs than up on the balcony overlooking the river. The patisserie, groaning with cakes and chocolate, is the main reason to come.

$ Hai Café, 111 Tran Phu St/98 Nguyen Thai Hoc St, T0510-386 3210, www.visit hoian.com. The central area of this back-to-back café has a photographic exhibition of the WWF's invaluable work in the threatened environment around Hoi An. It offers good food in a relaxing courtyard or attractive café setting. Cookery courses can be arranged.

WHAT TO DO

Cookery classes
Morning Glory, www.restaurant-hoian. com. Also runs cooking classes.
Red Bridge Cooking School, Thon 4, Cam Thanh, T0510-393 3222, www.visithoian. com. Visit the market to be shown local produce, then take a 20-min boat ride to the cooking school where you're shown the herb garden. Next, you watch the chefs make a number of dishes such as warm squid salad served in half a pineapple and grilled aubergine stuffed with vegetables. Move inside and you get to make your own fresh spring rolls and learn Vietnamese food carving, which is a lot harder than it looks. From US$27.

Diving and snorkelling
Cham Island Diving Center, 88 Nguyen Thai Hoc St, T0510-391 0782, www.cham islanddiving.com. Its Cham Island excursion is recommended for snorkellers as it gives time to explore the village on Cham Island, US$40; led by Italians who lived on the island for a year.

Handicrafts
Hoi An Handicraft Workshop, 9 Nguyen Thai Hoc St, T0510-391 0216, www.hoian handicraft.com. Traditional music performances Tue-Sun at 1015, 1515 and 1930, with the Vietnamese monochord and dancers. At the back there is a potter's wheel, straw mat making, embroiderers, conical hat makers, wood carvers and iron ornament makers.

HOI AN TO DALAT

Venturing away from the coast, Highway 14 winds its way up into the Central Highlands and the Truong Son Mountain Range, dotted with colonial hill stations and ethnic minority communities. Overlooked by many visitors, the area has started to develop a tourist infrastructure, with accommodation and transport in the main towns of Kontum, Pleiku, Buon Ma Thuot and Dalat, as well as homestay options. The cool climate of the plateau is a welcome respite from the heat of the lowlands, while the spectacular views make it well worth the detour from the coast.

→ INS AND OUTS

If pressed for time, there is the option to fly from Danang to the airports at Pleiku or Buon Ma Thuot and continue by road from there. Most people choose to hire a private car to explore the area though there are plentiful local buses. From Dalat there's the option to fly direct to Ho Chi Minh City. Alternatively, you could take the train or an Open Tour Bus south along the coast from Danang, visiting Quang Ngai and Son My (My Lai) en route (see 'South to Dalat via the coast', page 146).

HIGHWAY 14 TO KONTUM

From Hoi An, Highway 14 winds its way through the foothills towards Kontum. As you approach Dan Glei, you will pass through the most lush forests anywhere in Vietnam on the Lo-Xo Pass. Wild, dark green and luxuriant jungle tumbles down mountains carpeting the area in a thick, abundant forest. It is extremely beautiful and the height of the jungle-clad mountains are awe-inspiring.

To the east of the road is the **Ngoc Linh Nature Reserve** and the towering Ngoc Linh peak at 2116 m. There is a riot of ferns, waterfalls and astoundingly beautiful scenery all around. Continuing south towards Kontum, between Dak Nay and Plei Kan are Katu villages that speak a Mon-Khmer language.

→ KONTUM

Kontum, although being one of the larger provinces within Vietnam, is the least populated and one of the poorest. It was created in 1991 when it was decided to break up Gia Lai Province. The town is 49 km north of Pleiku with a population of 36,000, many of whom are from ethnic minorities.

The town itself is a small, sleepy market town and in itself is not remarkable except that it houses the **Wooden Church**, **Tan Huong Church** and the **Bishop's Seminary**. These alone are worth a trip to Kontum.

Twelve kilometres south of Kontum the road crosses the **Chu Pao Pass**. There is nothing to see in particular, but commanding views over the Kontum Plateau. The road descends past sugar cane plantations before crossing the Dakbla River.

ARRIVING IN KONTUM

Getting there Kontum is situated just off Highway 14 and is 44 km north of Pleiku. Buses from Hoi An (eight hours) are numerous and local buses ply the route from Pleiku and to

The Central Highlands have long been associated with Vietnam's hill tribes. French missionaries were active among the minorities of the Central Highlands (the colonial administration deterred ethnic Vietnamese from settling here) although with uneven success. Bishop Cuenot dispatched two missionaries from Quy Nhon to Buon Ma Thuot where they received a hostile reception from the Mnong, so travelled north to Kontum where among the Ba-na they found more receptive souls for their evangelizing. Today, many of the ethnic minorities in the Central Highlands are Roman Catholic, although some are Protestant (Ede around Buon Ma Thuot, for instance).

At the same time French businesses were hard at work establishing plantations to supply the home market. Rubber and coffee were the staple crops. The greatest difficulty they faced was recruiting sufficient labour. Men and women of the ethnic minorities preferred to cultivate their own small plots rather than accept the hard labour and slave wages of the plantation owners. Norman Lewis travelled in the Central Highlands and describes the situation in his book, *A Dragon Apparent*.

Since 1984 there has been a bit of a free-for-all and a scramble for land. Ethnic Vietnamese have encroached on minority land and planted it with coffee, pepper and fruit trees. From the air one sees neat rows of crops and carefully tended plots, interrupted only by large areas of scrub that are too dry to cultivate. The scene is reinforced at ground level where the occasional tall tree is the only reminder of the formerly extensive forest cover. The way of life of the minorities is disappearing with the forests – there are few trees to build their stilt houses from or shady forests in which to live and hunt.

The Mnong, Coho, Sedang and Bahnar people speak a language that stems from the Mon Khmer language. The language of the Ede, Giarai, Cham and Raglai originates from the Malayo-Polynesian language.

a lesser degree from Buon Ma Thuot and Quy Nhon. Kontum does not have an airport but shares the airport with Pleiku, an hour's drive away.

Getting around Starting from Dakbla Hotel 1 most of the city and sights are within walking distance. There are a few taxis available and also a few *Honda ôm* drivers. It is possible to rent cars and bikes from the tourist office.

Moving on There are daily bus departures to Pleiku (see page 153) and Buon Ma Thuot (see page 155). 12 km south of Kontum, the road crosses the Chu Pao Pass, from there are commanding views over the Kontum Plateau. The road descends past sugar cane plantations before crossing the Dakbla River.

Best time to visit Climatically the best time to visit is from November to April. It is warm with little to no rain. The main festival is on 14 November to celebrate the life of Bishop Cuenot.

Tourist information Kontum Tourist Office ① *2 Phan Dinh Phung St (on the ground floor of the Dakbla Hotel 1), T060-386 3333, www.kontumtourism.com, daily 0700-1100, 1300-1700,* for details about tours and further information.

BACKGROUND

The French Bishop Stephen Theodore Cuenot founded Kontum in the mid-1800s. He was a missionary priest endeavouring to convert the local tribes to Christianity. He succeeded, as many of the inhabitants are Christian. He was arrested on Emperor Tu Duc's orders (the Emperor did not like missionaries) and died in Binh Dinh prison on 14 November 1861, a day before the beheading instructions arrived. He was beatified Saint Etienne-Theodore Cuenot in 1909. His wooden church remain almost unchanged since that time.

In more recent years the area was the scene of some of the fiercest fighting during the American war.

PLACES IN KONTUM

The main sights within Kontum are the Wooden Church, Tan Huong Church, the Bishop's Seminary, a soon-to-open provinicial museum on the riverfront, surrounding Ba-na villages, and Kontum prison. **Tan Huong Church** ① *92 Nguyen Hué St (if the church is shut ask in the office adjacent and they will gladly open it).* The whitewashed façade bears an interesting depiction of St George and the dragon. It is not immediately evident that the church is built on stilts, but crouch down and look under one of the little arches that run along the side and the stilts, joists and floorboards are clear. The glass in the windows is all old, as the rippling indicates, although one of the two stained-glass windows over the altar has required a little patching up. Unfortunately the roof is a modern replacement, but the original style of fishscale tiling can still be seen in the tower. The interior of the church is exquisite, with dark wooden columns and a fine vaulted ceiling made of wattle and daub. The altar is a new, but rather fine addition, made of a jackfruit tree, as is the lectern. The original building was erected in 1853 and then rebuilt in 1860 following a fire. The current church dates from 1906.

Further east on the same street is the superb **Wooden Church**. Built by the French with Ba-na labour in 1913, it remains largely unaltered, with the original wooden frame and wooden doors. Unfortunately the windows are modern tinted-glass and the paintings on them depicting scenes from Christ's life as well as a couple of Old Testament scenes with Moses are a little crude. In the grounds stands a statue of Stephen Theodore Cuenot, the

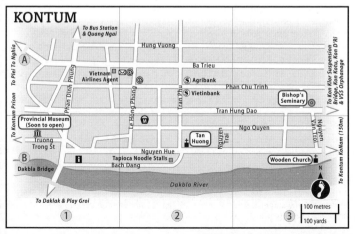

first Roman Catholic bishop of East Cochin China diocese. There is also an orphanage that is run by the church in the grounds that welcomes visitors.

The architecturally remarkable and prominent **Bishop's Seminary** is set in lovely gardens with pink and white frangipani trees. It was completed in 1935; the seminary was founded by French missionary Martial Jannin Phuoc. The upstairs **exhibition room** ① *Mon-Sat 0800-1130, by donation*, displays an eclectic collection of instruments, photos and scale models; some signs are in English.

Kontum prison ① *500 m along Truong Trong St, daily 0800-1100, 1400-1700, under US$1*, was built in 1915 and was home to several prominent revolutionaries. It was abandoned by the French in 1933 and later left to collapse. There is a small museum in some new buildings and a memorial depicting malnourished prisoners. The labels are in Vietnamese only.

AROUND KONTUM

There are scores of **Ba-na villages** around Kontum that can be reached by motorbike, and at least one that is easily accessible on foot. **Plei To Nghia** is at the westerly end of Phan Chu Trinh Street down a dusty track. Wattle and daub houses, mostly on stilts, can be seen and the long low white building on short stilts at the vilage entrance is the church. In the evening the elderly folk of the village go for communal prayers while the young people gather at the foot of their longhouses for a sunset chat. In and around the village are small fields heavily fortified with thorns and barbed wire, which seems a little strange considering the Ba-na do not lock their doors. In fact the defence is not against poachers but the village's large population of rooting, snuffling, pot-bellied pigs. Every family has a few pigs that roam loose. The pigs are sometimes given names and recognize the voice of their owner, coming when called.

Most houses are on stilts, with the animals living underneath. They are built from wattle and daub around a wooden frame, although brick is starting to appear as it is cheaper than declining wood resources, and modern tile is beginning to replace the lovely old fishscale tiling. Considering the tiny spaces in which most Vietnamese live, these houses are positively palatial. There is a large living room in the centre, a kitchen (with no chimney) at one end and bedroom at the other. **Kon D'Ri** (Kon Jori) is a fine example of a community almost untouched by modern life (apart from Celine Dion's voice competing with the cows and cockerels!). A perfect *rong* communal house dominates the hamlet, and all other dwellings in the village are made from bamboo, or mud and reeds. The Ba-na *rong* is instantly recognizable by its tall thatched roof. The height of the roof is meant to indicate the significance of the building and make it visible to all. It is a focal point of the village for meetings of the village elders, weddings and other communal events. The stilt house close by is in fact a small Roman Catholic church. Nearby **Kon Kotu** is similar. To get there follow Nguyen Hué Street and turn right into Tran Hung Dao Street, cross the suspension bridge (Kon Klor Bridge) over the Dakbla River (built in 1997 after a flood washed the old one away). After a few hundred metres turn left and continue for 3 km bearing left for Kon Kotu and right for Kon D'Ri. A private orphanage, simply titled "VS5 " is run in the area by Teresa Lung and her siblings, themselves orphans. Visitors are welcomed (contact lungdang2002@yahoo.com).

A more lively Ba-na community can be found at **Kontum KoNam** (turn right off Nguyen Hue past the wooden church). Here the stilt houses are crowded close together and the village bustles with activity.

Twenty kilometres from Kontum it's possible to visit the Gia-rai villages of Plei RoLay, Plei Bua and Plei Weh. Forty kilometres from Kontum you can visit Kon Biu, a Xo-dang village, 7 km further on is Kon Cheoleo, a Jolong village (there are only 15 known Jolong villages in Vietnam; their language is similar to Ba-na). The Xo-dang build the entrance to the *rong* on the east and west in harmony with the sun, unlike the Ba-na. The Xo-dang play the drums to ask for rain. It's also possible to visit Kon Hongor, a Ba-na Ro Ngao community (there are only 4000 Ro Ngao in Kontum Province).

→ PLEIKU (PLAY KU)

Pleiku is the provincial capital of Gia Lai Province. It is located in a valley at the bottom of a local mountain, Ham Rong, that is clear from 12 km away. It is a modern, thriving, bustling town. The area around Pleiku is more cultivated than that of Kontum. Rubber, pepper, coffee and tea plantations abound and rice and watermelon are grown. The city itself is sprawling although there are six main streets on which you'll find all that you will need in terms of restaurants, shops, internet cafés and hotels. There was fierce fighting here during the American War. According to government statistics which are not always accurate, there are some 300,000 Gia-rai and some 150,000 Ba-na living in the province.

ARRIVING IN PLEIKU

Getting there Pleiku is just off Highway 14 and is 44 km south of Kontum and 197 km from Buon Ma Thuot. It has a modern domestic airport that is 10 minutes' drive from the city centre with direct flights from Danang and Ho Chi Minh City. Plenty of local buses plough the routes to Kontum, Buon Ma Thuot and Tuy Hoa. There are also bus connections with Ho Chi Minh City and Hanoi.

Moving on From Pleiku it is possible to fly back to Danang to continue the journey south along the coast, or on towards Ho Chi Minh City. It is also a good base from which to explore the Central Highlands either by local bus or hiring a car. Buon Ma Thuot is a four-hour drive; Kontum is 1-1½ hours.

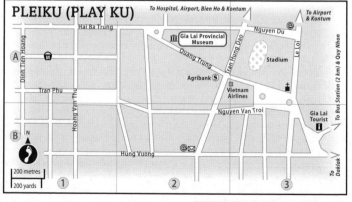

Getting around Starting from Laly Hotel most of the city and sights are within walking distance. There are a few taxis available, a local bus service that will take you within the city and surrounding environs and *Honda ôm* drivers are plentiful.

Best time to visit Climatically the best time to visit is from November to February when it is warm with little to no rain.

Tourist information Gia Lai Tourist ① *215 Hung Vuong St (on the ground floor of the Hung Vuong Hotel), T59-387 4571, www.gialaitourist.com, daily 0730-1100, 1330-1630.*

BACKGROUND

The town, with a population of 187,000, is located high on the Pleiku Plateau, one of many such structural features in the Central Highlands. It is the capital of Gia Lai Province which, with a population density of just 34 people per sq km, is one of the most sparsely inhabited areas of Vietnam. Historically, this was a densely forested part of the country and it remains home to a large number of ethnic minorities. Pleiku was the headquarters to two Corps, one of the four military tactical zones into which South Vietnam was divided during the war. John Vann (see Neil Sheehan's *Bright Shining Lie*) controlled massive B-52 bombing raids against the encroaching NVA from here until his death in a helicopter crash in June 1972. After the American departure in 1973, the South Vietnamese heavily fortified the town. The encroaching NVA decided to strike Buon Ma Thuot instead and soon controlled most of the highland region. President Thieu ordered his troops to withdraw and in doing so they torched Pleiku. This is the main reason there are very few old buildings here.

PLACES IN AND AROUND PLEIKU

The town itself has little to offer the tourist; during the monsoon the side streets turn into muddy torrents and chill damp pervades guesthouse rooms. The **Gia Lai Provincial Museum** ① *28 Quang Trung St, T59-382 4520, Mon-Fri 0730-1100, 1330-1630, 10,000d, Vietnamese signs only*, houses artefacts from the local minorities and from the war.

There are a number of places to visit on the Kontum road (hire a car or *Honda ôm*) **Bien Ho**, 5 km north of Pleiku, is a large **volcanic lake** and the main source of water for Pleiku, so no fishing or swimming. A raised platform on a promontory jutting out into the lake is a good place from which to appreciate the beauty and peace of the setting.

About 2 km further is the turn left to the once-spectacular **Yaly Falls**. Now that there is a hydroelectric plant to which the water is diverted there is not much to see, but along the road are several **Gia-rai villages** that are worth a visit, but a guide and permit is required and Gia Lai Tourist will only permit a visit to Plei Fun. **Plei Fun** is about 37 km along the Yaly road; around 16 km out of Pleiku you will pass a very colourful pink-patterned Rong house on the left-hand side. In the graveyard, tiled or wooden roofs which shelter the worldly possessions of the deceased – bottles, bowls, even the odd bicycle, cover the graves. Carved hardwood statues guard the graves, a peculiarly Gia-rai tradition. These are part of the grave abandonment ceremony and the statues represent minority life. Saplings are planted around the grave and will eventually grow to cover them. Until five year's ago the Gia-rai would reopen coffins to place their newly dead in them but the government forbade the practice on hygiene grounds. In 2010 there was a spectacularly coloured grave topped with carved metal figures and surrounded by numerous statues.

Trips to the Ba-na villages of **Dektu**, **Deron**, **DeDoa** and **Dekop**, 35 km east of Pleiku, can be arranged. At Dektu the government built a well next to the *rong* house (traditional communal lodge) but the Ba-na believe the water here is artificial and so have covered the well up. The jar on the pedestal in front of the *rong* represents the running water from the stream (ie real water). Inside the *rong* you will see drums, rice jars and truncated parts of buffalo that are sacrificed at harvest time. Here the graves are modern metal ones.

Tours for war veterans and those interested in war history can be arranged around Pleiku. Sites include Camp Enari, the former headquarters of 4th US infantry division, Hanzel Airstrip on Dragon Mountain, Camp Pleine, the base of US Special Services, the Catecka Teal Plantation, a US operational area, the 1st Cavalry Division base on Honcong Mountain, the Phoenix Airstrip near Dak To, the Airbase of 4th division at An Khe and Radcliff, the 1st Cavalry division base.

→BUON MA THUOT

Buon Ma Thuot is the provincial capital of Daklak Province. The city has changed from being a sleepy backwater town (similar to Kontum) to a thriving modern city within the last 15 years. Buon Ma Thuot has now surpassed its illustrious and renowned neighbour of Dalat to be the main centre for tea and coffee production, and the area has become the second largest producer of coffee in the world. The creation of the Trung Nguyen coffee empire in 1997 and the subsequent franchise of the names have meant that Trung Nguyen coffee shops are to be found everywhere in Vietnam (from the smallest communes to all the main cities). This has led to an unprecedented level of domestic coffee consumption. With the revenues that they have received it is pleasant to see that the money has to a great part been reinvested in the community (there are new schools, roads, hospitals aplenty). There is also a sports complex to rival any to be found in Ho Chi Minh City or Hanoi. Although it is a sprawling modern city, the heart of the city is located on the four streets that radiate out from the Thang Loi Hotel.

ARRIVING IN BUON MA THUOT
Getting there Buon Ma Thuot is located on Highway 14 and can also be reached by Highway 27 from Dalat and on Highway 26 from Nha Trang. There are direct flights from Ho Chi Minh City and Danang. There are innumerable local bus connections with major cities as well as smaller towns in the central highlands.

Moving on Local buses go to Pleiku (see page 153), Kontum (see page 149), Dalat (see page 158), Ho Chi Minh City (see page 185), Nha Trang (see page 170) and Hanoi (see page 27). It is also the base for visiting Yok Don National Park (see page 157); tours can be booked at operators within the town. There are hourly buses from Buon Ma Thuot to Lak Lake (see page 158), from where there are onward bus connections to Dalat.

Getting around There is good local bus service that runs within the city. There are also plenty of taxis and *Honda ôm* drivers.

Best time to visit Climatically the best time to visit is from November to April when there is little to no rain and the temperature is warm to hot.

Tourist information Daklak Tourist Office ⓘ *53 Ly Thuong Kiet St (within the grounds of Thang Loi Hotel), T0500-385 2246, www.daklaktourist.com.vn*, provides useful information about the province and has knowledgeable, English-speaking staff.

BACKGROUND

Up until the 1950s big game hunting was Buon Ma Thuot's main claim to fame. Tigers and elephants were plentiful. Hunting wild animals is now illegal in Vietnam, though poachers continue to aggressively hunt what little wildlife remains. Buon Ma Thuot was considered of vital strategic importance during the war, dominating a large region of the Central Highlands. The Americans had realized the importance of the city, as did the northern

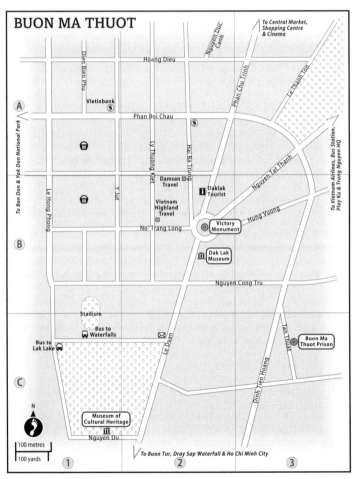

Vietnamese. Unfortunately the southern Vietnamese did not. In March 1975 the northern military which had infiltrated 30,000 troops and equipment to within striking distance of Buon Ma Thuot undetected launched an offensive against the city. Instead of a protracted two-year battle that the northern generals had anticipated, there was little resistance. The news was broadcasted on local Vietnamese radio and also on *Voice of America*. It demoralized the southern forces and within two months the war was over.

In the years following the war, the government instigated a resettlement programme primarily from Hanoi and the Red River Delta but also to a lesser degree from Ho Chi Minh City. The land that had belonged to the hill tribes was given to the new settlers. The Ede did not take kindly to having their land encroached upon by outsiders (Vietnamese). The tensions reached their peak in late 2001, early 2002 and again in 2004 when there was widespread rioting in Buon Ma Thuot. For a period of several weeks the whole area was closed to non-Vietnamese. Buon Ma Thuot nowadays is much more peaceful but there are numerous military barracks within the city and its nearby suburbs.

PLACES IN BUON MA THUOT

The town is dominated by the **Victory Monument** (Tuong Dai Chien Thang) complete with a replica tank from the 10 March 1975 battle whose gun is pointing towards the door of the Roman Catholic church on the city's main roundabout. The **Museum of Cultural Heritage** ① *2 Y Ngong St, T500-381 2770, daily 0800-1100, 1400-1700, 10,000d; explanations in English*, is in Emperor Bao Dai's hunting lodge built in 1927. It houses a selection of clothing and artefacts from some of the hill tribes, an Ede longhouse model, an Ede seat, rice and wine jars. There is a map showing Daklak Province onto which many of the ethnic minority villages are marked. There's also a photo of the Ban Don elephant race. A new museum complex is under construction and should be open by the time you read this.

The **Dak Lak Museum** ① *1 Le Duan St, T500-381 2770, Mon-Fri 0800-1100, 1400-1700, entry included with entrance to the Museum of Cultural Heritage*, is a dull museum recording revolution acts and the first battle between the north and south on the 10 March 1975.

At **Buon Ma Thuot Prison** ① *18 Tan Thuat St, daily 0730-1700, free; no signs in English*, you can visit guardrooms, watchtowers and tiny cells that housed revolutionary prisoners from the 1930s to the 1970s; the whole complex has been completely renovated. The governor's former residence now houses a small museum containing photos of prison life and also some of the more illustrious prisoners and items that were used to hide secret information.

Not really a sight, but if you are passing, you should stop by the headquarters of the **Trung Nguyen Coffee Empire** ① *268 Nguyen Tat Thanh St, www.trungnguyen.com.vn*, and pop your head around the door to see what money buys in terms of interior decor. Coffee can be bought at a kiosk next to the main entrance.

YOK DON NATIONAL PARK

① *Yok Don National Park, Buon Don District, T500-378 3049, yokdonecotourism@vnn.vn. Tour guide section Mr Hung T090-519 7501 (mob), daily 0700-2200. Tours range from elephant riding (US$40 for 2 hrs) to elephant trekking (US$190 for 2 people for 3 days) to animal spotting by night (US$70), to riverboat rides (US$20 for 1 hr) to trekking (US$15 for 3 hrs). There is an additional entry fee to the park, for under US$1. Accommodation is available.*

A 115,545-ha wildlife reserve about 40 km northwest of Buon Ma Thuot, Yok Don National Park (Vuon Quoc Gia Yok Don) contains at least 63 species of mammals, 17 of which are on the worldwide endangered list, and 250 species of bird, and is thought to be the home of several rare white elephants. There are known to be around 50 Asian elephants, 10 tigers, Samba deer, giant muntjac, leopard, the recently discovered golden jackal and green peafowl. The park is surprisingly flat – save Yok Don Mountain in the middle at 482 m and Yok Da Mountain (482 m) further north – and is, surprisingly, a less-than-dense deciduous forest which makes it easy to trek on an elephant though few wild animals congregate where elephant treks occur. There are 120 species of tree and 854 species of flora. Within its boundaries, also, there are 25 villages of different ethnic tribes who maintain a number of domesticated elephants. Trekking deep into the park and staying in tents near Yok Don Mountain is probably the only chance of seeing wildlife of any great rarity but, alas, the rare become rarer with each passing year. The less adventurous (or those with smaller elephant-trekking budgets) will have to make do with one-hour rides or simply watching one of the village's elephants at work. Note that the rainy season is from April to October.

LAK LAKE
The serene Lak Lake is about 50 km southeast of Buon Ma Thuot and can be explored by dugout. It is an attraction in its own right but is all the more compelling on account of the surrounding Mnong villages. Early morning mists hang above the calm waters and mingle with the columns of woodsmoke rising from the longhouses. The Mnong number about 50,000 and are matriarchal. They have been famed as elephant catchers for hundreds of years, although the elephants are now used for tourist rides rather than in their traditional role for dragging logs from the forest. In order to watch the elephants taking their evening wallow in the cool waters and to appreciate the tranquillity of sunrise over the lake, stay overnight at a Mnong village, such as Buon Juin. An evening supping with your hosts, sharing rice wine and sleeping in the simplicity of a Mnong longhouse is an ideal introduction to these genial people.

→ DALAT

Dalat is an attractive town situated on a plateau in the Central Highlands at an altitude of almost 1500m. The town itself, a former French hill station, is centred on a lake – Xuan Huong – amid rolling countryside and is dotted with more than 2000 French villas. To the north are five volcanic peaks of the Langbiang mountains, rising to 2400 m. In the area are forests, waterfalls, and an abundance of orchids, roses and other temperate flora.

ARRIVING IN DALAT
Getting there Dalat is on Highway 20. There are daily flights from Ho Chi Minh City and Hanoi. There are frequent bus connections with Pleiku, Kontum, Ho Chi Minh City, Nha Trang, Buon Ma Thuot, Phan Thiet, and Phan Rang. Open Tour Buses connect Dalat with Nha Trang, Mui Ne and Ho Chi Minh City.

Moving on From Dalat there are onward connections by plane for those short of time, or continue by bus to Nha Trang (see page 170). An alternative route from Dalat would be to head southwest along Highway 20 to Ho Chi Minh City, stopping off at the Nam Cat Tien National Park (see page 167) en route.

Getting around Dalat is rather a large town and there are a number of hills. A plentiful selection of taxis is available as are the ubiquitous *Honda ôm* drivers, including those from **Easy Riders**.

Best time to visit The best time to visit is from November to May when there is less rainfall and pleasant temperatures. At the weekends the centre is closed to traffic between 1900 and 2200 allowing for stalls to set up on Nguyen Thi Minh Khai Street. As different indigenous groups live in the Central Highlands, there are festivals all year round. Buffalo sacrifice ceremonies take place in Mnong, Sedang and Cotu communities after the spring harvest.

Tourist information Dalat Tourist ① *www.dalattourist.com.vn*, is the state-run travel company for Lam Dong Province. There are also a number of tour operators that offer good information and tours.

BACKGROUND

Dr Alexandre Yersin, a protégé of Louis Pasteur, founded Dalat in 1893. He stumbled across Dalat as he was trying to find somewhere cool to escape from the sweltering summer heat of the coast and lowlands. The lush alpinesque scenery of Dalat impressed the French and it soon became the secondary main city in the south after Saigon. (In the summer months the government moved lock, stock and barrel to Dalat where it was cooler). There are plenty of original French-style villas, many of which have been converted into hotels while some remain in private ownership; others are government offices. The last emperor of Vietnam, Bao Dai, lived here and it is possible to see his former imperial residence.

Dalat soon took on the appearance of Paris in the mountains. A golf course was made and a luxurious hotel was built. In both the Second World War and the American War high-ranking officials of the opposing armies would while away a pleasant couple of days playing golf against each other before having to return to the battlefields.

Of all the highland cities Dalat was the least affected by the American War. The main reason being that at the time the only entrance into Dalat was up the Prenn Pass. There was a small heliport at Cam Ly (part of Dalat) and also a radio listening station on Langbian Mountain but nothing else of note.

→ PLACES IN DALAT

The town is currently undergoing a huge renovation programme. New roads are being built and existing roads are being upgraded. A large new Phuong Trang bus station has been constructed near the cable car station. Dalat is the honeymoon capital of southern Vietnam. There is a quaint belief – not widely held – that unless you go on honeymoon to Dalat then you are not really married.

XUAN HUONG LAKE

Originally the Grand Lake, Xuan Huong Lake was renamed in 1954. It was created in 1919 after a small dam was constructed on the Cam Ly River. It is the attractive centrepiece of the town and a popular exercise area for the local inhabitants of whom many will, first thing in the morning, walk around the lake stopping every so often to perform t'ai chi exercises. Power-walking at dusk is also popular. The lake was drained in 2010 so as to remove accumulated silt and construct a new road across the center.

DALAT FLOWER GARDEN

ⓘ *Vuon Hoa Dalat, 2 Phu Dong Thien Vuong St, daily 0700-1800, 10,000d.*

At the northeast end of the lake is the Dalat Flower Garden. It supports a range of plants including orchids, roses, lilies and hydrangeas. Signs are not in English, only Latin and Vietnamese; the one English sign directs visitors to the orchidarium. There are kiosks selling drinks and ice creams and there's a lake with pedaloes.

COLONIAL VILLAS

Many of the large colonial villas – almost universally washed in pastel yellow – are 1930s and 1940s vintage. Some have curved walls, railings and are almost nautical in inspiration; others are reminiscent of houses in Provence. Many of the larger villas can be found along **Tran Hung Dao Street** and a number of these are now being converted into villa hotels. Sadly many of the villas have fallen into a very sorry state and are looking decidedly unloved. Given their architectural significance this is a great pity. Perhaps the largest and most impressive house on Tran Hung Dao is the former residence of the Governor General at 12 Tran Hung Dao Street – now the **Hotel Dinh 2**. The villa is 1930s in style, with large

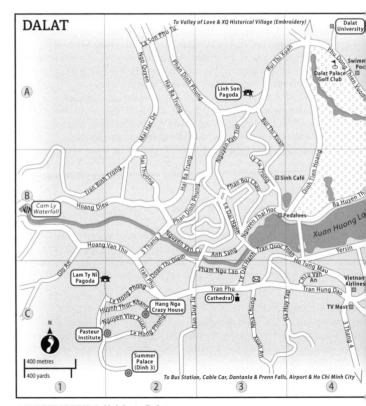

airy rooms and furniture and occupies a magnificent position set among mountain pines and overlooking the town and lake. The house is a popular place for domestic tourists to have their photographs taken. It is possible to stay here although it is often booked up and is popular with members of Lam Dong People's Committee.

DALAT CATHEDRAL

ⓘ *Tran Phu St. Mass is held twice a day Mon-Sat 0515 and 1715 and on Sun at 0515, 0700, 0830, 1600 and 1800. The recently painted tan and cream-coloured cathedral has a good choir and attracts a large and enthusiastic congregation.*

The single-tiered cathedral is visible from the lake and 100 m from the Novotel hotel. At the top of the turret is a chicken-shaped wind dial. It is referred to locally as the 'Chicken Cathedral'. Construction began in 1931, although the building was not completed until the Japanese 'occupation' in 1942. The stained-glass windows, with their vivid colours and use of pure, clean lines, were crafted in France by Louis Balmet, the same man who made the windows in Nha Trang and Danang cathedrals, between 1934 and 1940. Sadly, most have not survived the ravages of time. Lining the nave are blocks of woodcarvings of Christ and the crucifixion.

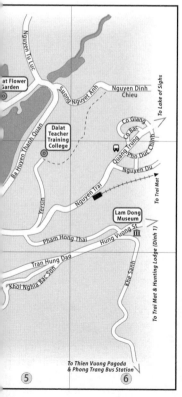

SUMMER PALACE (DINH 3) AND DINH 1

ⓘ *Le Hong Phong St, T63-382 6858, 0730-1100 and 1330-1600, 10,000d. Visitors have to wear covers over their shoes to protect the wooden floors. You can dress up in emperors' clothing and have your picture taken, 30,000d. Café, ice creams available.*

Vietnam's last emperor, Bao Dai, had a Summer Palace on Le Hong Phong Street, about 2 km from the town centre and now known as Dinh 3. Built on a hill with views on every side, it is art deco in style both inside and out, and rather modest for a palace. The palace was built between 1933 and 1938. The stark interior contains little to indicate that this was the home of an emperor – almost all of Bao Dai's personal belongings have been removed. The impressive dining room contains an etched-glass map of Vietnam, while the study has Bao Dai's desk, a few personal ornaments and photographs, noticeably of the family who, in 1954, were exiled to France where they lived. One of the family photos shows Bao Dai's son, the prince Bao Long, in full military dress uniform. He died in July 2007 in France aged 71.

Emperor Bao Dai's daughters are still alive and were, in a spirit of reconciliation, invited back to visit Vietnam in the mid-1990s. They politely declined (one of the reasons given was that as they were both in their 70s it would have been too much effort), although the grandchildren may one day return. The emperor's bedroom and bathroom are open to public scrutiny as is the little terrace from his bedroom where, apparently, on a clear night he would gaze at the stars. The family drawing room is open together with a little commentary on which chair was used by whom. The palace is very popular with rowdy Vietnamese tourists who have their photographs taken wherever they can. The gardens are colourful and well maintained, though have a carnival atmosphere. From the moon balcony you can see the garden has been arranged into the shape of the Bao Dai stamp.

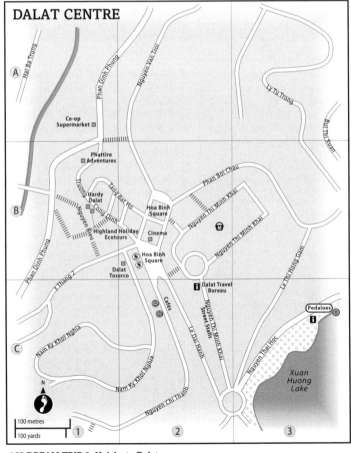

PASTEUR INSTITUTE
ⓘ *Le Hong Phong, not open to the public.*
The yellow-wash institute was opened in 1935 and was built to produce vaccines for keeping the colonial population healthy. Although small and modest it is quite an attractive building fashioned in a series of cubes.

LAM TY NI PAGODA
ⓘ *Down a track off Le Hong Phong St.*
Lam Ty Ni Pagoda is unremarkable save for a charming monk, Vien Thuc, who lives here. Vien Thuc arrived in 1968 and in 1987 he finished the gateway that leads up through a garden to the figure of Quan Am. Vien Thuc originally named his garden – which is almost Japanese in inspiration – An Lac Vien, or Peace Garden, but has now decided that Divine Calmness Bamboo Garden has a better ring to it. Vien Thuc is a scholar, poet, artist, philosopher, mystic, divine and entrepreneur but is best known for his paintings of which, by his own reckoning, there are more than 100,000. And, wandering through the maze of rustic huts and shacks tacked on to the back of the temple one can easily believe this: the walls are lined deep with hanging sheets which bear his simple but distinctive calligraphy and philosophy: "Living in the present how beautiful this very moment is", "Zen painting destroys millennium sorrows", "The mystique, silence and melody universal of love" and so on. Vien Thuc shows visitors around with a mixture of pride "I work very hard" and self-deprecating modesty, chuckling to himself as if to say, "I must be mad". His work is widely known: he has exhibited in Paris, New York and Holland as well as on the web. His paintings and books of poetry are for sale at prices that are creeping up to levels high enough for you to wish you could buy shares in him.

The main sanctuary of the pagoda was built in 1961 and contains an image of the Buddha with an electric halo. Nowadays, the gates are often locked; he is unwelcoming to Vietnamese and has been known to turn certain nationalities away.

HANG NGA CRAZY HOUSE
ⓘ *3 Huynh Thuc Khang, T63-382 2070, daily 0700-1800, 8000d.*
The slightly wacky theme is maintained at the nearby Tree House leading many to wonder what they put in the water for this corner of Dalat to nurture so many creative eccentrics. Doctor Dang Viet Nga has, over a period of many years, built up her hotel in organic fashion. The rooms and gardens resemble scenes taken from the pages of a fairy storybook. Guests sleep inside mushrooms, trees and giraffes and sip tea under giant cobwebs. There is a honeymoon room, an ant room and plenty more. It is not a particularly comfortable place to stay and the number of visitors limits privacy. (Dr Dang Viet Nga also built the Children's Centre at 38 Tran Phu Street.)

DALAT MARKET
ⓘ *At the end of Nguyen Thi Minh Khai St.*
Dalat Market (Cho Dalat) sells a dazzling array of exotic fruits and vegetables grown in the temperate climate of the area – plums, strawberries, carrots, persimmons, loganberries, mulberries, artichokes, durians and avocados. The forbidding appearance of the market is masked by the riot of colour of the flowers on sale, including gladioli, irises, roses, gerbera, chrysanthemums and marigolds. Sampling the immense variety of candied fruit here is the highlight of any visit to Dalat.

LINH SON PAGODA

ⓘ 120 Nguyen Van Troi St just up from the intersection with Phan Dinh Phung St.

The Linh Son Pagoda, built in 1942, is kept in immaculate condition. Perched on a small hillock, two dragon balustrades front the sanctuary, themselves flanked by two ponds with miniature mountain scenes. To the right is a small, Dutch-looking pagoda tower. Behind is a school of Buddhist studies attended by dozens of young, grey-clad men and women.

DALAT UNIVERSITY

ⓘ 1 Phu Dong Thien Vuong St.

Out near the golf course, Dalat University was founded as a Roman Catholic University in 1957 and taken over by the government in 1975. It provides for thousands of students from central and southern Vietnam and sits in grounds with cherry trees. It is strong on English teaching and science and has links with the Nuclear Research Institute. Symbolic of the change in political fortunes, a huge red communist star atop the grey obelisk in the University's grounds actually conceals a crucifix.

DALAT TEACHER TRAINING COLLEGE

ⓘ Yersin St.

Some of the finest buildings in town are educational. One of these is the Dalat Teacher Training College, the old Lycée Yersin. The long curved wall of the school can be seen from the outside. It ends in a blind tower the top of which can be seen from miles away. Sadly the college has neglected its architectural heritage and many of the buildings are abandoned and overgrown. Foreigners cannot walk into the grounds. The track that skirts around the side of the college has an interesting row of modest houses, perhaps originally for teachers.

DALAT RAILWAY STATION

ⓘ 20 m off Quang Trung St, T63-383 4409.

Dalat station is the last in Vietnam to retain its original French art deco architecture; the coloured-glass windows remain intact. Its steep pitched roofs could handle the heaviest of alpine snowfalls for which, presumably, they were designed. The waiting room, formerly segregated by race, is in good condition.

The station was opened in 1938, five years after the completion of the rack-and-pinion track from Saigon, and was closed in 1964. Despite the fact it is virtually unused, the building is surprisingly well maintained and beds of geraniums flourish under the sun and the careful hand of an unseen gardener. In 1991, a 7-km stretch to the village of Trai Mat was reopened and every day a small Russian-built diesel car makes the journey (daily at 0800, 0930, 1100, 1400, 1530, US$5 return, 30 minutes), minimum six people. There is also an old steam engine, which is occasionally fired up, and a Renault diesel car.

LAM DONG MUSEUM

ⓘ 4 Hung Vuong St, T63-382239, Tue-Sat 0730-1130, 1330-1630, 4000d.

The museum contains extensive tribal artefacts from the local Lam Dong Province tribes as well as natural history exhibits and old photos from when Dalat was founded up to the modern day. Particularly interesting are the ancient Dong Son relics and artifacts from Funnan-era temples recently discovered in Cat Tien National Park. At the time of this writing the museum was temporarily housed in the palace above the museum. The museum below will reopen in 2011 with extensive renovations and new collections.

THIEN VUONG PAGODA

ⓘ *4 km south of the centre of town, at the end of Khe Sanh St.*

Begun in the 1950s, this stark pagoda has recently been expanded and renovated. In the main sanctuary are three massive bronze-coloured, sandalwood standing figures with Sakyamuni, the historic Buddha, in the centre. The pagoda, though in no way artistically significant, is popular with local visitors and stalls nearby sell local jams, artichoke tea, cordials and dried mushrooms.

HUNTING LODGE (DINH 1)

Emperor Bao Dai also had a hunting lodge that used to be a museum. East of the town centre, Dinh 1 sported 1930s furniture, antique telephone switchboards, and although it was not sumptuous, nevertheless had a feel of authenticity. It has now closed and the talk is of it reopening as a casino.

WATERFALLS

Datanla Falls ⓘ *along a track, 5 km out of town on Highway 20 towards HCMC, T63-383 1804, 0700-1700, 5000d,* the path leads steeply downwards into a forested ravine; it is an easy hike there, but tiring on the return journey. However, the **Alpine Coaster**, a toboggan on rails (T63-383 1804, 35,000d return), makes the journey faster and easier. The falls – really a cascade – are hardly spectacular, but few people come here except at weekends so it is usually peaceful.

    Prenn Falls ⓘ *12 km from Dalat, on the route to HCMC, next to the road, T63-353 0785, 0700-1700, 10,000d,* the falls were dedicated to Queen Sirikit of Thailand when she visited them in 1959. Though it underwent renovations a few years ago, the falls began to suffer pollution and degredation in 2010 because dredged silt from Xuan Huong lake in Dalat was being dumped at the source of the falls. The falls are not that good but there is a pleasant rope bridge that can be crossed and pleasant views of the surrounding area.

    About 20 km north of Bao Loc on the Bao Loc Plateau are the Dambri Falls I Highway 20, 120 km from Dalat, July to November only; get a *xe ôm* from Bao Loc or take a tour. These are considered the most impressive falls in southern Vietnam and are worth an excursion for those who have time.

DALAT CABLE CAR (CÁP TREO)

ⓘ *It starts south of town off 3 April Rd, T63-383 7938, 35,000d single, 50,000d return, 0730-1700 and is widely popular with both locals and tourists.*

The journey from top to bottom takes about 15 minutes and leads to a Thien Vien Truc Lam Pagoda and Paradise Lake.

LAKE OF SIGHS AND VALLEY OF LOVE

ⓘ *The Lake of Sighs is 5 km northeast of Dalat (5000d) and the Valley of Love is 5 km due north (6000d). Because of the cool climate, it is very pleasant to reach the lakes, forests and waterfalls around Dalat by bicycle. In fact a day spent travelling is probably more enjoyable than the sights themselves.*

The lake is said by some to be named after the sighs of the girls being courted by handsome young men from the military academy in Dalat. Another unlikely theory is that the name was coined after a young Vietnamese maiden, Mai Nuong, drowned herself in the lake in the 18th century. The story is that her lover, Hoang Tung, had joined the army to fight the Chinese who were mounting one of their periodic invasions of the country, and had thoughtlessly failed to tell her. Devastated, and thinking that Hoang Tung no longer loved her; she committed suicide in the lake. Not long ago the lake was surrounded by thick forest; today it is a thin wood. The area is busy at weekends.

The Valley of Love does not refer to a Jimi Hendrix or other psychedelic-era song but to **Thung Lung Tinh Yeu** ① *8000d or free if you take a path to the side*. Boats can be hired on the lake here; there is also horse riding and a few refreshment stands.

TRAI MAT

① *7 km from the centre of Dalat. By motorbike, follow Tran Hung Dao St which becomes Hung Vuong St, past SOS Village on the left, and keep going. Every day a small Russian-built diesel railway car makes the return journey (US$5 return, 30 mins) at 0800, 0930, 1100, 1400, 1530.*

Trai Mat Village is home to the local Coho tribe and can be reached by train from Dalat. In 1991 a 7-km stretch of track from Dalat railway station to the village of Trai Mat was reopened after nearly 20 years of closure. The journey to Trai Mat village takes you near the Lake of Sighs and past immaculately tended vegetable gardens; no space on the valley floors or sides is wasted and the high-intensity agriculture is a marvellous sight. Trai Mat is a prosperous market village with piles of produce from the surrounding area. Walk 300m up the road and to the left a narrow lane leads down to Chua Linh Phuoc, an attractive Buddhist temple more than 50 years old. It is notable for its huge Buddha and mosaic-adorned pillars. The mosaics are made of broken rice bowls and fragments of beer bottle. Just outside of Trai Mat is the flower garden of professor Jan Sook Kim, who is a world-renowned expert on the cultivation and growing of orchids. On a hill above the town is a new Cai Dai temple; one of the largest in the country.

LAT VILLAGE AND LANGBIAN MOUNTAIN

① *You pass through the Lat village to reach Langbian Mountain. The main gate is normally open 0800-1700, 7000d.*

The village itself is a mixture of old and new – there are traditional wooden stilt houses that are opposite new two- to three-storey houses. The village itself has to a large degree lost its traditional ways (there was a charming tradition in which the local Lat teenagers would bathe in the local rivers au natural. This was practised until the mid-1990s when the voyeuristic Vietnamese put a stop to it).

Langbian Mountain itself is the highest mountain in southern Vietnam at just over 2000 m. It housed an American radar listening post during the war. Nowadays it is visited primarily for its stunning vistas of the surrounding areas and also for its abundant wildlife, in particular birds. It is a trek to get to the top and sensible walking shoes would be appropriate.

LANG GA (CHICKEN VILLAGE)

① *Just off the Dalat–HCMC road, 18 km from Dalat, Highway 20.*

This is a pleasant village of the Coho tribe of which the most noticeable sight is a 5-m-high concrete chicken in the middle of the village. There are numerous different stories as to why it was built with the more popular one being that it was constructed in honour of a local village wench who was tragically killed while searching for a nine-clawed chicken in the surrounding mountains to give to her fiancé for an engagement present. The local officials at the end of the war asked the inhabitants what they would like and were asked for the concrete chicken. The other version of the story of its origin is that it was built to commemorate the heroic peasant chicken farmers.

There are several weaving shops in the village that provide good-quality products at a fraction of what they would cost in Dalat or Ho Chi Minh City. Do stop and talk to the women who do the weaving; some of them speak excellent English learnt from visitors. They will show you the black bridal shawl with a red stripe (black for the wedding and red for good luck).

NAM CAT TIEN NATIONAL PARK

ⓘ *About 50 km south of Bao Loc (at the small town of Tan Phu) turn off Highway 20 to Nam Cat Tien, which is about 25 km down a rough road (not well signposted). 50,000d. Guides can be hired and accommodation is available. Take tough, long-sleeved and long-legged clothing, jungle boots and leech socks if possible and plenty of insect repellent.*

This newly created national park is about 150 km north of Ho Chi Minh City and is often visited as an excursion from the capital. The park is one of the last surviving areas of natural bamboo and dipterocarp forest in southern Vietnam. It is also one of the few places where populations of large mammals can be found in Vietnam – tiger, elephant, bear and the last few (possibly only four or five) remaining Javan rhino. There are also 300 species of bird, smaller mammals, reptiles and butterflies. The park is managed by 20 rangers who besides helping protect the flora and fauna also conduct research and show visitors around. They do not speak English.

DALAT TO NHA TRANG

The road is spectacular as it heads up to the **Ngoan Muc Pass** then descends sharply towards the coastal plain, past banana plantations and water pipes. In 2007, a new 54-km road between Dalat and Nha Trang opened, cutting the journey by 80 km and passing through the **Bidup National Park** of the Ba (Lady) Mountain. The road linked route 723 of Lam Dong Province to Provincial Route 2 of Khanh Hoa Province.

HOI AN TO DALAT LISTINGS

WHERE TO STAY

You'll find everything from homestay to regional hotel resorts to serviceable town hotels in the remote Central Highlands. At Dalat, itself, everything from a backpacker hostel, to a smart town hotel, to a beautiful spa resort in the pine hills can be found.

Pleiku
$ Ialy Hotel, 89 Hung Vuong St, T059-382 4843, ialyhotel@dng.vnn.vn. Excellent location opposite the main post office. Reasonable sized, good-value rooms with en suite facilities, a/c and satellite TV. Staff are friendly enough but no English is spoken. The restaurant on the 1st floor is only open for breakfast. ATM in the lobby.

Kontum
$$ Indochine (Dong Duong) Hotel, 30 Bach Dang St, T060-386 3334, www.indochinehotel.vn. The views from this hotel are fantastic. You can look right up the river to the mountains beyond. Decent-sized rooms with mod cons including hairdryer. The breakfasts could be better.

Buon Ma Thuot
$$$-$$ Damsan Hotel, 212-214 Nguyen Cong Tru St, T0500-385 1234, www.damsan hotel.com.vn. A good hotel with a pool and tennis court and large restaurant. Service is good and rooms are comfortable. There's a lovely balconied coffee shop and bar, **Da Quy**, opposite.

Lak Lake
It costs US$5 to stay in a Mnong longhouse at Buon Jun; contact **Daklak Tourist** (www.daklaktourist.com.vn, in Buon Ma Thuot, to make arrangements.).

Dalat
$$$$ Ana Mandara Villas Dalat Resort & Spa, Le Lai St, T063-355 5888, http://anamandara-resort.com. Restored French villas are perched on a hillside, surrounded by fruit farms. Each villa has a couple of bedrooms, a sitting room and dining room. The heated pool, buried amid the secluded hillside villas, is lovely. There is also a central villa that houses a French bistro and wine bar. The Spa Experience has been created in one of the villas.

$$$ Empress Hotel, 5 Nguyen Thai Hoc St, T063-383 3888, www.empresshotelvn.com. This is a particularly attractive hotel in a lovely position overlooking the lake. All rooms are arranged around a small courtyard that traps the sun and is a great place for breakfast or to pen a postcard. The rooms are large with very comfortable beds and the more expensive ones have luxurious bathrooms so try to get a room upgrade. Attentive and courteous staff. A great-value hotel with the best view of Xuan Huong Lake.

$$ Best Western Dalat Plaza Hotel, 9 Le Dai Hanh, T063-625 0999, www.bestwestern.com. The new **Best Western** is a breath of fresh air and affordably priced. Located in the city centre with views of the lake. The restaurant provides room service, which is uncommon in Vietnam. Facilities include a fitness centre, spa and free Wi-Fi.

$ Hoa Binh 1 (Peace Hotel 1), 64 Truong Cong Dinh St, T063-382 2787, peace12@hcm.vnn.vn. One of the better low-cost places with 16 rooms in a good location. The 5 rooms at the back are set around a small yard; quiet but not much view. Rooms at the front have a view but can be a bit noisy. The rooms have TV, fan and mosquito nets. A friendly place with an all-day café.

RESTAURANTS

All the Central Highlands towns offer good Vietnamese restaurants. At Dalat, the choice is much greater. Don't miss the coffee in Buon Ma Thuot, Vietnam's coffee capital.

Pleiku
$ Thien Thanh Restaurant, 22 Pham Van Dong St, off Le Loi past the Ialy Hotel, T59-382 7011. A modern restaurant that is tastefully decorated serving up a good selection of Vietnamese and international cuisine. The outdoor seating area has great views over the surrounding countryside. The food is plentiful, fresh and good value for money.

Kontum
$ Dakbla's Café, 168 Nguyen Hue St, T60-386 2584. Modern restaurant filled with ethnic minority artefacts, it has the most interesting decor in the region. The pleasant staff are conversant in several languages (English, French and German) and there's a good selection of food at reasonable prices.

Buon Ma Thuot
$$-$ Thang Loi Restaurant, Thang Loi Hotel, 1 Phan Chu Trinh St. This is arguably the best restaurant in town. Set on the ground floor of the hotel it overlooks Liberty Sq. It has a good selection of Vietnamese and international cuisine (their chips are particularly good) and plenty of noodle and rice dishes and fruit. Prices are reasonable and the service is friendly and efficient.

Dalat
$$-$ Empress Restaurant, Empress Hotel. Open all day and specializing in Chinese fare but with a good selection of Vietnamese and Western dishes. Ideal breakfast setting, al fresco around the fountain in the courtyard.
$ Stop and Go Café, 2A Ly Tu Trong St, T063-382 8458. A café and art gallery run by the local poet, Mr Duy Viet. Sit inside or on the terrace as he bustles around rustling up breakfast, pulling out volumes of visitors' books and his own collected works. The garden is an overrun wilderness.
$ Tu An's Peace Café, 57 Truong Cong Dinh St, T063-351 1524. Tu An insists that hers is the original **Peace Café**, as she is surrounded by several restaurants all by the same name. Both the foreign and Vietnamese food is fantastic. Try the pasta and goulash or just ask for any dish you want and she can almost always make it.

WHAT TO DO

Dalat
Tour operators
Dalat Toserco, No7, 3 Thang 2 St, T063-382 2125. Budget transport and a good selection of tours. Slightly more expensive than **Sinh Café**.
Easy-riders.net, The Hangout Bar, 71 Truong Cong Dinh St, T090-959 6580 (mob), www.easy-riders.net. Personalized motorbike tours from a fluent English-speaker and highly-trained graduate from a 4-year university tourism program.
Groovy Gecko Adventure Tours, 65 Truong Cong Dinh, T091-824 8976 (mob), www.groovygeckotours.net.
Offers trekking adventures on Langbiang Mountain, canyoning, mountain biking to Mui Ne, abseiling and rock climbing. Also offers trekking to hilltribe minority villages.
Phat Tire Adventures, 109 Nguyen Van Troi St, T063-382 9422, www.phattire ventures.com. Canyoning from US$29; rock climbing US$35; mountain biking from US$38; trekking from US$22; kayaking, US$30.
Sinh Tourist, 4a Bui Thi Xuan, T063-382 2663, www.thesinhtourist.vn. Part of the nationwide **Sinh Café** chain. Primarily provides cheap travel to HCMC and Nha Trang. Also arranges local tours.

NHA TRANG AND AROUND

Nha Trang is Vietnam's only real seaside city. It nestles amid the protective embrace of the surrounding hills and islands. The long golden beach, which only a very few years ago was remarkably empty, fills up quickly these days, and it is easy to see why. The light has a beautifully radiant quality and the air is clear; the colours are vivid, particularly the blues of the sea, sky and fishing boats berthed on the river.

An important Cham settlement, Nha Trang retains distinguished and well-preserved Cham towers. It is a centuries-old fishing town established in the sheltered mouth of the Cai Estuary. A port which can handle small coastal traders was built here in 1924. Its clear waters and offshore islands won wide acclaim in the 1960s and its new-found prosperity is based firmly on tourism with big name chain hotels opening along its shores.

ARRIVING IN NHA TRANG

Getting there Nha Trang's airport is 34 km away at Cam Ranh; there are flights from Hanoi, Ho Chi Minh City and Danang. There is an airport bus service into town (40 minutes, 40,000d) or taxis (US$10-15); some hotels arrange transfers. The town is on the main north–south railway line and there are connections with Ho Chi Minh City and Hanoi (and all stops between). The main bus terminal is west of the town centre; *xe ôms* take passengers into town. Nha Trang is also served by Open Tour Buses.

Moving on Buses to the airport leave from the bus station, 200 m from the main road, signposted 'Bus Station to Cam Ranh Airport', two hours before every flight. Long-distance buses to Ho Chi Minh City, Danang, Buon Ma Thuot, Dalat and Hué leave from the main bus station. Open Tour Buses depart from their relevant operator's café.

Getting around Nha Trang is negotiable on foot – just. But there are bicycles and motorbikes for hire everywhere and the usual cyclos. Some hotels and the tour companies have cars for out-of-town excursions.

Tourist information Khanh Hoa Tours ① *1 Tran Hung Dao St, T58-352 6753, www. nhatrangtourist.com.vn, daily 0700-1130, 1330-1700,* the official city tour office, can arrange visa extensions, car and boat hire and tours of the area. It's also a **Vietnam Airlines** booking office. It's not that helpful; plenty of the tour operators in town have good information.

Safety There have been a reports of revellers being mugged at night and men being relieved of their wallets by attractive women. Don't carry huge sums of money or your valuables with you on a night out. We've also received reports about money going missing during massage sessions.

BACKGROUND

Nha Trang is a firmly established favourite of Vietnamese as well as foreign visitors and Nha Trangites of all backgrounds and persuasions endeavour to ease the dollar from the traveller's sweaty paw. Nevertheless, there is a permanent relaxed holiday atmosphere, the streets are not crowded and the motorbikes still cruise at a leisurely pace.

The name Nha Trang is thought to be derived from the Cham word *yakram*, meaning bamboo river, and the surrounding area was a focal point of the Cham Kingdom – some of the country's best-preserved Cham towers lie close by. Nha Trang was besieged for nine months during the Tay Son rebellion in the late 18th century (see box, page 175), before eventually falling to the rebel troops. There are, in reality, two Nha Trangs: popular Nha Trang, which is a lively seaside town consisting of a long, palm and casuarina-fringed beach and one or two streets running parallel to it offering an active nightlife and popular bars and restaurants;, and commercial Nha Trang to the north of Yersin Street, which is a bustling city with an attractive array of Chinese shophouses.

→ PLACES IN NHA TRANG

THE BEACH
The beach and beachside promenade have been spruced up in recent years and it is now a pleasant place to relax although there are the occasional hawkers. Beach beds cost 25,000d per session; the nicest being in front of the Sailing Club and La Louisiane. There are fixed thatched umbrellas in the sand and public toilets.

PONAGAR CHAM TEMPLE COMPLEX
ⓘ *0600-1800, 15,000d. The best time to visit the towers is late afternoon, 1600-1700.*
On a hill just outside the city is the Ponagar Cham Temple complex, known locally as Thap Ba. Originally the complex consisted of eight towers, four of which remain. Their stylistic differences indicate they were built at different times between the seventh and 12th centuries. The largest (at 23 m high) was built in AD 817 and contains a statue of Ponagar, also known by the Vietnamese as Lady Thien Y-ana (who was the beautiful wife of Prince Bac Hai), as well as a fine and very large lingam. She taught the Cham people of the area weaving and new agricultural techniques, and they built the tower in her honour. The other towers are dedicated to gods: the central tower to Cri Cambhu (which has become a fertility temple for childless couples); the northwest tower to Sandhaka (woodcutter and foster-father to Ponagar); and the south tower to Ganeca (Ponagar's daughter).

To get to the temple complex you can either walk or catch a cyclo. Follow 2 Thang 4 Street north out of town; Cham Ponagar is just over the second of two bridges (Xom Bong bridge), a couple of kilometres from the city centre.

CAI RIVER ESTUARY AND FISHING BOATS
En route to the towers, the road crosses the Cai River estuary where there is a diversity of craft including Nha Trang's elegant fleet of blue fishing boats, lined with red and complete with painted eyes for warding off sea monsters, and coracles (*cái thúng*) for getting to the boats and mechanical fish traps. The traps take the form of nets which are supported by long arms; the arms are hinged to a platform on stilts and are raised and lowered by wires connected to a capstan which is turned, sometimes by hand but more commonly by foot.

LONG SON PAGODA
ⓘ *23 Thang 10 St.*
The best-known pagoda in Nha Trang is the Long Son Pagoda, built in 1963. Inside the sanctuary is an unusual image of the Buddha, backlit with natural light. Murals depicting the *jataka* stories decorate the upper walls. To the right of the sanctuary, stairs lead up to

a 9-m-high white Buddha, perched on a hill top, from where there are fine views. Before reaching the white pagoda, take a left on the stairs. Through an arch behind the pagoda you'll see a 14-m-long reclining Buddha. Commissioned in 2003, it is an impressive sight.

The pagoda commemorates the monks and nuns who died demonstrating against the Diem government – in particular those who, through self-immolation, brought the despotic nature of the Diem regime and its human rights abuses to the attention of the public.

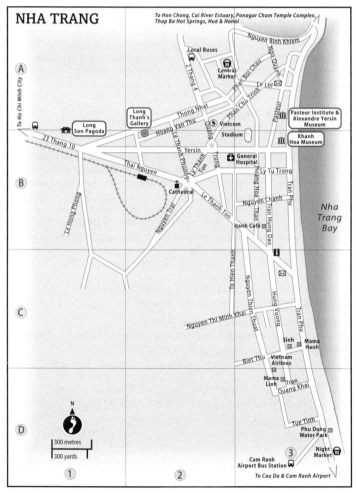

NHA TRANG

To Hon Chong, Cai River Estuary, Ponagar Cham Temple Complex,
Thap Ba Hot Springs, Hué & Hanoi

Nguyen Binh Khiem

To Ho Chi Minh City

Local Buses

Central Market

2 Thang 4

Phan Boi Chau

Ngo Quyen

Le Loi

A

Phan Chu Trinh

Long Thanh's Gallery

Thong Nhat

Pasteur Institute & Alexandre Yersin Museum

Long Son Pagoda

Hoang Van Thu

Vietcom

Khanh Hoa Museum

23 Thang 10

Yersin

Stadium

Le Thanh Phuong

Ly Thanh Ton

Quang Trung

Hoang Hoa Tham

General Hospital

Ly Tu Trong

Tran Phu

Thai Nguyen

B

Le Hong Phong

Nguyen Trai

Cathedral

Le Thanh Ton

Nguyen Chanh

Tran Hung Dao

Nha Trang Bay

Hanh Café

To Hien Thanh

Nguyen Thien Thuat

Nguyen Thi Minh Khai

Hung Vuong

C

Tran Phu

Sinh

Mama Hanh

Biet Thu

Vietnam Airlines

Mama Linh

Tran Quang Khai

Tue Tinh

Phu Dong Water Park

N

300 metres

300 yards

D

Cam Ranh Airport Bus Station

Night Market

3

To Cau Da & Cam Ranh Airport

1

2

ON THE ROAD
Alexandre Yersin

Alexandre John Emille Yersin was born in 1863 in Canton Vaud, Switzerland. He enrolled at the University of Lausanne and completed his medical education in Paris where he became an assistant to Louis Pasteur. In 1888, Yersin adopted French citizenship. To the astonishment of all he became a ship's doctor; he visited the Far East and in 1891 landed in Nha Trang.

Two years later, as part of his exploration of Vietnam he 'discovered' the Dalat Plateau which he recommended for development as a hill resort owing to its beauty and temperate climate. The following year, in 1894, he was urged to visit Hong Kong to assist in an outbreak of the plague. He identified the baccilus which was named *Yersinia pestis*.

In 1895 he set up a laboratory in Nha Trang which, in 1902, became a Pasteur Institute, the first to be established outside France. Here he developed an anti-serum for the treatment of plague. He established a cattle farm for the production of serum and vaccines and for the improvement of breeding stock at Suoi Dau, 25 km south of Nha Trang. Yersin was responsible for the introduction to Vietnam of commercial crops such as coffee, rubber and the cinchona (quinine) tree.

In his retirement he indulged his passions – astrology, photography and observation of the hydrographic conditions of Nha Trang Bay.

Yersin died in 1943 and was buried at Suoi Dau. His tombstone, simply engraved 'Alexandre Yersin 1863-1943', can be seen today at Suoi Dau. Take Highway 1, 25 km south of Nha Trang, look for the sign 'Tombeau de Alexandre Yersin'. The key to the gate is kept with a local family. The tomb is 1.5 km from the gate.

NHA TRANG CATHEDRAL
ⓘ *Mass Mon-Sat 0500 and 1630, Sun 0500, 0700, and 1630.*
Granite-coloured (though built of concrete) and imposing, the cathedral was built between 1928 and 1933 on a small rock outcrop. It was not until 1961, however, that the building was consecrated as a cathedral for the diocese of Nha Trang and Ninh Thuan. The cathedral has a single, crenellated tower, a fine, vaulted ceiling, with stained glass in the upper sections of its windows and pierced metal in the lower. The windows over the altar depict Jesus with Mary and Joseph, Joan of Arc and Sainte Thérèse. Like the windows in Dalat and Danang cathedrals they were made in Grenoble by Louis Balmet. Fourteen rather fine pictures depict the stations of the cross: they look French but there is no attribution and no one seems sure of their provenance. The path to the cathedral runs off Nguyen Trai Street.

ALEXANDRE YERSIN MUSEUM
ⓘ *10 Tran Phu St, T58-382 2355, Mon-Fri 0730-1100, 1400-1630, 26,000d. The curator is helpful, friendly and speaks fluent French and English.*
The Yersin Museum is contained within the colonnaded **Pasteur Institute** founded by the great scientist's protégé, Dr Alexandre Yersin. Swiss-born Yersin first arrived in Vietnam in 1891 and spent much of the rest of his life in Nha Trang (see box, above). The museum contains the lab equipment used by Yersin, his library and stereoscope through which visitors can see in 3-D the black-and-white slides, including shots taken by Yersin on his visits to the highlands.

KHANH HOA MUSEUM

① 16 Tran Phu St, T58-382 2277, Tue-Fri 0800-1100, 1400-1700, free. English-speaking curators will be pleased to show you around and should be tipped.

The Khanh Hoa Museum, which was renovated in 2010, contains a Dongson bronze drum and a Palaeolithic stone xylophone. There is a room of ethnographics and, of course, a Ho Chi Minh room which contains several items of interest.

CENTRAL MARKET

The **Cho Dam** (Central Market) close to Nguyen Hong Son Street is a good place to wander and browse and it is quite well-stocked with useful items. In the vicinity of the market, along **Phan Boi Chau Street**, for example, are some bustling streets with old colonial-style shuttered houses.

LONG THANH'S GALLERY

① 126 Hoang Van Thu St, not far from the railway station, T58-382 4875, www.longthanhart. com, open 0900-1900. Long Thanh is willing by pre-arrangement to meet photographers and organize photographic expeditions.

Long Thanh is one of Vietnam's most distinguished photographers and many of his famous pictures are taken in and around his native Nha Trang. He works only in black and white and his sensitive photographs capture the full gamut of human emotions. His outstanding images include cheerful children (often Cham) frolicking in the rain, young women and wistful old people who have witnessed generations of change in a single lifetime. Long Thanh has won a series of international awards and recognition for his work. His style is distinctive and many have tried to copy his technique. He speaks English and welcomes visitors to his gallery.

→ AROUND NHA TRANG

THE ISLANDS

① The best known are the tours run by Mama Hanh's/Hanh's Green Hat and Mama Linh (see page 178). These tours depart at 0900. They have established 100,000d as the benchmark price for a day trip, which should include a seafood lunch and snorkelling equipment: cold beers (not unreasonably) cost extra. It is also possible to charter your own boat. From Cau Da pier, boats can be taken to the islands in Nha Trang Bay. Prices vary according to the number of passengers.
On **Mieu Island** you can visit the **Tri Nguyen Aquarium** *① 35,000d*, a series of tanks in which fish and crustacea are reared, ostensibly for scientific purposes but, as the adjacent restaurant makes plain, it is the science of the tummy that is being served. Not a particularly noteworthy trip.

Other nearby islands are **Hon Mun** *① 40,000d*, and **Hon Mot**. Hon Tam is now off limits due to the building of a resort. The islands are usually a bit of an anticlimax for, as so often in Vietnam, to travel is better than to arrive; it's often a case of lovely boat trip, disappointing beach. The best part is anchoring offshore and jumping into the exquisitely cool water while your skipper prepares a sumptuous seafood feast and the beers chill in the ice bucket. These islands are sometimes known as the **Salangane islands** after the sea swallows that nest here in such profusion. The sea swallow (*yen* in Vietnamese) produces the highly prized bird's nest from which the famous soup is made (see box, page 270). **Hon Yen** (Swallow Island) is out of bounds and strictly government controlled, presumably to deter any would-be private nest collectors.

ON THE ROAD

Tay Son Rebellion (1771-1788)

At the time of the Tay Son rebellion in 1771, Vietnam was in turmoil and conditions in the countryside were deteriorating to the point of famine. The three Tay Son brothers found a rich lode of dissatisfaction among the peasantry, which they successfully mined. Exploiting the latent discontent, they redistributed property from hostile mandarins to the peasants and raised a motley army of clerks, cattle-dealers, farmers, hill people, even scholars, to fight the Trinh and Nguyen lords. Brilliant strategists and demonstrating considerable leadership skills, the brothers and their supporters swept through the country extending the area under their control south as far as Saigon and north to Trinh.

The Chinese, sensing that the disorder and dissent caused by the conflict gave them an opportunity to bring the entire nation under their control, sent a 200,000-strong army southwards in 1788. In the same year, the most intelligent (by all accounts) of the brothers, Nguyen Hue, proclaimed himself emperor under the name of Quang Trung and began to prepare for battle against the cursed Chinese. On the fifth day of Tet in1789, the brothers attacked the Chinese near Thang Long catching them unawares as they celebrated the New Year. (The Viet Cong were to do the same during the Tet Offensive nearly 200 years later.) With great military skill, they routed the enemy, who fled in panic back towards China. Rather than face capture, one of the Chinese generals committed suicide. This victory at the Battle of Dong Da is regarded as one of the greatest in the annals of Vietnamese history. Quang Trung, having saved the nation from the Chinese, had visions of recreating the great Nam Viet Empire of the second century BC, and of invading China. Among the reforms that he introduced were a degree of land reform, a wider programme of education, and a fairer system of taxation. He even tried to get all peasants to carry identity cards with the slogan 'the great trust of the empire' emblazoned on them. These greater visions were not to be, however: Quang Trung died suddenly in 1792, failing to provide the dynastic continuity that was necessary if Vietnam was to survive the impending French arrival.

As a postscript to the Tay Son rebellion, in 1802 the new Emperor Gia Long ordered his soldiers to exhume the body of the last of the brothers and urinate upon it in front of the deceased's wife and son. They were then torn apart by four elephants. Quang Trung and the other Tay Son brothers – like many former nationalist and peasant leaders – are revered by the Vietnamese and honoured by the communists.

NORTH OF NHA TRANG

From the Ponagar Cham Temple Complex (see page 171) proceed a few hundred metres north then turn off to the right down to the sea; from Nha Trang take Tran Phu Street north and over the new bridge, follow the new road around the coast until you see the promontory. **Hon Chong** (Husband Rocks) are perched at the end of the promontory which has a large, rather pudgy indentation in it – said to have been made by the hand of a male giant. It looks more like a paw print and is disfigured with graffiti. The rocks are quite fun and safe for children to scramble about on. There are numerous shacks selling drinks here and the appeal of the whole area is distinctly Vietnamese.

North of Hon Chong is the attractive **Hon Chong Bay**. The water of the bay is clear and calm and the beach sandy, gently shelving and good for children. The bay is rather more sheltered than Nha Trang Bay itself so may be safe for swimming when Nha Trang is too rough. But do look out for rocks, particularly towards the ends of the bay. There are now a few guesthouses and restaurants here.

Thap Ba Hot Springs ① *T58-383 5335, www.thapbahotspring.com.vn, charges vary for the different baths and services*, aren't far from the Cai River; go a short distance past Ponagar and turn left, then carry on for couple of kilometres. A soak in mineral water or mud bath is supposed to do you good. As the literature says, "you feel so freshly even it is hotly". Baths and pools of differing sizes for singles, couples and groups. The water is 40°C.

Twenty kilometres north up Highway 1, followed by a 2-km hike will bring you to **Ba Ho**, the name given to a sequence of three pools and rapids to be found in a remote and attractive woodland setting. Huge granite boulders have been sculpted and smoothed by the dashing torrent, but it is easy enough to find a lazy pool to soak in.

Some 40 km north of Nha Trang – turn right off Highway 1 at Ninh Hoa – is the beach area of **Doc Lech**. Take a taxi or hire a car from your hotel. The beach here is gentler and more protected than Hon Chong, which would appear to make it suitable for young children. The sea is quite beautiful with multicoloured boats bobbing on the small waves and the beach is dotted with fishing baskets. Doc Lech is very popular with groups of Vietnamese holiday makers. Given that it is a long haul from Nha Trang it is probably best to go only mid-week out of the holiday season. There are guesthouses and restaurants. On the way you will pass workers on the salt flats.

Ninh Van Bay, north of Nha Trang, is accessed from the private speedboat dock of the Evason group where they have a luxurious island hideaway. North of Doc Lech, off a long peninsula accessed by Dam Mon, is **Whale Island**, an island resort offering relaxation, diving and boat trips.

NHA TRANG AND AROUND LISTINGS

WHERE TO STAY

Nha Trang is one of Vietnam's premier beach resorts offering smart upscale beach accommodation, attractive resorts, and good, cheap town hotels.

$$$$ Evason Ana Mandara, Tran Phu St, T058-352 2222, www.sixsenses.com. Nha Trang's finest beach resort and, despite the increasing competition, still the loveliest resort in Vietnam, where those who can afford it relax in unashamed and exquisite luxury. The resort has 74 rooms in sea view or garden villas that are all beautifully furnished with special touches and outdoor bathtubs. Every conceivable facility is available in this enchanting retreat, including 2 pools, a tennis court, an enlarged gym, bicycles and restaurants. For those wanting further pampering there is the Six Senses Spa.

$$$$ Six Senses Ninh Van Bay, 30 km north of Nha Trang, T058-372 8222, www.sixsenses.com. Beach Villas, Rock Villas and Hilltop Villas are laid out in the full dramatic curve of Ninh Van Bay. Exceptional luxury; the Rock Villas are perched on rocks at the tip of the bay with bathrooms overlooking the sea and fronted by small infinity pools. The resort is large; from the Rock Villas to the main restaurant is an enormous hike. Beach Villas are more centrally located. While your days away in the herb garden, Six Senses Spa, library or bar and be attended by your personal butler. It's highly romantic, very secluded and very expensive; the food is exceptional. The resort is 1 hr ahead of real time which is far too confusing.

$$$ Whale Island Resort, off Nha Trang, T058-384 0501, www.iledelabaleine.com.

This is a great place in which to relax amid the aquamarine waters of the South China Sea. Bungalows right on this island beach, 2½ hrs north of Nha Trang. The price includes breakfasts. Activities include diving, windsurfing, canoeing and catamaran sailing and there's plenty of wildlife to observe. Return transfers to Nha Trang are arranged.

$$ Jungle Beach, Ninh Phuoc Village, T058-362 2384, www.junglebeachvietnam.com. **Jungle Beach** is located in Doc Let, about 1 hr north of Nha Trang, on one of the most pristine beaches in the country. The water is calm, shallow and clear year-round. Rates include 3 meals a day and unlimited water and lemonade. Rooms are rustic and set in the gardens on the beach.

$$-$ Backpackers' House, 54G Nguyen Thien Thuat St, T058-352 4500, www.backpackershouse.net. A super clean and bright new place with dorms and private rooms with cable TV and DVD players set up in a courtyard along with the attached **Green Apple Restaurant** and hang out joint. Tours also arranged. A dollar from each booking is invested in the Anh Dao Orphanage.

$$-$ Perfume Grass Inn (Que Thao), 4A Biet Thu St, T058-352 4286, www.perfume-grass.com. Well-run and friendly family hotel with 21 rooms. Restaurant and internet service. Good value for money. Book in advance.

$ Blue House, 12/8 Hung Vuong St, T058-382 4505, ngovietthuy57@yahoo.com.vn. Down a little alley in a quiet setting. 16 a/c and cheaper fan rooms in a small, neat blue building. Friendly, warm welcome and excellent value for money.

RESTAURANTS

As you'd expect from a seaside resort, you'll find plenty of good seafood and shellfish in Nha Trang. As it's an increasingly cosmopolitan resort, you'll also find good international offerings too.

$$$ Da Fernando, 96 Nguyen Thien Thuat St, T058-352 8034. Open daily. Fernando formerly helmed the **Good Morning Vietnam** eatery in Mui Ne, but has come into his own in Nha Trang. The menu includes

the usual Italian favourites – pizzas, pastas, gnocchi and risotto, but moves beyond the basics with a few delightful surprises. Easily the best Italian eatery in Nha Trang.
$$-$ La Mancha, 78 Nguyen Thien Tuat St, T091-456 9782 (mob). Open 1100-2400. Great atmosphere, with Spanish decor, barbecued meat on the street. Garlic galore and great dishes but not served together (ie tapas style) and sadly the chorizo is not real. Nonetheless, highly recommended.
$$-$ Sailing Club, 72-74 Tran Phu St, T058-352 4628, www.sailingclubnhatrang. com. Daily 0700-2300. Although best known as a bar, this busy and attractive beachfront area also includes several restaurants: Japanese, Italian and global cuisine. None is cheap but all serve good food and represent decent value. Look out for its new resort, **Mia**, south of the city (www.mianhatrang.com).

$ Cyclo, 130 Nguyen Thien Thuat St, T058-352 4208, khuongthuy@hotmail.com. Daily 0700-2400. Outstanding little family-run restaurant. Italian and Vietnamese dishes. Real attention to detail in the cooking.
$ Lac Canh, 44 Nguyen Binh Khiem St, T058-382 1391, www.laccanh.com. Specializes in beef, squid and prawns, which you barbecue at your table. Also excellent fish and a special dish of eel mixed with vermicelli. Smoky atmosphere and can be hard to get a table. Highly recommended.
$ Truc Linh, 11 Biet Thu St, T058-352 6742. Deservedly popular with sensible prices. Good fruit shake and *op la* (fried eggs). There's also **Truc Linh 2**, at 21 Biet Thu St, T058-352 1089, and **Truc Linh 3**, at 80 Hung Vuong St, T058-352 5259. Nos 2 and 3 are recommended as the best.

WHAT TO DO

Diving
Rainbow Divers, 90A Hung Vuong St, T090-878 1756, www.divevietnam.com. A full range of training and courses, including the National Geographic dive courses. Good reports regarding equipment and focus on safety. Qualified instructors speak a variety of European languages. Top professional operation. **Rainbow** also operates out of **Whale Island Resort**.

Therapies
Six Senses Spa, Evason Ana Mandara, www.sixsenses.com. Japanese and Vichy showers, hot tubs and massages in beautiful surroundings. Programmes for vitality, stress-management and meditation that include tailored spa treatments. 5-day lifestyle packages are US$990 (no accommodation).
Sú Spa, 93AB Nguyen Thien Thuat St, T058-352 3242, www.suspa.vn. An upmarket spa in zen-like surrounds.

Tour operators
The following tour operators can also arrange trips to Buon Ma Thuot and the Central Highlands.
Mama Hanh/Bien Dao Sea & Island Tours, 2 Nguyen Thi Minh Khai St, T058-352 6494, www.biendaotour.com. Boat trips (US$12 including lunch and pick-up from hotel, excluding entrance fees and Con Se Tre village fees). **Mama Hanh** also offers less crowded half-day and 1-day tours for US$15. Also other local tours, fishing tours, car, motorbike and bicycle hire.
Mama Linh, 144 Hung Vuong St, T058-352 2844, mamalinhvn@yahoo.com. Organizes standard boat trips 250,000d and sells minibus tickets to Hoi An, Phan Thiet, HCMC and Dalat. Not as helpful as **Mama Hanh**.
Sinh Tourist, 2A Biet Thu St, T058-352 1981, www.thesinhtouristvn. Offers tours and Open Tour Bus tickets. **Sinh Café** buses arrive and depart from here.

PHAN THIET AND MUI NE

Phan Thiet is a fishing town at the mouth of the Ca Ty River. Despite its modest appearance and unassuming nature it is the administrative capital of Binh Thuan Province. For the traveller the real attraction lies east of town in the form of the 20-km sweep of golden sand of Mui Ne. Here can be found Vietnam's finest collection of coastal resorts with some excellent watersports and two of the country's most attractive golf courses. Overdevelopment is a real issue, though. Water and electricity are intermittently available at budget accommodations, though luxury resorts usually have reserves. Both pollution and seasonal erosion, augmented by development, detract from the beach during busy season. Road safety has also become a serious concern with several foreign fatalities (and many more locals) in 2009 and 2010, as both passengers and pedestrians.

ARRIVING IN PHAN THIET AND MUI NE

Getting there and around The drive from Ho Chi Minh City takes five to six hours. The north–south Open Tour Buses all divert to Mui Ne and drop off/pick up from every hotel along the beach. The Express buses stop at the station in Phan Thiet and it is easy to take a motorbike taxi from there to Mui Ne. Hiring a car from Ho Chi Minh City is approximately US$100. From Nha Trang the journey is about as long, though much lengthier if stopping off to see the Cham Towers in Phan Rang. There are also rail connections from Phan Thiet to the mainline station at Muong Man, 12 km from Phan Thiet. A new line connects Ho Chi Minh City directly with Phan Thiet, leaving Phan Thiet daily at 1345 and 2235 at weekends. All other city connections are available via the Muong Man station. Both motorbike taxis and Mai Linh car taxis abound in the town and along the Mui Ne strip.

Moving on Open Tour Buses pick up in Mui Ne but for all other transport connections you'll need to return to Phan Thiet.

Best time to visit The weather in Phan Thiet always seems nice. It is, of course, better in the dry season, December through April. Phan Thiet is most popular with overseas visitors (and the growing number of package tour operators) in the Christmas to Easter period when prices at the some of the better hotels rise by 20% or more. From December to March, Mui Ne loses portions of its beach to the sea.

Tourist information Binh Thuan Tourist ① *82 Trung Trac St, T62-381 6821, binhthuantourist@hcm.vnn.vn*, arranges tours and car rentals.

PHAN THIET

Phan Thiet's 18-hole **golf course**, designed by Nick Faldo, is regarded by golfers as one of the best in Vietnam. Golfers come from all around the region to play it.

The most distinctive landmark in town is the municipal **water tower** completed in 1934. It is an elegant structure with a pagoda-like roof; built by the infamous "Red Prince" and first president of Laos. The tower icon features in the logos of many local businesses and agencies. There are a few **Ho Chi Minh relics**, including a **museum** on Nguyen Truong To Street and the **Duc Thanh school** next door, where Ho Chi Minh taught in 1911, but otherwise nothing of interest at the museum.

ON THE ROAD

Superior God of the Southern Sea

The whale has long been worshipped in Vietnam. Ever since the days of the early Champa the whale has been credited with saving the lives of drowning fishermen. The Cham believed that Cha-Aih-Va, a powerful god, could assume the form of a whale in order to rescue those in need.

Emperor Gia Long is said to have been rescued by a whale when his boat sank. After he ascended the throne, Gia Long awarded the whale the title Nam Hai Cu Toc Ngoc Lam Thuong Dang Than, (Superior God of the Southern Sea).

Coastal inhabitants always try to help whales in difficulty and cut them free of their nets. If a whale should die a full funeral is arranged. The person who discovered its dead body is considered to be the whale's 'eldest son' and will head the funeral procession dressed in white as if it were his own father's funeral.

The **Van Thuy Thu Temple** ① *20A Ngu Ong St, 0730-1130 and 1400-1700, 5000d*, is the oldest whale temple (built in 1762) in Vietnam. The temple houses more than 100 whale skeletons, including one specimen more than 22m in length. Like all whale temples, it was originally built by the sea, but as sea levels have receded, this temple is now stranded in the middle of the neighborhood.

MUI NE

Mui Ne (or Cape Ne) is the name of the famous sandy cape and the small fishing village that lies at its end. Mui Ne's claims to fame are its *nuoc mam* (fish sauce) and its **beaches** where it is possible to do a host of watersports including kiteboarding for which it is justly famous. Body boarding and surfing are better December to January when there are more waves. The wind dies down at the end of April, and May has virtually no wind. The cape is dominated by some impressive **sand dunes**; some are golden but in other parts quite red, a reflection of the underlying geology. Around the village visitors may notice a strong smell of rotting fish. This is the unfortunate but inevitable by-product of fish sauce fermenting in wooden barrels. The *nuoc mam* of Phan Thiet is made from anchovies, as *cá com* on the label testifies. The process takes a year but to Vietnamese palates it is worth every day. *Nuoc mam* from Phan Thiet is regarded highly but not as reverentially as that from the southern island of Phu Quoc.

There are still significant numbers of Cham (50,000) and Ra-glai (30,000) minorities, who until a century ago, were the dominnt groups in the region. There are many relics of the Champa kingdom here in Binh Thuan Province, the best and easiest to find being **Po Shanu**, two Cham towers dating from the late eighth century on a hill on the Mui Ne road. They are now somewhat broken down but the road leading up to them makes a nice evening ride; you can watch the sun set and from this vantage point you'll see the physical make-up of the coastal plain and estuaries to the south and the central highlands to the north. Driving up the long climb towards Mui Ne the towers are on the right-hand side of the road and quite unmissable. Like Cham towers elsewhere in this part of the country they were constructed of brick bound together with resin of the *day* tree. Once the tower was completed timber was piled around it and ignited; the heat from the flames melted the resin, which solidified on cooling.

PHAN THIET AND MUI NE LISTINGS

WHERE TO STAY

There's one decent upscale place to stay in Phan Thiet city. Most visitors are here, however, for the lovely golden arc of sand at Mui Ne which caters for everyone from backpackers to the smart set with boutique beach resorts on the sands.

Phan Thiet

$$$$ Du Parc Phan Thiet Ocean Dunes & Golf Resort, 1 Ton Duc Thang St, T62-382 2393, www.phanthietresorts.com. On the beach just outside Phan Thiet, this is set behind lovely gardens. 123 comfortable rooms in a bland building and new, well-appointed villas with beach views. Good facilities, 2 pools, 2 restaurants with tasty food , bar, tennis courts and gym. Guests enjoy a 30% discount on green fees at the adjacent 18-hole champion golf course, the Ocean Dunes Golf Club.

$$$$ Victoria Phan Thiet Beach Resort & Spa, T062-381 3000, www.victoriahotels. asia. Part of the French-run **Victoria Group**, the resort has thatch-roof bungalows with outdoor rain showers and 3 villas, built in country-house style in an attractive landscaped setting. It is well equipped with restaurants, several bars, an attractive pool and a spa.

Mui Ne

$$$$ Anantara Mui Ne Resort & Spa, KM10, Nguyen Dinh Chieu St, T062-374 1888, www.anantara.com. Formerly known as the **L'Anmien**, Anantara is the first 5-star resort in Mui Ne. Accommodation includes standard rooms, suites and villas, all with separate rain showers and bathtubs. Other facilities include a wine cellar, spa and fitness centre.

$$$$ Coco Beach (**Hai Duong**), T062-384 7111, www.cocobeach.net. Coco Beach was the first resort on Mui Ne and remains among the best. Not luxurious but friendly and impeccably kept. Wooden bungalows and 2-bedroom 'villas' facing the beach in a beautiful setting with a lovely pool. Price includes a decent buffet breakfast. There are 2 restaurants: the French **Champa** (Tue-Sun 1500-2200 only) and **Paradise Beach Club** (open all day).

$$$$-$$$ Mia Mui Ne, T062-384 7440, www.miamuine.com. This is a stunning resort, designed in the most charming style with bungalows and rooms that are simple and cool and surrounded by dense vegetation. Its pool has been extended and the bathrooms for the superior rooms enlarged. It has an excellent restaurant and bar. A good buffet breakfast is included.

$$$ Full Moon Beach, T062-384 7008, www.windsurf-vietnam.com. Visitors are assured of a friendly reception by the French and Vietnamese couple who own and run the place. Some rooms are spacious, others a little cramped, some brick, some bamboo. The most attractive rooms have a sea view. There is a good restaurant.

$$-$ Mui Ne Backpackers Resort, 88 Nguyen Dinh Chieu St, T062-384 7047, www.muinebackpackers.com. One of the nicest options in the budget category, and one of the original hotels on the beach. There is a small swimming pool, and a variety of room styles to choose from, as well as dorms.

$ Hiep Hoa, T062-384 7262, T091-812 4149 (mob), hiephoatourism@yahoo.com. Attractive and simple little place with 25 a/c rooms. It's quiet, clean and with its own stretch of beach. Popular and should be booked in advance. Rates are excellent value for Mui Ne, with discounts in low season.

RESTAURANTS

International restaurants and cafes are popular in Mui Ne due to the international flavour of this beach resort. Vietnamese options are also to be found all the way along the beach.

Mui Ne

$$ Forest Restaurant, 7 Nguyen Dinh Chieu St, T062-384 7589. Local dishes and lots of seafood, this atmospheric garden-jungle setting puts on live music and dance shows throughout the evening.

$$ Luna D'Autonno, T062-384 7591. One of the best Italian restaurants in the country. Inspired menu that goes way beyond the standard pizzas and pasta with daily fish specials and barbecues. Huge portions, good wine.

ENTERTAINMENT

Mui Ne

Joe's Cafe, 86 Nguyen Dinh Chieu St, T062-384 7177, www.joescafegardenresort. com. **Joe's** offers live music, free Wi-Fi, great coffee and a large selection of sandwiches, pasta and all-day breakfasts.

Sankara, 78 Nguyen Dinh Chieu St, T062-374 1122, www.sankaravietnam.com. This chic new beachside bar with pool has made a lot of noise since its much-anticipated opening in 2009. The place to see and be seen on weekends and holidays.

WHAT TO DO

Ocean Dunes Golf Club, 1 Ton Duc Thang St, T062-382 3366, www.oceandunesgolf.vn. Phan Thiet's 18-hole golf course, designed by Nick Faldo, is highly regarded. Fully equipped club house with bar and restaurant. Green fees from US$60 including caddie fees. Discounts for hotel guests and members.
Xanh Spa, Mia Resort (**Sailing Club**), T062-384 7440, www.miamuine.com. Massage treatments are available in special cabins in the grounds.

Windsurfing, kitesurfing and other watersports are popular in Mui Ne, the watersports capital of Vietnam. The wind is normally brisk and the sight of the kitesurfers zooming around on the waves is great for those of us too cowardly to try. Equipment and training is offered by a couple of resorts. Make sure your operator is licensed.

DREAM TRIP 3:
Ho Chi Minh City→Mekong Delta→Angkor Wat
21 days

Ho Chi Minh City 3 nights, page 185

Con Dao 2 nights, page 210
By plane from HCMC (45 mins)

My Tho 1 night, page 215
By road from HCMC (2 hrs)

Ben Tre 1 night, page 218
By road from My Tho (20-30 mins)

Tra Vinh 1 night, page 219
By road from Ben Tre 1½-2 hrs

Vinh Long 1 night, page 220
By road from Tra Vinh (60-80 mins)

Can Tho 2 nights, page 223
By road from Vinh Long (1 hr)

Sa Dec 1 night, page 225
By road from Can Tho (60-90 mins)

Cao Lanh (for Xeo Quit) 1 night,
page 227
By road from Sa Dec (30-45 mins)
From Sa Dec to Xeo Quit (45 mins-1 hr)

Chau Doc 2 nights, page 231
By road from Cao Lanh (2 hrs)
or from Sa Dec (2 hrs)

Phu Quoc Island 3 nights, page 236
By plane from HCMC (55 mins),
Rach Gia (40 mins) or Can Tho (45 mins)
By boat from Rach Gia (hydrofoil 2½ hrs)
or Ha Tien (1½ hrs hydrofoil)

Siem Reap (for Angkor) 3 nights,
page 241
By plane from HCMC (1 hr)
By boat from Chau Doc to Phnom Penh
(5 hrs); then by bus from Phnom Penh
to Siem Reap (5 hrs)

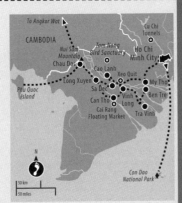

DREAM TRIP 3
Ho Chi Minh City→Mekong Delta→Angkor Wat

Ho Chi Minh City, Pearl of the Orient, is the largest city in Vietnam. During the 1960s and 1970s Saigon boomed and flourished under the American occupation; today it is the nation's foremost commercial and industrial centre. It is frenetic, exciting, riddled with traffic and enlivened by great shops, bars and restaurants. Surrounding the city are a number of fascinating historical sites including the Viet Cong tunnels at Cu Chi and the fantastical Cao Dai temple at Tay Ninh.

To the south of the city, the Mekong region is a veritable Garden of Eden, stuffed full of bountiful fruit trees, decorated in pink bougainvillea and carpeted with brilliant green rice paddies. Waterways are as busy as highways, with fishing boats chugging their way along the brown river.

Boat trips along canals and down rivers are the highlights of this region, as is a visit to Vietnam's offshore islands. Phu Quoc – Vietnam's largest island – lying off the southwest coast, remains largely undeveloped with beautiful sandy beaches along much of its coastline and forested hills inland. While the tiny archipelago that makes up Con Dao National Park is one of Vietnam's few pristine wilderness areas.

From Ho Chi Minh City, it's a short flight to the petite town of Siem Reap to visit the exceptional ruins of Angkor, ancient capital of the powerful Khmer Empire, one of the archaeological treasures of Asia.

HO CHI MINH CITY AND AROUND

Ho Chi Minh City is a manic, capitalistic hothouse, clogged with traffic, bustling with energy and enlivened by top restaurants, shops and bars. Its streets are evidence of a vibrant historical past with pagodas and temples and a bustling Chinatown. During the 1960s and early 1970s, Saigon, the Pearl of the Orient, boomed and flourished under the American occupation. In more recent times it was the seat of the South Vietnam government until the events that led to the country's reunification.

Today, Ho Chi Minh City is dedicated to commerce and hedonistic pleasures. Officially renamed in 1975, it remains to most the bi-syllabic, familiar 'Saigon'. It is the largest city in Vietnam and still growing at a prodigious rate. It is also the nation's foremost commercial and industrial centre, a place of remorseless, relentless activity and expanding urban sprawl. For the visitor, Ho Chi Minh City is a fantastic place to shop, eat and drink, while admiring its historical past and enjoying its energetic present. The striking Bitexco Tower, which now stands in the heart of the city, encapsulates its growth and ambition.

→ ARRIVING IN HO CHI MINH CITY

GETTING THERE

Ho Chi Minh City (HCMC) may not be Vietnam's capital, but it is the economic powerhouse of the country and the largest city. Reflecting its premier economic position, it is well connected with the wider world – indeed, more airlines fly into here than into Hanoi; it is also connected to all the domestic airports bar one. **Tan Son Nhat Airport** is 30-40 minutes from the centre. By taxi the cost is 150,000-200,000d. Taxi drivers may try and demand a flat fee in US dollars but you should insist on using the meter, which is the law, and pay in dong – staff now issue tickets complete with your driver's numer making the situation better. On the right of the international terminal is the domestic terminal. Bus No 152 runs roughly every 50 minutes for 4000d plus 3000d per piece of luggage to Ben Tranh Market.

The **railway station** is northwest of the city centre and there are regular connections with Hanoi and all stops on the line north. With the ring road around Ho Chi Minh City, few long-distance public buses actually come into town. To avoid an additional 45-minute journey, try to catch a bus heading to Ben Xe Mien Dong or join the large number of visitors who arrive in Ho Chi Minh City on one or other of the many competing Open Tour Buses.

MOVING ON

As well as air connections to Siem Reap in Cambodia (see page 244) there are daily international bus services via the ferry crossing at Chau Doc (see page 231). From Ho Chi Minh City there are buses to most larger towns in the central and northern regions, and with many places in the Mekong Delta. Open Tour Buses generally depart from offices in Pham Ngu Lao District. There are daily flights to Phu Quoc Island (see page 236) and three flights daily to the Con Dao archipelago (see page 210).

GETTING AROUND

Ho Chi Minh City has abundant transport – which is fortunate, because it is a hot, large and increasingly polluted city. Metered taxis, motorcycle taxis and a handful of cyclos vie for business in a healthy spirit of competition. Many tourists who prefer some level of independence opt to hire (or even, buy) a bicycle or motorbike.

ORIENTATION

Until virtually all of Ho Chi Minh City was located to the west of the Saigon River. However, the eastern side of the river, District 2, is changing dramatically, with modern condo developments, popular with expats and moneyed Vietnamese (who prefer property to bank deposits) going up at a rate of knots. Most visitors to the city head straight for hotels in Districts 1 (the historic centre) or 3. Many will arrive on buses in De Tham or Pham Ngu Lao streets, the backpacker area, in District 1, not far from the city centre. Cholon or Chinatown (District 5) is a mile west of the centre. The Port of Saigon lies downstream of the city centre in districts 4 and 8. Few visitors venture here although cruise ships berth in District 4.

SAFETY

Be careful with handbags, particularly on the back of motorbikes as drive-by snatchings are on the increase. Jewellery should not be worn. Cameras should be held tightly at all times and passports, tickets and money kept in the safe of your hotel.

BEST TIME TO VISIT

Ho Chi Minh City is a fun and exciting place to visit all year around.

TOURIST INFORMATION

A **Tourist Information Center** ① *92-96 Nguyen Hue St, T8-3825 0615, www.ticvietnam. com, daily 0800-2100*, provides free information, hotel reservationsand tour bookings; currency exchange on site and free internet. A useful tour operator and Southeast Asian specialist is **Asian Trails** ① *9th Floor, HMC Tower, 193 Dinh Tien Hoang St, District 1, T8-3910 2871, www.asiantrails.travel.*

→ BACKGROUND

Before the 15th century, Saigon was a small Khmer village surrounded by a wilderness of forest and swamp. Through the years it had ostensibly been incorporated into the Funan and then the Khmer empires, although it is hard to believe that these kingdoms had any direct, long-term influence on the inhabitants of the community. The Khmers, who called the region *Prei Nokor*, used the area for hunting.

By 1623 Saigon had become an important commercial centre, and in the mid-17th century it became the residence of the so-called Vice-King of Cambodia. In 1698, the Viets managed to extend their control this far south and finally Saigon was brought under Vietnamese control and hence celebrated the city's tercentenary in 1998. By 1790, the city had a population of 50,000 and before Hué was selected as the capital of the Nguyen Dynasty, Emperor Gia Long made Saigon his place of residence.

In the middle of the 19th century, the French began to challenge Vietnamese authority in the south of Vietnam and Saigon. Between 1859 and 1862, in response to the Nguyen persecution of Catholics in Vietnam, the French attacked and captured Saigon, along with the southern provinces of Vinh Long, An Giang and Ha Tien. The Treaty of Saigon in 1862 ratified the conquest and created the new French colony of Cochin China. Saigon was developed in French style: wide, tree-lined boulevards, street-side cafés, elegant French architecture, boutiques and the smell of baking baguettes. The map of French Saigon in the 1930s was a city that owed more to Haussmann than Vietnamese geomancers.

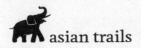

The population of Ho Chi Minh City today is officially more than seven million and rising fast as the rural poor are lured by the tales of streets paved with gold. Actual numbers are thought to be considerably higher when all the recent migrants without residence cards are added. But it has been a roller-coaster ride over the last 40 years. During the course of the Vietnam War, as refugees spilled in from a devastated countryside, the population of Saigon almost doubled from 2.4 million in 1965 to around 4.5 million by 1975. With reunification in 1976, the new communist authorities pursued a policy of depopulation, believing that the city had become too large, that it was parasitic and was preying on the surrounding countryside. Certainly, most of the jobs were in the service sector, and were linked to the United States' presence. For example, Saigon had 56,000 registered prostitutes alone (and many, many, more unregistered), most of them country girls.

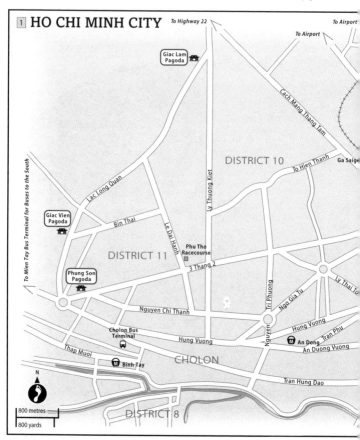

Vietnam's economic reforms are most in evidence in Ho Chi Minh City and the average annual income here, at US$3000, is more than double the national average (US$1000). It is here that the highest concentration of Hoa (ethnic Chinese) is to be found – numbering around 500,000 – and, although once persecuted for their economic success, they still have the greatest economic influence and acumen. Most of Ho Chi Minh City's ethnic Chinese live in the district of Cholon, and from there control two-thirds of small-scale commercial enterprises. The reforms have encouraged the Hoa to begin investing in business again. Drawing on their links with fellow Chinese in Taiwan, Hong Kong, Bangkok and among the overseas Vietnamese, they are viewed by the government as crucial in improving prospects for the economy. The reforms have also brought economic inefficiencies into the open. Although the changes have brought wealth to a few, and increased the range of goods on sale, they have also created a much clearer division between the haves and the have-nots.

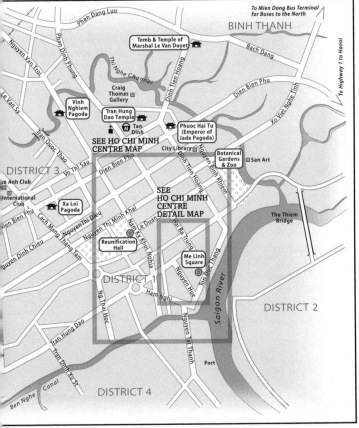

In its short history Saigon has had a number of keepers. Each has rebuilt the city in their own style. First the Khmer, then the early Vietnamese, followed by the French who tore it all down and started from scratch and were succeeded by the Americans and the 'Puppet' Regime, and finally the communist north who engineered society rather than the buildings, locking the urban fabric in a time warp.

Under the current regime, best described as crony capitalist, the city is once more being rebuilt. Ever larger holes are being torn in the heart of central Ho Chi Minh City. Whereas a few years ago it was common to see buildings disappear, now whole blocks fall to the wrecker's ball. From the holes left behind, concrete, steel and glass monuments emerge. There is, of course, a difference from earlier periods of remodelling of the city. Then, it was conducted on a human scale and the largest buildings, though grand, were on a scale that was in keeping with the dimensions of the streets and ordinary shophouses. French buildings in Dong Khoi Street, for example, were consistent with the Vietnamese way of life: street-level trading with a few residential floors above. Now glitzy modern buildings on an altogether vaster scale dwarf every building from an earlier age. The latest overblown development is Times Square opposite the Grand Hotel on Dong Khoi St.

Ho Chi Minh City is divided, administratively, into 12 urban districts, or *quan*, and nine suburban districts, or *huyen*. These are further sub-divided into wards and the wards into neighbourhoods; each district and ward has its own People's Committee or local government who guard and protect their responsibilities and rights jealously and maintain a high degree of administrative autonomy. A city-wide People's Committee, elected every four years, oversees the functioning of the entire metropolis.

The future growth of Ho Chi Minh City will focus mostly on the southern and eastern sides. Saigon port did extend right up into the heart of the city into District 4 but has been relocated to Cat Lai and Hiep Phuoc in the suburbs. It is almost certain that in the coming years the valuable riverfront sites will be developed into desirable flats and offices – rather like London's Docklands. To the south, Saigon South, a huge new flank of the city is rising out of the marsh and mangrove. A site of 1336 ha has so far been converted from swamp into 'executive homes' and international schools; the infrastructure that will support the livelihoods of hundreds of thousands of people is materializing out of nothing. It may sound like propaganda but the fact is that parcels of what was recently disregarded wasteland are now changing hands for millions of dollars. Serious investors and land speculators are moving in and the city is expanding fast. Land prices in District 2, the marshy area to the east of the Saigon River, soared to previously unimaginable heights as speculators snapped up land in advance of the construction of new river crossings.

PLACES IN HO CHI MINH CITY

All the sights of Central Ho Chi Minh City can be reached on foot in no more than 30 minutes from the major hotel areas of Nguyen Hue, Dong Khoi and Ton Duc Thang streets. Visiting all the sights described below will take several days, not that we would particularly recommend visiting them all. Quite a good first port of call, however, is the **Panorama 33 Café** *on the 33rd floor of* **Saigon Trade Center** ① *37 Ton Duc Thang St, Mon-Fri 1100-2400, Sat-Sun 0900-2400. From this vantage point you can see the whole city stretching before you, and its position and layout in relation to the river and surrounding swampland becomes strikingly clear. Another good spot to survey the river and downtown building work, is* **Chique** ① *15th floor, Landmark Building, 5B Ton Duc Thang St, 1400-2300. Its interior isn't chic but the views are front row.*

→ CITY CENTRE

The core of Ho Chi Minh City is, in many respects, the most interesting and historical. Remember, of course, that 'historical' here has a very different meaning from that in Hanoi. In Ho Chi Minh City a 100-year-old building is ancient – and, alas, increasingly rare. Still, a saunter down **Dong Khoi Street**, in District 1, the old rue Catinat can still give one an impression of life in a more elegant and less frenzied era. Much remains on a small and personal scale and within a 100-m radius of just about anywhere on Dong Khoi or Thai Van Lung streets there are dozens of cafés, restaurants and increasingly snazzy boutiques. However, the character of the street has altered with the opening of luxury chain names and will alter further with the completion of the Saigon Times Square mega hotel/apartments and convention centre development. A little bit of Graham Greene history was lost in 2010 when the Givral Café in the Eden Centre, which featured in *A Quiet American*, was closed as Vincom Towers built another tower block on Lam Son Square.

LAM SON SQUARE AND AROUND

The once-impressive, French-era **Opera House (Nha Hat Thanh Pho)** ① *7 Lam Son Sq, T8-3832 2009, nhahat_ghvk@hcm.fpt.vn*, dominates Lam Son Square. It was built in 1897 to the design of French architect Ferret Eugene and restored in 1998. It once housed the National Assembly; nowadays, when it is open, it provides a varied programme of events, for example, traditional theatre, contemporary dance and gymnastics.

North of the Opera House is the repainted **Continental Hotel**, built in 1880 and an integral part of the city's history. Graham Greene stayed here and the hotel features in the novel *The Quiet American*. Old journalists' haunt **Continental Shelf** was "a famous verandah where correspondents, spies, speculators, traffickers, intellectuals and soldiers used to meet during the war to glean information and pick up secret reports, half false, half true or half disclosed. All of this is more than enough for it to be known as Radio Catinat". It has a delightful enclosed garden ("I sometimes went there for a late evening drink among the frangipani and hibiscus blossom ... It was the reverse of the frenzy of the war, and a good place to think," wrote war journalist Jon Swain).

The **Continental** lines **Dong Khoi Street** (formerly the bar-lined Tu Do Street, the old Rue Catinat), which stretches from Cong Xa Paris down to the river. All the shops specialize in, or sell a mix of silk clothes and accessories, jewellery, lacquerware and household goods.

Facing the **Continental**, also adjoining Dong Khoi Street, is the opulent **Hotel Caravelle**, which houses boutique shops selling luxury goods. The **Caravelle** opened for business in 1959. The famous **Saigon Saigon** bar on the 10th floor was a favourite spot for wartime reporters and during the 1960s the *Associated Press*, *NBC*, *CBS*, the *New York Times* and *Washington Post* based their offices here. The press escaped casualties when, on 25 August 1964, a bomb exploded in room 514, on a floor mostly used by foreign reporters. The hotel suffered damage and there were injuries but the journalists were all out in the field. It was renamed Doc Lap (Independence Hotel) in 1975 but not before a Vietnamese tank trundled down the rue Catinat to Place Garnier (now Lam Son Square) and aimed its turret at the hotel; to this day nobody knows why it did not fire. During the filming of Graham Greene's *The Quiet American*, actors Michael Caine and Brendan Fraser stayed at the hotel.

At the northwest end of Nguyen Hue Boulevard is the yellow and white **City Hall**, formerly the French Hôtel de Ville built in 1897 and now the Ho Chi Minh City People's Committee building, which overlooks a **statue of Bac Ho** (Uncle Ho) offering comfort, or perhaps advice, to a child. This is a favourite spot for Vietnamese to have their photograph taken, especially newly-weds who believe old Ho confers some sort of blessing.

South of City Hall, the **Rex Hotel**, a pre-Liberation favourite with US officers, stands at the intersection of Le Loi and Nguyen Hue boulevards. This was the scene of the daily 'Five O'Clock Follies' where the military briefed an increasingly sceptical press corps during the Vietnam War. Fully renovated and smartly expanding, the crown on the fifth-floor terrace of the **Rex** (a good place to have a beer) is rotating once again following a number of years of immobility. Some maintain that it symbolizes Ho Chi Minh City's newly discovered (or rediscovered) vitality.

On weekend evenings thousands of young Saigon men and women and young families cruise up and down Nguyen Hue and Le Loi boulevards and Dong Khoi Street on motorbikes; this whirl of people and machines is known as *chay long rong* 'cruising' or *song voi*, 'living fast'. There are now so many motorbikes on the streets of Ho Chi Minh City that intersections seem lethally confused. Miraculously, the riders miss each other (most of the time) while pedestrians safely make their way through waves of machines.

NOTRE DAME CATHEDRAL

ⓘ *Visiting times are described as being 0500-1100 and 1500-1730. Communion is celebrated here 7 times on Sun (drawing congregations Western churches can only dream of) and 3 times on weekdays.*

North up Dong Khoi Street, in the middle of **Cong Xa Paris** (Paris Square), is the imposing, austere red-brick, twin-spired Notre Dame Cathedral, overlooking a grassed square in which a statue of the Virgin Mary stands holding an orb. The statue was the subject of intense scrutiny in 2006 as it was said that it had shed tears. The cathedral was built between 1877 and 1880 and is said to be on the site of an ancient pagoda. A number of the homeless sleep under its walls at night; unfortunately the signs asking Vietnamese men not to treat the walls as a public urinal do not deter this unpleasant but widespread practice. Mass times are a spectacle as crowds, unable to squeeze through the doors, listen to the service while perched on their parked motorbikes in rows eight or nine deep.

GENERAL POST OFFICE

ⓘ *2 Cong Xa Paris, daily 0730-1930.*

Facing onto the Paris Square is the General Post Office, built in the 1880s in French style, it is a particularly distinguished building. The front façade has attractive cornices with

French and Khmer motifs and the names of notable French men of letters and science. Inside, the high, vaulted ceiling and fans create a deliciously cool atmosphere in which to scribble a postcard. Note the old wall-map of Cochin China that has miraculously survived. The enormous portrait of Ho Chi Minh, hanging at the end of the hall, completes the sense of grandeur.

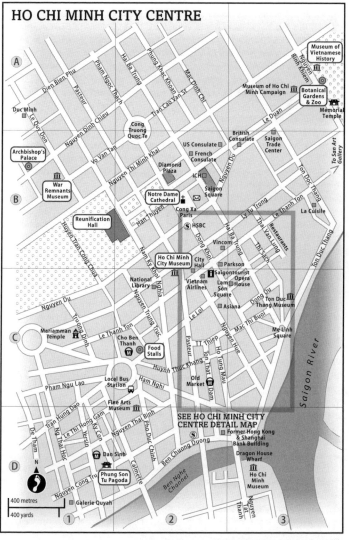

HO CHI MINH CITY CENTRE

Museum of Vietnamese History

Nguyen Binh Khiem

Museum of Ho Chi Minh Campaign

Botanical Gardens & Zoo

Memorial Temple

Dien Bien Phu

Pham Ngoc Thach

Hai Ba Trung

Phung Khac Khoan

Tran Cao Van St

Mac Dinh Chi

Pasteur

Duc Minh

Le Quy Don

Nguyen Dinh Chieu

Cong Truong Quoc Te

Le Duan

British Consulate

Saigon Trade Center

To San Art Gallery

Archbishop's Palace

Vo Van Tan

Nguyen Thi Minh Khai

US Consulate

French Consulate

Nguyen Du

Ton Duc Thang

War Remnants Museum

Diamond Plaza

ICH

Saigon Square

Notre Dame Cathedral

La Cuisile

Reunification Hall

Han Thuyen

Cong Xa Paris

HSBC

Le Thanh Ton

Ly Tu Trong

Thai Van Lung

Le Thanh Ton

Ton Duc Thang

Huyen Tran Cong Chua

Dong Khoi

Vincom

Hai Ba Trung

Thi Sach

Restaurants

Nam Ky Khoi Nghia

Ho Chi Minh City Museum

City Hall

Parkson

Nguyen Trung Truc

National Library

Saigontourist

Opera House

Vietnam Airlines

Lam Son Square

Dong Du

Ton Duc Thang Museum

Nguyen Du

Truong Dinh

Le Loi

Asiana

Mariamman Temple

Le Thanh Ton

Pasteur

Mac Thi Buoi

Me Linh Square

Saigon River

Cho Ben Thanh

Food Stalls

Thiep

Ho Tung Mau

Nguyen Hue

Huynh Thuc Khang

Ton That Dam

Pham Ngu Lao

Local Bus Station

Ham Nghi

Old Market

Tran Hung Dao

Le Thi Hong Gam

Ky Con

Nguyen Thai Binh

Pho Duc Chinh

Fine Arts Museum

SEE HO CHI MINH CITY CENTRE DETAIL MAP

De Tham

Ng Thai Hoc

Yersin

Calmette

Nguyen Cong Tru

Ben Chuong Duong

Former Hong Kong & Shanghai Bank Building

Dragon House Wharf

Ho Chi Minh Museum

N

Dan Sinh

Phung Son Tu Pagoda

400 metres

400 yards

Galerie Quyah

Ben Nghe Channel

Nguyen Tat Thanh

1   2   3

REUNIFICATION HALL

ⓘ *135 Nam Ky Khoi Nghia St, T8-3822 3652, www.dinhdoclap.gov.vn, daily 0730-1100, 1300-1600, 30,000d. The guides are friendly, but their English is not always very good. Tours every 10 mins. The hall is sometimes closed for state occasions.*

Ngo Dinh Diem's **Presidential Palace**, now renamed Reunification Hall, or the **Thong Nhat Conference Hall**, is in a large park to the southeast of Nguyen Thi Minh Khai Street and southwest of Nam Ky Khoi Nghia Street. The residence of the French governor was built on this site in 1868 and was later renamed the Presidential Palace. In February 1962, a pair of planes took off to attack Viet Cong emplacements – piloted by two of the south's finest airmen – but they turned back to bomb the Presidential Palace in a futile attempt to assassinate President Diem. The president, who held office between 1955-1963, escaped with his family to the cellar, but the palace had to be demolished and replaced with a new building. (Diem was later assassinated after a military coup.) One of the two pilots, Nguyen Thanh Trung is a Vice President of **Vietnam Airlines** and still flies government officials around every couple of months to keep his pilot's licence current. One of the most memorable photographs taken during the war was of a North Vietnamese Army (NVA) tank crashing through the gates of the Palace on 30 April 1975 – symbolizing the end of South Vietnam and its government. The President of South Vietnam, General Duong Van Minh, along with his entire cabinet, was arrested in the Palace shortly afterwards. The hall has been preserved as it was found in 1975 and visitors can take a guided tour. In the **Vice President's Guest Room**, there is a lacquered painting of the Temple of Literature in Hanoi, while the **Presenting of Credentials Room** contains a fine 40-piece lacquer work showing diplomats presenting their credentials during the Le Dynasty (15th century). In the basement there are operations rooms, military maps, radios and other paraphernalia. In essence, it is a 1960s-style building filled with 1960s-style official furnishings that now look very kitsch. Not only was the building designed according to the principles of Chinese geomancy but the colour of the carpets – lurid mustard yellow in one room – was also chosen depending on whether it was to calm or stimulate users of the rooms. Visitors are shown an interesting film about the Revolution and some fascinating photographs and memorabilia from the era. A replica of the tank that bulldozed through the gates of the compound heralding the end of South Vietnam is displayed in the forecourt.

WAR REMNANTS MUSEUM

ⓘ *28 Vo Van Tan St, Q3, T8-3930 6325, www.baotangchungtichchientranh.vn, daily 0730-1200, 1330-1700, 15,000d.*

All the horrors of the Vietnam War from the nation's perspective – photographs of atrocities and action, bombs, military tanks and planes and deformed foetuses – are piled up in a new museum building. In the courtyard are tanks, bombs and helicopters, while the new museum, arranged in five new sections, records man's inhumanity. The display covers the Son My (My Lai) massacre on 16 March 1968 (see box, page 145), the effects of napalm and phosphorous, and the after-effects of Agent Orange defoliation (this is particularly disturbing, with bottled malformed human foetuses). There's also a new feature on Senator John Kerry's Vietnam involvement. Unsurprisingly, there is no record of North Vietnamese atrocities to US and South Vietnamese troops. This museum has gone through some interesting name changes in recent years. It began life as the Exhibition House of

American and Chinese War Crimes. In 1990, 'Chinese' was dropped from the name, and in 1994 'American' was too. Since 1996 it has simply been called the War Remnants Museum.

ARCHBISHOP'S PALACE

ⓘ *330 Nguyen Dinh Chieu St and corner of Tran Quoc Thao St.*

Around this area are a number of very fine French-era buildings still standing; some have been allowed to fall into decay but others have been well maintained. In particular the Archbishop's Palace and the high schools, **Le Qui Don** ⓘ *2 Le Qui Don St*, and **Marie Curie** ⓘ *Nam Ky Khoi Nghia St*. All have had extensions built in recent years, but at least the schools (unlike the archbishop) have attempted to blend the new buildings in with the old. The palace is believed to be the oldest house in Ho Chi Minh City, built in 1790 (although not originally on this spot) for the then French bishop of Adran, Pierre Pigneau de Behaine.

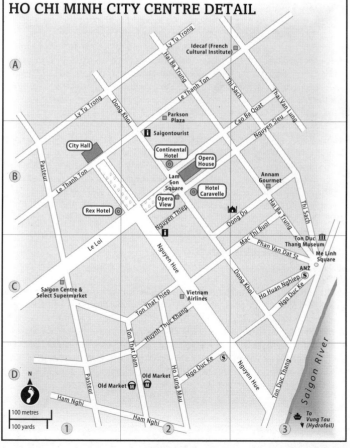

HO CHI MINH CITY CENTRE DETAIL

XA LOI PAGODA

ⓘ 89 Ba Huyen Thanh Quan St, daily 0630-1100, 1430-1700.

Ho Chi Minh City has close to 200 pagodas – far too many for most visitors to see. Many of the finest are in Cholon (see page 200), although there is a selection closer to the main hotel area in central Ho Chi Minh City. The Xa Loi Pagoda is not far from the War Remnants Museum and is surrounded by food stalls. Built in 1956, the pagoda contains a multi-storeyed tower, which is particularly revered, as it houses a relic of the Buddha. The main sanctuary contains a large, bronze-gilded Buddha in an attitude of meditation. Around the walls are a series of silk paintings depicting the previous lives of the Buddha (with an explanation of each life to the right of the entrance into the sanctuary). The pagoda is historically, rather than artistically, important as it became a focus of dissent against the Diem regime (see box, page 199).

LE DUAN STREET

North of the cathedral is Le Duan Street, the former corridor of power with Ngo Dinh Diem's Palace at one end, the zoo at the other and the former embassies of the three major powers, France, the USA and the UK, in between. Quite who was aping who and who was the puppet and who was the master was a tangled question. Nearest the Reunification Hall is the compound of the **French Consulate**. A block away is the **former US Embassy**. After diplomatic ties were resumed in 1995 the Americans lost little time in demolishing the 1960s building which held so many bad memories. The US Consulate General now stands on this site. Outside, a queue of hopeful visa supplicants forms every day come rain or shine. This office has the distinction of being the busiest overseas US mission for marriage visas, a title for which it vies closely with the US Embassy in Manila. A **memorial** outside, on the corner of Mac Dinh Chi Street, records the attack by Viet Cong special forces during the Tet offensive of 1968 and the final victory in 1975. On the other side of the road, a little further northeast at 25 Le Duan, is the **former British Embassy**, erected in the late 1950s, now the British Consulate General and British Council. At 2 Le Duan Street is the **Museum of Ho Chi Minh Campaign** (Bao Tang Quan Doi) *ⓘ T8-3822 9387, Tue-Sun 0730-1100, 1330-1630, 15,000d,* with a tank and warplane in the front compound. It contains an indifferent display of photographs and articles of war.

BOTANICAL GARDENS AND ZOO

ⓘ 2 Nguyen Binh Khiem St, T8-3829 3728, daily 0700-2000, entrance to gardens and zoo, 12,000d.

At the end of Le Duan Street are the Botanical Gardens which run alongside Nguyen Binh Khiem Street at the point where the Thi Nghe channel flows into the Saigon River. The gardens were established in 1864 by French botanist Jean-Batiste Louis Pierre; by the 1970s they had a collection of nearly 2000 species, and a particularly fine display of orchids. With the dislocations of the immediate postwar years, the gardens went into decline, a situation from which they are still trying to recover. In the south quarter of the gardens is a mediocre zoo with a rather moth-eaten collection of animals which form a backdrop to smartly dressed Vietnamese families posing for photographs.

MUSEUM OF VIETNAMESE HISTORY

ⓘ *2 Nguyen Binh Khiem St, T8-3829 8146, www.baotanglichsuvn.com, Tue-Sun 0800-1130, 1330-1700,15,000d. Photography permit, 32,000d. Labels in English and French. Water puppet shows are held here daily 0900, 1000, 1100, 1400, 1500 and 1600, 15 mins, 20,000d.*

The history museum (Bao Tang Lich Su Viet Nam) is an elegant building constructed in 1928 and is pagoda-esque in style. It displays a wide range of artefacts from the prehistoric (300,000 years ago) and the Dongson periods (3500 BC-AD 100), right through to the birth of the Vietnamese Communist Party in 1930. Particularly impressive are the Cham sculptures, of which the standing bronze Buddha, dating from the fourth to sixth century, is probably the finest. There is also a delicately carved Devi (Goddess) dating from the 10th century as well as pieces such as the head of Shiva, Hindu destroyer and creator, from the eighth to ninth century and Ganesh, elephant-headed son of Shiva and Parvati, also dating from the eighth to ninth century.

There are also representative pieces from the Chen-la, Funan, Khmer, Oc-eo and Han Chinese periods, and from the various Vietnamese dynasties together with some hill tribe artefacts. Labelling is in English, French and Vietnamese.

Other highlights include the wooden stakes planted in the Bach Dang riverbed for repelling the war ships of the Mongol Yuan in the 13th century, a beautiful Phoenix head from the Tran dynasty (13th to 14th century) and an Hgor (big drum) from the Jarai people, made from the skin of two elephants. It belonged to the Potauoui (King of Fire) family in Ajunpa district, Gia Lai Province. There are some fine sandstone sculptures too including an incredibly smooth linga from Long An Province (seventh to eighth century) in the Mekong Delta. The linga represents the cult of Siva and signifies gender, energy, fertility and potency.

Near the History Museum is the **Memorial Temple** ⓘ *Tue-Sun 0800-1130, 1300-1600*, constructed in 1928 and dedicated to famous Vietnamese.

HO CHI MINH CITY MUSEUM AND AROUND

ⓘ *65 Ly Tu Trong St, T8-3829 9741, www.hcmc-museum.edu.vn, daily 0800-1700, 15,000d.*

This museum includes a mixed bag of displays concerning the revolution, with a display of photographs, a few pieces of hardware (helicopter, anti-aircraft guns) in the back compound, and some memorabilia. Other exhibits chart the development of the city and its economy. The building itself is historically important. Dominating a prominent intersection, the grey-white classical French-designed building was built as a museum before it became the palace for the governor of Cochin China in 1890. After the 1945 revolution it was used for administrative offices before returning to the French as the High Commissioner's residence in September 1945. During the War, Ngo Dinh Diem resided here under its new name as Southern Governor's Palace; during the reign of Nguyen Van Thieu (1967-1975), it operated as the supreme court.

Southwest from the museum on the corner of Ly Tu Trong Street and Nam Ky Khoi Nghia is the National Library.

MARIAMMAN HINDU TEMPLE

ⓘ *45 Truong Dinh St.*

Although clearly Hindu, with a statue of Mariamman flanked by Maduraiveeran and Pechiamman, the temple is largely frequented by Chinese worshippers, providing the strange sight of Chinese Vietnamese clasping incense sticks and prostrating themselves in front of a Hindu deity, as they would to a Buddha image. The Chinese have always been pragmatic when it comes to religion.

BEN THANH MARKET (CHO BEN THANH)

A large, covered central market, Ben Thanh Market faces a statue of Tran Nguyen Han (a Le Dynasty general) at a large and chaotic roundabout, the Ben Thanh gyratory system, which marks the intersection of Le Loi, Ham Nghi and Tran Hung Dao streets. Ben Thanh is well stocked with clothes (cheap souvenir T-shirts), household goods, a wide range of soap, shampoo and sun cream, a good choice of souvenirs, lacquerware, embroidery and so on, as well as some terrific lines in food, including cold meats, fresh and dried fruits. It is not cheap (most local people window-shop here and purchase elsewhere) but the quality is high and the selection probably without equal. It is a terrific experience just to wander through and marvel at the range of produce on offer, all the more so now most of the beggars have been eased out. Outside the north gate (*cua Bac*) on Le Thanh Ton Street are some tempting displays of fruit (the oranges and apples are imported) and cut flowers.

The **Ben Thanh Night Market** has flourished since 2003. Starting at dusk and open until after midnight the night market is Ho Chi Minh City's attempt to recreate Bangkok's Patpong market. As the sun sinks and the main market closes stalls spring up in the surrounding streets. Clothes and cheap jewellery and an abundance of food stalls are the key attractions. The clear fact is that every night and often way beyond midnight the night market remains well and truly open. This may not sound unusual to new visitors but as the city authorities have been engaged in a tireless war against open-air eating for the past half dozen years the fact that it is now possible to sit in the open and eat well and cheaply is a positive achievement.

Opposite the south gate of Ben Thanh Market is a swirling current of traffic negotiating (by and large successfully) the Benh Thanh gyratory system, one of Ho Chi Minh City's busiest roundabouts and immediately to the south of that is the central (local) bus station. You can obtain a highly useful map inside the station and attempt to ask questions but very little English is spoken. Buses are air-conditioned too.

Ho Chi Minh City has a number of markets, but this one and the Binh Tay Market in Cholon (see page 203) are the largest. Many of the markets are surprisingly well stocked for a country that not too long ago was close to economic collapse.

FINE ARTS MUSEUM

① 97A Pho Duc Chinh St, T8-3829 4441, daily 0900-1700, 10,000d. Not everything is labelled and what is labelled is not in English

The so-called Fine Arts Museum (Bao Tang My Thuat), housed in an impressive cream-coloured mansion is a distinctly unimpressive and unloved collection of dusty works of art. The third floor contains artefacts from the ancient civilizations of Oc-eo through to the Cham era. More recent collections include some attractive Dong Nai ceramics of the early 20th century. Highlights include a 12th-century sculpture of kala, a monster guarding the temple, from My Son. It is a fanged beast with a big protuberance for a nose, bulging eyes and forest-thick eyebrows. Hindu god sculptures are made of soft sandstone: Laksmi, found in Soc Trang in the Mekong Delta (seventh to eighth century) is the goddess of beauty and good fortune. A line of funeral statues (gaunt-looking, wooden folk) made by the Tay Nguyen people in the early 20th century in the central Highlands, line a corridor. These figures are crafted by the living as substitutes of their late relatives.

Part of the second floor is devoted to more recent events. Lacquered pictures appear, such as the interior of Cu Chi by Quach Phong (1997). There's a small collection of propaganda art posters (undated) and a vast bronze mural of the nation indicating anti-

ON THE ROAD
Buddhist martyrs: self-immolation as protest

In August 1963 there was a demonstration of 15,000 people at the Xa Loi Pagoda, with speakers denouncing the Diem regime and telling jokes about Diem's sister-in-law, Madame Nhu (who was later to call monks "hooligans in robes"). Two nights later, ARVN special forces (from Roman Catholic families) raided the pagoda, battering down the gate, wounding 30 and killing seven people. Soon afterwards Diem declared martial law. The pagoda became a focus of discontent, with several monks committing suicide through self-immolation to protest against the Diem regime.

The first monk to immolate himself was 66-year-old Thich Quang Du, from Hué. On 11 June 1963, his companions poured petrol over him and set him alight as he sat in the lotus position. Pedestrians prostrated themselves at the sight; even a policeman threw himself to the ground in reverence. The next day, the picture of the monk in flames filled the front pages of newspapers around the world. Some 30 monks and nuns followed Thich's example in protesting against the Diem government and US involvement in South Vietnam. Two young US protesters also followed suit, one committing suicide by self-immolation outside the Pentagon and the other next to the UN, both in November 1968.

Madame Nhu, a Catholic, is reported as having said after the monks' death: "Let them burn, and we shall clap our hands." Within five months Diem had been killed in a military coup.

In May 1993, a Vietnamese man immolated himself at the Thien Mu Pagoda in Hué – the pagoda where the first monk-martyr was based (see page 114).

American sentiment by Nguyen Sang (undated). Some of the most interesting work is by Americans who have produced work that reflects on the war – namely montage and photographs. The ground floor is given over to temporary exhibitions.

The building itself is worthy of note having been built in the early 20th century by a Chinese man whose fortune was made by selling empty bottles.

PHUNG SON TU PAGODA
① *338 Nguyen Cong Tru St.*
This is a small temple built just after the Second World War by Fukien Chinese; its most notable features are the wonderful painted entrance doors with their fearsome armed warriors. Incense spirals hang in the open well of the pagoda, which is dedicated to Ong Bon, the Guardian of Happiness and Virtue.

The **War Surplus Market** (**Dan Sinh**) ① *Yersin between Nguyen Thai Binh St and Nguyen Cong Tru St*, is not far from the Phung Son Tu Pagoda. Merchandise on sale includes dog tags and military clothing and equipment (not all of it authentic). The market is popular with Western visitors looking for mementoes of their visit, so bargain particularly hard.

OLD MARKET AND RIVERSIDE
The Old Market is on Ton That Dam Street, running between Ham Nghi Street and Ton That Thiep Street. It is the centre for the sale of black market goods (particularly consumer electronics) – now openly displayed. There is also a good range of foodstalls and fruit sellers. Close by is the old and rather splendid **Hong Kong and Shanghai Bank building** ① *Ben Chuong Duong St*. It no longer houses the HSBC bank, which returned

ON THE ROAD
Betel nut

Betel nut has been a stimulant for the Vietnamese for hundreds of years. The ingredients combine the egg-shaped betel palm (*Areca catechu*) nut (*cau*) with Piper betel vine leaves (*trau*) and lime. When chewed (known as *An trau*) the ingredients stain the mouth and lips and red juice can often be seen dribbling down the chins of users. It often stains teeth black due to the polyphenol in the nut and leaf, which is considered attractive. The origin of the substance lies in Vietnamese legend and its use is found at weddings where a betel quid (a combination of powdered betel nut, betel leaves, lime and other flavourings) is laid out for guests. The areca nut is also a customary wedding gift given to the bride's family by the bridegroom's family. Betel and areca nuts are also presented at Tet (Lunar New Year).

to Vietnam in 1994; this is now to be found on Dong Khoi Street facing the cathedral. Nguyen Tat Thanh Street runs south from here over the Ben Nghe Channel to **Dragon House Wharf**, at the confluence of the Ben Nghe Channel and the Saigon River. The former customs building, dating from 1863, has been converted into the **Ho Chi Minh Museum** ⓘ *1 Nguyen Tat Thanh St, 0730-1130, 1330-1630, 10,000d,* (predominantly on the first floor), celebrating the life and exploits of Ho Chi Minh, mostly through pictures and the odd piece of memorabilia. School children are brought here to learn about their country's recent history, and people of all ages have their photographs taken with a portrait of Bac Ho in the background.

A short distance north up Ton Duc Thang Street from the broad Me Linh Square (in the centre of which is an imposing statue of Vietnamese hero Tran Hung Dao) is the rarely visited **Ton Duc Thang Museum** ⓘ *5 Ton Duc Thang St, T8-3829 7542, Tue-Sun 0730-1130, 1330-1700, free.* Opened in 1989, it is dedicated to the life of Ton Duc Thang or Bac (Uncle) Ton. Bac Ton, a comrade who fought with Ho Chi Minh, was appointed President of Vietnam following Ho's death, remaining in office until his own death in 1980. The museum contains an array of photographs and other memorabilia.

→ PHAM NGU LAO

Most backpackers arriving overland in Ho Chi Minh City are dropped off in this bustling district, a 10- to 15-minute walk from downtown. Those arriving by air tend to head straight here too. The countless hotels, guesthouses and rooms to rent open and close and change name or owner with remarkable speed. The area is littered with restaurants, cafés, bars, email services, laundries, tour agencies and money changers, all fiercely competitive; there are mini-supermarkets and shops selling rucksacks, footwear, CDs, DVDs, pirated software and ethnic knick-knacks.

→ CHOLON (CHINATOWN)

This is the heart of Ho Chi Minh City's Chinese community. Cholon is an area of commerce and trade; not global but nevertheless international. In typical Chinese style it is dominated by small and medium-size businesses and this shows in the buildings' shop fronts (look for the Chinese characters on signs over the door). The Chinese do less on the pavements than the Vietnamese and this is apparent on a tour through Cholon. Cholon is home to a great many temples and pagodas – some of which are described below. As one would expect from a Chinese trading district, there is plenty of fabric for sale in the markets.

Cho lon or 'big market' or Chinatown, is inhabited predominantly by Vietnamese of Chinese origin. However, since 1975 the authorities have alienated many Chinese, causing hundreds of thousands to leave the country. In making their escape many have died – either through drowning, as their perilously small and overladen craft foundered, or at the hands of pirates in the East Sea. In total, between 1977 and 1982, 709,570 refugees were recorded by the UNHCR as having fled Vietnam. By the late 1980s, the flow of boat people was being driven more by economic, rather than political, forces; there was little chance of making good in a country as poor, and in an economy as moribund, as that of Vietnam. Even with this flow of Chinese out of the country, there is still a large population of Chinese Vietnamese living in Cholon, an area which encompasses District 5 to the southwest of the city centre. Cholon appears to the casual visitor to be the most populated, noisiest and in general the most vigorous part of Ho Chi Minh City, if not Vietnam. It is here that entrepreneurial talent and private funds are concentrated; both resources that the government are keen to mobilize in their attempts to reinvigorate the economy.

Cholon is worth visiting not only for the bustle and activity, but also because the temples and assembly halls found here are the finest in Ho Chi Minh City. As with any town in Southeast Asia boasting a sizeable Chinese population, the early settlers established meeting rooms which offered social, cultural and spiritual support to members of a dialect group. These assembly halls (*hoi quan*) are most common in Hoi An and Cholon. There are temples in the buildings which attract Vietnamese as well as Chinese worshippers, and indeed today serve little of their former purpose. The elderly meet here occasionally for a natter and a cup of tea.

NGHIA AN ASSEMBLY HALL
ⓘ *678 Nguyen Trai St, not far from the Arc en Ciel Hotel.*
A magnificent, carved, gold-painted wooden boat hangs over the entrance to the Nghia An Assembly Hall. To the left, on entering the temple, is a larger-than-life representation of Quan Cong's horse and groom. (Quan Cong was a loyal military man who lived in China in the third century.) At the main altar are three figures in glass cases: the central red-faced figure with a green cloak is Quan Cong himself; to the left and right are his trusty companions, General Chau Xuong (very fierce) and the mandarin Quan Binh respectively. On leaving, note the fine gold figures of guardians on the inside of the door panels.

TAM SON ASSEMBLY HALL
ⓘ *118 Trieu Quang Phuc St, just off Nguyen Trai St.*
The temple, built in the 19th century by Fukien immigrants, is frequented by childless women as it is dedicated to Chua Thai Sanh, the Goddess of Fertility. It is an uncluttered, 'pure' example of a Chinese/Vietnamese pagoda – peaceful and quiet. Like Nghia An Hoi Quan, the temple contains figures of Quan Cong, his horse and two companions.

THIEN HAU TEMPLES
ⓘ *710 and 802 Nguyen Trai St.*
The Thien Hau Temple at 710 Nguyen Trai Street is one of the largest in the city. Constructed in the early 19th century, it is Chinese in inspiration and is dedicated to the worship of both the Buddha and to the Goddess Thien Hau, the goddess of the sea and the protector of

sailors. Thien Hau was born in China and as a girl saved her father from drowning, but not her brother. Thien Hau's festival is marked here on the 23rd day of the third lunar month. One enormous incense urn and an incinerator can be seen through the main doors. Inside, the principal altar supports the gilded form of Thien Hau, with a boat to one side. Silk paintings depicting religious scenes decorate the walls. By far the most interesting part of the pagoda is the roof, which can be best seen from the small open courtyard. It must be one of the finest and most richly ornamented in Vietnam, with the high-relief frieze depicting episodes from the Legends of the Three Kingdoms. In the post-1975 era, many would-be refugees prayed here for safe deliverance before casting themselves adrift on the East Sea. A number of those who survived the perilous voyage sent offerings to the merciful goddess and the temple has been well maintained since. On busy days it is very smoky. Look up on leaving to see over the front door a picture of a boiling sea peppered with sinking boats. A benign Thien An looks down mercifully from a cloud. The temple has its own shop stocked with joss sticks, paper offerings and temple tat. Most people seem to buy their gear from the vendors outside who presumably don't have to pass on any 'overhead' costs. The shop also sells chilled water and Coca Cola.

A **second temple** dedicated to Thien Hau is a couple of blocks away at 802 Nguyen Trai St. This was built by migrants from Fukien Province in China in the 1730s although the building on the site today is not old. The roof can be seen from the road and in addition to the normal dragons are some curious models of what appear to be miniature Chinese landscapes carried by bowed men. Inside it is less busy than the first Thien Hau temple but on good days worshippers hurry from one image of Thien Hau (depicted here with a black face) to another waving burning joss sticks in front of her. Whatever happens in these temples is not religious in the sense of worshipping a god but more a superstition, entreating the spirits for good fortune (hence the lottery ticket sellers outside) or asking them to stave off bad luck. Note that these are not pagodas in the sense that they are not a place for the worship of Buddha and you will see no Buddhist monks here and have no sense of serene or enlightened calm. This temple has some nicely carved stone pillars of entwined dragons and on the wall to the right of the altars is a frieze of a boat being swamped by a tsunami. The walls are festooned with calendars from local Chinese restaurants and gold shops.

MING DYNASTY ASSEMBLY HALL
ⓘ *380 Tran Hung Dao St.*

The Ming Dynasty Assembly Hall (Dinh Minh Huong Gia Thanh) was built by the Cantonese community which arrived in Saigon via Hoi An in the 18th century. The assembly hall was built in 1789 to the dedication and worship of the Ming Dynasty although the building we see today dates largely from an extensive renovation carried out in the 1960s. There is some old furniture, a heavy-marble topped table and chairs which arrived in 1850 from China. It appears that the Vietnamese Emperor Gia Long used the Chinese community for cordial relations with the Chinese royal court and one of the community, a man called Trinh Hoai Duc was appointed Vietnamese ambassador to the Middle Dynasty. In the main hall there are three altars which, following imperial tradition, are: the central altar dedicated to the royal family (Ming Dynasty in this case), the right-hand altar dedicated to two mandarin officers (military) and the left-hand altar dedicated to two mandarin officers (civil).

The hall behind is dedicated to the memory of the Vuong family who built the hall and whose descendants have lived here ever since. The custodian is in fact the third generation of this family and he will explain the complexities in broken English or polished French. There is, in addition, a small side chapel where childless women can seek divine intercession from a local deity, Ba Me Sanh.

QUAN AM PAGODA

① *12 Lao Tu St (just off Luong Nhu Hoc St).*

The Quan Am Pagoda is thought to be one of the oldest in the city. Its roof supports four sets of impressive mosaic-encrusted figures, while inside, the main building is fronted with old, gold and lacquer panels of guardian spirits. The main altar supports a seated statue of A-Pho, the Holy Mother. In front of the main altar is a white ceramic statue of Quan Am, the Goddess of Purity and Motherhood (Goddess of Mercy) – see box, page 44. The pagoda complex also contains a series of courtyards and altars dedicated to a range of deities and spirits. Outside, hawkers sell caged birds and vast quantities of incense sticks to pilgrims.

BINH TAY MARKET

The Binh Tay Market, sandwiched between Thap Muoi and Phan Van Khoe streets, is one of the most colourful and exciting markets in Ho Chi Minh City, with a wonderful array of noises, smells and colours. It sprawls over a large area and is contained in what looks like a rather decayed Forbidden Palace. Beware of pickpockets here. A new high-rise market – the five-storey **An Dong Market** – opened at the end of 1991 in Cholon. It was built with an investment of US$5 million from local ethnic Chinese businessmen.

→ OUTER HO CHI MINH CITY

Outer Ho Chi Minh City includes a clutch of scattered pagodas in several districts, namely Districts 3, 10, 11 and Binh Thanh. All are accessible by cyclo, moto or taxi. There's also a new museum of traditional medicine in District 10.

PHUNG SON PAGODA

① *A 40-min walk or 8-min motorbike ride from the Binh Tay Market, set back from the road at 1408 3 Thang 2 Blvd.*

The Phung Son Pagoda, also known as **Go Pagoda**, was built at the beginning of the 19th century on the site of an earlier Cambodian structure and has been rebuilt several times. At one time, it was decided to move the pagoda, and all the temple valuables were loaded on to the back of a white elephant. The beast stumbled and the valuables tumbled out into the pond that surrounds the temple. This was taken as a sign from the gods that the pagoda was to stay where it was. In the sanctuary, there is a large, seated, gilded Buddha, surrounded by a variety of other figures from several Asian and Southeast Asian countries. This, being a pagoda, has a very different atmosphere from the temples of Chinatown. There is no frenzied scrum in front of the altars and only a few whisps of smoke. Monks sit in contemplation.

GIAC VIEN PAGODA

① *At the end of a narrow and rather seedy 400-m-long alley running off Lac Long Quan St (just after No 247). There is a also a temple down here of no interest whatsoever, the pagoda is right at the end.*

Giac Vien Pagoda (Buddha's Complete Enlightenment) is similar in layout, content and inspiration to Giac Lam Pagoda (see below). Visiting just one of the two pagodas would be enough for most visitors. The Giac Vien Pagoda was built in 1771 and dedicated to the worship of the Emperor Gia Long. Although restored, Giac Vien remains one of the best-preserved temples in Vietnam. It is lavishly decorated, with more than 100 carvings of various divinities and spirits, dominated by a large gilded image of the Buddha of the Past (Amitabha or *A Di Da Phat* in Vietnamese). It is everything a pagoda should be: demons and gods jump out around every corner, a confusion of fantastic characters. With the smoke and smells, the richness of colour and the darkness, it's an assault on the senses. Among the decorations, note the 'Buddha lamp', funerary tablets and urns with photographs of the deceased. Outside there is a small pavilion in which the ashes of the dead are stored in small urns.

GIAC LAM PAGODA

ⓘ *118 Lac Long Quan St, Ward 10, Q Tan Binh, T8-865 3933, about 2 km northeast of Giac Vien Pagoda, through an arch and down a short track about 300 m from the intersection with Le Dai Hanh St. Near the intersection is a modern 7-storey tower and beyond a giant Buddha statue which is also modern. Daily 0500-1200, 1400-2100.*

The Giac Lam Pagoda (Forest of Enlightenment) was built in 1744 and is the oldest pagoda in Ho Chi Minh City. There is a sacred Bodhi tree in the temple courtyard and the pagoda is set among fruit trees and vegetable plots. Inside Giac Lam it feels, initially, like a rather cluttered private house. In one section, there are rows of funerary tablets with pictures of the deceased – a rather moving display of man's mortality. The main altar is impressive, with layers of Buddhas, dominated by the gilded form of the Buddha of the Past. Note the 49-Buddha oil lamp with little scraps of paper tucked in. On these scraps are the names of the mourned. The number seven is very important in Buddhism and most towers have seven storeys. Behind the main temple in the section with the funerary tablets is a bust of Ho Chi Minh. At the very back of the pagoda is a hall with murals showing scenes of torture from hell. Each sin is punished in a very specific and appropriate way. The monks are very friendly and will probably offer tea. Some speak good English and French as well as having detailed knowledge of the history of the pagoda. It is a small haven of peace. An unusual feature is the use of blue and white porcelain plates to decorate the roof and some of the small towers in the garden facing the pagoda. These towers are the burial places of former head monks.

PHUOC HAI TU (EMPEROR OF JADE PAGODA) AND AROUND

ⓘ *73 Mai Thi Luu St off Dien Bien Phu St, 0700-1800.*

The Phuoc Hai Tu can be found, nestling behind low pink walls, just before the Thi Nghe Channel. Women sell birds that are set free to gain merit, and a pond to the right contains large turtles. The Emperor of Jade is the supreme god of the Taoists, although this temple, built in 1900, contains a wide range of other deities. These include the archangel Michael of the Buddhists, a Sakyamuni (historic) Buddha, statues of the two generals who tamed the Green Dragon (representing the east) and the White Dragon (representing the west), to the left and right of the first altar respectively, and Quan Am (see box, page 44). The Hall of Ten Hells in the left-hand sanctuary has reliefs depicting the 1000 tortures of hell.

Nearby, the architecturally interesting **city library** ⓘ *3 Nguyen Dinh Chieu*, has a cool, modern façade; there is a memorial at the front of the building.

TRAN HUNG DAO TEMPLE

ⓘ *Near the Emperor of Jade Pagoda at 34 Vo Thi Sau St, daily 0700-1100, 1430-1700.*

The small Tran Hung Dao Temple, built in 1932, was dedicated to the worship of the victorious 13th-century General Hung Dao and contains a series of bas-reliefs depicting the general's successes, along with weapons and carved dragons. In the front courtyard is a larger-than-life bronze statue of this hero of Vietnamese nationalism.

VINH NGHIEM PAGODA
ⓘ *To the west, on Nguyen Van Troi St, and just to the south of the Thi Nghe Channel.*
Another modern pagoda, the Vinh Nghiem Pagoda, was completed in 1967 and is one of the largest in Vietnam. Built in the Japanese style, it displays a classic seven-storey pagoda in a large and airy sanctuary. On either side of the entrance are two fearsome warriors; inside is a large Japanese-style Buddha in an attitude of meditation, flanked by two goddesses. Along the walls are a series of scrolls depicting the *jataka* tales, with rather quaint (and difficult to interpret) explanations in English.

TOMB AND TEMPLE OF MARSHAL LE VAN DUYET
ⓘ *126 Dinh Tien Hoang St, a 10- to 15-min cyclo ride across the Thi Nghe Channel and almost into the suburbs, 0500-1800.*
Le Van Duyet was a highly respected Vietnamese soldier who put down the Tay Son Rebellion (see box, page 175) and who died in 1831. The pagoda was renovated in 1937 – a plaque on the left lists those who made donations to the renovation fund. The main sanctuary contains a weird assortment of objects: a stuffed tiger, a miniature mountain, whale baleen, spears and other weapons of war. Much of the collection is made up of the Marshal's personal possessions. In front of the temple is the tomb itself, surrounded by a low wall and flanked by two guardian lions and two lotus buds. The pagoda's attractive roof is best seen from the tomb.

MUSEUM OF VIETNAMESE TRADITIONAL MEDICINE
ⓘ *41 Hoang Du Khuong St, District 10, T8-386 42430, www.fitomuseum.com.vn, open daily 0830-1730.*
A fascinating exploration into traditional medicine with 3000 exhibits including instruments, manuscripts, ceramic jars and model of a 19th-century pharmacy.

→ AROUND HO CHI MINH CITY

Unlike Hanoi, which is so rich in sights to visit on a day out, the Ho Chi Minh City region is woefully under-endowed. The Cu Chi Tunnels nd Cao Dai Temple are the most popular day trip, followed closely by an excursion to the Mekong Delta, especially My Tho (see page 215).

CU CHI TUNNELS
ⓘ *Most visitors reach Cu Chi on a tour or charter a car and include a visit to Tay Ninh – see below. Regular buses leave for Cu Chi town from the Mien Tay station (Cholon) and the Ham Nghi station; from Cu Chi it is necessary to take a Honda ôm to the tunnels or the infrequent Ben Suc bus, 10 km. It is also possible to take a motorbike from Ho Chi Minh City and back but the road (now the Bangkok to Ho Chi Minh City highway) is becoming increasingly dangerous with fast and heavy traffic. Go up Cach Mang Thang Tam St, which turns into Highway 22. Continue to Cu Chi. Go over the flyover and take the next turning to the right which is signed to the Cu Chi Tunnels. From here the tunnels are quite badly signed and you will almost certainly need to ask. Daily 0700-1700, 90,000d.*
Cu Chi Tunnels are about 40 km northwest of Ho Chi Minh City. Cu Chi town is on the main road to Tay Ninh and the Cao Dai temple and both the tunnels and the temple can be

visited in a single day trip. Dug by the Viet Minh, who began work in 1948, they were later expanded by the People's Liberation Armed Forces (PLAF, or Viet Cong, VC) and used for storage and refuge, and contained sleeping quarters, hospitals and schools. Between 1960 and 1970, 200 km of tunnels were built. At the height of their usage, some 300,000 were living underground. The width of the tunnel entry at ground level was 22 cm by 30 cm. The tunnels are too narrow for most Westerners, but a short section of the 250 km of tunnels has been especially widened to allow tourists to share the experience. Tall or large people might still find it a claustrophobic squeeze.

Cu Chi was one of the most fervently communist of the districts around Ho Chi Minh City and the tunnels were used as the base from which the PLAF mounted the operations of the Tet Offensive in 1968. Communist cadres were active in this area of rubber plantations, even before the Second World War. Vann and Ramsey, two American soldiers, were to notice the difference between this area and other parts of the south in the early 1960s: "No children laughed and shouted for gum and candy in these hamlets. Everyone, adult and child, had a cold look" (*A Bright Shining Lie*, Sheehan 1989).

When the Americans first discovered this underground base on their doorstep (Dong Du GI base was nearby) they would simply pump CS gas down the tunnel openings and then set explosives. They also pumped river water in and used German Shepherd dogs to smell out air holes. The VC, however, smothered the holes in garlic to deter the dogs. They also used cotton from the cotton tree – kapok – to stifle the smoke from cooking; 40,000 VC were killed in the tunnels in 10 years. Later, realizing that the tunnels might also yield valuable intelligence, volunteer 'tunnel rats' were sent into the earth to capture prisoners.

Cu Chi district was a free-fire zone and was assaulted using the full battery of ecological warfare. Defoliants were sprayed and 20 tonne Rome Ploughs carved up the area in the search for tunnels. It was said that even a crow flying over Cu Chi district had to carry its own lunch. Later it was also carpet bombed with 50,000 tonnes dropped on the area in 10 years.

At **Cu Chi 1** (Ben Dinh) ① *90,000d*, visitors are shown a somewhat antique but nevertheless interesting film of the tunnels during the war before being taken into the tunnels and seeing some of the rooms and the booby traps the GIs encountered. The VC survived on just cassava for up to three months and at both places you will be invited to taste some dipped in salt, sesame, sugar and peanuts. You will also be invited to a firing range to try your hand with ancient AK47s at a buck a bang.

Cu Chi 2 (Ben Duoc), has a temple, the **Ben Duoc Temple**, in memory of the 50,000 Saigon dead; the exterior is covered in mosaic murals. It stands in front of a rather beautiful sculpture of a tear called *Symbol of the Country's Spiritual Soul*.

Near the tunnels is the Cu Chi graveyard for patriots with 8000 graves. It has a very interesting large and striking bas-relief of war images along the perimeter of the entrance to the cemetery.

CAO DAI GREAT TEMPLE
① *Ceremonies are held each day at 0600, 1200, 1800 and 2400, visitors can watch from the cathedral's balcony. Visitors should not enter the central portion of the nave – keep to the side aisles – and also should not wander in and out during services. If you go in at the beginning of the service you should stay until the end (1 hr). Photography is allowed. Take a tour, or charter a car in Ho Chi Minh City. Regular buses leave for Tay Ninh, via Cu Chi, from Mien Tay station (2½ hrs) or motorbike.*

Tay Ninh, the home of the temple, is 96 km northwest of Ho Chi Minh City and 64 km further on from Cu Chi town. It can be visited on a day trip from the city and can easily be combined with a visit to the Cu Chi tunnels. The idiosyncratic Cao Dai Great Temple, the 'cathedral' of the Cao Dai religion, is the main reason to visit the town.

The Cao Dai Great Temple, built in 1880, is set within a very large complex of schools and administrative buildings, all washed in pastel yellow. The twin-towered cathedral is European in inspiration but with distinct oriental features. On the façade are figures of Cao Dai saints in high relief and at the entrance is a painting depicting Victor Hugo flanked by the Vietnamese poet Nguyen Binh Khiem and the Chinese nationalist Sun Yat Sen. The latter holds an inkstone, symbolizing, strangely, the link between Confucianism and Christianity. Novelist Graham Greene in *The Quiet American* called it "The Walt Disney Fantasia of the East". Monsieur Ferry, an acquaintance of Norman Lewis, described the cathedral in even more outlandish terms, saying it "looked like a fantasy from the brain of Disney, and all the faiths of the Orient had been ransacked to create the pompous ritual...". Lewis himself was clearly unimpressed with the structure and the religion, writing in *A Dragon Apparent* that "This cathedral must be the most outrageously vulgar building ever to have been erected with serious intent".

After removing shoes and hats, women enter the cathedral through a door to the left, men to the right, and they then proceed down their respective aisles towards the altar, usually accompanied by a Cao Dai priest dressed in white with a black turban. During services they don red, blue and yellow robes signifying Confucianism, Taoism and Buddhism respectively. The men in coloured robes sporting an embroidered divine eye on their costumes are more senior. During services, on the balcony at the back of the cathedral, a group of men play a stringed instrument called a Dan Co between their feet using a bow; women sing as they play.

Two rows of pink pillars entwined with green dragons line the nave, leading up to the main altar which supports a large globe on which is painted a single staring eye – the divine, all-seeing-eye. The roof is blue and dotted with clouds, representing the heavens, and the walls are pierced by open, lattice-work windows with the divine eye as the centrepiece to the window design. At the back of the cathedral is a sculpture of Pham Com Tac, the last pope and one of the religion's founders who died in 1957. He stands on flowers surrounded by huge brown snakes and is flanked by his two assistants; one is the leader of spirits, the other the leader of materialism.

There are nine columns and nine steps to the cathedral representing the nine steps to heaven. Above the altar is the Cao Dai pantheon: at the top in the centre is Sakyamuni Buddha. Next to him on the left is Lao Tzu, master of Taosim. Left of Lao Tzu, is Quan Am, Goddess of Mercy, sitting on a lotus blossom. On the other side of the Buddha statue is Confucius. Right of the sage is the red-faced Chinese God of War and Soldiers, Quan Cong. Below Sakyamuni Buddha is the poet and leader of the Chinese saints, Li Ti Pei. Below him is Jesus and below Christ is Jiang Zhia, master of Geniism.

About 500 m from the cathedral (turn right when facing the main façade) is the **Doan Ket**, a formal garden.

The town of Tay Ninh also has a good **market** and some **Cham temples** 1 km to the southwest of the town.

HO CHI MINH CITY LISTINGS

WHERE TO STAY

Ho Chi Minh City has upped its hotel game. In the last 10 years, the city has seen the opening of the **Park Hyatt**, **Sheraton** and **Novotel**, and the historic **Rex** received a makeover. In addition to the 5-star hotels, there are smart town hotels and backpacker hostels in the backpacker district of Pham Ngu Lao.

$$$$ Caravelle, 19-23 Lam Son Sq, T08-3823 4999, www.caravellehotel.com. Central and one of HCMC's top hotels and recently renovated. Comfortable with well-trained and friendly staff. **Restaurant Nineteen** serves a fantastic buffet lunch and dinner with free flow of fine French wine included and **Saigon Saigon**, the rooftop bar, draws the crowds until the early hours of the morning. Also has boutique shops and ATM.

$$$$ Rex, 141 Nguyen Hué Blvd, T08-3829 2185, www.rexhotelvietnam.com. A historically important hotel in the heart of Saigon with unusual interior decor and a newer fabulous side extension that has become the principal entrance complete with high-end shopping arcade. New wing premium rooms are very smart, if a little business-like; cheaper 'Superior' rooms in the old wing have small bathtub and are interior facing.

$$$$ Majestic, 1 Dong Khoi St, T08-3829 5517, www.majesticsaigon.com.vn. Built in 1925, this riverside hotel has character and charm and has been tastefully restored and recently expanded. More expensive and large rooms have superb views over the river; from the bar on the top floor there are magnificent views especially at night.

$$$$-$$$ Novotel Saigon, 167 Hai Ba Trung St, T08-3822 4866, www.accorhotels. com. This new hotel has a fresh, sharp look, and its modern rooms have a homely feel. There's a great swimming pool and spa, a cool bar and an international buffet served in space-age surroundings.

$$$ Lan Lan Hotel, 246 Thu Khoa Huan St, T08-3822 7926, www.lanlanhotel.com.vn. Excellent-value rooms. Those on the upper floors have expansive views of the city. Helpful staff, buffet breakfast and in-room Wi-Fi. Has a 2nd location on the same road.

$$ Spring, 44-46 Le Thanh Ton St, T08-3829 7362, www.springhotelvietnam.com. Central, comfortable with charming and helpful staff. Book well in advance if you want to stay in this well-run family hotel that is excellent value; breakfast included. Recommended.

$$ Beautiful Saigon, 62 Bui Vien St, Pham Ngu Lao, T08-3836 4852, www.beautiful saigonhotel.com. A relatively new addition to the backpacker zone, this is more for the flashpackers and welcome it is too. Very nice smart and tidy rooms all with mod cons, Wi-Fi and breakfast. Recommended by happy guests.

$ Hong Hoa, 185/28 Pham Ngu Lao St, T08-3836 1915, www.honghoavn.com. A well-run family hotel with 9 rooms, all a/c, hot water and private bathroom. Downstairs has free email and a supermarket.

RESTAURANTS

HCMC has a rich culinary tradition and, as home to people from most of the world's imagined corners, its cooking is diverse. Do not overlook street-side stalls, staples include *pho* (noodle soup, 30-50,000d), *bánh xeo* (savoury pancakes, 30,000d), *cha giò* (spring rolls, around 10,000d) and *banh* *mi pate* (baguettes stuffed with pâté and salad, from 10,000d) all served fresh.

The internationalization of Ho Chi Minh City is evidenced by the number of fast food chains opening up, with **Pizza Hut**, **KFC**, **Domino's** and even **Burger King** now in town. Hong Kong-based

Al Fresco's group dominate, with **Papa Joes**, **Al Fresco's** (pizzas and ribs) and **Pepperoni's** (pasta and salads) outlets all around town. Check www.alfrescosgroup.com for a full list of addresses. For some more authentically Vietnamese fast food (although any street food could really be classed as fast) look out for the various **Pho 24** outlets scattered around town – this is street food, sanitized and as the name suggests, some are open 24 hrs.

$$$ Hoa Tuc, 74 Hai Ba Trung St, T08-3825 1676. Open 1000-2230. Set in a popular courtyard dining space. Dine amid the art deco accents on soft shell crab or a salad of pink pomelo, squid and crab with herbs. The desserts are tantalizing. Try the Earl Grey tea custard. Portions a tad on the small side. Cooking classes available (www.saigoncookingclass.com).

$$$ La Fourchette, 9 Ngo Duc Ke St, T08-3829 8143. Daily 1200-1430, 1830-2230. Truly excellent and authentic French bistro offering a warm welcome, well-prepared dishes and generous portions of tender steak. Booking advised. Recommended.

$$$-$$ Pacharan, 97 Hai Ba Trung St, T08-3825 6024. Daily 1100-late. A hit from the beginning, this Spanish restaurant is nearly full every night with happy and satisfied customers. The open-air rooftop bar that overlooks the **Park Hyatt Hotel** is a winner when there's a cool breeze blowing through the terrace. Fans of Spanish fare will love the (expensive) Iberian cured ham from rare, semi-wild, acorn-fed black-footed pigs as well as staples such as anchovies, olives, mushrooms and prawns; all the tapas are beautifully presented.

$$$-$$ Temple Club, 29 Ton That Thiep St, T08-3829 9244. Daily 1100-1400, 1830-2230. Beautifully furnished club and restaurant open to non-members. French-colonial style and tasty Vietnamese dishes. Excellent value. The restaurant is popular so it's wise to book.

$$ Elbow Room, 52 Pasteur St, T08-3821 4327, www.elbowroom.com.vn. Cosy, bare brick American diner serving the best burgers in town and awesome shakes – don't miss the vanilla version.

$$ Guc Cach, 10 Dang Tat St, T08-4801 4410. The 2nd restaurant run by a local architect, **Guc Cach**, is known for its great atmosphere, old school Saigon decor, and excellent Vietnamese fare. The soft shell crab is superb. Recommended.

$$ The Refinery, 74 Hai Ba Trung St, T08-3823 0509. Open 1100-2300. This former opium factory (through the arch and on the left) is a little understated in its reincarnation. The herb-encrusted steak and grilled barramundi are delicious but the seared tuna with lentil salad is outstanding. Braised rabbit and duck and apple tagine with raisin and butter couscous are other menu offerings.

$ 13 Ngo Duc Ke, 15 Ngo Duc Ke St, T08-3823 9314. Daily 0600-2230. Fresh, well cooked, honest Vietnamese fare. Chicken in lemongrass (no skin, no bone) is a great favourite and *bo luc lac* melts in the mouth. Popular with locals, expats and travellers.

ENTERTAINMENT

The city's bar scene is on the up with new rooftop bars and sleek cocktail lounges appearing all the time. Long-time backpacker haunts in the Pham Ngu Lao area tend to be busy later at night and stay open longer than those in the centre.

Evening cafés
Many younger Vietnamese prefer non-alcohol drinks. Romantic couples sit in virtual darkness listening to Vietnamese love songs whilst sipping coffee and fruit shakes. these cafés are an agreeable way of relaxing after dinner in a more typically Vietnamese way.

CON DAO

Con Dao, a name given to the 14 islands that make up this tiny archipelago, is Vietnam's last untouched wilderness with possibilities for wildlife viewing but not for too much longer. A few years ago the government approved a tourism strategy that would see it attracting 500,000 to 700,000 tourists a year by 2020. The biggest and only permanently settled island is Con Son with a population of approximately 6000 people.

ARRIVING IN CON DAO
Getting there There are now three flights a day between Con Dao and Ho Chi Minh City (45 minutes).

Best time to visit Between June and September is sea turtle nesting season (records show that the 1st and 15th of the month are best) although good weather is not guaranteed. February to April can be incredibly windy. The wet season lasts from May to November.

BACKGROUND
The Portuguese arrived on Con Dao in 1516 but it wasn't until 1702 that a trading post was set up here by the East India Trading Company. Because of the millions of sea birds that inhabited it, it was then called Bird Island. In 1773, it became the home of Nguyen Anh and many mandarin families who fled there after being defeated by the armies of the Tay Son. In 1832, the Con Dao archipelago was handed over to the French by Emperor Tu Duc. Prisons were built in 1862 by Admiral Bonard in which the French incarcerated their more obstinate political prisoners. Up to 12,000 people could be held in the completed prisons. The Con Dao prisons were later used by the government of South Vietnam to hold political prisoners. In 113 years of prison existence 200,000 people were incarcerated here and one tenth of those people died in prison. Remarkably, 153 prisoners volunteered to stay on in Con Son to live after 1975.

Now targeted as the next hot tourist destination the province is to spend US$23 million upgrading the islands' infrastructure. US-based MH Golden Sands is to develop a tourism, commercial and convention complex worth US$30-50 million near the airport. A Japanese project is in the pipeline and Indochina Capital has invested in an Evason resort.

PLACES IN CON DAO
The combination of its mountains and islands, cultural diversity as well as its biodiversity, make Con Dao quite special. It is also one of Vietnam's last relatively pristine areas. There are just a few main roads around Con Son and an unbelievable lack of traffic. The main hotels face out onto Con Son Bay behind the coastal road. The colourful fishing boats that used to bob and work the sea here have been moved to Ben Dam port in the west of the island. Here you can see the docked squid boats if the timing is right.

The prison system operated between 1862 and 1975, first by the French and then by the Americans. **Prison Phu Hai**, which backs on to parts of the **Saigon Con Dao Resort**, was built in 1862 and is the largest prison on the islands with 10 detention rooms and 20 punishment cells. The chapel inside was built by the Americans in 1963. Next door is **Phu Son Prison** built in 1916. The third prison, **Phu Tho**, plus **Camp Phu Tuong** and **Camp Phu Phong** (built in 1962) contained the infamous **'tiger cages'** where prisoners were chained

Vo Thi Sau was born in Ba Ria Province in 1933 and was executed in Con Dao in 1952. At the age of 14 this Vietnamese revolutionary heroine developed an interest in politics and a passionate hatred for the French.

In 1949 she obtained three hand-grenades and, with one, killed a French soldier and injured 20 others. She became a messenger and supplied food and ammunition to the Viet Minh.

In 1950 she tried to assassinate a village headman working for the French but the hand-grenade failed to go off. She was caught, tortured and sentenced to death. She was executed on 23 January 1952 at the age of 18.

and tortured; the enclosures still stand. Metal bars were placed across the roofs of the cells and guards would throw excrement and lime onto the prisoners. In addition, many prisoners were outside in areas known as 'sun-bathing compartments'. Not content on limiting torture methods, a cow manure enclosure was used to dunk prisoners in sewage up to 3 m deep. American-style tiger enclosures were built in 1971 at **Camp Phu Binh**. In total there were 504 tiger cages. Beyond the prisons, inland, is the **Hang Duong cemetery** where many of the victims of the prison are buried. The grave of Le Hong Phong, the very first General Secretary of the Communist Party in Vietnam (1935-1936) and Vo Thi Sau (1933-1952) can be seen among them. A tour of the prisons and cemetery costs 50,000d per person and is arranged through the museum, see below.

There is a **museum** (**Bao Tang Tong Ho Tinh**) ① *Mon-Sat 0700-1130, 1330-1700, 1000d*, in the town of Con Dao in the house of the former prison governor (built 1862) containing artefacts relating to the island's past. Con Dao museum has an interesting display of old photographs, and can arrange walking tours of the old prisons.

Opposite the museum is **Wharf 914**, the main ferry access point to the islands, so-called because of the number of prisoners who died building it.

There is a small museum and explanatory displays at the **National Park office headquarters** ① *see below, Mon-Fri 0700-1130, 1330-1700, Sat 0730-1100, 1400-1630*.

CON DAO NATIONAL PARK

① *29 Vo Thi Sau St, T64-383 0650, www.condaopark.com.vn. There are a number of activities that can be organized in the national park, from snorkelling and swimming, to forest walks and birdwatching. Diving is available to see some of Con Dao's underwater features, such as its caves, as well as the coral reefs. The national park will rent out snorkelling gear and you can also rent one of their speedboats if you are in a group that can share the cost.*

In 1984 the forests on all 14 islands of the Con Dao archipelago were given official protection, and in 1993, 80% of the land area was designated a national park. In 1998 the park boundaries were expanded to include the surrounding sea.

Con Dao is a special place ecologically, though it is not the most diverse protected area in Vietnam. In 1995, with support from the World Wildlife Fund, the park began a sea-turtle conservation project. Con Dao is the most important sea-turtle nesting site in Vietnam, with several hundred female green turtles (*Chelonia mydas*) coming ashore to lay their eggs every year. Occasionally the hawksbill turtle visits too. Park staff attach a tag to every turtle

ON THE ROAD
Turtles

Although the turtle is a symbol of longevity in Vietnam, its marine turtle population is under threat. In the last 30 years their numbers have declined. In an attempt to save the world's five species, all threatened with extinction according to the World Conservation Union (IUCN), the Ministry of Fisheries has launched a plan with IUCN to save the creature. Most of the turtles, the hawksbill (*Eretmochelys imbricata*), green (*Chelonia mydas*), loggerhead (*Caretta caretta*), Olive Ridley (*Lepidochelys olivacea*) and leatherback (*Dermochelys coriacea*) nest on the Con Dao islands. With populations of not more than 300 in total for all species in Vietnam they have faced decimation because of poaching, egg collecting and illegal trading of stuffed animals and products such as jewellery and ornaments. In a 2004 study by TRAFFIC, the wildlife trade monitoring network, more than 28,000 items made of mainly hawksbill tortoiseshell were being sold in Vietnam.

in order to identify returning turtles, and move the turtles' eggs if they are in danger of being flooded at high tide. The rest of the year the turtles migrate long distances. Recently, a turtle tagged in Con Dao was found in a fishing village in Cambodia – unfortunately the tag was insufficient protection to prevent it being eaten. Also in 1995, park staff identified the presence of dugongs (sea cows), which are mammals that feed on seagrass and can live to more than 70 years. Unfortunately, before the park was established dugongs were caught for meat so now the population in Con Dao is small and endangered.

The coral reefs surrounding the islands are among the most diverse in the country. Scientists have identified more than 200 species of coral and coral fish. In November 1997, typhoon *Linda* struck the islands and many of Con Dao's coral reefs were damaged.

In the forests scientists have identified more than 1000 plant species, of which several are unique to Con Dao and include many valuable medicinal and timber species. Bird life is also significant with rare species such as the pied imperial pigeon (*Ducula bicolor*) – Con Dao is the only place in Vietnam where you can see this bird – the red-billed tropicbird (*Phaethon aethereus*) – found on only a few islands in the world – and the brown booby (*Sula leucogaster*) – a rare sea bird that inhabits the park's most remote island, Hon Trung (Egg Island). Egg Island, a speedboat ride northeast of Con Son, is a rugged outcrop hosting thousands of seabirds including sooty and crested terns, white-bellied sea eagles, and the rare, in Vietnam, masked booby. Most of the threats to the islands' natural resources come from development in the form of new roads, houses and the new fishing port built in Ben Dam Bay – an area of once-beautiful coral reef and mangrove forest.

BEACHES AND BAYS

Ong Dung Beach can be reached by walking across Con Son Island downhill on a track through the jungle. Plenty of birds can be seen if you trek at the right time of day. You can snorkel around 300 m offshore. There is a forest protection centre at the bay where you can buy food and drink and hire snorkelling gear and a boat. **Bai Nhat Beach**, just before Ben Dam Bay, is a beautiful wild stretch of sand where good swimming is possible. North of Con Son is **Tre Lon Island**, said to be one of the best places in the archipelago to see coral reefs and reef fish; this was also used as an isolated French prison. Le Duan, former General Secretary of the Communist Party, was imprisoned here from 1931-1936. Close to the airport is one of the island's best and most wild beaches at **Dam Trau**. Golden sands in a tight curved bay backed by casuarinas can be found here but there are no island views. Signposted 'Mieu Cau' on the left just before the airport, it is a 15-minute walk, passing a pagoda flanked by two white horses.

Bay Canh Island is a major sea turtle nesting site; there is also a functioning French-built lighthouse dating from 1883. If you are interested in seeing the turtles arrange to stay overnight through the national park. **Cau Island**, east of Bay Canh Island is the only other island in the archipelago with fresh water. It harbours the swifts that make the nests and turtles that come to lay their eggs. It was also an isolated French prison at one time. Pham Van Dong, a former prime minster of both North Vietnam and the reunited Vietnam (1955-1987), was incarcerated here for seven years, from 1929 to 1936.

For swimming, **Lo Voi Beach**, east of the hotels, is good for swimming as is **An Hai Beach** at the other end of the bay. Birdwatching is also possible around the freshwater lake – **Quang Trung** – swamps and tree-covered sand dunes near the park headquarters. Spotters could see the Brahminy kite (*Haliastur Indus*), white-bellied sea eagle, Javan pond heron and cinnamon bittern. On the way to **Ong Dung** you can see the white-rumped shama, greater racket-tailed drongo, the rare pied imperial pigeon and the even rarer red-billed tropicbird.

At Dat Doc, east of Con Son, is a very attractive and pristine bay backed by a sheer cliff face. The **Evason Hideaway & Six Senses Spa** company have built a hotel complex here.

CON DAO LISTINGS

WHERE TO STAY

Con Dao now offers a premier beach and spa resort, **Six Senses Con Dao**, as well as more affordable but limited town options.

$$$$ Six Senses Con Dao, Dat Doc Beach, T64-3831 222, www.sixsenses.com/sixsensescondao. 50 beautifully furnished villas with infinity pools and butler service plus a Six Senses Spa stretch their way around the curve of Dat Doc Beach in luxurious isolation.

$$$ Saigon Con Dao, 18 Ton Duc Thang St, T64-383 0336, www.saigoncondao.com. These buildings on the seafront have had an upgrade and rooms are nicely furnished. The **Poulo Condore** restaurant is on site. Staff are efficient and friendly.

$$$-$$ Con Dao Resort, 8 Nguyen Duc Thuan St, T64-383 0939, www.condaoresort.com.vn. Some 41 rooms including some in villas facing the beach. The rooms feature a/c bathtubs, TV and balconies. There's a pool and a tennis court. There's also a restaurant – the **Du Gong**. Staff can arrange walking and motorbike tours of the area.

WHAT TO DO

Boat tours
The national park offices runs boat tours depending on the number of people and the weather. These include trips to Hon Tre Lon, Hon Tre No, Hon Bay Canh and Hon Cau as well as points around Con Son Island.

Diving
Dive Vietnam, www.divevietnam.com, offers diving and snorkelling in the best dive waters off Vietnam.

MY THO AND AROUND

My Tho is an important riverside market town, 5 km off the main highway to Vinh Long, and is the capital of Tien Giang Province. It is the stepping-off point for boat trips to islands in the Tien River. Visitors enjoy the chance to wander among abundant fruit orchards and witness at first hand local industries. My Tho is 71 km southwest of Ho Chi Minh City on the banks of the Tien River, a distributary of the Mekong. The drive from Ho Chi Minh City is dispiriting, nose-to-tail traffic and virtually uninterrupted ribbon development testify to the population pressure in so much of this land. The town has had a turbulent history: it was Khmer until the 17th century, when the advancing Vietnamese took control of the surrounding area. In the 18th century Thai forces annexed the territory, before being driven out in 1784. Finally, the French gained control in 1862. Around My Tho are the northern delta towns of Ben Tre, Vinh Long, Tra Vinh, Sa Dec and Cao Lanh.

ARRIVING IN MY THO

Getting there and around The much-improved Highway 1 is the main route from Ho Chi Minh City to My Tho (two hours). There is an efficient public bus service, taxis aplenty, a few river taxis and boats and *Honda ôm*. However, most people choose to visit the area using a combination of private car and boat trips.

Moving on The bus station is 3-4 km out of town towards Ho Chi Minh City with regular connections every 30 minutes to Ho Chi Minh City's Mine Tay station; buses to Ben Tre (see page 218) take 20-30 minutes but there are also connections to other delta towns including Vinh Long (2½ hours), Cao Lanh (2½ hours), Can Tho and Chau Doc.

Tourist information Tien Giang Tourist ⓘ *8 30 Thang 4 St on the river, Ward 1, T730-387 3184, www.tiengiangtourist.com*, has improved its services and attitude a good deal. Competition has opened up in the area but it has a near monopoly on the popular boat trips. The staff are friendly and helpful and have a good command of several languages.

→ MY THO

On the corner of Nguyen Trai Street and Hung Vuong Street, and five minutes' walk from the central market, is **My Tho church** painted with a yellow wash with a newer, white campanile. The **central market** covers a large area from Le Loi Street down to the river. The river is the most enjoyable spot to watch My Tho life go by.

It is a long walk to **Vinh Trang Pagoda** ⓘ *60 Nguyen Trung Trac St, daily 0900-1200, 1400-1700 (best to go by bicycle or* Honda ôm*)*. The entrance to the temple is through an ornate porcelain-encrusted gate. The pagoda was built in 1849 and displays a mixture of architectural styles: Chinese, Vietnamese and colonial. The façade is almost fairytale in inspiration. Two huge new statues of the Buddha now dominate the area.

There has been a flurry of municipal activity in the past couple of years not much of it beneficial. All the bustling cafés along Trung Trac Street by the side of the small Bao Dinh River have been swept away and in their place is a broad, scorched pavement devoid of any shade. The saving grace, however is the new corner café from where you can idly pass the time watching the river and passing motorbikes.

ON THE ROAD

Hydrology of the Mekong Delta

The Mekong River enters Vietnam in two branches known traditionally as the Mekong and the Bassac but now called the Tien and the Hau. Over the 200-km journey to the sea they divide to form nine mouths, the so-called Nine Dragons or *Cuu Long*.

In response to the rains of the Southwest monsoon, river levels begin to rise in June, usually reaching a peak in October and falling to normal in December. This seasonal pattern is ideal for rice growing, around which the whole way of life of the delta has evolved.

The Mekong has a unique natural flood regulator in the form of Cambodia's great lake, the Tonlé Sap. As river levels rise the water backs up into the vast lake which more than doubles in size, preventing more serious flooding in the Mekong Delta. Nevertheless, the Tien and Hau still burst their banks and water inundates the huge Plain of Reeds (*Dong Thap Muoi*) and the Rach Gia Depression, home to thousands of water birds.

The annual flood has always been regarded as a blessing bringing, as it does, fertile silt and flushing out salinity and acidity from the soil. Since the 1990s, however, frequent serious flooding has made this annual event less benign and an increasingly serious problem.

From 1705 onwards Vietnamese emperors began building canals to improve navigation in the delta. This task was taken up enthusiastically by the French in order to open up new areas of the delta to rice cultivation and export. Interestingly it is thought the canals built prior to 1975 had little effect on flooding.

Since 1975 a number of new canals have been built in Cambodia and Vietnam and old ones deepened. The purpose of some of these predominantly west–east canals is to carry irrigation water to drier parts. Their effect has been to speed up the flow of water across the delta from about 17 days to five. Peak flows across the border from Cambodia have tripled in 30 years, partly as a result of deforestation and urbanization upriver.

In addition, the road network of the delta has been developed and roads raised above the normal high-water levels. This has the effect of trapping floodwater, preventing it from reaching the Gulf of Thailand or East Sea and prolonging floods. Many canals have gates to prevent the inundation of sea water; the gates also hinder the outflow of floodwaters.

Information taken from a paper by Quang M Nguyen

→ AROUND MY THO

THE ISLANDS

There are four islands in the Tien River between My Tho and Ben Tre: Dragon, Tortoise, Phoenix and Unicorn. The best way of getting to them is to take a tour. A vast pier and boat service centre has been built on 30 Thang 4 Street where all the tour operators are now concentrated. To avoid the hundreds of visitors now descending on these islands, go in the afternoon after the tour buses have gone. Hiring a private boat (US$10) is not recommended due to the lack of insurance, the communication difficulties and lack of explanations. Prices vary according to the number of people and which islands you choose to visit.

Immediately opposite My Tho is **Dragon Island (Tan Long Island)**. It is pleasant to wander along its narrow paths. Tan Long is noted for its longan production but there are many other fruits to sample as well as honey and rice whisky.

The Island of the Coconut Monk, also known as **Phoenix Island (Con Phung)**, is about 3 km from My Tho. The 'Coconut Monk' established a retreat on this island shortly after the end of the Second World War where he developed a new 'religion', a fusion of Buddhism and Christianity. He is said to have meditated for three years on a stone slab, eating nothing but coconuts – hence the name. Persecuted by both the South Vietnamese government and by the communists, the monastery has fallen into disuse.

Unicorn Island is a garden of Eden – stuffed with longan, durian, roses, pomelo and a host of other fruit trees. Honey is made on this island too.

The main attraction of **Tortoise Island** is to sample the coconut sweets and to visit the handicrafts workshop.

AP BAC

Not far from My Tho is the hamlet of Ap Bac, the site of the communists' first major military victory against the ARVN. The battle demonstrated that without direct US involvement the communists could never be defeated. John Paul Vann was harsh in his criticism of the tactics and motivation of the South Vietnamese Army who failed to dislodge a weak Viet Cong position. As he observed from the air, almost speechless with rage, he realized how feeble his Vietnamese ally was; an opinion that few senior US officers heeded – to their cost (see *Bright Shining Lie* by Neil Sheehan).

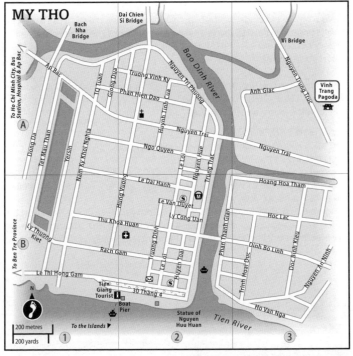

Ben Tre is a typical Vietnamese delta town with a charming riverfront feel. The small bridge over the river is wooden slatted but with iron supports. Bountiful fruit stalls are laid out on the waterfront and locals sell potted plants on barges by the river. Small cargo ships pass dilapidated shacks falling into the muddy waters. Ben Tre used to be a bit of a cul-de-sac but this is changing due to the opening of the new bridge linking it to My Tho. Consequently, it doesn't attract a lot of foreign or, for that matter, Vietnamese visitors. Its main claim to fame is that it is the birthplace of Nguyen Dinh Chieu, a blind and patriotic poet. The province is essentially a huge island of mud at one of the nine mouths of the Mekong. It depends heavily on farming, fishing and coconuts although there are some light industries engaged in processing the local farm output and refining sugar. During the wars of resistance against the French and Americans, Ben Tre earned itself a reputation as a staunch Viet Minh/Viet Cong stronghold. Ben Tre in recent years has improved its tourism facilities.

ARRIVING IN BEN TRE
Getting there and around Ben Tre is 70 km from My Tho, 32 km from Can Tho and 147 km from Ho Chi Minh City via the My Thuan toll bridge. There are regular buses from My Tho, which take 20-30 minutes. In the city itself there are taxis and *Honda ôms*. There are also river taxis.

Moving on Buses run from Ben Tre to Tra Vinh (see page 219) and take 1½ to two hours. It is also possible to travel to Vinh Long along route 60 then 57, which takes one hour to the ferry crossing from Long Ho (15,000d). This tarmacked route passes plenty of small bridges and village life.

Tourist information Ben Tre Tourist ① *16 Hai Ba Trung St, T75-382 2392, www.bentre tourist.vn*, is friendly and helpful. The tours that it offers are not particularly cheap but it does provide a reasonable selection.

PLACES IN BEN TRE
Vien Minh Pagoda is located on Nguyen Dinh Chieu Street and is the centre for the association of Buddhists in Ben Tre Province. It was originally made of wood but was rebuilt using concrete in 1958.

At **Binh Phu** village, 2 km from downtown, you can see rice wine being made. **Phu Le** village also makes rice wine.

Nguyen Dinh Chieu Temple is 36 km from the town centre in An Duc village. The temple is dedicated to the poet Nguyen Dinh Chieu who is Ben Tre's most famous son. It is well kept and photogenic and worth a visit. The monks are friendly and helpful.

Tra Vinh is the capital of the province of the same name and has a large Khmer population – 300,000 people (30% of the province's population) are Khmer, and at the last count there were 140 Khmer temples. The large Khmer population is a bit of an enigma, for while Khmer people can be found across the Mekong Delta the concentration is highest in this, the most distant Mekong province from Cambodia. For whatever reason, Tra Vinh established itself as a centre of population some 500 years ago; then, as Vietnamese settlers began fanning across the delta displacing the Khmer, the population of this area remained firmly rooted creating a little pocket of Cambodian ethnicity and culture far from home. The modern market building, adorned with a huge picture of Ho Chi Minh, is the pivot of the city.

ARRIVING IN TRA VINH

Getting there and around The bus station is about 500 m south of town and there is a reasonable domestic bus service. Buses from Ben Tre take 1½ to two hours. There are quite a few taxis and *Honda ôm*.

Moving on The road is direct to Vinh Long and regular buses ply the route (60-80 minutes). If travelling on to Can Tho, it is best to go via Vinh Long and take a bus from there.

Tourist information Tra Vinh Tourist ① *64-66 Le Loi St, T74-385 8556, travinhtourist@yahoo. com*, owns the Cuu Long Hotel and is friendly and helpful. City tour by moto from US$18.

BACKGROUND

For those interested in religious edifices Tra Vinh is the place to visit. In one of the more obscure surveys undertaken to calculate the number of religious buildings per head of population it was found that with more than 140 Khmer temples, 50 Vietnamese pagodas, five Chinese pagodas, seven mosques and 14 churches serving a town of only 70,000 souls Tra Vinh was the outright winner by miles.

So many attractive buildings coupled with the tree-lined boulevards – some trees are well over 30 m tall – make this one of the more attractive cities in the Delta. It is well worth an overnight stay here to recharge the batteries.

PLACES IN TRA VINH

The **market** is on the central square between Dien Bien Phu Street – the town's main thoroughfare – and the Tra Vinh River, which is a relatively small branch of the Mekong compared with most Delta towns. A walk through the market and along the river bank makes a pleasant late afternoon or early evening stroll. Otherwise there is not a lot to do in Tra Vinh, although it's a nice enough place to spend some time. The **Ong Met Pagoda** on Dien Bien Phu Street north of the town centre dates back to the mid-16th century. It is a gilded Chinese-style temple where the monks will be only too happy to ply you with tea and practise their English, although the building itself is fairly unremarkable.

AROUND TRA VINH

The two best reasons to come to Tra Vinh are to see the storks and the Khmer temples. Fortunately, these can be combined at the nearby **Hang Pagoda**, also known as Ao Ban Om, about 5 km south of town and 300 m off the main road. It is not particularly special architecturally, but the sight of the hundreds of storks that rest in the grounds and wheel around the pointed roofs at dawn and dusk (1600-1800) is truly spectacular.

There's also the **Bao Tang Van Hoa Dan Toc Khmer** (0700-1100, 1300-1700) a small collection of artefacts next to the square-shaped lotus filled pond of Ba Om just south of town (there are plans for a hotel here). Labels are in Vietnamese and Khmer only; naga heads, Hanuman masks and musical instruments feature. Opposite is the **Chua Angkorajaborey** (**Ang**) or Chua Van Minh in Vietnamese dating from AD 990, which is rather peaceful.

→ VINH LONG

Vinh Long is a rather ramshackle, but nonetheless clean, riverside town on the banks of the Co Chien River and is the capital of Vinh Long Province. It is the launch pad for lovely boat trips through **An Binh Island** via the small floating market at **Cai Be**. An Binh is the centre of the Mekong homestay industry (see box, page 221).

At sunset families cluster along the river promenade to fly colourful kites in animal shapes. In the mornings, puppies and watermelons are for sale along Hung Dao Vuong Street and teenagers play ball and throw home-made shuttlecocks in the afternoons along Hung Vuong Street.

Vinh Long was one of the focal points in the spread of Christianity in the Mekong Delta and there is a cathedral and Roman Catholic seminary in town. The richly stocked and well-ordered Cho Vinh Long (central market), is on 1 Thang 5 Street down from the **Cuu Long** hotel and stretches back to near the local bus station. A new market building has also been built opposite the existing market. There is a Cao Dai church not far from the second bridge leading into town from Ho Chi Minh City and My Tho, visible on the right-hand side. In the countryside around Vinh Long you will see dozens of egg-shaped brick mounds – these are terracotta-coloured kilns for the brick works and are an attractive sight. Vinh Long makes a reasonable stopping-off point on the road to Long Xuyen, Rach Gia and Ha Tien.

ARRIVING IN VINH LONG
Getting there The road runs direct from Ho Chi Minh City via the My Thuan bridge. The bus station is about 500 m south of town; there is a good bus service and *Honda ôms*.

Moving on There are good bus connections to all Mekong towns including Can Tho (one hour), see page 223.

Tourist information Cuu Long Tourist ① *inside the hotel of the same name No 1, 1 Thang 5 St, T70-382 3616, http://cuulongtourist.com, daily 0700-1700*. Ask for Mr Phu, he is helpful, and has a good understanding of English and French. This is one of the friendlier and more helpful of the state-run companies and runs tours and homestays.

PLACES IN VINH LONG
The **river trips** taking in the islands and orchards around Vinh Long are as charming as any in the delta, but getting there can be expensive. Local boatmen are prepared to risk a fine and take tourists for one-tenth of the operators' charge. **Binh Hoa Phuoc Island** and An Binh, generally collectively known as An Binh, make a pleasant side trip, see also Sleeping. There is a **floating market** at **Cai Be**, about 10 km from Vinh Long. This is not quite so

ON THE ROAD
Mekong homestays

Facing Vinh Long town in the Co Chien River, a tributary of the Mekong, is a large island known as An Binh that is further sliced into smaller islands by ribbons of canals. **Cuu Long Tourist** (see page 222) runs several homestays on the island – a wonderful way to immerse yourself in local life.

The accommodation is basic with camp beds, shared bathrooms and mosquito nets and a home-cooked dinner of the fruits of the delta (elephant ear fish with abundant greens including mint and spring rolls and beef cooked in coconut). Sunset and drinks in patios or terraces or riverfront lookouts chatting with the owner completes the night. A dawn paddle in the Mekong, surrounded by floating water hyacinth and watching the sun rise is the reward for early risers. These tranquil islands are stuffed with fruit-bearing trees and flowers. Travel is by sampan or you can walk down the winding paths that link the communities. During your stay you will take tea and fruit at a traditional house, see rice cakes and popcorn being made, and visit a brick factory and watch terracotta pots being created close to the unusually shaped kilns that dot this area of the delta.

spectacular as the floating markets around Can Tho (see page 225) but nevertheless make for a diverting morning's trip.

An Binh Island, just a 10-minute ferry ride from Phan Boi Chau Street, represents a great example of delta landscape. The island can be explored either by boat, paddling down narrow canals, or by following the dirt tracks and crossing monkey bridges on foot. Monkey bridges are those single bamboo poles with, if you are lucky, a flimsy handrail which is there for psychological reassurance rather than to stop you from falling off. But don't worry, the water is warm and usually shallow and the mud soft. On the island is the ancient **Tien Chau Pagoda** and a *nuoc mam* (**fish sauce factory**).

The **Vinh Long Museum** ① *T70-382 3181, daily 0800-1100 and 1330-1630, Fri-Sun 1800-2100, free,* displays photographs of the war including the devastation of the town in 1968, some weaponry and a room dedicated to Ho Chi Minh.

The **Van Thieu Mieu Temple** ① *0500-1100, 1300-1900*, a charming mustard yellow cluster of buildings is 2 km from town along Tran Phu Street. In the first building to the right on entering the complex is an altar dedicated to Confucius.

The Khmer Temples at Tra Vinh (see page 219) can be visited on a day trip from Vinh Long.

MY THO AND AROUND LISTINGS

WHERE TO STAY

My Tho

$$ Nha Co Huynh Thuy Le, 255A Nguyen Hué St, Ward 2, T067-377 3937. Run by **Dong Thap Tourist**, this lovely home has 2 fan rooms with stained-glass windows and carved wooden doors. The shared bathroom is at the back with cold water. The price includes breakfast.

$$ Song Tien Annex, 33 Trung Trac St, T0730-397 7883, www.tiengiangtourist.com. This place has undergone a remarkable transformation into a lovely 20-room hotel boasting large beds and bathtubs on legs. Price includes breakfast and it's now the best place in town.

$ Song Tien Hotel, 101 Trung Truc St, T0730-387 2009. Centrally located near the river and market, the renovated **Song Tien**'s rooms vary widely, ranging from large, bright doubles with huge beds, to smaller windowless twins, so be sure to check a few. All rooms have a/c and TVs. Good value.

Vinh Long

$ Cuu Long (B), No 1, 1 Thang 5 St (ie No 1 May St), T070-382 3656, www.cuulong tourist.com. Set back from the river, in the centre of the action. 34 comfortable a/c rooms; price includes breakfast. The **Hoa Vien Club** in the grounds next to the hotel is also good for a drink. Wi-Fi available.

$ Mekong Homestays, An Binh Island, Vinh Long. Organized by **Cuu Long Tourist** or **Mekong Travel** (see below). Accommodation is basic, with camp beds, shared bathrooms and mosquito nets, and a home-cooked dinner of the fruits of the delta. Evening entertainment consists of chatting with the owner. The price includes a boat trip around the island, transfers from Vinh Long, guide, 1 dinner and 1 breakfast.

RESTAURANTS

My Tho

A local speciality is *hu tieu my tho* (a spicy soup of vermicelli, sliced pork and dried shrimp). At night, noodle stalls spring up on the pavement at Le Loi St/Le Dai Han St.

$ Banh Xeo 46, 11 Trung Trac St. Serves *bánh xèo*, savoury pancakes filled with beansprouts, mushrooms and prawns.

$ Hu Tien 44, 44 Nam Ky Khoi Nghia St. Daily 0500-1200. Specializes in *hu tien my tho*. Good value at 16,000d for a large bowl.

$ Lac Hong 63, 30 Thang 4 St. This is the latest place to be seen. Sip your coffee in the cool and watch the world go by.

Vinh Long

$ Phuong Thuy Restaurant, No 1, 1 Thang 5 St, T070-382 4786. Daily 0600-2100. A 'stilt' restaurant on the river with Vietnamese and Western dishes and welcoming service. Cuttlefish and shrimp feature strongly.

WHAT TO DO

Tour operators

Cuu Long Tourist, No 1, 1 Thang 5 St, T070-382 3616, www.cuulongtourist.com. Trips to An Binh Island include a visit to the small floating market of Cai Be. A tour of the area including homestay, dinner and breakfast can be arranged.

Mekong Travel, No 8, 30 Thang 5 St, T070-383 6252, www.mekongtravel.com.vn. Offers the same homestay and floating market options as **Cuu Long Tourist**.

Tien Giang Tourist, No 8, 30 Thang 4 St, by the docks, T0730-625 0065, www.tiengiangtourist.com. A 3 hr, 2-island tour including breakfast and lunch from 400,000d.

CAN THO AND AROUND

Can Tho is a large and rapidly growing commercial city situated in the heart of the Mekong Delta. Lying chiefly on the west bank of the Can Tho River it is the capital of Can Tho Province, the largest city in the delta, and the region's principal transport hub, with roads and canals running to most other important towns. It is also one of the most welcoming of the delta towns and is the launch pad for trips to see some of the region's floating markets. South of Can Tho are the towns of Soc Trang, Bac Lieu and Ca Mau.

→ CAN THO

A small settlement was established at Can Tho at the end of the 18th century, although the town did not prosper until the French took control of the delta a century later and rice production for export began to take off. Despite the city's rapid recent growth there are still strong vestiges of French influence apparent in the broad boulevards flanked by flame trees, as well as many elegant buildings. Can Tho was also an important US base. Paul Theroux in *The Great Railway Bazaar* wrote: "Can Tho was once the home of thousands of GIs. With the brothels and bars closed, it had the abandoned look of an unused fairground after a busy summer. In a matter of time, very few years, there will be little evidence that the Americans were ever there. There are poisoned rice fields between the straggling fingers of the Mekong Delta and there are hundreds of blond and fuzzy-haired children, but in a generation even these unusual features will change."

ARRIVING IN CAN THO

Getting there Virtually all visitors arrive by road. With the My Thuan Bridge (near Vinh Long) and the new bridge linking Vinh Long and Can Tho, journey times have fallen. The bus station is about 2 km northwest of the town and has regular connections from Ho Chi Minh City (four hours), Vinh Long (one hour) and other towns in the delta. There is an airport at Can Tho, 7 km from the city centre, which has flights from Hanoi and Phu Quoc Island.

Moving on From Can Tho it's possible to travel by road to Chau Doc (see page 231) via Long Xuyen, which takes approximately four hours; or by private charter boat. There are also buses to Rach Gia (five hours) for connections with Phu Quoc Island (see page 236); or you could return to Vinh Long and continue on to Sa Dec (see page 225) or Cao Lanh (see page 227). There are also hourly buses to Ho Chi Minh City (see page 185), which take four to five hours, as well as other towns in the Mekong Delta. It is also now possible to fly from Can Tho directly to Phu Quoc Island (45 minutes).

Getting around Quite a lot of Can Tho can be explored on foot. *Xe lôi* the Mekong cyclo is no longer able to trade between 0600-1800 due to traffic problems but a motorbike taxi can be picked up. Some of the sites, the floating markets for instance, are best visited by boat. There are also river taxis and an efficient public bus service.

Best time to visit As in all the other Mekong cities the best time is from December to April when the temperatures are warm and there is no rain. May to November is the monsoon season and as such it is prone to flooding (although it does fare better than other cities).

Background Can Tho has its own university, founded in 1966 and also a famous rice research institute, located at O Mon, 25 km away on Highway 91. Like the **International Rice Research Institute** (IRRI), its more famous counterpart at Los Baños in the Philippines (and to which it is attached), one of the Can Tho institute's key functions is developing rice hybrids that will flourish in the varied conditions of the delta. Near the coast, rice has to be tolerant of salt and tidal flooding. In Dong Thap Province, near Cambodia, floating rice grows stalks of 4-5 m in order to keep its head above the annual flood. The task of the agronomists is to produce varieties which flourish in these diverse environments and at the same time produce decent yields.

PLACES IN CAN THO

Hai Ba Trung Street, alongside the river, is the heart of the town; at dusk families stroll in the park here in their Sunday best. Opposite the park is **Chua Ong Pagoda** ① *34 Hai Ba Trung St*, dating from 1894 and built by Chinese from Guangzhou. Unusually for a Chinese temple it is not free-standing but part of a terrace of buildings. The right-hand side of the pagoda is dedicated to the Goddess of Fortune, while the left-hand side belongs to General Ma Tien, who, to judge from his unsmiling statue, is fierce and warlike and not to be trifled with. The layout is a combination of typical pagoda – with a small open courtyard

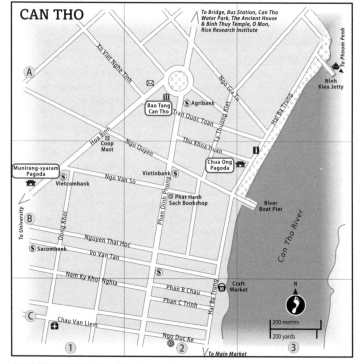

for the incense smoke to escape – and typical meeting house, complete with its language school, of the overseas Chinese in Southeast Asia.

The bustling market that used to operate on Hai Ba Trung Street along the bank of the river, and gave the town a bit of character, has been moved 1 km downriver. A new riverside promenade has been created. There's also a new crafts market building with a riverside restaurant.

The **Munirang-syaram Pagoda** ① *36 Hoa Binh Blvd (southwest of post office)*, was built just after the Vietnam War and is a Khmer Hinayana Buddhist sanctuary. **Bao Tang Can Tho** ① *Hoa Binh St, Tue-Thu 0800-1100, 1400-1700, Sat-Sun 0800-1100, 1830-2100*, in an impressive building, is the local history museum.

Binh Thuy Temple, 7 km north along the road to Long Xuyen, dates from the mid-19th century; festivals are held here in the middle of the fourth and 12th lunar months. Nearby, 500 m down Bui Huu Nghia Road, opposite Binh Thuy temple, visit **Nha Co Binh Thuy** aka the **ancient house** ① *10,000d to go inside the house; ask the owners,* (also known as Vuon Lan if you get a moto to take you there), which was used as a setting in the film *The Lover.*

FLOATING MARKETS

① *The daily markets are busiest at around 0600-0900. Women with sampans to rent will approach travellers in Hai Ba Trung St near the market waving a book of testimonials from previous satisfied customers. Expect to pay about US$15 for 2 people for 3 hrs. Set off as early as possible to beat the flotilla of tour boats. A trip of at least 5 hrs is recommended to see the landscape at a leisurely pace. If you take a larger boat you will not be able to manoeuvre in and out of the market.*

There are boat trips to the floating markets at **Phung Hiep**, 33 km away (an eight-hour round trip by sampan or take a bus to Phung Hiep and rent a boat there) and **Phong Dien**, 15 km down the Can Tho River (a five-hour trip). **Cai Rang** is 7 km away and is easy to visit for those with only a couple of hours to spare. Bustling affairs, the vendors attach a sample of their wares to a bamboo pole to attract customers. Up to seven vegetables can be seen dangling from staffs – wintermelon, pumpkin, spring onions, giant parsnips, grapefruit, garlic, mango, onions and Vietnamese plums. Housewives paddle their sampans from boat to boat and barter, haggle and gossip in the usual way. At the back of the boats, the domesticity of life on the water is in full glare – washing is hung out and motors are stranded high above the water.

Phung Hiep also features yards making traditional fishing boats and rice barges. Orchards and gardens abound, small sampans are best as they can negotiate the narrowest canals to take the visitor into the heart of the area, a veritable Garden of Eden.

→ TOWARDS CHAU DOC

SA DEC

Sa Dec's biggest claim to fame is that it was the birthplace of French novelist Marguerite Duras, and the town's three main avenues – Nguyen Hue, Tran Hung Dao and Hung Vuong garlanded with fragrant frangipani – together with some attractive colonial villas betray the French influence on this relatively young town. Sa Dec is also renowned for its flowers and bonsai trees. There are many flower nurseries on the fringes of the city. It is untouched by tourism and offers an untainted insight into life in one of the last attractive towns of the delta.

The town was formerly the capital of Dong Thap Province, a privilege that was snatched by Cao Lanh in 1984 but a responsibility that Sa Dec is better off without. It is a small and friendly town about 20 km west of Vinh Long. The delightful journey between the two towns passes brick kilns, and bikers transporting their wares (namely tropical fish in bottles and dogs).

Getting there and around Sa Dec is 143 km from Ho Chi Minh City and 102 km from Chau Doc, and 20 km from Vinh Long along Highway 80. The most direct route is by crossing My Thuan Bridge and following the signs to Sa Dec. Local options include taxis, *Honda ôms* and sampans.

Moving on The bus station is 500 m southeast of town on the main road just before the bridge. Buses to Cao Lanh (see page 227) Vinh Long, Long Xuyen and other delta towns leave from here.

Tourist information There is no tourist information in Sa Dec. Dong Thap Tourist Company keeps some leaflets at the Sa Dec Hotel, and has a contact at the Huynh Thuy Le House (see below) but its main office is in Cao Lanh.

Places in Sa Dec Sa Dec's bustling riverside market on Nguyen Hue Street is worth a visit. Many of the scenes from the film adaptation of Duras' novel *The Lover* were filmed in front of the shop terraces and merchants' houses here. Sit in one of the many riverside cafés to watch the world float by – which presumably, as a young woman, is what Duras did.

Huynh Thuy Le was Duras' lover and his house, **Nha Co Huynh Thuy Le** ① *255A Nguyen Hue St, Ward 2, T67-377 3937, nhaco-huynhthuyle@yahoo.com, Mon-Sat 0730-1700, Sun 0830-1700, 20,000d,* is a lovely Sino-influenced building on the main street. There are stunning gold-leaf carved animal figures framing arches and the centrepiece is a golden shrine to Chinese warrior Quan Cong. The Ancient House was built in 1895 and restored in 1917. There are photographs of the Huynh family (he later married and had five daughters and three sons; he died in 1972), Duras and the Sa Dec school. The building was a police station and cared for from 1975-2006. The two friendly women who run the place, Xuan and Tuyen, speak French and English will offer you tea and crystallised ginger; this is a wonderful way to pass the afternoon. Reserved lunch and dinner is possible, as is a stay in the house. **Duras' childhood home** is not across the river as some guidebooks say; it no longer exists. She lived in a house near the Ecole de Sa Dec (now Truong Vuong primary school on the corner of Hung Vuong and Ho Xuan Huong St), which is pictured inside the Nha Co Huynh Thuy Le.

Phuoc Hung Pagoda ① *75/5 Hung Vuong St,* is a splendid Chinese-style pagoda constructed in 1838 when Sa Dec was a humble one-road village. Surrounded by ornamental gardens, lotus ponds and cypress trees, the main temple to the right is decorated with fabulous animals assembled from pieces of porcelain rice bowls. Inside are some marvellous wooden statues of Buddhist figures made in 1838 by the venerable sculptor Cam. There are also some superbly preserved gilded wooden beams and two antique prayer tocsins. The smaller one was made in 1888 and its resounding mellow tone changes with the weather. The West Hall contains a valuable copy of the 101 volume Great Buddhist Canon. There are also some very interesting and ancient photos of dead devotees and of pagoda life in the past.

A few kilometres west of Sa Dec is the **Tu Ton Rose Garden (Vuon Hong Tu Ton)** ① *28 Vuon Hong St, Khom 3, Ward 3, T67-376 1685, 0600-2000, free*. The garden is next to a lemon yellow building with yellow gates. This 6000-ha nursery borders the river and is home to more than 40 varieties of rose and 540 other types of plant, from medicinal herbs to exotic orchids. Wander amid the potted hibiscus, beds of roses and bougainvillea and enjoy the visiting butterflies. The garden can be reached either on foot or by taking a *Honda ôm* to Tan Qui Don village.

CAO LANH

Cao Lanh for many years was a small, underdeveloped Mekong town. However, since becoming the capital of Dong Thap Province, an honour previously bestowed on Sa Dec, it has changed and has become a thriving market town. It also benefits from being the closest main city to the Xeo Quit base (Rung Cham forest) and Tram Chim Nature Reserve, both of which are main tourist attractions. In fact, the excursions are the only real reason to visit Cao Lanh, particularly if you are a bird lover or a Ho Chi Minh biographer.

Getting there and around The bus station is located at the corner of Ton Tung and Doc Binh Kieu St and receives buses from Ho Chi Minh City (three hours) and most delta towns including Can Tho (60-90 minutes). There are a few taxis, *Honda ôm* and sampans.

Moving on Cao Lanh is a base for visiting the Xeo Quit Base (see page 228) either by hiring a car or booking a tour. From here, buses continue along the route towards Chau Doc (see page 231) or return to Ho Chi Minh City to take a flight.

Tourist information Dong Thap Tourist Co ① *2 Doc Binh Kieu St, T67-385 5637, www. dongthaptourist.com, Mon-Sat 0700-1130, 1330-1700*. Some staff have a reasonable command of English and are helpful and provide excellent value for the services it provides.

Places in and around Cao Lanh To the northeast along Nguyen Hue Street is the **war memorial**, containing the graves of Vietnamese who fell in the war with the USA. The **Tomb of Ho Chi Minh's father** ① *Nguyen Sinh Sac (Tham Quan Khu Di Tich Nguyen Sinh Sac), next to Quan Nam restaurant at 137 Pham Huu Lau St, open 0700-1130, 1330-1700, 8000d*, set under a shell structure and sits in front of a lotus pond. A small stilt-house museum sits in the tranquil grounds.

The vast **Plain of Reeds (Dong Thap Muoi)** is a swamp that extends for miles north towards Cambodia, particularly in the late monsoon season (September to November). It is an important wildlife habitat (see below) but in the wet season, when the water levels rise, getting about on dry land can be a real problem. Extraordinarily, the Vietnamese have not adapted the stilt house solution used by the Khmer and every year get flooded out. In the rural districts houses are built on the highest land available and in a good year the floor will be just inches above the lapping water. At these times all transport is by boat. When the sky is grey the scene is desolate and the isolation of the plain can truly feel like the end of the Earth has been reached.

Tower Mound (Go Thap) is the best place from which to get a view of the immensity and beauty of the surrounding Plain of Reeds. There was a watchtower here although no one seems sure if it was 10 storeys high or the last in a chain of 10 towers. There are earthworks from which General Duong and Admiral Kieu conducted their resistance against the French between 1861 and 1866.

Tam Nong Bird Sanctuary (Tram Chim) is an 8000-ha reserve 45 km northwest of Cao Lanh (T67-382 7436). It contains 182 species of bird at various times of year, but most spectacular is the red-headed crane (sarus), rarest of the world's 15 crane species. Between August and November these spectacular creatures migrate across the nearby Cambodian border to avoid the floods (cranes feed on land), but at any other time, and particularly at dawn and dusk, they are a magnificent sight. Floating rice is grown in the area around the bird sanctuary and although the acreage planted diminishes each year this is another of nature's truly prodigious feats. The leaves float on the surface while the roots are anchored in mud as much as 4-5 m below; but as so much energy goes into growing the stalk little is left over for the ears of rice, so yields are low.

About 20 km east of Cao Lanh is the **Xeo Quit Base** ⓘ *6 km off the main road at My Long where it is signposted to the on-site restaurant, T67-350 4733, kdtxeoquit@yahoo.com. vn, 0730-1700, 5000d for entrance and boat trip. Nguyen Thanh Nguyen is the only English-speaking guide at the site, T91-827 3125, he requires 1-2 days' notice*. Xeo Quit was home to Viet Cong generals who planned the war from the safety of the base. There was so little vegetation cover here that fast-growing eucalyptus trees were planted; but even these took three years to provide sufficient cover to conceal humans. As the waterlogged ground prevented tunnelling, waterproof chambers sealed with plastic and resin were sunk into the mud. Stocked with rice, water and candles communist cadres coordinated their resistance strategy from here for almost 15 years. Despite frequent land and air raids the US forces never succeeded in finding or damaging the base. Today, the appeal of visiting the base is to explore the dense jungle by way of canoe. Paddling along the tunnel-like streams that cut through the trees to dug-outs and bunkers used by the Viet Cong is incredibly atmospheric. It's a fascinating historical site and the dense jungle is a refuge for wildlife. There is a restaurant at the site.

CAN THO AND AROUND LISTINGS

WHERE TO STAY

Can Tho is the most popular place to stay in the delta and offers a good variety of accommodation for a beautiful riverside resort to backpacker options.

Can Tho

$$$$ Golf Hotel, 2 Hai Ba Trung St, T0710-381 2210, www.vinagolf.vn. No longer the tallest hotel in town with its 10 floors. The services and facilities are on a par with the better hotels in HCMC and Hanoi but it always seems empty. The staff are friendly, knowledgeable and multilingual. The rooms are well equipped with all mod cons and en suites. The restaurants on the 8th, 9th and 10th floors provide fine dining and the views from the **Windy Sky Bar** (8th floor) are superb. The swimming 'fool' is a draw. ATM on site.

$$$$ Victoria Can Tho Resort, Cai Khe Ward, T0710-381 0111, www.victoriahotels.asia. This is one of the most beautiful hotels in Vietnam. With its riverside garden location, combined with a harmonious interior, breezy reception area, emphasis on comfort and plenty of genuine period features, it inspires relaxation. The centrepiece is the gorgeous, flood-lit pool, flanked by the lobby bar and restaurant. Rooms are elegantly decorated. Other facilities include a tennis court and therapies in divine massage cabins. The hotel offers a complimentary shuttle bus and boat to the town centre.

$$ Kim Tho, 1A4 Ngo Gia Tu St, T0710-222 7979, www.kimtho.com. The closest thing to boutique hotel in the delta with low-slung beds and white linens. Don't bother paying extra for a room with a view. Choose a standard with a bathtub. The standout attraction is the rooftop café with fabulous views. Price includes breakfast and in-room Wi-Fi.

$ Tay Ho, 42 Hai Ba Trung St, T0710-382 3392, tay_ho@hotmail.com. This lovely place has a variety of rooms and a great public balcony that can be enjoyed by those paying for back rooms. All rooms now have private bathrooms. Riverview rooms, inevitably, cost more. The staff are friendly.

RESTAURANTS

Can Tho

Hai Ba Trung St by the river has a range of excellent and well-priced little restaurants; the riverside setting is attractive.

$$-$ Sao Hom, Nha Long Cho Can Tho, T0710-381 5616, http://saohom.transmekong.com. This very busy restaurant on the riverfront serves plentiful food and provides very good service. Watching the river life and the floating pleasure palaces at night is a good way to spend an evening. Shame about the illuminated billboards on the opposite bank. This place is hugely popular with very large tour groups that alter the character of the restaurant when they swarm in.

$ Mekong, 38 Hai Ba Trung St. Perfectly good little place near the river in this popular restaurant strip. Serves decent Vietnamese fare at reasonable prices.

$ Nam Bo, 50 Hai Ba Trung St, T0710-382 3908. Delightful French house on the corner of a street. Its balcony seating area overlooks the market clutter and riverside promenade. Tasty Vietnamese and French dishes. The set menu is 170,000d. Small café downstairs. Recommended.

$ Phuong Nam, 48 Hai Ba Trung St, T0710-381 2077. Similar to the next door **Nam Bo**, good food, less stylish, a popular travellers' haunt and reasonable prices.

Sa Dec

$$ Nha Co Huynh Thuy Le, 255A Nguyen Hué St, Ward 2, T067-377 3937. Run by **Dong Thap Tourist**; reserve a day in advance for the chance to dine in the home of Marguerite Duras' lover. Attended to by Xuan and Tuyen who are guides at the house, dine on spring rolls, fried fish, lotus salad, noodles, fried vegetables with pork and fruit. Set lunch and dinner menus are 130,000d.

WHAT TO DO

Can Tho
Boat trips

Trans Mekong, 144 Hai Ba Trung St, P Tan An, T0710-382 9540, www.transmekong. com. Operates 3 *bassac* boats (converted rice barges) that sleep passengers in a/c cabins with private bathrooms.

   Buffalo Tours and **Victoria Can Tho** offer the 1-day Mekong Delta cruise on converted rice barge, *Le Jarai* as well as longer Mekong trips.

Tour operators

Can Tho Tourist, 50 Hai Ba Trung St, T0710-382 1854, www.canthotourist.vn. It's quite expensive and organizes tours in both small boats and powerful boats – the latter not the best way to see the delta. The staff are helpful and knowledgeable. Tours include trips to Cai Rang, Phong Dien and Phung Hiep floating markets, to Soc Trang, city tours, canal tours, bicycle tours, trekking tours, stork sanctuary tour and homestays that involve working with farmers in the fields. General boat tours also arranged. It charges US$67.50 for a 1-night tour for 2 people including floating market and bike tour.

Sa Dec
Dong Thap Tourist, based at the **Huynh Thuy Le Old House**, T67-377 3937, www.dongthaptourist.com. Trips to Xeo Quit and Cao Lanh organized.

Cao Lanh
Birdwatching at the nearby sanctuaries is the most common activity. It is also possible to hire boats from **Dong Thap Tourist Company**, 2 Doc Binh Kieu St, T67-385 5637. Dong Thap also organizes trips to the mausoleum of Nguyen Sinh Sac, Xeo Quit, Sa Dec and the Gao Giong Ecotourism Zone.

CHAU DOC AND AROUND

Chau Doc was once an attractive bustling riverside town (formerly called Chau Phu) in An Giang Province on the west bank of the Hau or Bassac River and bordering Cambodia. It is still a bustling market town but no longer so appealing. The town is an important trading and marketing centre for the surrounding agricultural communities. One of its biggest attractions is the nearby Nui Sam (Sam Mountain), which is dotted with pagodas and tombs and from whose summit superb views of the plains below can be enjoyed. Around Chau Doc are the towns of Rach Gia, Ha Tien and, capital of the province, Long Xuyen. The nearby Tra Su Nature Reserve is home to water birds and bats.

ARRIVING IN CHAU DOC

Getting there Chau Doc is an increasingly important border crossing into Cambodia. There are connections by boat with Phnom Penh as well as by road. It is also possible (but expensive) to get to Chau Doc by boat from Can Tho (private charter only or by the Victoria Hotel group boat for guests only). Road and bus connetions with Can Tho, Vinh Long, Cao Lanh, Sa Dec and Ho Chi Minh City are good. The bus station is 3 km south of the town centre; minibuses stop in town on Quang Trung Street.

Moving on There are daily boat departures to Phnom Penh from where it is possible to arrange onwards travel to Siem Reap (see page 244); a couple of tour operators in town organize tickets. The **Victoria Hotel** run speedboats to Phnom Penh (US$100) for guests. There is also a 10-hour bus ride from Chau Doc to Phnom Penh. Cambodian visas can be bought at the border. However, the quickest route is to return to Ho Chi Minh City (six hours) from where it is a one-hour flight direct to Siem Reap.

To access Phu Quoc Island from Chau Doc there are various options: travel to Ha Tien (four hours) to catch a hydrofoil (1½ hours); travel to Rach Gia (four hours) and either take a hydrofoil (2½ hours) or a plane (40 minutes); travel to Can Tho and take a plane (45 minutes); or return to Ho Chi Minh City and take a flight from there (55 minutes).

Getting around Chau Doc itself is easily small enough to explore on foot. By means of a bridge or sampan crossing, some nearby Cham villages can be reached and explored on foot too. Nui Sam, the nearby sacred mountain, can be reached by motorbike or bus.

Best time to visit Chau Doc suffers not only from the universal Mekong problem of the monsoon floods, but also from the fact that Nui Sam is one of the holiest sites in southern Vietnam and, as such, attracts vast numbers of pilgrims on auspicious days. From a climatic viewpoint then the best time to visit is December to April.

Tourist information Tour operators in town are a good source of information.

BACKGROUND

Until the mid-18th century Chau Doc was part of Cambodia: it was given to the Nguyen lord, Nguyen Phuc Khoat, after he had helped to put down a local insurrection. The area still supports a large Khmer population, as well as the largest Cham settlement in the Delta. Cambodia's influence can be seen in the tendency for women to wear the *kramar*,

Cambodia's famous chequered scarf, instead of the *non lá* conical hat, and in the people's darker skin, indicating Khmer blood. Chau Doc district (it was a separate province for a while) is the seat of the **Hoa Hao religion**, which claims about one to 1.5 million adherents and was founded in the village of Hoa Hao in 1939.

→ CHAU DOC

A large market sprawls from the riverfront down and along Le Cong Thanh Doc, Phu Thu, Bach Dang and Chi Lang streets. It sells fresh produce and black-market goods smuggled across from Cambodia. Near the market and the river, at the intersection of Tran Hung Dao Street and Nguyen Van Thoai Street, is the **Chau Phu Pagoda**. Built in 1926, it is dedicated to Thai Ngoc Hau, a former local mandarin. The pagoda is rather dilapidated, but has some fine carved pillars, which miraculously are still standing. A **Cao Dai temple**, which welcomes visitors, stands on Louise Street.

The **Vinh Te Canal**, north of town, is 90 km long and is a considerable feat of engineering, begun in 1819 and finished in 1824 using 80,000 workers. Its purpose was twofold: navigation and defence from the Cambodians. So impressed was Emperor Minh Mang in the achievement of its builder, Nguyen Van Thoai (or Thoai Ngoc Hau), that he named the canal after Thoai's wife, Chau Thi Vinh Te.

→ AROUND CHAU DOC

Easily visited from Chau Doc is the holy mountain, Nui Sam, covered in pagodas. Across the river you can boat over to Cham villages and see the floating fish farms. South of Chau Doc the road passes the sorrowful Ba Chuc ossuary. There are also three international border crossings to Cambodia, two to the southwest and one to the north of Chau Doc.

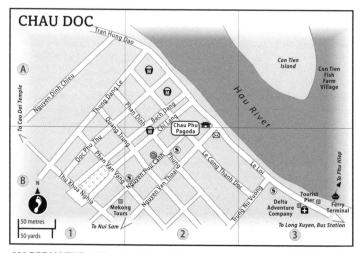

NUI SAM (SAM MOUNTAIN)

ⓘ *Take a bus (there is a stop at the foot of the mountain) or* xe lôi.

Nui Sam lies about 5 km southwest of town and is one reason to visit Chau Doc. This mountain was designated a 'Famed Beauty Spot' in 1980 by the Ministry of Culture. It is one of the holiest sites in southern Vietnam. Rising from the flood plain, Nui Sam is a favourite spot for Vietnamese tourists who throng here, especially at festival time.

The mountain, really a barren, rock-strewn hill, can be seen at the end of the continuation of Nguyen Van Thoai Street. It is literally honeycombed with tombs, sanctuaries and temples. Most visitors come only to see Tay An Pagoda, Lady Xu Temple, and the tomb of Thoai Ngoc Hau. But it is possible to walk or drive right up the hill for good views of the surrounding countryside: from the summit it is easy to appreciate that this is some of the most fertile land in Vietnam. At the top is a military base formerly occupied by American soldiers and now by Vietnamese watching their Cambodian flank. Near the top the Victoria Hotel group has built a hotel which it plans to reopen as a Victoria training hotel.

The **Tay An Pagoda** is at the foot of the hill, facing the road. Built originally in 1847, it has been extended twice and now represents an eclectic mixture of styles – Chinese, Islamic, perhaps even Italian. The pagoda contains a bewildering display of more than 200 statues. A short distance on from the pagoda, to the right, past shops and stalls, is the **Chua Xu**. This temple was originally constructed in the late 19th century, and then rebuilt in 1972. It is rather a featureless building, though highly revered by the Vietnamese and honours the holy Lady Xu whose statue is enshrined in the new multi-roofed pagoda. The 23rd to the 25th of the fourth lunar month is the period when the holy Lady is commemorated, during which time, hundreds of Vietnamese flock to see her being washed and reclothed. Lady Xu is a major pilgrimage for traders and business from Ho Chi Minh City and the south, all hoping that sales will thereby soar and profits leap. On the other side of the road is the **tomb of Thoai Ngoc Hau** (1761-1829); an enormous head of the man graces the entranceway. Thoai is a local hero having played a role in the resistance against the French but more for his engineering feats in canal building and draining swamps. He is also known as Nguyen Van Thoai and this name is given to one of Chau Doc's streets. The real reason to come here is to watch the pilgrims and to climb the hill.

Hang Pagoda, a 200-year-old temple situated halfway up Nui Sam, is worth visiting for several reasons. In the first level of the temple are some vivid cartoon drawings of the tortures of hell. The second level is built at the mouth of a cave which last century was home to a woman named Thich Gieu Thien. Her likeness and tomb can be seen in the first pagoda. Fed up with her lazy and abusive husband she left her home in Cholon and came to live in this cave, as an ascetic supposedly waited on by two snakes.

Nui Sam is the most expensive burial site in southern Vietnam. Wealthy Vietnamese and Chinese believe it is a most propitious last resting place. This is why the lower flanks are given over almost entirely to tombs. Demand for burial plots has reached such levels that a new complex is being developed to help ease the demands on the land at Sam Mountain.

CHAM VILLAGES

There are a number of Cham villages around Chau Doc. **Phu Hiep, Con Tien** and **Chau Giang** are on the opposite bank of the Hau River. There are several mosques in the villages as the Cham in this part of Vietnam are Muslim. At **Chau Phong** visitors can enjoy homestays. To reach the villages, take a sampan from the ferry terminal near the **Victoria Chau Doc Hotel**.

A visit to the **floating fish farm villages** (some 3000 floating houses), such as **Con Tien**, is a worthwhile and informative experience. A floating farm will have some 150,000 carp contained in a 6-m-deep iron cage beneath the house. Fish are worth around 600d for a baby and up to 25,000d for 500 g for a five-month-old fish. Catfish and mullet are also raised. (Chau Doc has a catfish monument on the riverfront promenade). When the fish are ready for sale, boats with nets under them are used to transport the fish to Long Xuyen.

CHAU DOC TO HA TIEN AND RACH GIA
Ha Tien can be reached either by boat or by road. The road is in a pitiful state but can be traversed by 4WD, Minsk or bicycle. Nevertheless, it is well worth attempting as it means the south coast can be reached without trailing back the 38 km to Long Xuyen. Also, the scenery as the road skirts the Cambodian border is beautiful and the local way of life little changed in hundreds of years. The road passes **Ba Chuc Ossuary** where the bones of 1000 Vietnamese killed in 1978 by the Khmer Rouge are displayed in a glass-sided memorial. Skulls are also stacked up in a glass-sided memorial, and each section is categorized by gender and by age – from children to grandparents. Nearby, there is a house in a small row of shops where photographs of the massacre are displayed; they are grisly and abhorrent.

An alternative route to Ha Tien is to follow Highway 91 to Nha Ban town. Turn right and follow the signs to Tri Ton town (along the way you drive through the Plain of Reeds, pass Cam Mountain and also various Khmer temples that are beautiful and thankfully tourist free. Upon arrival in Tri Ton town (some of the shops have signs in Khmer script) turn right and head for the Vam Ray ferry. Once across the Ha Tien-Rach Gia canal you are on Highway 80. Turn left to **Rach Gia** and right to Ha Tien.

CHAU DOC AND AROUND LISTINGS

WHERE TO STAY

Chau Doc

$$$$ Victoria Chau Doc, 1 Le Loi St, T076-386 5010, www.victoriahotels.asia. This old, cream building with its beautiful riverfront deck and pool complete with loungers and view of the river confluence is the perfect place to relax. All rooms are attractively decorated. The hotel runs a daily speedboat to and from Phnom Penh. A refined place with superb service.

$ Thuan Loi, 18 Tran Hung Dao St, T076-386 6134, hotelthuanloi@hcm.vnn.vn. A/c and good river views, clean and friendly. The expanded and attractively designed restaurant enjoys a great location right on the river and is recommended especially in the late afternoon for coffee. This is a highly popular place; reserve in advance if possible. Good floating restaurant attached.

$ Vinh Phuoc, 12-14 Quang Trung St, T012-1828 9964, www.hotels-chaudoc. com. Run by the friendly Ms Le Diem. 12 a/c rooms with private bathroom. Basic, but good enough for the price. Great information service (**Mekong Tours**) and Wi-Fi throughout. Includes breakfast. Bus pick ups for onward boat travel.

Ha Tien

$ Du Hung, 17A Tran Hau St, T077-395 1555, www.dongtamhotel.com. A hotel with spacious rooms and all facilities close to the ferry dock. Recommended.

Rach Gia

$ Kim Co, 141 Nguyen Hung Son St, T77-387 9610, www.kimcohotel.com. The pastel shades of this hotel are incongruous in the setting, but it's well located and has Wi-Fi.

RESTAURANTS

Chau Doc

$$$-$$ Bassac, in **Victoria Chau Doc**. The French and Vietnamese menus at this suave riverside restaurant with stunning terrace include buffalo paillard with shallot confit, and and *basa* in banana leaf with saffron. Daily specials board too. The bar is a lovely spot for a pre-dinner drink.

$ Mekong, 41 Le Loi St, T076-386 7381, opposite **Victoria Chau Doc**. Open for lunch and dinner. Located right beside

a lovingly restored French villa. Good selection of food including grilled prawns and fried rice dishes. The staff are friendly.

$ Sunrise Palace, next to the tourist pier, T076-385 4793. The beef in Chau Doc is probably the best in Vietnam and here the *bo nuong* (grilled beef), served with herbs, is excellent. Good *de nuong* (goat) too. Serves delicious Russian live beer that goes perfectly with the food. The outdoor seating is best – inside is a wedding venue space.

WHAT TO DO

Chau Doc

Mekong Tours, Vinh Phuoc Hotel, and at 14 Nguyen Huu Canh St, T076-386 8222, and at the **Thanh Nam 2 hotel** where they are particularly helpful, www.mekongtours. net. Local trips include the fish farms, floating markets and Cham village. Arranges bus and boat tickets further afield including Phu Quoc, Phnom Penh, Ha Tien

and My Tho. Also helps with air ticketing and visa applications.

Ha Tien

Mekong Tours, 200 Mac Thien Tich St, T077-395 2259, www.mekongtours.net. For bus and boat tickets locally and further afield. Cambodian visa organized, US$23. Very helpful.

PHU QUOC ISLAND

Phu Quoc is Vietnam's largest island, lying off the southwest coast of Vietnam. The island remains largely undeveloped with beautiful sandy beaches along much of its coastline and forested hills and pepper plantations inland. Most of the beaches benefit from crystal-clear waters, particularly in the dry season (the sea can be very rough during monsoon), making it perfect for swimming and a place well worth visiting for those with some time to spend in southern Vietnam. The island's remoteness and lack of infrastructure has meant that it is only recently that tourism has started developing and the pace of development has been slower than in other parts of the country owing to the lack of power and water supplies to much of the island.

However, Phu Quoc is set to expand at a phenomenal rate as multi-million dollar projects have been given the green light with roads as well as resorts being constructed. The opening of a new international airport (due mid-2013) is set to be a watershed moment for the island and the islanders, many of whom have been relocated from their beach-side fishing villages to make way for hotels. The island's status as a remote, undeveloped bolt hole, is over.

Phu Quoc's northernmost tip lies just outside Cambodian territorial waters and, like other parts of present-day Vietnam in this area, it has been fought over, claimed and reclaimed by Thai, Khmer and Viet. At the moment some of the island is reserved for military use and hence certain areas are restricted but, despite this, there remains plenty to explore.

PHU QUOC ISLAND

ARRIVING IN PHU QUOC ISLAND

Getting there You can get to Phu Quoc by boat from Rach Gia or Ha Tien or by plane from Ho Chi Minh City, Rach Gia, Can Tho and the Central Highlands. Most hotels will provide a free pick-up service from the airport if accommodation is booked in advance. The same does not apply to transfers from the ferry port. *Xe ôm* drivers meet the ferries.

Moving on To contine with the itinerary, the easiest option is to fly to Ho Chi Minh City (55 minutes) and take a plane to Siem Reap (see page 244). Another option would be to fly to Rach Gia and continue overland to Cambodia to there via Chau Doc or Ha Tien.

Getting around While some of the island's roads are surfaced many are still dirt tracks and so the best way to get around the entire island is by motorbike, although this could prove desperately hot and dusty. There are plenty of motorbike taxis and motorbikes are easily available and cheap to hire. The only problem that visitors are likely to encounter is the very limited signposting which can make some places pretty hard to find without some form of local assistance. Cars with drivers at fairly reasonable costs are available. Ask at hotels.

Tourist information Most of the resorts are very happy to arrange tours and they are a good source of up-to-date information. There are several tour operators which will provide plenty of information.

BACKGROUND
Historically, the island is renowned for its small part in the triumph of the Nguyen Dynasty. In 1765 Pigneau de Behaine was sent here as a young seminarist to train Roman Catholic missionaries; by chance he was on the island when Nguyen Anh (son of emperor-to-be Gia Long) arrived, fleeing the Tay Son. Pigneau's role in the rise of the Nguyen Dynasty is described on page 116. Another link between the island and Vietnamese history is that it was here, in 1919, that the civil servant Ngo Van Chieu communed with the spirit world and made contact with the Supreme Being, leading to the establishment of the Cao Dai religion.

AROUND THE ISLAND
Duong Dong is the main town on the island and many of the hotels and resorts are near here on Truong Beach. Millions of fish can be seen laid out to dry on land and on tables – all destined for the pot. Before being bottled they are fermented. At the Khai Hoan **fish sauce factory** ① *free*, huge barrels act as vats, each containing fish and salt. If the sauce is made in concrete vats, the taste is lost and so the sauce is cheaper.

The **Coi Nguon Museum** ① *149 Tran Hung Dao St, T77-398 0206, www.coi nguonphuquoc. com, daily 0700-1700, 1 English-speaking guide*, displays a huge amount of island creatures, fishing paraphernalia, old currency and Chinese ceramics from shipwrecked boats. The guide could not explain, however, how a private collector has amassed such a large haul of natural and man-made treasures.

About 10 km south of Dong Duong is the gloriously kitsch **Phu Quoc Pearl Gallery** ① *T91-399 3202, www.treasuresfromthedeep.com, 0800-1800*. Just offshore 10,000 South Sea pearls are collected each year. A video demonstrates the farming operation and the tasting of pearl meat and the pearl process is illustrated in the gallery. Jewellery is for sale. Some 100 m south of the pearl farm on the coastal road there are two **whale dedication temples**, Lang Ca Ong. In front of one is a crude whale/dolphin statue.

Ganh Dau, at the northwest tip, is 35 km from Duong Dong. The townsfolk speak Khmer because refugees escaping the Khmer Rouge came here and settled with the locals. The Cambodian coast is 4-5 km away and can be seen, as can the last island of Vietnam. (The Cambodians actually claim Phu Quoc as their own). The beach has a few palms and rocks to clamber on and there is a restaurant. **Dai Beach**, south of Ganh Danh, is a strip of white sand backed by casuarinas overlooking Turtle Island. The water is clear but there are no facilities. Inland from here the area is heavily forested but the wood is protected by law. In this part of the island fish are laid out to dry on large trestle-tables or on the ground for use as fertilizer. South of Dai Beach is **Ong Lang Beach** where there are a couple of resorts (see Where to stay).

The dazzling white sands of **Sao Beach** on the southeast coast are stunning and well worth visiting. Finding the beach can be difficult so you may need to ask directions. There are now two places to stay here and numerous restaurants by the sand, but it remains undeveloped.

The inland streams and waterfalls (**Da Ban** and **Chanh** streams) are not very dramatic in the dry season but still provide a relaxing place to swim and walk in the forests. The national park is home to plenty of animal species including monkeys, which can sometimes be spotted along the roads.

One of the biggest draws are the boat trips around the **An Thoi islands**, scattered islands, like chips off a block, off the southern coast, which offer opportunities for swimming, snorkelling, diving and fishing. It is also possible to stop off to visit an interesting fishing village at **Thom Island**.

PHU QUOC ISLAND LISTINGS

WHERE TO STAY

During peak periods, such as Christmas and Tet, it is advisable to book accommodation well in advance. Most of the resorts lie along the west coast to the south of Duong Dong and are within a few kilometres of the airport. Others are on On Lang Beach. **Fusion Maia Phu Quoc**, Asia's first all-inclusive spa on the water, will open in summer 2013.

$$$$ Chen Sea Resort & Spa, Ong Lang Beach, T077-399 5895, www. centarahotelsresorts.com/cpv. A very inviting resort with lovely villas set back from the yellow-sand beach. Smaller-roomed semi-detached bungalows face the sea with sunken bathtubs on generous verandas, and outdoor rain showers off gorgeous bathrooms with dual stone basins. The narrow strip of golden sand is dotted with paprika-coloured umbrellas, and there's an infinity pool, spa, watersports and atmospheric restaurant. Excellent buffet breakfast. Highly recommended.

$$$$ La Veranda, Tran Hung Dao St, Long Beach, T077-398 2988, www.laveranda resort.com. A beautiful luxury resort with rooms and villas set in luscious gardens leading on to the main beach on the island. All rooms are beautifully furnished and come with TV, DVD player and Wi-Fi. De luxe rooms and villas come with gorgeous 4-poster beds and drapes. There's a spa, pool and the delicious food of the **Pepper Tree Restaurant**. The welcome and service is exceptional.

$$$$-$$$ Mai House Resort, Long Beach, T077-384 7003, maihouseresort@ yahoo.com. This is a really lovely resort run by the lovely Tuyet Mai and her husband. The architecture and design is all Mai's work – tasteful with plenty of attention to detail. Set in large flourishing gardens in front of a delicious slice of beach dotted with palms. The 20 a/c bungalows feature 4-poster beds, beamed roofs, pretty tiled bathrooms and balconies with carved balustrades. Sea view rooms are bigger. Adjoining bungalows available for families. The open-fronted restaurant (with Wi-Fi access and places to lounge) overlooks the beach. One of the best places to eat on the island.

$$$$-$$$ Mango Bay Resort, Ong Lang Beach, T077-398 1693, www.mangobay phuquoc.com. An environmentally friendly resort located on the beach close to some pepper farms. Some bungalows are made from rammed earth and come with fans and coconut doorknobs and are kitted out with bamboo furniture and tiled floors. There are some 40 rooms scattered across the complex. There's information on birds and fish, and the restaurant provides a mixture of Vietnamese and Western food at very reasonable prices.

$$$-$$ Freedomland, Ong Lang Beach, 12 mins' walk from beach, T01-226 586802, www.freedomlandphuquoc.com. Run by Peter, this laidback resort creates a community vibe as all guests eat together at the large dinner table. Wooden stilt bungalows with thatched roofs and private bathrooms are scattered around the grounds. Recommended.

$$ Lang Toi, Sao Beach T09-8233 7477, langtoi_restaurant@yahoo.com.vn. With just 4 beautiful rooms complete with deep bathtubs, large balconies and tasteful wooden furnishings, this house is the best of the 2 options on the stunning Sao Beach. Beachfront restaurant serves all manner of seafood and simpler rice and noodle dishes. Recommended.

RESTAURANTS

The night market in Duong Dong is a great place for fresh local seafood, with plenty of vendors springing up each night. Along the river road a few restaurants also serve good Vietnamese dishes and seafood and are very popular with locals and Vietnamese tourists. **Truong Duong**, 30/4 Thanh Tu St, T09-146 1419, is one of the best. Be warned – the smell of the fish sauce factories can be a little overpowering at those nearer the port. **La Veranda** and **Mai House Resort** (see Where to stay) house the best upmarket kitchens near town, serving high quality international and Vietnamese food.

$$-$ Amigos, next to **La Veranda**, T091-707 0456. Run by the affable 'Speedy' (Mr Hai) and his Aussie partner, this beachfront bar and restaurant has a huge deck for great sunset views. Pizzas and burgers, grilled seafood, and a large range of cocktails. Happy hours and dancing later on.

$ German B, 78 Trung Hung Dao St, T016 6405 3830. Funky, orange-painted café serving cakes, pizza, and German breads. Music and cocktails by night.

WHAT TO DO

John's Tours, 143 Tran Hung Dao St, T091-910 7086, http://johnsislandtours.com. Run by the super-helpful and friendly John Tran out of an office next to the alley to **La Veranda** and various kiosks on the beach as well as hotel desks. John can organize anything for any budget and knows the island like the back of his hand. Snorkelling, squid fishing, island tours and car hire can all be arranged. Prices from US$17. Car hire with driver starts from 1,100,000d per day; motorbike with driver 500,000d per day. He can also help with motorbike rental (from 100,000d per day).

Rainbow Divers, 11 Tran Hung Dao St, close to the market, T091-340 0964 (mob), www.divevietnam.com. Long-standing operation with a very good reputation. Best diving Oct-Apr.

ANGKOR WAT AND SIEM REAP

The huge temple complex of Angkor, the ancient capital of the powerful Khmer Empire, is one of the archaeological treasures of Asia and the spiritual and cultural heart of Cambodia. Angkor Wat is arguably the greatest temple within the complex, both in terms of grandeur and sheer magnitude. After all, it is the biggest religious monument in the world, its outer walls clad with one of the longest continuous bas-relief ever created. The diverse architectural prowess and dexterity of thousands of artisans is testified by around 100 brilliant monuments in the area. Of these the Bayon, with its beaming smiles; Banteay Srei, which features the finest intricate carvings; and the jungle temple of Ta Prohm are unmissable. Others prefer the more understated but equally brilliant temples of Neak Pean, Preah Khan and Pre Rup.

The petite town of Siem Reap sits nearby the Angkor complex, and is home to a gamut of world-class hotels, restaurants and bars. A hop, skip and a jump from the town is Southeast Asia's largest lake, the Tonlé Sap, with floating villages, teeming with riverine life.

→ PLACES IN ANGKOR

GETTING THERE

Air The **airport** ① *T063-963148*, is 7 km from Siem Reap, the town closest to the Angkor ruins, with flights from Phnom Penh and Ho Chi Minh City. A moto into town is US$1, a taxi US$7. Guesthouse owners often meet flights. Visas can be issued upon arrival US$20 (฿1000), photo required.

By bus/boat There are regular bus connections with Phnom Penh (five hours) where the boat/bus from Vietnam arrives for those travelling overland.

MOVING ON

It's possible to return to Vietnam by bus and boat, however, the quickest option is to fly back to Ho Chi Minh City to complete the route.

GETTING AROUND

Most of the temples within the Angkor complex (except the Roluos Group) are located in an area 8 km north of Siem Reap, with the area extending across a 25 km radius. The Roluos Group are 13 km east of Siem Reap and further away is Banteay Srei (32 km).

Cars with drivers and guides are available from larger hotels from around US$25 to US$30 per day plus US$25 for a guide. An excellent guiding service by car is provided by **Mr Hak** ① *T012-540336, www.angkortaxidriver.com*, who offers a variety of packages and tours around Angkor and the surrounding area. The **Angkor Tour Guide Association** and most other travel agencies can also organize this. Expect to pay around US$10-12 per day for a moto unless the driver speaks good English, in which case the price will be higher. This price will cover trips to the Roluos Group of temples but not to Banteay Srei. No need to add more than a dollar or two to the price for getting to Banteay Srei unless the driver is also a guide and can demonstrate to you that he is genuinely going to show you around. Tuk-tuks have appeared in recent years and a trip to the temples on a motorbike-drawn cart is quite a popular option for two people, US$14-17 a day.

ON THE ROAD
Beating the crowds

These days avoiding traffic within the Angkor complex is difficult but still moderately achievable. As it stands, there is a pretty standard one-day tour itinerary that includes: Angkor Wat (sunrise), Angkor Thom, the Bayon, etc (morning), break for lunch, Ta Prohm (afternoon), Preah Khan (afternoon) and Phnom Bakheng (sunset). If you reverse the order, peak hour traffic at major temples is dramatically reduced. As many tour groups troop into Siem Reap for lunch this is an opportune time to catch a peaceful moment in the complex, just bring a packed lunch or eat at 1100 or 1400.

To avoid the masses at the draw-card attraction, Angkor Wat, try to walk around the temple, as opposed to through it. Sunset at Phnom Bakheng has turned into a circus fiasco, so aim for Angkor or the Bayon at this time as they are both quiet in comparison.

Sunrise is still relatively peaceful at Angkor, grab yourself the prime position behind the left-hand pond (you need to depart Siem Reap no later than 0530), though there are other stunning early morning options, such as Srah Srang or Bakong. Bakheng gives a beautiful vista of Angkor in the early-mid morning.

Bicycle hire, US$2-3 per day from most guesthouses, represents a nice option for those who feel reasonably familiar with the area. The White Bicycles scheme, set up by Norwegian expats, offers bikes for US$2 per day with US$1.50 of that going straight into local charities and no commission to the hotels and is recommended. If you are on a limited schedule and only have a day or two to explore you won't be able to cover an awful lot of the temples on a pedal bike as the searing temperatures and sprawling layout can take even the most advanced cyclists a considerable amount of time. Angkor Wat and Banteay Srei have official parking sites, 1000 riel and at the other temples you can quite safely park and lock your bikes in front of a drink stall.

You can also charter a helicopter. Elephants are stationed near the Bayon or at the South Gate of Angkor Thom during the day. In the evenings, they are located at the bottom of Phnom Bakheng, taking tourists up to the summit for sunset.

BEST TIME TO VISIT
Angkor's peak season coincides with the dry season, November-February. Not only is this the driest time of year it is also the coolest (which can still be unbearably hot). The monsoon lasts from June to October/November. At this time it can get very muddy.

TOURIST INFORMATION
Guides can be invaluable when navigating the temples, with the majority being able to answer most questions about Angkor as well as providing additional information about Cambodian culture and history. Most hotels and travel agents will be able to point you in the direction of a good guide. The **Khmer Angkor Tour Guide Association** ① *on the road to Angkor, T063-964347, www.khmerangkortourguide.com*, has pretty well-trained guides. Most of the guides here are well briefed and some speak English better than others. The going rate is US$20-25 per day. There is a new **tourist office** ① *at the far end of Sivatha Street (towards the crocodile farm), 0730-1100 and 1430-1700*.

Temple fees and hours A one-day pass costs US$20, three-day pass US$40, seven-day pass US$60. The seven-day pass is valid for any seven days (they don't have to be consecutive) one month from the purchase date. Most people will be able to cover the majority of the temples within three days. If you buy your ticket after 1715 the day before, you get a free sunset thrown in. Th compex is open daily 0500-1800. You will need to pay additional fees if you wish to visit Beng Melea (US$5), Phnom Kulen (US$20) or Koh Ker (US$10); payable at the individual sites.

Safety Landmines were planted on some outlying paths to prevent Khmer Rouge guerrillas from infiltrating the temples; they have pretty much all been cleared by now, but it is safer to stick to well-used paths. Be wary of snakes in the dry season. The very poisonous Hanuman snake (lurid green) is fairly common in the area.

Photography A generalization, but somewhat true is that black and white tends to produce better-looking tourist pictures than those in colour. The best colour shots usually include some kind of contrast against the temples, a saffron-clad monk or a child. Don't forget to ask if you want to include people in your shots. In general, the best time to photograph the great majority of temples is before 0900 and after 1630.

ITINERARIES
The temples are scattered over an area in excess of 160 sq km. A half-day would only allow enough time to visit the South Gate of Angkor Thom, Bayon and Angkor Wat. There are three so-called 'circuits'. The **Petit Circuit** takes in the main central temples including Angkor Wat, Bayon, Baphuon and the Terrace of the Elephants. The **Grand Circuit** takes a wider route, including smaller temples like Ta Prohm, East Mebon and Neak Pean. The **Roluos Group Circuit** ventures further afield still, taking in the temples near Roluos: Lolei, Preah Ko and Bakong. Here are some options for visiting Angkor's temples:

One day Angkor Wat (sunrise or sunset), South Gate of Angkor Thom, Angkor Thom Complex (Bayon, Elephant Terrace, Royal Palace) and Ta Prohm. This is a hefty schedule for one day; you'll need to arrive after 1615 and finish just after 1700 the following day.

Two days The same as above but with the inclusion of the rest of the Angkor Thom, Preah Khan, Srah Srang (sunrise), and at a push, Banteay Srei.

Three days **Day 1** Sunrise at Angkor Wat; morning South Gate of Angkor Thom, Angkor Thom complex (aside from Bayon); Ta Prohm; late afternoon-sunset at the Bayon. **Day 2** Sunrise Srah Srang; morning Banteay Kdei and Banteay Srei; late afternoon Preah Khan; sunset at Angkor Wat. **Day 3** Sunrise and morning Roluos; afternoon Ta Keo and sunset either at Bakheng or Angkor Wat. Those choosing to stay one or two days longer should try to work Banteay Samre, East Mebon, Neak Pean and Thomannon into their itinerary. A further two to three days warrants a trip to Prasat Kravan, Ta Som, Beng Melea and Kbal Spean.

→ SIEM REAP

The nearest town to Angkor, Siem Reap is a bustling tourism hub with a growing art and fashion crowd; however, it's still true to say that without the temples few people would ever find themselves here. Siem Reap is also an easy place to stay for volunteers looking to do a stint in saving the world, but perhaps too many nights spent in crowded Bar Street distracts from the task in hand. Visitors exhausted by the temple trail might care

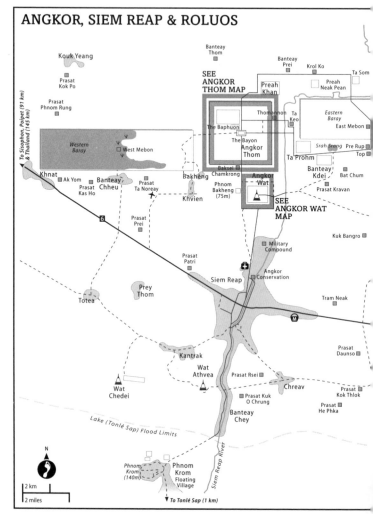

ANGKOR, SIEM REAP & ROLUOS

Kouk Yeang

Prasat
Kok Po

Prasat
Phnom Rung

Banteay
Thom

SEE
ANGKOR
THOM MAP

Banteay
Prei

Krol Ko

Preah
Neak Pean

Ta Som

Preah Khan

Thomannon

Ta
Keo

Eastern
Baray

East Mebon

Western
Baray

West Mebon

The Baphuon

The Bayon
Angkor
Thom

Srah Srang

Pre Rup

East Mebon

Khnat

Ak Yom

Banteay
Chheu

Prasat
Ta Noreay

Bakheng

Baksei
Chamkrong

Angkor
Wat

Ta Prohm

Banteay
Kdei

Bat Chum

Prasat
Kas Ho

Phnom
Bakheng
(75m)

SEE
ANGKOR WAT
MAP

Prasat Kravan

Khvien

Prasat
Prei

Kuk Bangro

Prasat
Patri

Military
Compound

Totea

Prey
Thom

Siem Reap

Angkor
Conservation

Tram Neak

Kantrak

Wat
Athvea

Prasat Rsei

Prasat
Daunso

Wat
Chedei

Chreav

Prasat
Kok Thlok

Prasat Kuk
O Chrung

Prasat
He Phka

Banteay
Chey

Lake (Tonlé Sap) Flood Limits

Siem Reap River

N

2 km

2 miles

Phnom
Krom
(140m)

Phnom Krom
Floating
Village

▼ To Tonlé Sap (1 km)

To Sisophon, Poipet (91 km)
& Thailand (145 km)

to while away a morning or afternoon in Siem Reap itself. The town has developed quite substantially in the past couple of years and, with the blossoming of hotels, restaurants and bars, it is now a pleasant place in its own right. Hotel building has pretty much kept pace with tourist arrivals so the town is a hive of activity.

The town is laid out formally and because there is ample land on which to build, it is pleasantly airy. Buildings are often set in large overgrown grounds resembling mini wildernesses. The current level of unprecedented growth and development is set to continue, so this may not be the case five years from now. The growth spurt has put a great strain on the city's natural resources.

The Old Market area is the most touristy part of the town. Staying around here is recommended for independent travellers and those staying more than two or three days. A sprinkling of guesthouses are here but a much greater selection is offered just across the river, in the Wat Bo area. This part of Siem Reap has recently become a popular place to stay with a range of accommodation available. It's not so crowded as the old market area and less traffic than airport road.

The **Angkor National Museum** ① *on the road to the temples, www.angkornational museum.com, daily 0830-1800, US$12,* is a short walk from the town centre. Due to the high entry price this museum is usually empty and it does seem rather incongruous that the artefacts on display here are not actually still in-situ at the temples themselves. Having said that, it isn't a bad museum and you can gather a lot of useful information about the development of Angkor. There are also some intriguing background details such as the 102 hospitals built during the reign of Jayavarman VII and the 1960 boxes of haemorrhoid cream that were part of their annual provisions. There are also some displays on the clothes the average Angkorian wore but it's a shame there isn't more about the daily lives of these ancients.

Map labels:
To Banteay Srei (10 km) & Phnom Kulen
Wat Phnom Bok
Phnom Bok (212m)
Prasat To
Pradak
Rolling River
Banteay Samre
Prei Pasat
Pasat Komnap
To Chau Srei Vibol Temple Complex (5km approx)
Kuk Taleh
Prasat Pou Teng
Lolei
To Phnom Penh
Prasat O Kaek
Preah Ko
Bakong
Roluos
Prahu
Prasat Prei Monti
Svay Pream
Prasat Totoeng O Thngai
Prasat Trapeang Phong
6

KHMER EMPIRE

Under **Jayavarman VII** (1181-1218) the complex stretched more than 25 km east to west and nearly 10 km north to south, approximately the same size as Manhattan. For five centuries (ninth-13th), the court of Angkor held sway over a vast territory. At its height Khmer influence spanned half of Southeast Asia, from Burma to the southernmost tip of Indochina and from the borders of Yunnan to the Malay Peninsula. The only threat to this great empire was a river-borne invasion in 1177, when the Cham used a Chinese navigator to pilot their canoes up the Mekong. Scenes are depicted in bas-reliefs of the Bayon temple.

Jayavarman II (AD 802-835) founded the Angkor Kingdom, then coined Hariharalaya to the north of the Tonlé Sap, in the Roluos region (Angkor), in AD 802. Later he moved the capital to Phnom Kulen, 40 km northeast of Angkor, where he built a Mountain Temple and Rong Shen shrine. After several years he moved the capital back to the Roluos region. **Jayavarman III** (AD 835-877) continued his father's legacy and built a number of shrines at Hariharalaya. Many historians believe he was responsible for the initial construction of the impressive laterite pyramid, Bakong, considered the great precursor to Angkor Wat. Bakong, built to symbolize Mount Meru, was later embellished and developed by Indravarman. **Indravarman** (AD 877-889) overthrew his predecessor violently and undertook a major renovation campaign in the capital Hariharalaya. The majority of what stands in the Roluos Group today is the work of Indravarman. A battle between Indravarman's sons destroyed the palace and the victor and new king **Yasovarman I** (AD 889-900) moved the capital from Roluos and laid the foundations of Angkor itself. He dedicated the temple to his ancestors. His new capital at Angkor was called Yasodharapura, meaning 'glory-bearing city', and here he built 100 wooden ashramas, retreats (all of which have disintegrated today). Yasovarman selected Bakheng as the location for his temple-mountain and after flattening the mountain top, set about creating another Mount Meru. The temple he constructed was considered more complex than anything built beforehand, a five-storey pyramid with 108 shrines. A road was then built to link the former and present capitals of Roluos and Bakheng. Like the Kings before him, Yasovarman was obliged to construct a major waterworks and the construction of the reservoir – the East Baray (now completely dry) – was considered an incredible feat. After Yasovarman's death in AD 900 his son **Harshavarman** (AD 900-923) assumed power for the next 23 years. During his brief reign, Harshavarman is believed to have built Baksei Chamkrong (north-east of Phnom Bakheng) and Prasat Kravan (the 'Cardamom Sanctuary'). His brother, **Ishanarvarman II** (AD 923-928), resumed power upon his death but no great architectural feats were recorded in this time. In 928, **Jayavarman IV** moved the capital 65 km away to Koh Ker. Here he built the grand state temple Prasat Thom, an impressive seven-storey, sandstone pyramid. Following the death of Jayavarman, things took a turn for the worst. Chaos ensued under **Harshavarman's II** weak leadership and over the next four years, no monuments were known to be erected. Jayavarman's IV nephew, **Rajendravarman** (AD 944-968), took control of the situation and it's assumed he forcefully relocated the capital back to Angkor. Rather than moving back into the old capital Phnom Bakheng, he marked his own new territory, selecting an area south of the East Baray as his administrative centre. Here, in AD 961 he constructed the state temple, Pre Rup, and constructed the temple, East Mebon (AD 953), in the middle of the baray. Srah Srang, Kutisvara and Bat

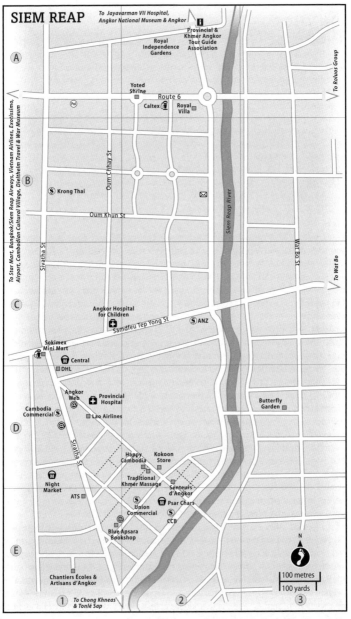

SIEM REAP

To Jayavarman VII Hospital,
Angkor National Museum & Angkor

Provincial &
Khmer Angkor
Tour Guide
Association

Royal
Independence
Gardens

To Roluos Group

Yoted
Shrine

Route 6

Caltex

Royal
Villa

Pol

Krong Thai

Oum Chhay St

Oum Khun St

Siem Reap River

To Star Mart, Bangkok/Siem Reap Airways, Vietnam Airlines, Exotissimo,
Airport, Cambodian Cultural Village, Diethelm Travel & War Museum

Sivatha St

Wat Bo St

To Wat Bo

Angkor Hospital
for Children

Samdeu Tep Yong St

ANZ

Sokimex
Mini Mart

Central

DHL

Angkor
Web

Provincial
Hospital

Cambodia
Commercial

Lao Airlines

Butterfly
Garden

Sivatha St

Night
Market

ATS

Happy
Cambodia

Kokoon
Store

Traditional
Khmer Massage

Senteurs
d'Angkor

Union
Commercial

Psar Chars

CCB

Blue Apsara
Bookshop

Chantiers Écoles &
Artisans d'Angkor

To Chong Khneas
& Tonlé Sap

N

100 metres
100 yards

ON THE ROAD
The Churning of the Sea

The Hindu legend, the Churning of the Sea, relates how the gods and demons resolved matters in the turbulent days when the world was being created. The elixir of immortality was one of 13 precious things lost in the churning of the cosmic sea. It took 1000 years before the gods and demons, in a joint dredging operation – aided by Sesha, the sea snake, and Vishnu – recovered them all.

The design of the temples of Angkor was based on this ancient legend. The moat represents the ocean and the gods use the top of Mount Meru – represented by the tower – as their churning stick. The cosmic serpent offered himself as a rope to enable the gods and demons to twirl the stick.

Paul Mus, a French archaeologist, suggests that the bridge with the naga balustrades which went over the moat from the world of men to the royal city was an image of the rainbow. Throughout Southeast Asia and India, the rainbow is alluded to as a multi-coloured serpent rearing its head in the sky.

Chum were also constructed, with the help of his chief architect, Kavindrarimathana. It was towards the end of his reign that he started construction on Banteay Srei, considered one of the finest examples of Angkorian craftsmanship in the country. Rajendravarman's son **Jayavarman V** (AD 968-1001) became the new king in 968. The administrative centre was renamed Jayendranagari and yet again, relocated. More than compensating for the unfinished Ta Keo was Jayavarman's V continued work on Banteay Srei. Under his supervision the splendid temple was completed and dedicated to his father.

Aside from successfully extending the Khmer Empire's territory **King Suryavarman I** (1002-1049), made a significant contribution to Khmer architectural heritage. He presided over the creation of a new administrative centre – the Royal Palace (in Angkor Thom) – and the huge walls that surround it. The next in line was Udayadityavarman II (1050-1066), the son of Suryavarman I. The Baphuon temple-mountain was built during his relatively short appointment. After overthrowing his Great-Uncle Dharanindravarman, **SuryavarmanII** (1112-1150), the greatest of Angkor's god-kings, came to power. His rule marked the highest point in Angkorian architecture and civilization. Not only was he victorious in conflict, having beaten the Cham whom couldn't be defeated by China, he was responsible for extending the borders of the Khmer Empire into Myanmar, Malaya and Siam. This aside, he was also considered one of the era's most brilliant creators. Suryavarman II was responsible for the construction of Angkor Wat, the current-day symbol of Cambodia. Beng Melea, Banteay Samre and Thommanon are also thought to be the works of this genius. He has been immortalized in his own creation – in a bas-relief in the South Gallery of Angkor Wat the glorious King Suryavarman II sitting on top of an elephant. After a period of political turmoil, which included the sacking of Angkor, **Jayavarman VII** seized the throne in 1181 and set about rebuilding his fiefdom. He created a new administrative centre – the great city of Angkor Thom. The mid-point of Angkor Thom is marked by his brilliant Mahayana Buddhist state temple, the Bayon. It is said that the Bayon was completed in 21 years. Jayavarman took thousands of peasants from the rice fields to build it, which proved a fatal error, for rice yields decreased and the empire began its decline as resources were drained. The temple, which consists of sculptured faces of

Avolokiteshvara (the Buddha of compassion and mercy) are often said to also encompass the face of their great creator, Jayavarman VIII. He was also responsible for restoring the Royal Palace, renovating Srah Srang and constructing the Elephant Terrace, the Terrace of the Leper King and the nearby baray (northeast of Angkor Thom), Jayatataka reservoir. At the centre of his reservoir he built Neak Pean. Jayavarman VII adopted Mahayana Buddhism; Buddhist principles replaced the Hindu pantheon, and were invoked as the basis of royal authority. This spread of Buddhism is thought to have caused some of the earlier Hindu temples to be neglected. The king paid tribute to his Buddhist roots through his monastic temples – Ta Prohm and Preah Khan.

THE FRENCH AT ANGKOR

Thai ascendency and eventual occupation of Angkor in 1431, led to the city's abandonment and the subsequent invasion of the jungle. Four centuries later, in 1860, Henri Mouhot – a French naturalist – stumbled across the forgotten city, its temple towers enmeshed in the forest canopy. Locals told him they were the work of a race of giant gods. Only the stone temples remained; all the wooden secular buildings had decomposed in the intervening centuries. In 1873 French archaeologist Louis Delaporte removed many of Angkor's finest statues for 'the cultural enrichment of France'. In 1898, the École Française d'Extrême Orient started clearing the jungle, restoring the temples, mapping the complex and making an inventory of the site. Delaporte was later to write the two-volume *Les Monuments du Cambodge*, the most comprehensive Angkorian inventory of its time, and his earlier sketches, plans and reconstructions, published in *Voyage au Cambodge* in 1880 are without parallel.

ANGKOR TEMPLES

The temples at Angkor were modelled on those of the kingdom of Chenla (a mountain kingdom centred on northern Cambodia and southern Laos), which in turn were modelled on Indian temples. They represent Mount Meru – the home of the gods of Indian cosmology. The central towers symbolize the peaks of Mount Meru, surrounded by a wall representing the earth and moats and basins representing the oceans. The devaraja, or god-king, was enshrined in the centre of the religious complex, which acted as the spiritual axis of the kingdom. The people believed their apotheosized king communicated directly with the gods.

The central tower sanctuaries housed the images of the Hindu gods to whom the temples were dedicated. Dead members of the royal and priestly families were accorded a status on a par with these gods. Libraries to store the sacred scriptures were also built within the ceremonial centre. The temples were mainly built to shelter the images of the gods – unlike Christian churches, Moslem mosques and some Buddhist pagodas, they were not intended to accommodate worshippers. Only priests, the servants of the god, were allowed into the interiors. The 'congregation' would mill around in open courtyards or wooden pavilions.

The first temples were of a very simple design, but with time they became more grandiose and doors and galleries were added. Most of Angkor's buildings are made from a soft sandstone which is easy to work. It was transported to the site from Phnom Kulen, about 30 km to the northeast. Laterite was used for foundations, core material, and enclosure walls, as it was widely available and could be easily cut into blocks. A common feature of Khmer temples was false doors and windows on the sides and backs of sanctuaries and other buildings. In most cases there was no need for well-lit rooms and corridors as hardly anyone

ON THE ROAD
Motifs in Khmer sculpture

Apsaras These are regarded as one of the greatest invention of the Khmers. The gorgeous temptresses – born, according to legend, 'during the churning of the Sea of Milk' – were Angkor's equivalent of pin-up girls and represented the ultimate ideal of feminine beauty. They lived in heaven where their sole raison d'être was to have eternal sex with Khmer heroes and holy men. The apsaras are carved in seductive poses with splendidly ornate jewellery and clothed in the latest Angkor fashion. Different facial features suggest the existence of several races at Angkor. Together with the five towers of Angkor Wat they have become the symbol of Khmer culture. The god-king himself possessed an apsara-like retinue of court dancers – impressive enough for Chinese envoy Chou Ta-kuan to write home about it in 1296.

Garuda Mythical creature – half-man, half-bird – was the vehicle of the Hindu god, Vishnu, and the sworn enemy of the nagas. It appeared relatively late in Khmer architecture.

Kala Jawless monster commanded by the gods to devour his own body – made its first appearance in lintels at Roluos. The monster represented devouring time and was an early import from Java.

Makara Mythical water-monster with a scaly body, eagles' talons and an elephantine trunk.

Naga Sacred snake. These play an important part in Hindu mythology and the Khmers drew on them for architectural inspiration. Possibly more than any other single symbol or motif, the naga is characteristic of Southeast Asia and decorates objects throughout the region. The naga is an aquatic serpent and is intimately associated with water (a key component of Khmer prosperity). In Hindu mythology, the naga coils beneath and supports Vishnu on the cosmic ocean. The snake also swallows the waters of life, these only being set free to reinvigorate the world after Indra ruptures the serpent with a bolt of lightning. Another version has Vishnu's servants pulling at the serpent to squeeze the waters of life from it (the so-called churning of the sea, see box, page 248).

Singha Lion in stylized form; often the guardians to temples.

ever went into them. That said, the galleries round the central towers in later temples, such as Angkor Wat, indicate that worshippers did use the temples for ceremonial circumambulation when they would contemplate the inspiring bas-reliefs from the important Hindu epic, *Ramayana* and *Mahabharata* (written between 400 BC and AD 200).

Despite the court's conversion to Mahayana Buddhism in the 12th century, the architectural ground-plans of temples did not alter much – even though they were based on Hindu cosmology. The idea of the god-king was simply grafted onto the new state religion and statues of the Buddha rather than the gods of the Hindu pantheon were used to represent the god-king. One particular image of the Buddha predominated at Angkor in which he wears an Angkor-style crown, with a conical top encrusted with jewellery.

→ ANGKOR WAT

The awe-inspiring sight of Angkor Wat, first thing in the morning, is something you're not likely to forget. Angkor literally means 'city' or 'capital' and it is the biggest religious monument ever built and certainly one of the most spectacular. The temple complex covers 81 ha. Its five towers are emblazoned on the Cambodian flag and the 12th-century masterpiece is considered by art historians to be the prime example of classical Khmer art and architecture. It took more than 30 years to build and is dedicated to the Hindu god Vishnu, personified in earthly form by its builder, the god-king Suryavarman II, and is aligned east to west.

Angkor Wat differs from other temples, primarily because it is facing westward, symbolically the direction of death, leading many to originally believe it was a tomb. However, as Vishnu is associated with the west, it is now generally accepted that it served both as a temple and a mausoleum for the king. Like other Khmer temple-mountains, Angkor Wat is an architectural allegory, depicting in stone the epic tales of Hindu mythology. The central sanctuary of the temple complex represents the sacred Mount Meru, the centre of the Hindu universe, on whose summit the gods reside. Angkor Wat's five towers symbolize Meru's five peaks; the enclosing wall represents the mountains at the edge of the world and the surrounding moat, the ocean beyond.

The temple complex is enclosed by a square moat – more than 5 km in length and 190 m wide – and a high, galleried wall, which is covered in epic bas-reliefs and has four

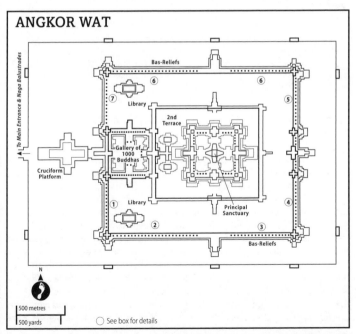

ANGKOR WAT

To Main Entrance & Naga Balustrades

Bas-Reliefs

⑥ ⑥

⑦

Library ⑤

2nd
Terrace

Gallery of
1000
Buddhas

Cruciform
Platform

① Library

Principal
Sanctuary

② ③ ④

Bas-Reliefs

N

500 metres
500 yards

◯ See box for details

ON THE ROAD

Anti-clockwise around Angkor Wat's bas-reliefs

1 Western gallery The southern half represents a scene from the *Mahabharata* of a battle between the Pandavas (with pointed head dresses, attacking from the right) and the Kauravas. The two armies come from the two ends of the panel and meet in the middle. The southwest corner has been badly damaged – some say by the Khmer Rouge – but shows scenes from Vishnu's life.

2 Southern gallery The western half depicts Suryavarman II (builder of Angkor Wat) leading a procession. He is riding a royal elephant, giving orders to his army before leading them into battle against the Cham. The rank of the army officers is indicated by the number of umbrellas. The undisciplined, outlandishly dressed figures are the Thais.

3 Southern gallery The eastern half was restored in 1946 and depicts the punishments and rewards one can expect in the after life. The damned are depicted in the bottom row, while the blessed, depicted in the upper two rows, are borne along in palanquins surrounded by large numbers of bare-breasted apsaras.

4 Eastern gallery The southern half is the best-known part of the bas-relief – the churning of the sea of milk by gods and demons to make ambrosia (the nectar of the gods which gives immortality). In the centre, Vishnu commands the operation. Below are sea animals and above, apsaras.

5 Eastern gallery The northern half is an unfinished representation of a war between the gods for the possession of the ambrosia. The gate in the centre was used by Khmer royalty and dignitaries for mounting and dismounting elephants.

6 Northern gallery Represents a war between gods and demons. Siva is shown in meditation with Ganesh, Brahma and Krishna. Most of the other scenes are from the *Ramayana*, notably the visit of Hanuman to Sita.

7 Western gallery The northern half has another scene from the *Ramayana* depicting a battle between Rama and Ravana who rides a chariot pulled by monsters and commands an army of giants.

ceremonial tower gateways. The main gateway faces west and the temple is approached by a 475-m-long road, built along a causeway, which is lined with naga balustrades. At the far end of the causeway stands a **cruciform platform**, guarded by stone lions, from which the devaraja may have held audiences; his backdrop being the three-tiered central sanctuary. Commonly referred to as the Terrace of Honour, it is entered through the colonnaded processional gateway of the outer gallery. The transitional enclosure beyond it is again cruciform in shape. Its four quadrants formed galleries, once stocked full of statues of the Buddha. Only a handful of the original 1000-odd images remain.

The cluster of **central towers**, 12 m above the second terrace, is reached by 12 steep stairways, which represent the precipitous slopes of Mount Meru. Many historians believe that the upwards hike to this terrace was reserved for the high priests and king himself. Today, anyone is welcome but the difficult climb is best handled slowly by stepping sideways up the steep incline. The five lotus flower-shaped sandstone towers – the first appearance of these features in Khmer architecture – are believed to have once been covered in gold. The eight-storey towers are square, although they appear octagonal, and give the impression of a sprouting bud. The central tower is dominant, as is the Siva shrine and principal sanctuary, whose pinnacle rises more than 30 m above the third level and, 55m above ground level. This sanctuary would have contained an image of Siva in the likeness of King Suryavarman II, as it was his temple-mountain. But it is now a Buddhist shrine and contains statues of the Buddha.

More than 1000 sq m of bas-relief decorate the temple. Its greatest sculptural treasure is the 2-m-high **bas-reliefs**, around the walls of the outer gallery. It is the longest continuous bas-relief in the world. In some areas traces of the paint and gilt that once covered the carvings can still be seen. Most famous are the hundreds of figures of deities and apsaras in niches along the walls.

→ THE ROYAL CITY OF ANGKOR THOM

Construction of Jayavarman VII's spacious walled capital, Angkor Thom (which means 'great city'), began at the end of the 12th century: he rebuilt the capital after it had been captured and destroyed by the Cham. Angkor Thom was colossal: the 100-m-wide moat surrounding the city, which was probably stocked with crocodiles as a protection against the enemy, extended more than 12 km. Inside the moat was an 8-m-high stone wall, buttressed on the inner side by a high mound of earth along the top of which ran a terrace for troops to man the ramparts.

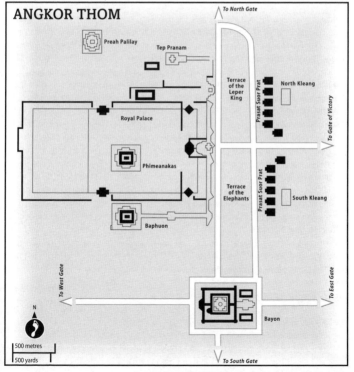

Four great gateways in the city wall face north, south, east and west and lead to the city's geometric centre, the Bayon. The fifth, Victory Gate, leads from the royal palace (within the Royal Enclosure) to the East Baray. The height of the gates was determined by the headroom needed to accommodate an elephant and howdah, complete with parasols. The flanks of each gateway are decorated by three-headed stone elephants, and each gateway tower has four giant faces, which keep an eye on all four cardinal points. Five causeways traverse the moat, each bordered by sculptured balustrades of nagas gripped, on one side, by 54 stern-looking giant gods and on the other by 54 fierce-faced demons. The balustrade depicts the Hindu legend of the Churning of the Sea (see box, page 248).

The **South Gate** provides the most common access route to Angkor Thom, predominantly because it sits on the path between the two great Angkor complexes. The gate is a wonderful introduction to Angkor Thom, with well-restored statues of asuras (demons) and gods lining the bridge. The figures on the left, exhibiting serene expression, are the gods, while those on the right, with grimaced, fierce-looking heads, are the asuras.

The **Bayon** was Jayavarman VII's own temple-mountain, built right in the middle of Angkor Thom; its large faces have now become synonymous with the Angkor complex. It is believed to have been built between the late 12th century to early 13th century, around 100 years after Angkor Wat. The Bayon is a three-tiered, pyramid-temple with a 45-m-high tower, topped by four gigantic carved heads. These faces are believed to be the images of Jayavarman VII as a Bodhisattra, and face the four compass points. They are crowned with lotus flowers, symbol of enlightenment, and are surrounded by 51 smaller towers each with heads facing north, south, east and west. There are more than 2000 large faces carved throughout the structure. The first two of the three levels feature galleries of bas-relief (which should be viewed clockwise); a circular central sanctuary dominates the third level.

The **bas-reliefs** which decorate the walls of the Bayon are much less imposing than those at Angkor Wat. The sculpture is carved deeper but is more naive and less sophisticated than the bas-reliefs at Angkor Wat. The relief on the outside depicts historical events; those on the inside are drawn from the epic world of gods and legends, representing the creatures who were supposed to haunt the subterranean depths of Mount Meru. In fact the reliefs on the outer wall illustrating historical scenes and derring-do with marauding Cham were carved in the early 13th century during the reign of Jayavarman; those on the inside which illuminate the Hindu cosmology were carved after the king's death when his successors turned from Mahayana Buddhism back to Hinduism. Two recurring themes in the bas-reliefs are the powerful king and the Hindu epics. Jayavarman is depicted in the throes of battle with the Cham – who are recognizable thanks to their unusual and distinctive headdress, which looks like an inverted lotus flower. The other bas-reliefs give a good insight into Khmer life at the time – the warrior elephants, ox carts, fishing with nets, cockfights and skewered fish drying on racks. Other vignettes show musicians, jugglers, hunters, chess players, palm-readers and scenes of Angkor citizens enjoying drinking sessions. In the naval battle scenes, the water around the war-canoes is depicted by the presence of fish, crocodiles and floating corpses.

The **Royal Palace**, to the north of the Bayon, had already been laid out by Suryavarman I: the official palace was in the front with the domestic quarters behind, its gardens surrounded by a laterite wall and moat. Suryavarman I also beautified the royal city with ornamental pools. Jayavarman VII simply improved his designs. In front of the Royal Palace, at the centre of Angkor Thom, Suryavarman I laid out the first Grand Plaza with the **Terrace of the Elephants** (also called the Royal Terrace). The 300-m-long wall derives its name from the large, life-like carvings of elephants in a hunting scene, adorning its walls. The 2.5-m wall also features elephants flanking the southern stairway. It is believed it was the foundations of the royal reception hall. Royalty once sat in gold-topped pavilions at the centre of the pavilion, and here there are rows of garudas (bird-men), their wings lifted as if in flight. They were intended to give the impression that the god-king's palace was floating in the heavens, like the imagined flying celestial palaces of the gods. At the northeast corner of the 'central square' is the 12th-century **Terrace of the Leper King**, which may have been a cremation platform for the aristocracy of Angkor. The 7-m-high double terrace has bands of bas-reliefs, one on top of the other, with intricately sculptured scenes of royal pageantry and seated apsaras as well as nagas and garudas which frequented the slopes of Mount Meru. Above is a strange statue of an earlier date, which probably depicts the god of death, Yama, and once held a staff in its right hand. The statue's naked, lichen-covered body gives the terrace its name – the lichen gives the uncanny impression of leprosy. The **Phimeanakas** (meaning Celestial or Flying Palace in Sanskrit) inside the Royal Palace was started by Rajendravarman and used by all the later kings. Lions guard all four stairways to the central tower. It is now ruined but was originally covered in gold.

South of the Royal Palace is the **Baphuon**, built by Udayadityavarman II. The temple was approached by a 200-m-long sandstone causeway, raised on pillars, which was probably constructed after the temple was built. **Preah Palilay**, just outside the north wall of the Royal Palace, was also built by Jayavarman VII.

→ AROUND ANGKOR THOM

PHNOM BAKHENG
ⓘ *Either climb the steep hill (slippery when wet), ride an elephant to the top of the hill (US$15) or walk up the gentle zig-zag path the elephants take.*

Yasovarman's temple-mountain stands at the top of a natural hill, Phnom Bakheng, 60 m high, affording good views of the plains of Angkor. A pyramid-temple dedicated to Siva, Bakheng was the home of the royal linga and Yasovarman's mausoleum after his death. It is composed of five towers built on a sandstone platform. There are 108 smaller towers scattered around the terraces. The main tower has been partially demolished and the others have completely disappeared. It was entered via a steep flight of steps which were guarded by squatting lions. The steps have deteriorated with the towers. Foliate scroll relief carving covers much of the main shrine – the first time this style was used. This strategically placed hill served as a camp for various combatants, including the Vietnamese, and suffered accordingly.

TA PRO
The temple of Ta Prohm is the perfect lost-in-the-jungle experience. Unlike most of the other monuments at Angkor, it has been only minimally cleared of its undergrowth, fig trees and creepers. It is widely regarded as one of Angkor's most enchanting temples.

Ta Prohm was consecrated in 1186 – five years after Jayavarman VII seized power. It was built to house the divine image of the Queen Mother. The outer enclosures of Ta Prohm are somewhat obscured by foliage but reach well beyond the temple's heart (1 km by 650 m). The temple proper consists of a number of concentric galleries, featuring corner towers and the standard gopuras. Other buildings and enclosures were built on a more ad hoc basis.

Within the complex walls lived 12,640 citizens. It contained 39 sanctuaries or prasats, 566 stone dwellings and 288 brick dwellings. Ta Prohm literally translates to the 'Royal Monastery' and that is what it functioned as, home to 18 abbots and 2740 monks. By the 12th century, temples were no longer exclusively places of worship – they also had to accommodate monks, so roofed halls were increasingly built within the complexes.

The trees burgeoning their way through the complex are predominantly the silk-cotton tree and the aptly named strangler fig. Naturally, the roots of the trees have descended towards the soil, prying their way through the temples foundations in the process. As the vegetation has matured, growing stronger, it has forced its way further into the temples structure, damaging the man-built base and causing untold destruction.

BANTEAY KDEI, SRAH SRANG, PRASAT KRAVAN AND PRE RUP

The massive complex of **Banteay Kdei**, otherwise known as 'the citadel of cells', is 3 km east of Angkor Thom. Some archaeologists think it may be dedicated to Jayavarman VII's religious teacher. The temple has remained in much the same state it was discovered in – a crowded collection of ruined laterite towers and connecting galleries lying on a flat plan, surrounded by a galleried enclosure. It is presumed that the temple was a Buddhist monastery and in recent years hundreds of buried Buddha statues were excavated from the site. Like Ta Prohm it contains a Hall of Dancers (east side), an open-roof building with four separate quarters. The second enclosure runs around the perimeters of the inner enclosure. The third inner enclosure contains a north and south library and central sanctuary. The central tower was never finished. The square pillars in the middle of the courtyard still cannot be explained by scholars. There are few inscriptions here to indicate either its name or purpose, but it is almost certainly a Buddhist temple built in the 12th century, about the same time as Ta Prohm. The Lake (baray) next to Banteay Kdei is called **Srah Srang** – 'Royal Bath' – and was used for ritual bathing. The steps down to the water face the rising sun and are flanked with lions and nagas. This sandstone landing stage dates from the reign of Jayavarman VII but the Lake itself is thought to date back two centuries earlier. A 10th-century inscription reads 'this water is stored for the use of all creatures except dyke breakers', eg elephants. The baray (700 m by 300 m), has been filled with turquoise-blue waters for more than 1300 years. With a good view of Pre Rup across the lake, some archaeologists believe that this spot affords the best vista in the whole Angkor complex.

Prasat Kravan, built in AD 921, means 'Cardamom Sanctuary' and is unusual in that it is built of brick. By that time brick had been replaced by laterite and sandstone. It consists of five brick towers arranged in a line. The Hindu temple, surrounded by a moat, consists of five elevated brick towers, positioned in a north-south direction. Two of the five decorated brick towers contain bas-reliefs (the north and central towers). The central tower is probably the most impressive and contains a linga on a pedestal. The sanctuary's three walls all contain pictures of Vishnu.

Northeast of Srah Srang is **Pre Rup**, the State Temple of King Rajendravarman's capital. Built in AD 961, the temple-mountain representing Mount Meru is larger, higher and artistically superior than its predecessor, the East Mebon, which it closely resembles. Keeping with tradition of state capitals, Pre Rup marked the centre of the city, much of which doesn't exist today. The pyramid-structure, which is constructed of laterite with brick prasats, sits at the apex of an artificial, purpose-built mountain. The central pyramid-level consists of a three-tiered, sandstone platform, with five central towers sitting above. Its modern name, 'turning the body', derives from local legend and is named after a cremation ritual in which the outline of a body was traced in the cinders one way and then the other. The upper levels of the pyramid offer a brilliant, panoramic view of the countryside.

PREAH KHAN

The 12th-century complex of Preah Khan, one of the largest complexes within the Angkor area, was Jayavarman VII's first capital before Angkor Thom was completed. Preah Khan means 'sacred sword' and is believed to have derived from a decisive battle against the Cham, which created a 'lake of blood', but was invariably won by Jayavarman VII. It is similar in ground-plan to Ta Prohm but attention was paid to the approaches: its east and west entrance avenues leading to ornamental causeways are lined with carved-stone boundary posts. Evidence suggests that it was more than a mere Buddhist monastery but most likely a Buddhist university. Nonetheless an abundance of Brahmanic iconography is still present on site. Around the rectangular complex is a large laterite wall, surrounded by large garudas wielding the naga (each more than 5 m in height), the theme continues across the length of the whole 3-km external enclosure, with the motif dotted every 50 m. Within these walls lies the surrounding moat.

PREAH NEAK PEAN

To the east of Preah Khan is the Buddhist temple Preah Neak Pean built by Jayavarman VII. The temple of Neak Pean is also a fountain, built in the middle of a pool and representing the paradisiacal Himalayan mountain-lake, Anaavatapta, from Hindu mythology. It is a small sanctuary on an island in the baray of Preah Khan. Two nagas form the edge of the island, and their tails join at the back. The temple pools were an important part of the aesthetic experience of Preah Khan and Neak Pean – the ornate stone carving of both doubly visible by reflection.

→ OUTLYING TEMPLES

THE ROLUOS GROUP

The Roluos Group receives few visitors but is worth visiting if time permits. Jayavarman II built several capitals including one at Roluos, at that time called Hariharalaya. This was the site of his last city and remained the capital during the reigns of his three successors. The three remaining Hindu sanctuaries at Roluos are **Preah Ko**, **Bakong** and **Lolei**. They were finished in AD 879, AD 881 and AD 893 respectively by Indravarman I and his son Yashovarman I and are the best-preserved of the early temples. All three temples are built of brick, with sandstone doorways and niches. Sculptured figures which appear in the Roluos group are the crouching lion, the reclining bull (Nandi - Siva's mount) and the naga (snake).

Preah Ko, meaning 'sacred ox', was named after the three statues of Nandi (the mount of the Hindu god, Siva) which stand in front of the temple. Orientated east-west, there is a cluster of six brick towers arranged in two rows on a low brick platform, the steps up to which are guarded by crouching lions while Nandi, looking back, blocks the way. The front row of towers was devoted to Indravarman's male ancestors and the second row to the female. Indravarman's temple-mountain, **Bakong**, is a royal five-stepped pyramid-temple with a sandstone central tower built on a series of successively receding terraces with surrounding brick towers. Indravarman himself was buried in the temple.

Bakong is the largest and most impressive temple in the Roluos Group by a long way. A bridge flanked by a naga balustrade leads over a dry moat to the temple. The central tower was built to replace the original one when the monument was restored in the 12th century and is probably larger than the original. The Bakong denotes the true beginning of classical Khmer architecture and contained the god-king's Siva linga. **Lolei** was built by Yashovarman I in the middle of Indravarman's baray. The brick towers were dedicated to the king's ancestors, but they have disintegrated; of the four, two have partly collapsed.

BANTEAY SREI

Banteay Srei, 25 km from Ta Prohm along a decent road (closes at 1700), was built by the Brahmin tutor to King Rajendravarman, Yajnavaraha, grandson of Harshavarman, and founded in AD 967. Banteay Srei translates to 'Citadel of Women', a title bestowed upon it in relatively recent years due to the intricate apsara carvings that adorn the interior. The temple is considered by many historians to be the highest achievement of art from the Angkor period. The explicit preservation of this temple reveals covered terraces, of which only the columns remain, which once lined both sides of the primary entrance. In keeping with tradition, a long causeway leads into the temple, across a moat, on the eastern side. The main walls, entry pavilions and libraries have been constructed from laterite and the carvings from pink sandstone. The layout was inspired by Prasat Thom at Koh Ker. Three beautifully carved tower-shrines stand side by side on a low terrace in the middle of a quadrangle, with a pair of libraries on either side enclosed by a wall. Two of the shrines, the southern one and the central one, were dedicated to Siva and the northern one to Vishnu; both had libraries close by, with carvings depicting appropriate legends. The whole temple is dedicated to Brahma. Having been built by a Brahmin priest, the temple was never intended for use by a king, which goes some way towards explaining its small size – you have to duck to get through the doorways to the sanctuary towers. Perhaps because of its modest scale Banteay Srei contains some of the finest examples of Khmer sculpture. Finely carved and rare pink sandstone replaces the plaster-coated carved-brick decoration, typical of earlier temples. All the buildings are covered in carvings: the jambs, the lintels, the balustered windows. Banteay Srei's ornamentation is exceptional – its roofs, pediments and lintels are magnificently carved with tongues of flame, serpents' tails, gods, demons and floral garlands.

ANGKOR WAT AND SIEM REAP LISTINGS

WHERE TO STAY

It is not uncommon for taxi, moto and tuk-tuk drivers to tell new arrivals that the guesthouse they were booked into is now 'closed' or full. They will try to take you to the place where they get the best commission. One way around this is to arrange for the guesthouse or hotel to pick you up for free or a small fee.

Siem Reap

$$$$ Angkor Village Resort, T063-963561, www.angkorvillage.com. The resort contains 40 rooms set in Balinese-style surroundings. Traditional massage services, 2 restaurants, theatre shows and lovely pool. Elephant, boat and helicopter rides can be arranged. Recommended.

$$$$ Le Meridien Angkor, main road towards temples, T063-963900, www.le meridien.com/angkor. From the outside this 5-star hotel is severe with angled architecture with small, dark slits for windows. Walk into the lobby and it is immediately transformed into space and light. Rooms are nicely designed and sized and all come with a/c, en suite and cable TV. Other facilities include spa, restaurants and pool. The garden is a lovely spot to take breakfast. Recommended.

$$$$ Sokha Angkor, Sivatha St, T063-969999, www.sokhahotels.com. One of the few Cambodian-owned 5-star hotels in the country, the rooms and services here are top notch, even if the decor is a little gaudy (check out the incredibly over-the-top swimming pool, complete with faux temple structures and waterfalls). Excellent Japanese restaurant. Recommended.

$$$$ Victoria Angkor Hotel, Route 6, T063-760428, www.victoriahotels-asia.com. Perfection. A beautiful hotel, with that 1930s East-meets-West style that exemplifies the French tradition of *art de vivre*. The superb decor makes you feel like you are staying in another era. Each room is beautifully decorated with local fabrics and fantastic furniture. Swimming pool, open-air salas, jacuzzi and spa. Highly recommended.

$$$$-$$$ Steung Siem Reap Hotel, St 9, T063-965167, www.steungsiemreaphotel. com. This new-build colonial-era-style hotel is an excellent addition to the central market area of Siem Reap. The pleasant rooms come with cooling wooden floors and many overlook a verdant and very quiet pool. There are all the trimmings you'd expect in this price range, including gym, sauna, free Wi-Fi, free breakfast, a/c, huge bathtubs and good, friendly service. Recommended.

$$$$-$$$ Villa Kiara, just outside eastern edge of town, Sala Kamroeuk village, T063-764156, www.villakiara.com. Set in a very peaceful, private garden compound this 17-room/suite 'boutique' resort is unpretentious yet stylish. There's free breakfast, Wi-Fi, a restaurant and complimentary transfers to and from town. The pool is cute as well. All rooms are, of course, a/c with TV and en suite hot-water facilities. Recommended.

$$$-$$ La Noria, on road running on east side of the river, just past the 'stone' bridge, T063-964242, www.lanoriaangkor.com. Almost perfect riverside setting for this gorgeous small resort. Tranquil gardens, a small pool and a real away-from-it-all vibe seduces guests who stay in brightly coloured a/c and en suite rooms each with their own balcony. No TV, very quiet and decent restaurant. Recommended.

$$$-$$ Soria Moria, Wat Bo Rd, T063-964768, www.thesoriamoria.com. Excellent, well-run small hotel that has a roof-top bar and a decent restaurant. Rooms – all en suite, with contemporary Asian flourishes, a/c and colour TVs – are quiet; the upper ones have nice airy views over the town. The enlightened owners have now transferred half the ownership to their Khmer staff as part of an ongoing project to create sustainable, locally owned hotels in the area. Highly recommended.

$$-$ Bopha, on the east side of the river, T063-964928, www.bopha-angkor.com. Stunning hotel. Good rooms with all the amenities, decorated with local furniture and fabrics. Brilliant Thai-Khmer restaurant. Highly recommended.

$$-$ Jasmine Lodge, Airport Rd near to town centre, T012-784980, www.jasmine lodge.com. One of the best budget deals in town, **Jasmine** is often fully booked, and with good reason. The super-friendly owner Kunn and his family go out of their way to make this a superlative place to stay; there's free internet and Wi-Fi, breakfast can be included in the rate on request, there are huge shared areas for sitting, a book exchange, tour bookings, bus tickets, etc. There is a huge spread of rooms from basic ones with a fan and shared facilities to sparkling new accommodation with a/c, TV and hot-water bathrooms. Highly recommended.

$ Bou Savy, just outside town off the main airport road, T063-964967, www.bousavy guesthouse.com. One of the best budget options in town this tiny and very friendly family-owned guesthouse is set in soothing gardens and offers a range of rooms with fan or a/c. Also offers breakfast, internet and has some nice public areas. Recommended.

RESTAURANTS

Near the moat there are a number of cheap food and drink stalls, bookshops and a posse of hawkers selling film, souvenirs, etc. Outside the entrance to Angkor Wat is a larger selection of cafés and restaurants including the sister restaurant to **Blue Pumpkin**, serving good sandwiches and breakfasts, ideal for takeaway.

Siem Reap

$$$ Abacus, Oum Khun St, off Sivatha St, T012-644286. A little further out from the main Old Market area, this place is considered one of the best restaurants in town. Offering French and Cambodian, everything is fantastic here. The fish is superb, the steak is to die for. Recommended.

$$$ Barrio, Sivatha St, away from the central area. Fantastic French and Khmer food. A favourite of the expats. Recommended.

$$$-$$ Sala Bai Restaurant School. See Where to stay. Open for breakfast and lunch only. Taking in students from impoverished backgrounds from the poorest areas of Cambodia, **Sala Bai** trains them in catering skills and places them in establishments around town. Service is not the best as students are quite shy practising their English, but a little bit of patience will help them through. Highly recommended.

$$ Bopha, on the east side of the river, slightly up from Passagio, T063-964928. Fantastic Thai-Khmer restaurant in lovely, tranquil garden setting. One of the absolute best in town. Highly recommended.

$$ Singing Tree, Wat Bo Rd, T09-263 5500, www.singingtreecafe.com. Tue-Sun 0800-2100. Brilliant diner-cum-community centre with tasty European and Khmer home cooking, with plenty of veggie options. Also hosts a DVD library and a fairtrade shop.

ENTERTAINMENT

Siem Reap
Shadow puppetry

This is one of the finest performing arts of the region. The **Bayon Restaurant**, Wat Bo Rd, has regular shadow puppet shows in the evening. Local NGO, Krousar Thmey, often tour its shadow puppet show to Siem Reap. The show is performed by underprivileged children (who have also made the puppets) at **La Noria Restaurant** (Wed 1930 but check as they can be irregular). Donations accepted.

PRACTICALITIES

262 Ins and outs
262 Best time to visit Vietnam
262 Getting to Vietnam
265 Transport in Vietnam
268 Where to stay in Vietnam
269 Food and drink in Vietnam

271 Essentials A-Z

275 Index

287 Photography credits

288 Credits

INS AND OUTS

→ BEST TIME TO VISIT VIETNAM

Climatically the best time to see Vietnam is around December to March when it should be dry and not too hot. In the south it is warm with lovely cool evenings. Admittedly the north and the highlands will be a bit chilly but they should be dry with clear blue skies. The tourist industry high season is normally November to May when hotel prices tend to rise and booking flights can be hard. Travel in the south and Mekong Delta can be difficult at the height of the monsoon (particularly September, October and November). The central regions and north sometimes suffer typhoons and tropical storms from May to November. Hué is at its wettest from September to January.

Despite its historic and cultural resonance Tet, or Vietnamese New Year, is not a good time to visit. This movable feast usually falls between late January and March and, with aftershocks, lasts for about a fortnight. It is the only holiday most people get in the year. Popular destinations are packed, roads are jammed and for a couple of days almost all restaurants are shut. All hotel prices increase, and car hire prices are increased by 50% or more. The best prices are from May to October.

During the school summer holidays some resorts get busy. At Cat Ba, Sapa, Phan Thiet and Phu Quoc, for example, prices rise, there is a severe squeeze on rooms and weekends are worse. The Central Highlands tend to fare much better with cool temperatures and a good availability of rooms.

→ GETTING TO VIETNAM

AIR

Most international flights arrive in Ho Chi Minh City, which is well connected with the rest of the country. However, it is often cheaper and more flexible to fly via Bangkok, Hong Kong or Singapore. Ho Chi Minh City, and to a lesser extent Hanoi, is well connected with other Southeast Asian countries, and the rise of budget airlines has increased the number of flights. Prices vary according to high (November to April, July and August) and low season.

Flights from Europe There are direct flights to Vietnam from London (four times weekly to Ho Chi Minh City and Hanoi), Paris, Frankfurt and Moscow with **Vietnam Airlines** ① *T020-3263 2062 (UK), www.vietnamairlines.com*. Vietnam Airlines also codeshares flights from Amsterdam, Rome and Prague. **Air France** codeshares with Vietnam Airlines from Paris to Hanoi but also flies direct to Ho Chi Minh City. Flights last 12 hours. Return flights from London cost between £450-650. Non-Vietnam Airline flights from London and other European hubs go via Bangkok, Singapore, Kuala Lumpur, Hong Kong and the Gulf states. Non-direct flights from London to Vietnam takes around 16-18 hours, depending on the length of stopover. Airlines include **Air France, Cathay Pacific, Emirates, Lufthansa, Thai, Singapore Airlines, Malaysia Airlines** and **Qatar**. It is also possible to fly into Hanoi and depart from Ho Chi Minh City although this does seem to rack up the return fare. Check details with flight agents and tour operators. The best deals may involve flying to Bangkok and then on from there to your destination.

ON THE ROAD

HAPPY NEW YEAR

Tet is the traditional new year. The biggest celebration of the year, the word Tet is the shortened version of *tet nguyen dan* (first morning of the new period). Tet is the time to forgive and forget and to pay off debts. It is also everyone's birthday – the Vietnamese tend not to celebrate their birthdays; instead everyone adds a year to their age at Tet. Enormous quantities of food are consumed (this is not the time to worry about money), new clothes are bought, houses painted and repaired and firecrackers lit to welcome in the new year – at least they were until the government ban imposed in 1995. Cumquat trees are also bought and displayed. They are said to resemble coins and are a symbol of wealth and luck for the coming year. As a Vietnamese saying has it: 'Hungry all year but Tet three days full.' It is believed that before Tet, the spirit of the hearth, Ong Tao, leaves on a journey to visit the palace of the Jade Emperor where he must report on family affairs. To ensure that Ong Tao sets off in good cheer, a ceremony is held before Tet, Le Tao Quan, and during his absence a shrine is constructed (Cay Neu) to keep evil spirits at bay until his return. On the afternoon before Tet, Tat Nien, a sacrifice is offered at the family altar to dead relatives who are invited back to join in the festivities. Great attention is paid to the preparations for Tet, because it is believed that the first week of the new year dictates the fortunes for the rest of the year. The first visitor to the house on New Year's morning should be an influential, lucky and happy person, so families take care to arrange a suitable caller.

There are countless airlines flying to Bangkok from Europe and lots of good deals, so shop around.

Flights from the USA and Canada   There are flights to Vietnam from 15 major US hubs. Vietnam Airlines flies from Los Angeles and San Francisco to both Hanoi and Ho Chin Minh City via Taipei. The approximate flight time from Los Angeles to Ho Chi Minh City is 21 hours. United flies to Ho Chi Minh City via Hong Kong, Seoul and Tokyo. It is often cheaper to fly via Bangkok, Taipei, Tokyo or Hong Kong and from there to Vietnam, Cambodia or Laos. Thai, Delta, and United fly to Bangkok from a number of US and Canadian cities.

Flights from Australia and New Zealand Vietnam Airlines flies direct from Melbourne to Ho Chi Minh City and then on to Hanoi. There are also direct flights to Bangkok from all major Australian and New Zealand cities with Cathay Pacific, Korean Airlines, Qantas, Malaysia Airlines, Singapore Airlines and Thai, among others. There is also the option of flying into Hanoi and out of Ho Chi Minh City, or vice versa.

Flights from Asia Thai flies from Bangkok to Ho Chi Minh City and Hanoi. AirAsia flies from Bangkok and Kuala Lumpur to Ho Chi Minh City and from Kuala Lumpur and Bangkok to Hanoi. Vietnam Airlines flies from Bangkok, Phnom Penh, Siem Reap, Vientiane, Luang Prabang, Beijing, Guangzhou, Kunming, Hong Kong, Kuala Lumpur, Singapore, Manila, Busan, Seoul, Japan and Taipei. Laos Airlines flies from Luang Prabang and Vientiane. Malaysia Airlines flies from Kuala Lumpur to Hanoi and Ho Chi Minh City. Tiger Airways flies from Singapore to Ho Chi Minh City and Hanoi. Cathay Pacific flies from Hong Kong. **China Airlines** flies from Taipei to Ho Chi Minh City. **Japan Airlines** flies from Tokyo to Ho Chi Minh City and Hanoi. **Korean Air** flies from Seoul to Ho Chi Minh City and Hanoi. **Philippine Airlines** flies from Manila to Ho Chi Minh City. **Singapore Airlines** flies to Hanoi and Ho Chi Minh City. **Thai International** flies from Bangkok to Ho Chi Minh City and from Sydney and Melbourne to Ho Chi Minh City and Hanoi.

Airport information   There are two main international airports in Vietnam: **Tan Son Nhat Airport** (SGN) in Ho Chi Minh City, see page 185, and **Noi Bai Airport** (HAN) in Hanoi, see page 27. **Danang** (DAD), see page 130, has a couple of international flights. International departure tax is included in the price of the ticket.

RAIL
Vietnam's only international rail connection is with China. There are connections with Beijing via Nanning to Hanoi crossing at Lang Son. The lines are slow and distances are great.

ROAD
From Cambodia   There is a road crossing at Moc Bai on Highway 1 connecting Phnom Penh in Cambodia with Ho Chi Minh City via Tay Ninh Province. Further south, there is a second crossing to Phnom Penh via Chau Doc at Vinh Xuong in the Mekong Delta by boat. Further south still there is another road crossing into Cambodia at Tinh Bien, approximately 22 km south of Chau Doc. And, right at the very south of the country, you can cross at Xà Xía.

From China   There are three land crossings between China and Vietnam: at Lao Cai, Dong Dang and Mong Cai. There is no train across the border at Lao Cai at the moment. The train from Hanoi does cross at Dong Dang. The Mong Cai crossing is by road. If you enter Vietnam by land your visa must specify the exact road crossing.

From Laos   There is a popular road crossing open at Lao Bao, north of Hué, which enables travel through to Savannakhet in Laos. In the north there is a crossing at Tay Trang near Dien Bien Phu. Closer to Hanoi are the crossings at Nam Can (Nghe An Province) and Cau Treo (Ha Tinh Province) accessible from Vinh. You can also cross close to Kontum at Bo-Y (Kontum Province).

RIVER AND SEA
There are no normal sea crossings into Vietnam although an increasing number of cruise liners sail into Vietnamese waters. The only other international connection by boat is the Mekong River crossing from Phnom Penh to Chau Doc.

AIR

If you only have a short time to spend in the region, you will need to factor in some flights if you want to cover a lot of ground. There are regular flights between Ho Chi Minh City and Hanoi, as well as major towns and cities on the Dream Trip itineraries, including Haiphong, Hué and Danang. Taking flights to remote areas, such as the Northern Highlands (Dien Bien Phu) or Central Highlands (Pleiku, Buon Ma Thuot, Dalat) can save lengthy bus and train journeys. Access to the islands of Phu Quoc or the Con Dao archipelago is also quickest by plane. Siem Reap (for Angkor Wat) is a short flight from Ho Chi Minh City. **Vietnam Airlines** is the national carrier and flies to multiple domestic destinations. **Vietnam Airlines** changes its schedule every six months so check before making any plans. Refunds, rebookings and re-routing may not be allowed on certain ticket fares. Remember that during holiday periods flights get extremely busy.

RAIL

Train travel is exciting and overnight journeys are a good way of covering long distances. The Vietnamese rail network extends from Hanoi to Ho Chi Minh City. **Vietnam Railways** (www.vr.com.vn) runs the 2600-km rail network down the coast. With overnight stays at hotels along the way to see the sights, a rail sightseeing tour from Hanoi to Ho Chi Minh City should take a minimum of 10 days but you would need to buy tickets for each separate section of the journey.

The difference in price between first and second class is small and it is worth paying the extra. There are three seating classes and four sleeping classes including hard and soft seats and hard and soft sleepers; some are air-conditioned, others are not. The prices vary according to the class of cabin and the berth chosen; the bottom berth is more expensive than the top berth. All sleepers should be booked three days in advance. The kitchen on the Hanoi to Ho Chi Minh City service serves soups and simple, but adequate, rice dishes (it is a good idea to take additional food and drink on long journeys). First-class long-distance tickets include the price of meals. The express trains (**Reunification Express**) take between an advertised 29½ to 34 hours; odd-numbered trains travel from Hanoi to Ho Chi Minh City, even-numbered trains vice versa.

Most ticket offices have some staff who speak English. Queues can be long and some offices keep unusual hours. If you are short of time and short on patience it may well pay to get a tour operator to book your ticket for a small commission or visit the Ho Chi Minh City railway office in Pham Ngu Lao or the Hanoi agency in the Old Quarter.

There are also rail routes from Hanoi to Haiphong, to Lang Son and to Lao Cai. The **Victoria** hotel chain (www.victoriahotels-asia.com) runs a luxury carriage on the latter route.

RIVER AND SEA

In the south, there are services from Chau Doc to Phnom Penh. The **Victoria** hotel chain (www.victoriahotels-asia.com) runs a Mekong Delta service for its guests, or it is sometimes possible to charter a private boat. Ferries operate between Ho Chi Minh City and Vung Tau; Rach Gia and Phu Quoc; Ha Tien and Phu Quoc; Haiphong and Cat Ba Island; and Halong City and Cat Ba and Mong Cai.

ROAD

Open Tour Buses, see below, are very useful and cheap for bridging important towns. Many travellers opt to take a tour to reach remote areas because of the lack of self-drive car hire and the dangers and slow speed of public transport.

Bus Roads in Vietnam are notoriously dangerous. As American humourist PJ O'Rourke wrote: "In Japan people drive on the left. In China people drive on the right. In Vietnam it doesn't matter." Since Highway 1 is so dangerous and public transport buses are poor and slow, most travellers opt for the cheap and regular **Open Tour Bus** (private minibus or coach) that covers the length of the country. Almost every Vietnamese tour operator/ travellers' café listed in this guide will run a minibus service or act as an agent. The ticket is a flexible one-way ticket from Ho Chi Minh City to Hanoi and vice versa. The buses run daily from their own offices and include the following stops: Ho Chi Minh City, Mui Ne, Nha Trang, Dalat, Hoi An, Hué, Ninh Binh and Hanoi. They will also stop off at tourist destinations along the way such as Lang Co, Hai Van Pass, Marble Mountains and Po Klong Garai for quick visits. You may join at any leg of the journey, paying for one trip or several as you go. The Hanoi to Hué and vice versa is an overnight trip but although you might save on a night's accommodation you are unlikely to get much sleep.

If you do opt for **public buses** note that most bus stations are on the outskirts of town; in bigger centres there may be several stations. Long-distance buses invariably leave very early in the morning (0400-0500). Buses are the cheapest form of transport, although sometimes foreigners find they are being asked for two to three times the correct price. Prices are normally prominently displayed at bus stations. It helps if you can find out what the correct fare should be in advance. Less comfortable but quicker are the minibus services, which ply the more popular routes.

Car hire Self-drive car hire is not available in Vietnam. It is, however, possible to hire cars with drivers and this is a good way of getting to more remote areas with a group of people. Cars with drivers can be hired for around US$60-110 per day. Longer trips would see a reduced cost. All cars are air-conditioned. Car hire prices increase by 50% or more during Tet.

Motorbike and bicycle hire Most towns are small enough to get around by bicycle, and this can also be a pleasant way to explore the surrounding countryside. However, if covering large areas (touring around the Central Highlands, for example) then a motorbike will mean you can see more and get further off the beaten track.

Motorbikes and bicycles can be hired by the day in the cities, often from hotels and travellers' cafés. You do not need a driver's licence or proof of motorbike training to hire a motorbike in Vietnam, however, it became compulsory in 2007 to wear a helmet. Take time to familiarize yourself with road conditions and ride slowly. Motorbikes cost around US$6 per day including helmet; bicycles can be hired for US$1-2 including a lock. Always park your bicycle or motorbike in a *gui xe* (guarded parking place) and ask for a ticket. The small cost is worth every dong, even if you are just popping into the post office to post a letter.

ON THE ROAD

RULES OF THE ROAD

The speed with which Vietnam has developed in the last decade means that people who, five years ago, were sitting on the back of trundling buffalo carts, are now driving 30-ton trucks down Highway 1. This has led to an enormous increase in road casualties.

Vietnam also has 21 million motorbikes, one of the highest densities of motorbikes in the world.

Debates in the press on road carnage concentrate almost exclusively on technical shortcomings – old cars, antique trucks, absence of road signs – and neatly sidestep the true cause: absence of respect for other road users. However, attention to road safety is now improving.

There are far more traffic lights and road dividers than before and more traffic police on the junctions ready to pounce on offenders. The Vietnamese are now more likely to heed the traffic lights and there is less of a tendency to carry on regardless of whether the lights are red or green.

Traffic police actively collect fines for supposed breaches of traffic law. If you are invited to make a contribution to the police widows and orphans fund, but clearly you have committed no offence, refuse point blank. Feign total ignorance of English. If this does not work and your motorbike keys have been confiscated, try to negotiate the size of your donation downwards.

Motorbike taxi and cyclo Motorcycle taxis, known as *honda ôm* or *xe ôm* (*ôm* means to cuddle) are ubiquitous and cheap. You will find them on most street corners, outside hotels or in the street. With their baseball caps and dangling cigarette, *xe ôm* drivers are readily recognizable. If they see you before you see them, they will shout 'moto' to get your attention. In the north and upland areas the Honda is replaced with the Minsk. The shortest hop would be at least 10,000d. Always bargain though.

Cyclos are bicycle trishaws. Cyclo drivers charge double or more that of a *xe ôm*. A number of streets in the centres of Ho Chi Minh City and Hanoi are one-way or out of bounds to cyclos, necessitating lengthy detours which add to the time and cost. Do not take a cyclo after dark unless the driver is well known to you or you know the route. It is a wonderful way to get around the Old Quarter of Hanoi, though, and for those with plenty of time on their hands it is not as hazardous in smaller towns.

Taxi Taxis ply the streets of Hanoi and Ho Chi Minh City and other large towns and cities. They are cheap, around 12,000d per kilometre, and the drivers are better English speakers than cyclo drivers. Always keep a small selection of small denomination notes with you so that when the taxi stops you can round up the fare to the nearest small denomination. At night use the better known taxi companies rather than the unlicensed cars that often gather around popular nightspots.

ON THE ROAD

VIETNAMESE ADDRESSES

Unlike neighbouring countries, addresses in Vietnam generally follow quite a logical pattern. There are, however, a few points to note:

Odd numbers usually run consecutively on one side of the street, evens on the other; *bis* after a number – as in 16 bis Hai Ba Trung Street – means there are two houses with the same number, and *ter* after the number means there are three houses with the same number.

Large buildings with a single street number are usually subdivided 21A, 21B, etc; some buildings may be further subdivided 21B1, 21B2, etc.

An oblique (/ means *sec* or *tren* in Vietnamese) in a number, as in 23/16 Dinh Tien Hoang Street, means that the address is to be found in a small side street (*hem*) – in this case running off Dinh Tien Hoang Street by the side of No 23; the house in question will probably be signed 23/16 rather than just 16. Usually, but by no means always, a *hem* will be quieter than the main street and it may be worth looking at a guesthouse with an oblique number for that reason (especially in the Pham Ngu Lao area of Ho Chi Minh City).

An address will sometimes contain the letter F followed by a number, as in F6; this is short for *phuong* (ward, a small administrative area); its inclusion as part of an address is a reflection of the tidy nature of the Vietnamese mind rather than an aid to locating one's destination.

The letter Q in an address stands for *quân* (district); this points you in the right general direction and will be important in locating your destination as a long street in Hanoi or Ho Chi Minh City may run through several *quân*. In suburban and rural areas districts are known as *huyên*, Huyên Nha Be, for instance.

Note that there are no postcodes or zip codes in Vietnam.

→ WHERE TO STAY IN VIETNAM

Accommodation ranges from luxury suites in international five-star hotels and spa resorts to small, family hotels (mini hotels) and homestays with local people in the Mekong Delta and with the ethnic minorities in the Central Highlands and northern Vietnam. During peak seasons – especially December to March and particularly during busy holidays such as Tet, Christmas, New Year's Eve and around Easter – booking is essential. Expect staff to speak English in all top hotels. Do not expect it in cheaper hotels or in more remote places, although most places employ someone with a smattering of a foreign language.

Private mini hotels are worth seeking out as, being family-run, guests can expect quite good service. Mid-range and tourist hotels may provide a decent breakfast which is often included in the price. Some luxury and first-class hotels charge extra for breakfast and, on top of this, also charge VAT and service charge. There are world-class beach resorts in Phu Quoc, Nha Trang, Mui Ne, Hoi An and Danang. In the northern uplands, in places like Sapa, Ha Giang province and Mai Chau, it is possible to stay in an ethnic minority house. Bathrooms are basic and will consist of a cold or warm shower and an alfresco or Western toilet. To stay in a homestay, you can book through a tour operator or through the local tourist office, or call direct where telephone numbers are available. Homestays are also possible on farms and in orchards in the Mekong Delta. Here, guests sleep on

PRICE CODES

WHERE TO STAY

Price codes refer to the cost of two people sharing a double room in the high season.

$$$$ over US$100 Luxury: mostly found in Bangkok, Ho Chi Minh City, Hanoi, Danang, Phu Quoc, Luang Prabang, Phnom Penh and Siem Reap. Some beach and mountain resorts also fall into this category.

$$$ US$46-100 First class: there are a number of hotels in this category found in all the major cities and some smaller ones plus resorts across the region. Hotels in this category should offer reasonable business services, a range of recreational facilities, restaurants and bars, although these services will be more limited in Cambodia and Laos.

$$ US$20-45 Tourist class: all rooms will have air conditioning and an attached bathroom with hot water. Other services should include one or more restaurants, a bar and room service. In Bangkok and Vietnamese beach resorts, a pool may be available.

$ under US$20 Medium to budget: some air-conditioned en suite rooms in Vietnam and Laos although not necessarily in Cambodia but at the cheaper end rooms will usually be fan-cooled with shared bathrooms with basic facilities. Bed linen should be provided, towels may not be. Rooms are small and facilities few.

RESTAURANTS

$$$ over US$12   **$$** US$6-12   **$** under US$6

Price codes refer to the cost of a two-course meal for one person excluding drinks or service charge.

---

camp beds and share a Western bathroom with hot and cold water. National parks offer everything from air-conditioned bungalows to shared dormitory rooms to campsites where, sometimes, it is possible to hire tents. Visitors may spend a romantic night on a boat in Halong Bay or on the Mekong Delta. Boats range from the fairly luxurious to the basic. Most people book through tour operators.

You will have to leave your passport at hotel reception desks for the duration of your stay. It will be released to you temporarily for bank purposes or buying an air ticket. Credit cards are widely accepted but there is often a 2-4% fee for paying in this manner. Tipping is not expected in hotels in Vietnam. See box above for details of what to expect within each price category.

→ FOOD AND DRINK IN VIETNAM

Vietnam offers outstanding Vietnamese, French and international cuisine in restaurants that range from first class to humble foodstalls. At either the quality will be, in the main, exceptional. The accent is on local, seasonal and fresh produce and the rich pickings from the sea, along Vietnam's 2000-km coastline will always make it far inland too. You will find more hearty stews in the more remote north and more salad dishes along the coast. All restaurants offer a variety of local cuisine and some specialize in certain types of food – Hué cuisine, Cha Ca Hanoi, etc. *Pho* (pronounced *fer*), noodle soup, is Vietnam's best known dish and is utterly delicious.

All Vietnamese food is dipped, whether in fish sauce, soya sauce, chilli sauce, peanut sauce or pungent prawn sauce (*mam tom*) before eating. As each course is served, a new

ON THE ROAD

BIRD'S NEST SOUP

The tiny nests of the brown-rumped swift (*Collocalia esculenta*), also known as the edible-nest swiftlet or sea swallow, are collected for bird's nest soup, a Chinese delicacy, throughout Southeast Asia.

The semi-oval nests are made of silk-like strands of saliva secreted by the birds which, when cooked in broth, softens and becomes a little like noodles. Like so many Chinese delicacies, the nests are believed to have aphrodisiac qualities and the soup has even been suggested as a cure for HIV. The red nests are the most highly valued, and the Vietnamese Emperor Minh Mang (1820-1840) is said to have owed his extraordinary vitality to his inordinate consumption of bird's nest soup. This may explain why restaurants serving it are sometimes associated with massage parlours.

Collecting the nests is a precarious but profitable business and in some areas mafias of concessionaires vigorously guard and protect their assets. The men who collect the nests on a piecework basis risk serious injury climbing rickety ladders to cave roofs in sometimes almost total darkness, save for a candle strapped to their heads.

set of dips will accompany. Follow the guidance of your waiter or Vietnamese friends to get the right dip with the right dish.

Locally produced fresh beer is called *bia hoi*. Bar customers have a choice of Tiger, Heineken, Carlsberg, San Miguel, 33, Saigon Beer or Huda. Many major cities in Vietnam produce their own beer, most of which are light, refreshing and far better than better known Thai and Indonesian beers. Rice and fruit wines are produced and consumed in large quantities in upland areas, particularly in the north of Vietnam. The Chinese believe that snake wines increase their virility and as such are normally found in areas of high Chinese concentration. Soft drinks and bottled still and sparkling mineral water are widely available. Tea and coffee is widely available. Coffee is served with condensed milk.

ESSENTIALS A-Z

Accident and emergency
Contact the relevant emergency service and your embassy. Make sure you obtain police/medical records in order to file insurance claims. If you need to report a crime, visit your local police station and take a local with you who speaks English.
Ambulance T115, **Fire** T114, **Police** T113.

Electricity
Voltage 110-240. Sockets are round 2-pin. Sometimes they are 2 flat pin. A number of top hotels now use UK 3 square-pin sockets.

Embassies and consulates
For embassies and consulates of Vietnam, see www.embassiesabroad.com.

Health
See your doctor or travel clinic at least 6 weeks before your departure for general advice on travel risks, malaria and vaccinations (see also below). Make sure you have travel insurance, get a dental check-up (especially if you are going to be away for more than a month), know your own blood group and if you suffer a long-term condition such as diabetes or epilepsy make sure someone knows or that you have a **Medic Alert** bracelet/necklace with this information on it (www.medicalert.co.uk).

Health risks
Malaria exists in rural areas in Vietnam. However, there is no risk in the Red River Delta and the coastal plains north of Nha Trang. Neither is there a risk in Hanoi, HCMC, Danang and Nha Trang. The choice of malaria prophylaxis will need to be something other than chloroquine for most people, since there is such a high level of resistance to it. Always check with your doctor or travel clinic for the most up-to-date advice.

Malaria can cause death within 24 hrs. It can start as something just resembling an attack of flu. You may feel tired, lethargic, headachy, feverish; or more seriously, develop fits, followed by coma and then death. Have a low index of suspicion because it is very easy to write off vague symptoms, which may actually be malaria. If you have a temperature, go to a doctor as soon as you can and ask for a malaria test. On your return home if you suffer any of these symptoms, get tested as soon as possible, even if any previous test proved negative; the test could save your life.

The most serious viral disease is **dengue fever**, which is hard to protect against as the mosquitos bite throughout the day as well as at night. Bacterial diseases include **tuberculosis** (TB) and some causes of the more common traveller's **diarrhoea**. Lung fluke (**para-gonimiasis**) occurs in Vietnam. A fluke is a sort of flattened worm. In the Sin Ho district the locals like to eat undercooked or raw crabs, but our advice is to leave them to it. The crabs contain a fluke which, when eaten, travels to the lungs. The lung fluke may cause a cough, coughing 'blood', fever, chest pain and changes on your X-ray which will puzzle a British radiologist. The cure is the same drug that cures schistosomiasis (another fluke which can be acquired in some parts of the Mekong Delta).

Each year there is the possibility that **avian flu** or **SARS** may again rear their ugly heads. Check the news reports. If there is a problem in an area you are due to visit you may be advised to have an ordinary flu shot or to seek expert advice. Vietnam has had a number of fatalities from Avian influenza. Consult the WHO website, www.who.int, for further information and heed local advice on the ground. There are high rates of **HIV** in the region, especially among sex workers.

Medical services

Western hospitals staffed by foreign and Vietnamese medics exist in Hanoi and HCMC. **Columbia Asia** (Saigon International Clinic), 8 Alexander de Rhodes St, HCMC, T08-3823 8888, www.columbiaasia.com. International doctors offering a full range of services. **International SOS**, Central Building, 51 Xuan Dieu, Tay Ho, Hanoi, T04-3934 0666, and 167A Nam Ky Khoi Nghia St, Q3, T08-3829 8424, www.internationalsos.com/countries/vietnam. Open 24 hrs for emergencies, routine and medical evacuation. It provides dental service too.

Useful websites

www.btha.org British Travel Health Association (UK).
www.cdc.gov US government site that gives excellent advice on travel health and details of disease outbreaks.
www.fitfortravel.scot.nhs.uk A-Z of vaccine/health advice for each country.
www.who.int The WHO *Blue Book* lists the diseases of the world.

Vaccinations

The following vaccinations are advised: BCG, Hepatitis A, Japanese Encephalitis, Polio, Rabies, Tetanus, Typhoid and Yellow Fever.

Language

You are likely to find some English spoken wherever there are tourist services but outside tourist centres communication can be a problem for those who have no knowledge of Vietnamese. Furthermore, the Vietnamese language is not easy to learn. For example, pronunciation presents enormous difficulties as it is tonal: it has 6 tones, 12 vowels and 27 consonants. On the plus side, Vietnamese is written in a Roman alphabet making life much easier; place and street names are instantly recognizable. French is still spoken and often very well by the more elderly and educated Vietnamese.

Money → *US$1=20,816d, £1=33,334d, €1=27,183d (Jan 2013)*

The unit of currency is the **dong**. Under law, shops should only accept dong but in practice this is not enforced and dollars are accepted almost everywhere. If possible, however, try to pay for everything in dong as prices are usually lower and in more remote areas people may be unaware of the exchange rate. Also, to ordinary Vietnamese, 18,000d is a lot of money, while US$1 means nothing.

ATMs are plentiful in HCMC and Hanoi and are now pretty ubiquitous in other major tourist centres, but it is a good idea to travel with US dollars cash as a back up. Try to avoid tatty notes. ATM withdrawals are limited to 2 million dong per transaction. Banks in the main centres will change other major currencies including UK sterling, Hong Kong dollars, Thai baht, Swiss francs, Euros, Australian dollars, Singapore dollars and Canadian dollars. **Credit cards** are increasingly accepted, particularly Visa, MasterCard, Amex and JCB. Large hotels, expensive restaurants and medical centres invariably take them but beware a surcharge of between 2.5% and 4.5%. Most hotels will not add a surcharge onto your bill if paying by credit card. Traveller's cheques are best denominated in US dollars and can only be cashed in banks in the major towns. Commission of 2-4% is payable if cashing into dollars but not if you are converting them direct to dong.

Cost of travelling

On a budget expect to pay around US$8-15 per night for accommodation and about US$8-12 for food. A good mid-range hotel will cost US$15-30. There are comfort and cost levels anywhere from here up to more than US$200 per night. For travelling, many use the Open Tour Buses as they are inexpensive and, by Vietnamese standards, 'safe'. Slightly more expensive are trains followed by planes.

Safety

Do not take any valuables on to the streets of HCMC as bag and jewellery snatching is a common problem. Thieves work in teams, often with beggar women carrying babies as a decoy. Beware of people who obstruct your path (pushing a bicycle across the pavement is a common ruse); your pockets are being emptied from behind. Young men on fast motorbikes also cruise the central streets of HCMC waiting to pounce on victims. The situation in other cities is not so bad but take care in Nha Trang and Hanoi. Never go by cyclo in a strange part of town after dark.

Lone women travellers have fewer problems than in many other Asian countries. The most common form of harassment usually consists of comic and harmless displays of macho behaviour.

Unexploded ordnance is still a threat in some areas. It is best not to stray too far from the beaten track and don't unearth bits of suspicious metal.

Single Western men will be targeted by prostitutes on street corners, in tourist bars and those cruising on motorbikes. Do not hire a motorbike if you have never ridden before; fatal accidents involving tourists are on the increase. Vietnam's roads can be highly dangerous.

Beware of the following scams: being overcharged on credit cards; the pretend tearing up of a credit card transaction and the issuing of a new one; massage parlours where your money is stolen when you're having a massage; newspapers being sold for 5 times their value; and motorbikes that go 'wrong' and need repairs costing the earth.

Travel advisories

The US State Department's travel advisory: **Travel Warnings & Consular Information Sheets**, www.travel.state.gov, and the **UK Foreign and Commonwealth Office**'s travel warning section, www.fco.gov.uk, are useful.

Telephone → *Country code: +84*

To make a domestic call dial 0 + area code + phone number. Note that all numbers in this guide include the 0 and the area code. Most shops or cafés will let you call a local number for 2000d: look for the blue sign '*dien thoai cong cong*' (meaning public telephone). All post offices provide international telephone services. The cost of calls has greatly reduced but some post offices and hotels still insist on charging for a minimum of 3 mins. You start paying for an overseas call from the moment you ring even if the call is not answered. By dialling 171 or 178 followed by 0 or 00 to make an international call, it is approximately 30% cheaper. Vietnam's country code is +84; IDD is 0084; directory enquires 1080; operator-assisted domestic long-distance calls 103; international directory enquiries 143; Yellow pages 1081. Numbers beginning with 091, 090, 098 and 0123 are mobile numbers. Pay-as-you-go sim cards are available and calls are cheap.

Time

Vietnam is 7 hrs ahead of GMT.

Tipping

Vietnamese do not normally tip if eating in small restaurants but may tip in expensive bars. Foreigners leave small change, which is appreciated. Big hotels and restaurants add 5-10% service charge and the government tax of 10% to the bill. Taxis are rounded up to the nearest 5000d, hotel porters 20,000d.

Tourist information

Contact details for tourist offices and other resources are given in the relevant Ins and outs sections throughout the text.

The national tourist office is **Vietnam National Administration of Tourism** (www.vietnamtourism.com), whose role is to promote Vietnam as a tourist destination rather than to provide tourist information. Visitors to its offices can get some information and maps but they are more likely to be offered tours. Good tourist information is available from tour operators in the main tourist centres.

Visas and immigration

Tourist visa extensions need careful planning as, although hotels will accept photocopies of passports and visas, you cannot buy a ticket or fly with Vietnam Airlines without the original.

Valid passports with visas issued by a Vietnamese embassy are required by all visitors, irrespective of citizenship. Visas are normally valid only for arrival by air at Hanoi and HCMC. Those wishing to enter or leave Vietnam by land must specify the border crossing when applying. It is possible to alter the point of departure at immigration offices in Hanoi and HCMC. Contact the Vietnamese embassy in your country for specific application details. Visas on arrival at land crossings are not available and visas on arrival at airports are not exactly as they appear; they must be arranged in advance with licensed companies, paperwork signed before arriving and handed at desks at airports to get the visa. This may or may not work out cheaper than the embassy approach.

The standard **tourist visa** is valid for 30 days for 1 entry (*mot lan*) only. Tourist visas cost £54 and generally take 5 working days to process (Express 2-day service £69; next day service £75). 90-day tourist visas are now available and cost £85 (Express 2-day service £105; next day service £115).

If you are planning on staying for a while or making a side trip to Laos or Cambodia with the intention of coming back to Vietnam then a **multiple entry tourist visa** will make life much simpler. 30-day multiple entry visas cost £95 (Express 2-day service £110; next day service £121). 90-day multiple entry visas cost £120 (Express 2-day service £140; next day service £150).

Business visas are also available. Visa regulations are ever changing; contact www.vietnamembassy.org.uk for the latest information.

It is usually possible to apply for a **visa extension** while in Vietnam. Travel agencies and hotels will probably add their own mark-up but for many people it is worth paying to avoid the difficulty of making 1 or 2 journeys to an embassy. Visas can be extended for 1 month. Depending on where you are it will take between 1 day and a week. A visa valid for 1 month can only be extended for 1 month; a further 1 month extension is then possible. Citizens of Sweden, Norway, Denmark, and Finland may visit, visa free, for not more than 15 days.

Vietnam now operate a quasi 'visa on arrival' programme. An online application must be made through a company such as www.visa-vietnam.org. A pre-approved letter is granted and a service fee paid but payment for the actual visa is made on collection at the airport.

INDEX

A

accidents 271
addresses 268
air travel
  departure tax 264
  getting around 265
  getting there 262
ambulance 271
An Binh Island 221
Angkor 241
  Angkor Thom 253
  Angkor Wat 251
  Banteay Kdei 256
  Banteay Srei 258
  Baphuon 255
  Bayon 254
  best time to visit 242
  Phnom Bakheng 255
  Prasat Kravan 256
  Pre Rup 256
  Preah Khan 257
  Preah Neak Pean 257
  Roulos Group 257
  Srah Srang 256
  Ta Pro 255
  transport 241
Angkor Kingdom 246
Angkor Wat 251
Ap Bac 217
avian flu 271

B

B-52 memorials, Hanoi 48
Ba Be National Park 89
Bac Ha 81
Bach Ma National Park and Hill Station 124
Ba Chuc Ossuary 234
Bai Chay 98
Ba-na villages 152
Ban Co 64
Banteay Srei 258
Ben Tre 218
best time to visit 262

betel nut 200
Bich Dong 54
bicycle hire 266
Bidup National Park 167
bird's nest soup 270
boat travel 265
border with Cambodia
  Chau Doc 231
border with China
  Lao Cai 80
Buon Ma Thuot 155
bus travel 266

C

Cai Be 220
Can Tho and around 223
  floating markets 225
Cao Dai Great Temple 206
Cao Daism 206
Cao Dai Temple 134
Cao Lanh 227
car hire 266
Cat Ba Island 99
Cat Ba National Park 101
Cat Cat 79
Central Highlands 150
Cham kingdom 170
Champa 132
Cham villages 233
Chau Doc 231
Chieng Yen 62
China Beach 134
Chu Pao Pass 149
Churning of the Sea 248
Con Dao 210
Con Dao National Park 211
cookery classes 148
Cua Dai Beach 142
Cuc Dua 62
Cu Chi Tunnels 205
Cuc Phuong National Park 56
cyclos 267

D
Dalat 158
  cable car 165
  colonial villas 160
  flower garden 161
  Hang Nga Crazy House 163
  Hunting Lodge 165
  Lake of Sighs 165
  Lam Dong Museum 164
  Lam Ty Ni Pagoda 163
  Linh Son Pagoda 164
  market 163
  Pasteur Institute 163
  railway station 164
  Summer Palace 161
  Teacher Training College 164
  Thein Vuong Pagoda 165
  university 164
  Valley of Love 165
  waterfalls 165
  Xuan Huong Lake 159
Danang 130
  Cai Dai Temple 134
  Museum of Cham Sculpture 133
Demilitarized Zone (DMZ) 123
dengue fever 271
departure tax 264
diarrhoea 271
Dien Bien Phu 65
  battle sights 68
DMZ 123
Doc Lech 176
dong 272
Dong Van 88
Dong Van-Meo Vac Region 86
Dong Xuan Market, Hanoi 36
Dragon Island 216
Dragon's Jaw Hill, Sapa 77
drink 269
Duras, Marguerite 226

E
electricity 271
embassies 271
Endangered Primate Rescue Center 56
ethnic groups 60
exchange rate 272

F
Fan Si Pan 78
fire brigade 271
floating markets
  Cai Bai 220
  Can Tho 225
food 269

G
General de Castries 68
Graham Greene 126, 191
grottoes 61

H
Ha Giang 84
Haiphong 94
Hai Van Pass 127
Halong Bay 92
Halong City 97
handicraft villages, Hanoi 50
Hanoi 27
  36 Streets 33
  87 Ma May Street 35
  accommodation 51
  Ambassadors' Pagoda 40
  B-52 memorials 48
  Ba Dinh Square 43
  citadel 42
  Cua Quan Chuong 36
  Dai Liet Si 43
  Dong Xuan market 36
  Fine Arts Museum 47
  French Quarter 39
  Hai Ba Trung Temple 49
  Hang Be Market 35
  Hanoi Hilton 40
  history 31
  Hoa Lo Prison 40
  Hoan Kiem Lake 32
  Ho Chi Minh Museum 44
  Ho Chi Minh's house 43
  Ho Chi Minh's Mausoleum 42
  Ly Quoc Su Pagoda 37
  Military History Museum 42
  Museum of Ethnology 47
  Museum of the Vietnamese
    Revolution 38

Museum of Vietnamese History 39
Ngoc Son Temple 32
Old City and 36 Streets 33
One Pillar Pagoda 44
Opera House 37
Paul Doumer Bridge 47
Presidential Palace 43
Quan Am 44
Quan Thanh Pagoda 47
restaurants 51
Saint Joseph's Cathedral 37
Sofitel Metropole 37
Stone Lady Pagoda 37
street names 34
Tay Ho Pagoda 48
Temple of Literature
  (Van Mieu Pagoda) 44
The Huc (Sunbeam) Bridge 32
tourist information 28
Tran Quoc Pagoda 47
tube houses 34
Vietnamese Women's Museum 40
West Lake 47
Ha Tien 234
health 271
Heaven's Gate 86
Hien Hao 100
Hmong Kings 87
Hoa Lu 53
Hoang Khai 36
Ho Chi Minh City 185
  Archbishop's Palace 195
  Ben Thanh Market (Cho Ben Thanh) 198
  Binh Tay Market 202
  Botanical Gardens and Zoo 196
  Cholon (Chinatown) 200
  Continental Hotel 191
  Fine Arts Museum 198
  General Post Office 192
  Giac Lam Pagoda 204
  Giac Vien Pagoda 203
  history 186
  Lam Son Square 191
  Le Duan Street 196
  Mariamman Hindu Temple 197
  Ming Dynasty Assembly Hall 202
  Museum of Vietnamese History 197

Museum of Vietnamese Traditional
  Medicine 204
Nghia An Assembly Hall 201
Notre Dame Cathedral 192
opera house 191
Pham Ngu Lao 200
Phung Son Pagoda 203
Phung Son Tu Pagoda 199
Phuoc Hai Tu 204
Quan Am Pagoda 203
Reunification Hall 194
Rex Hotel 192
Thien Hau Temples 201
Tomb and Temple of
  Marshal Le Van Duyet 205
tourist information 186
Tran Hung Dao Temple 204
Vinh Nghiem Pagoda 205
War Remnants Museum 194
Xa Loi Pagoda 196
Ho Chi Minh's Mausoleum, Hanoi 42
Ho Chi Minh Trail 125
Hoi An 137
  Assembly Halls 140
  Merchants' houses 142
Hon Chong 175
honda ôm 267
Hon Gai 98
Hon Mot 174
Hon Mun 174
Hon Tam 174
hospitals 272
hotels 268
  price codes 269
Hué 107
  Amphitheatre and Elephant Temple 123
  best time to visit 107
  city centre 113
  homestays 268
  Imperial City 110
  Perfume River 114
  sights 110
  Thien Mu Pagoda 114
  Tomb of Dong Khanh 121
  Tomb of Duc Duc 120
  Tomb of Emperor Gia Long 116
  Tomb of Emperor Minh Mang 118

Tomb of Khai Dinh 121
Tomb of Thieu Tri 119
Tomb of Tu Duc 119
train to Danang 126
Hung Kia 62
Huong Giang 107

I
Imperial City, Hué 110
International Rice Research Institute 224
Island of the Coconut Monk 216

J
Japanese Covered Bridge, Hoi An 139

K
Khai, Hoang 36
Khe Sanh 124
Khmer Empire 246
Khmer sculpture 250
Kingdom of Champa 132
Kontum 149

L
Lac (White Thai village) 61
Lai Chau (Tam Duong) 72
Lak Lake 158
Lake of Sighs 165
Langbian Mountain 166
Lang Co 126
Lang Ga (Chicken Village) 166
language 272
Lao Cai 80
Lao Chai 79
La To 33
Lat village 166
Lung Cu 88
Lung Phin 88
Ly Thanh Tong 44

M
Mai Chau 60
malaria 271
Ma Pi Leng Pass 88
Marble Mountains (Nui Non Nuoc) 134
medical services 272
Mekong Delta
floating markets 225
hydrology 216

Meo Vac 88
Mieu Island 174
minibuses 266
Moc Chau 62
money 272
exchange rate 272
Monkey Island 100
motorbike hire 266
motorbike taxi 267
Mount Fan Si Pan 78
Mount Meru 251
Mui Ne 180
Muong Lay (Lai Chau) 70
My Khe Beach 134
My Lai (Son My) 146
My Son 143
My Tho 215
My Tho's islands 216

N
Nam Cam 80
Nam Cat Tien National Park 167
Nam O 127
Nam Sai 80
Ngoc Son Temple, Hanoi 32
Nguyen Dynasty 108
Nha Trang 170
Alexandre Yersin Museum 173
beach 171
Cai River Estuary 171
cathedral 173
central market 174
islands 174
Khanh Hoa Museum 174
Long Son Pagoda 171
Long Thanh's Gallery 174
Ponagar Cham Temple complex 171
Ninh Binh 53
Ninh Van Bay 176
Non Nuoc Beach 135
Nui Sam 233

O
Open Tour Bus 266

P

Perfume Pagoda 50
Perfume River 114
Phan Thiet 179
Phat Diem Cathedral 55
Phi Hay 71
Pho Bang 86
Phu Quoc Island 236
Plain of Reeds 227
Pleiku (Play Ku) 153
police 267, 271
Ponagar Cham Temple complex 171
Preah Khan 257
Preah Neak Pean 257
price codes
  hotels 269
  restaurants 269
Pu Ka village 69
Pu Luong Nature Reserve 62

Q

Quan Am 44
Quan Ba 86
Quang Ngai 146
Quan Vu 33
Quiet American, The 191

R

Rach Gia 234
rail, *see train*
restaurants 269
  price codes 269
Rex Hotel 192
river travel
  getting there 264
  getting around 265
road travel
  getting there 264
  getting around 266
Roulos Group 257

S

Sa Dec 225
safety 273
Saigon, *see Ho Chi Minh City*
Salangane islands 174
Sam Mountain 233

Sao Beach
  Phu Quoc 237
Sapa and around 75
  people 77
  trekking 77
Sa Phin 87
SARS 271
Siem Reap 244
silk worms 143
Sin Chai 79
Sin Ho 72
sleeping
  prices 269
snake wines 270
Sofitel Metropole, Hanoi 37
Son La 62
Son My (My Lai) 146
Son My (My Lai) Massacre 145
Sunbeam Bridge, Hanoi 32

T

Tam Coc 54
Tam Nong Bird Sanctuary 228
Tan Quang 88
Ta Van 79
taxi 267
Tay Ninh 207
Tay Son Rebellion 175
Temple of Literature, Hanoi 44
Tet 263
Thac Ba Lake 88
Tham Coong 63
Thap Ba Hot Springs 176
Thuan Chau 64
time zone 273
tipping 273
tourist information 273
Trai Mat 166
train travel
  getting around 265
  getting there 264
  Hué to Danang 126
Tran Hung Dao 33
transport
  bicycle 266
  buses 266
  cyclo 267

getting there 264
honda ôm 267
motorbike 266
motorcycle taxi 267
river boat services 265
taxis 267
train 265
Tra Vinh 219
trekking 77
Trung sisters 49
Truong Yen 53
Tuan Giao 64
tuberculosis 271
Tunnels of Cu Chi 205
Tunnels of Vinh Moc 124
turtles 212
Tu Ton Rose Garden 227

V

vaccinations 272
Valley of Love 165
Vinh Long 220
Vinh Moc Tunnels 124
Vinh Te Canal 232
visas 274

W

war veterans tours 155
water puppetry
    Hanoi 52
    HCMC 197
websites
    health 272
Whale Island 176
when to go 262
where to stay 268
White Silk Lake, Hanoi 47

X

Xa Linh 62
xe ôm 267
Xeo Quit Base 228
Xuan Thieu Beach 127

Y

Yen Minh 86
Yen Tu Mountains 98
Yersin, Alexandre 159, 173
Yok Don National Park 157

NOTES

NOTES

NOTES

NOTES

NOTES

NOTES